WHEN MOVEMENTS MATTER

PRINCETON STUDIES IN AMERICAN POLITICS:
HISTORICAL, INTERNATIONAL, AND COMPARATIVE
PERSPECTIVES

IRA KATZNELSON, MARTIN SHEFTER, AND THEDA SKOCPOL, EDS.

A LIST OF TITLES IN THIS SERIES APPEARS AT THE BACK OF THE BOOK

WHEN MOVEMENTS MATTER

THE TOWNSEND PLAN AND THE
RISE OF SOCIAL SECURITY

Edwin Amenta

PRINCETON UNIVERSITY PRESS   PRINCETON AND OXFORD

Copyright © 2006 by Princeton University Press
Published by Princeton University Press, 41 William Street,
Princeton, New Jersey 08540
In the United Kingdom: Princeton University Press, 6 Oxford Street,
Woodstock, Oxfordshire OX20 1TW

Second printing, and first paperback printing, 2008
Paperback ISBN: 978-0-691-13826-8

The Library of Congress has cataloged the cloth edition of this book as follows

Amenta, Edwin, 1957–
    When movements matter : the Townsend plan and the rise of social security / Edwin Amenta.
        p.   cm.—(Princeton studies in American politics)
    Includes bibliographical references and index.
    ISBN-13: 978-0-691-12473-5 (hardcover : alk. paper)
    ISBN-10: 0-691-12473-6 (hardcover : alk. paper)
    1. Old age pensions—United States.   2. Individual retirement accounts—United States.
3. Social security—United States.   I. Title.   II. Series.
    HD7105.35.U6A45 2006
    368.4'300973—dc22   2005032896

British Library Cataloging-in-Publication Data is available

This book has been composed in Goudy

Printed on acid-free paper. ∞

press.princeton.edu

Printed in the United States of America

10 9 8 7 6 5 4 3 2

CONTENTS

PREFACE

In 2005, the Social Security Act celebrated its seventieth birthday. But it was a troubled one, with President George W. Bush and his Republican allies rallying the nation to replace the venerable Social Security program with "personal investment" accounts, while congressional Democrats refused to address the program's problems until "privatization" was dropped.

Despite their conflict, both sides seemed to believe that Social Security enjoyed a kind of immaculate conception. Democrats and their allies, including the AARP, claimed that President Franklin Roosevelt envisioned the program as insurance that would always be needed by substantial numbers of the elderly. Republicans and their allies in conservative think tanks agreed, but argued that Bush was Roosevelt's true heir by foreseeing the retirement of Social Security and an affluent future in which all Americans would have the wherewithal to invest for their golden years. Republicans and Democrats alike claimed that when the Social Security Act was adopted in 1935, there was a consensus about the Social Security program's goals and desirability. Burned in our minds is the famous photo of a smiling FDR, surrounded by many happy supporters, signing the legislation.

There was no such agreement, however, and this distortion of the historical record makes it difficult to make sense of the recent predicament. It is more appropriate to say that Social Security turned fifty-five years old in 2005, and Roosevelt, though elected four times, never lived to see its birth. Only on August 28, 1950, when Harry S. Truman signed Social Security Act Amendments, did the advocates of old-age insurance—mainly Democrats, organized labor, and the Social Security Administration—win and their Republican opponents concede over the type and meaning of support for the American elderly.

The political sides and arguments back then resembled those of 2005. Republicans and their organized business allies initially disparaged Social Security as a hoax, a shell game, and a Ponzi scheme. In 1936 Republican presidential nominee Alf Landon asserted that Americans were being taxed to secure their old age, but Roosevelt was dissipating their premiums on "boondoggles" like the Works Progress Administration. Either future "oldsters" would lose out, vast debts would be foisted on their grandchildren, or, most frightening of all, the businesses that paid payroll taxes would have to pick up the tab. Roosevelt crushed Landon, but ex-president Hoover and Republican senator Arthur Vandenburg of Michigan saw traction in the anti–Social Security issue and assumed leadership of the anti-Security cause.

The organized elderly were also involved. They were not, however, requesting merely that Social Security be adjusted at the margins, and hoping that Democratic allies would win the day. Instead, the elderly demanded senior citizens' pensions, with benefits far more generous than imagined by Roosevelt and to be provided to all Americans—not for having paid payroll taxes but for lifelong social contributions, whether as wage earners, farmers, or housekeepers.

Leading this pension movement was the Townsend Plan, which emerged in 1934 as the Roosevelt administration started planning for Social Security. The Townsend Plan, symbolized by an aged peripatetic physician, soon rallied an astounding fifth of Americans over sixty-five years behind the idea that generous pensions were their right and that the spending of them would end the Depression. Through the 1940s, the Townsend Plan and the wider pension movement contested the administration and its opponents on the right.

Only a minority in Congress favored such generous treatment of the elderly, and so the pension movement took the battle to the states. The efforts of the Townsend Plan and state-level pension-advocacy organizations like Colorado's National Annuity League and California's Ham and Eggs advanced Old-Age Assistance programs, also provided through the Social Security Act, so far that their benefits greatly surpassed those of Social Security, which had been starved by conservative Congresses, led by Senator Vandenburg, in the 1940s.

In these pages I tell the story of battles between the pension movement, the allies of old-age policy in the administration and among northern Democrats, radical party representatives, and some progressive Republicans, and the forces arrayed against them, including Republicans and organized business, during the formative years of Social Security.

In 1950, Republicans and their allies finally acceded to President Truman's and the Social Security Administration's proposals to upgrade Social Security so that its benefits were competitive with Old-Age Assistance and its payroll taxes would cover most American workers and future commitments. The pension movement wanted something more generous, and Truman wanted health insurance, too, but an upgraded Social Security is what they could get.

The real prehistory of Social Security is a story of extensive political contestation led by the elderly. Take a careful look at the photo of FDR signing and try to identify any Republicans—or members of the Townsend Plan. The difference today is that the Republicans are mobilizing people, while the Democrats, and the AARP, hang back, anticipating that it will remain easier to defend an existing popular program than to gut and transform it. If this formative episode suggests anything about the future, it is that as the debate over Social Security continues, it will be a struggle, too, and perhaps lead to a result that none of initial participants intended. And it will probably turn out better for Social Security if old-age organizations and advocates make more extensive efforts to fight for their constituents.

WHEN MOVEMENTS MATTER

INTRODUCTION _____

The Townsend Plan's Image Problem

Because of the efforts of our national membership,
the aged people of this nation today are receiving
millions of dollars annually in the form of old-age
pensions which they had never received before. This
is the result of the individual work of our members
carrying forward the message of security and thus
making our nation pension-conscious.
   —Francis E. Townsend, 1943.[1]

With the exception of probably not more than a
half-dozen members [of the House of
Representatives], all felt that the Townsend
[pension-recovery bill] was utterly impossible; at the
same time they hesitated to vote against it. The
Townsend [Plan] had the effect of taking away from
the economic security bill its strongest natural
support—that of the old people.
   —Edwin E. Witte, 1937.[2]

IN THE GREAT DEPRESSION, older Americans rallied behind a proposal. Francis
E. Townsend, a sixty-seven-year-old physician from Long Beach, California,
suggested that the government pay $200 per month for Americans sixty years
old or older who agreed not to work and to spend the money right away. This
pension-recovery plan would free jobs, end the Depression, and provide the
aged with security. Dr. Townsend landed on the cover of *Newsweek* when a
bill based on his idea was introduced in Congress in January 1935, as President
Franklin D. Roosevelt forwarded his own social security legislation. Led by
its secretary Robert Earl Clements, the Townsend Plan,[3] the name affixed
both to the idea and to the organization promoting it, called on its affiliated
Townsend clubs to flood Washington with letters. Soon the Townsend Plan
spread from its western outpost across the nation. Townsend clubs claimed
nearly a fifth of Americans over sixty years old, 2 million altogether, a size
never reached by any organization in the civil rights or women's movement,
and the Townsend Plan was raising funds at a more rapid clip than the Democratic Party. Townsend was back on the cover of *Newsweek*, and the Townsend

TABLE I.1.

Top 25 Social Movement Organizations in the Twentieth Century, by Number of Articles in Peak Year, in the *New York Times*

	Group	Year	Total
1	American Federation of Labor	1937	1,050
2	Black Panthers	1970	1,028
3	Congress of Industrial Organizations	1937	786
4	NAACP	1963	762
5	Ku Klux Klan	1924	672
6	Congress of Racial Equality	1964	418
7	Anti-Saloon League	1930	409
8	Townsend Plan	1936	402
9	Students for a Democratic Society	1969	381
10	American Legion	1937	362
11	America First Committee	1941	280
12	John Birch Society	1964	255
13	American Civil Liberties Union	1977	252
14	League of Women Voters	1937	246
15	Moral Majority	1981	221
16	Southern Christian Leadership Conference	1968	215
17	German American Bund	1939	200
18	Student Nonviolent Coordinating Committee	1966	195
19	Veterans of Foreign Wars	1950	180
20	American Liberty League	1936	175

Note: No individual labor unions are included.

Plan was featured in the nation's movie theaters. In terms of yearly coverage in the *New York Times*, the Townsend Plan's for 1936 ranks it as the eighth-most publicized U.S. social movement organization of the twentieth century.

Instead of passing the Townsend Plan's bill, however, Congress adopted the Social Security Act. With far less generous and more restricted benefits than Townsend's proposal, the security act addressed the immediate poverty of the aged with Old-Age Assistance (OAA), a federal-state matching program, and also created a national old-age annuity program. The Townsend Plan kept the pressure on for years, and although the doctor's pension-recovery proposal never passed, old-age benefits were increased again and again, and the fledgling annuity program was eventually transformed into Social Security as we know it today. In his 1943 autobiography *New Horizons*, Townsend was not shy about taking credit for these developments, and many of his contemporaries were inclined to agree. In *Social Security in the United States* (1936), Paul Douglas, economist, reformer, and no fan of Townsend, conceded that the mobilization behind his proposal "probably did weaken the die-hard opposition to the security bill." Scholarship often concurs. The political scientist

Abraham Holtzman concludes that the Townsend Plan's impact was substantial, as do the historian Arthur M. Schlesinger Jr. and the social scientists Frances Fox Piven and Richard A. Cloward.[4]

Yet the Townsend Plan may not have been so influential. It reached its zenith in membership and attention after the passage of the Social Security Act, and when Social Security was greatly upgraded in 1950, the Townsend Plan was a spent force. Today it is largely forgotten. It seems possible, too, that the Townsend Plan had some detrimental effects. It fought the social security legislation in 1935, and its congressional endorsements usually went to Republicans, whose party often combated augmentations in old-age security. In his seminal book *The Development of the Social Security Act*, Edwin Witte, the University of Wisconsin economist and executive secretary of the committee that wrote the bill, complained that the Townsend Plan impeded the cause of old-age security, and President Roosevelt considered himself, not Dr. Townsend, to be the author of Social Security.[5] Also, Townsend's proposal was attacked as wildly extravagant by virtually the entire economics profession—despite the fact that in 1935 the Townsend Plan reduced the amount of its pension to about $60 per month. More soberly, the historian Edward D. Berkowitz shows that the movement for old-age security had generated great momentum before 1934, and the sociologist Ann Shola Orloff argues that the Townsend Plan may have induced Witte and his colleagues to make old-age policy more conservative than it would have been.[6] The standard view is a weak version of Witte's argument. The Townsend Plan may have helped to keep old age foremost in the Social Security Act, but it was erratic in action and faded in influence once that act went into effect.

This dispute among contemporaries and scholars suggests several historical questions: Did the Townsend Plan bring about the Social Security Act? Did it influence the process by which Social Security as we know it was created? Why and how, if at all, did the Townsend Plan—and social spending challengers like Huey Long's Share Our Wealth and other groups in the old-age pension movement—contribute to the development of social policy? Is the conventional wisdom true? Or did the Townsend Plan and the pension movement produce other long-lasting benefits for the aged—such as increasing their possibilities for future organization, providing an identity that was useful in politics and elsewhere, or simply improving their image or what people called them? Witte had no qualms about employing the undignified construction "the old people" to refer to the elderly, who also were often referred to by many a jocular label, such as "oldsters." Was Townsend, as he portrayed himself, a hero for the aged?

In addressing this dispute about the impact of the Townsend Plan, I follow it from its origins through its heyday and beyond, examining the different ways it and the pension movement it led attempted to influence old age in America. Social scientists want to do more, however, than to assess whether this or that challenger influenced one or another social change, no matter how important. We want to know something more general about social movements and their impacts and to uncover what lessons a case has for other challengers and their efforts. So I also seek to understand what it means for a social movement to have an impact and why movements are sometimes influential and sometimes not.

The Townsend Plan and the pension movement seem to fit contradictory images of social movements in the social science literature. The old-style view, based on movements of the 1930s, was that they make unrealistic demands, attract the disengaged and credulous, and are prey to unscrupulous political leaders.[7] Having migrated to California and having recently lost his job to the Depression, Townsend seemed to many scholars and journalists of the day to be an embodiment of rootlessness and despair. Richard Neuberger and Kelley Loe's book *An Army of the Aged* (1936) attributed Townsend's idea to his unemployment-induced "disturbed state of mind" and charged that the Townsend Plan was a racket, noting that Clements left the organization in 1936 after having made great profits. Hadley Cantril's book *The Psychology of Social Movements* (1941) dismisses the Townsend Plan as "just another one of a long procession of schemes" and wedges the discussion of the Townsend Plan between accounts of lynch mobs and the Nazi Party.[8] This negative image of social movements was reinforced in popular culture. In Sinclair Lewis's best-selling *It Can't Happen Here* (1935), a demagogue modeled on Huey Long manipulates organizations like the Townsend Plan to win the presidency and implement fascism. In Frank Capra's film *Meet John Doe* (1941), a publisher modeled partly on William Randolph Hearst and played by Edward Arnold pursues his sinister political ambitions by inducing Gary Cooper to create a nationwide network of "John Doe clubs." The Cooper character is as simpleminded as he is good-hearted—just as many viewed Townsend—and ultimately loses control of his followers. In addition, the March of Time documentary series labeled Dr. Townsend, along with Huey Long, Father Charles Coughlin, and Gerald L. K. Smith, as leaders of a "lunatic fringe."

The currently dominant view is that social movements are rational and often highly skilled political actors. Participants in movements are seen as more socially engaged than average, seeking to make the best of their poor access to institutional democratic politics through protest and unorthodox political tactics. From this point of view, usually social mobilization and protest have some impact and sometimes work spectacularly. The aged may have joined Townsend clubs not because they were frustrated but because they were "biographically available"—a sociological way of saying that they had free time on their hands. Making dramatic demands like a $200 pension—which was more than twice the median income in the Depression—may be the only way to win followers and gain passable results.[9] This view of social movements has been highlighted by nonfiction writing and, especially, documentary films portraying postwar American challengers. In Henry Hampton's *Eyes on the Prize*, civil rights activists are portrayed as poor in resources but courageous, cohesive, and canny—willing to face and even elicit violent responses from their opponents in order to overturn segregated institutions. Ken Burns's *Huey Long* and Alan Brinkley's *Voices of Protest* suggest that the impact of Share Our Wealth was far from all negative, but there have been no documentaries or books that treat the Townsend Plan or the pension movement as a serious political challenge.

Challenging Issue: The Consequences of Social Movements

That the Townsend Plan evokes conflicting images may not be so damaging for my plan to make sense of why social movements have influence when and where they do. To put it in a way that social scientists can readily relate to, there is variance to be explained. Yet only recently have scholars started to address the issue of the consequences of social movements. In part this was because the older scholarship assumed that movements were ineffective, or possibly dangerous, whereas today's scholars tend to assume movements matter. Now that scholars have been examining the consequences of social movements, they have identified specific conceptual, theoretical, and methodological problems that this subject poses.[10]

The central conceptual issue falls under the heading "What Is the Meaning of Success?" The currently conventional answer, provided first by the sociologist William Gamson in his highly influential book *The Strategy of Social Protest* (1975), is that the greatest "success" means "new advantages," understood as the degree to which a challenger's program was realized.[11] But this conception of success limits thinking about the possible consequences of challenges. For instance, a challenger may not achieve its demands, and thus be deemed a "failure," but still achieve a great deal. Although Townsend's pension plan was never adopted, if the Townsendites were responsible for Social Security, the largest item in the federal budget today, the Townsend Plan would have to be counted as one of the most influential challengers in U.S. history. Also, the standard definition cannot deal with the possibility of a challenger doing something worse than failing. What if the activity of the Townsendites backfired, as Witte and some early scholarship suggest?

The theoretical issues surrounding the impact of social movements can be summarized under the heading "What Else Matters?" A challenger has to make claims and mobilize people and a variety of resources in order to engage in collective action and attempt to have an impact.[12] But most scholars thus argue that mobilization is necessary, though not sufficient, to produce social change. They go beyond it, in two main directions. One is by Gamson, who wanted to know whether some goals, strategies, and forms of organization were more productive than others. Other scholars have followed this line of thought by identifying strategies of claims making and framing as being key. The second view is that once a state-oriented challenger is mobilized, the main thing standing in the way of its having an impact is the political context or "opportunity structure."[13]

Resolving this controversy between strategy and context seems simple enough, but there are at least two obstacles to doing so. First, scholars need to specify what constitutes a favorable political context and what does not. Otherwise, it is possible merely to say retrospectively that a given context was helpful. If the mid-1930s were particularly favorable to the claims of challengers, for instance, it is important to indicate how this period differed from what went before it and came after it. The second obstacle is that the productivity of goals, strategies, and forms of challengers seems likely to vary with the contexts in which they contend. Any arguments about the effectiveness of strategies by themselves, taken out of context, might be misleading.

Making sense of the consequences of social movements faces methodological and logistical hurdles that I classify under the heading "How Can You Tell?" To determine what accounts for the consequences of challengers, it is necessary to establish first if there were any consequences—but that is easier said than done. As we have seen, scholars do not agree on whether the Townsend Plan and the old-age pension movement had an impact. The empirical challenge comes down to demonstrating that important changes would not have occurred, or not in the way they did, in the absence of the challenger or the actions it took.

Often other conditions or actors, typically more powerful than challengers, are pressing toward similar sorts of change. For that reason, other potential determinants of social change need to be taken into account in assessing the impact of challengers. When the United States adopted new programs benefiting the aged, they may have been a result not of the Townsend Plan but of the Depression itself, the rise to power of Roosevelt, a liberal Democratic president backed by an overwhelmingly Democratic Congress, or the actions of the domestic reformers within the administration, as various scholars have argued. Premature declarations of significance disregard the deflating possibility that other conditions may have induced both the challenger and what it is presumed to have influenced. The rise of the Townsend Plan may have been the result of circumstances—the economic crisis, the liberal government, favorable bureaucrats—that also caused what some may mistakenly see as the impact of this challenger.

Ascertaining the consequences of any challenger involves historical interpretation. But for radical challengers like the Townsend Plan the record is littered with more than the usual amounts of disingenuousness. After 1935, Townsend Plan leaders found themselves in an awkward position. They had every reason to claim that the organization had provoked the existing old-age programs—in order to inspire Townsend clubbers and show potential new recruits how effective the organization was. Townsend eventually took credit for the old-age benefits promoted by the Roosevelt administration. At the same time the Townsend Plan leadership had to downplay the significance of these benefits, often dismissing programs as suitable only for "paupers," to arouse the membership to press for further gains. What is more, political leaders hoping to steal the thunder of a movement organization by proposing something new to win over its constituents rarely give the challenger much credit. Not surprisingly, political officials in the Roosevelt administration dismissed Townsend's plan as fanciful, long after it was greatly reduced in amount. In his memoir of the Social Security Act, Witte brushes off the pension proposal as fantastic, and to hear him tell it, he and his administration counterparts are all the more heroic for having overcome the meddling of the Townsendites. Then again, Roosevelt administration officials liked to invoke the Townsend Plan to try to scare conservatives into supporting the administration's more moderate old-age legislation.[14] Where the significance of the Townsend Plan is at issue, few principals are to be believed.

Demonstrating that challenges have results is also often hindered by the fact that they are usually case studies, which often have too many potential explanations chasing too few observations. There may be several explanations consistent with the basic facts. Also we scholars tend not to choose case studies randomly, but according to suspected significance. Many of us want to study the civil rights or feminist or environmental movements, but only few are eager to pursue the kind of ill-fated challengers that sometimes popped up in Gamson's randomly selected sample—such as the quixotic American Proportional Representation League and North Carolina Manumission Society.[15] However effective it may have been, the Townsend Plan had a very high public profile and its experience may have little to say about other challengers.

Consequences, Collective Benefits, and Political Mediation

Although I address conceptual, theoretical, and methodological issues in chapter 1, I hope to demonstrate briefly here that they are manageable. Conceptually speaking, I refer to the consequences or impact of social movements rather than their success and failure. I understand potential consequences in terms of collective goods—groupwise advantages or disadvantages from which nonparticipants in a challenge cannot be easily excluded. Collective goods can be material, such as categorical social spending programs, but can also be less tangible, such as new ways to refer to members of a group. Social movement organizations almost invariably claim to represent more than the leaders and adherents of the organization. To employ collective benefits as a standard is to focus on the consequences for that larger group.

This definition has the advantage of being able to address both intended and unintended consequences of challengers. A challenger may fail to achieve its stated program but still win substantial collective benefits for its constituents. It may be false, moreover, to assume that the formal discourse and plans of social movement organizations capture all their constituents' aspirations for change. A focus on collective benefits makes it possible to take these other aims into account. This way of looking at matters turns a colder eye on some actions that might be viewed as successful by others, such as parts of a challenger's program that would provide benefits only to the leaders or participants in a challenge. The collective benefits definition can extend on the negative side beyond failure, addressing the possibility that a challenger's actions may backfire. In short, examining the consequences of social movements by way of collective goods provides a more flexible way to understand the impact of a challenger.

On the theoretical side, I propose what I call a political mediation model of movement consequences. The argument is that the productivity of the collective action of state-oriented challengers is mediated by political circumstances. Political conditions influence the relationship between challengers' mobilization and collective actions, on the one hand, and policy and other outcomes, on the other. The U.S. polity in the first half of the twentieth century dampened the influence of challengers. An underdemocratized political system—with restricted voting rights and a lack of choices among parties—produces officials with little reason to aid challengers, and the U.S. polity was underdemocratized, especially in the South. The many checks and balances across the American polity—in which legislative, executive, and judicial authorities all have autonomy—also harm the prospects of challengers by making it easier for the politically powerful to veto new policies. The U.S. electoral system, with its winner-take-all elections, punishes challengers that attempt to exert influence by building new parties. Patronage-oriented political parties tend to regard challengers as menacing contenders and consider programmatic spending policies to be a threat, and patronage-oriented parties predominated in the Northeast. And the two major U.S. parties are skewed to the political right.

But medium-range and short-term political conditions also influence the prospects of challengers, and these are not always unhelpful in the U.S. setting. Two key political actors are the political regime in power and domestic bureaucrats. A political regime or government favorable to the goal or constituency of a challenger is likely to amplify the impact of its mobilization and collective action, even in a catchall party system with diminished ideological differences. Although it is has been difficult to construct U.S. governmental regimes oriented toward social policy reforms and advances, much of the Democratic Party outside the South has been pro-reform, and in some times and places this faction has held power. The missions, activities, and powers of state bureaus in charge of domestic programs related to the challenger also matter. Bureaucrats with missions similar to those proposed by challengers may enforce laws sympathetically or propose valuable new legislation. Although the United States historically has been characterized by relatively small and inefficient domestic bureaucracies, they have grown throughout the twentieth century.

I am also arguing that the ability of a social movement to win collective benefits depends partly on conditions it can control. To get results the strategies of state-oriented challengers need to fit the political situation. Different sorts of strategies are likely to be necessary to win collective benefits in different political circumstances. The more favorable these circumstances are, the less a mobilized challenger has to do to win collective benefits; the more difficult these circumstances, the more the challenger has to do. Some strategies are more inherently suited to political contexts like the U.S. one. I also argue that strategies aimed at political institutions, which are generally treated by scholars as similarly restrained, can vary greatly in their assertiveness and in the constraints they may impose on political actors.

In situations where change is possible, challengers need to match appropriate strategies to the political situations. What this means is that less assertive strategies, such as educational efforts and publicity, are likely to work only in the most favorable circumstances. Although more assertive strategies, such as targeted electoral activity, are likely to work in many settings, they are needed in unfavorable contexts. Moreover, to effect radical change like that demanded by the Townsend Plan requires extensive organization and mobilization and the skillful use of assertive strategies, as well as a favorable context. Specifying these circumstances and strategies is key here—otherwise it would be possible merely to claim after the fact that a particular strategy did or did not fit the circumstances in a particular instance.

To appraise my arguments I address whether what happened regarding old-age would have happened in the absence of the Townsend Plan and the pension movement and the lines of action they took. I employ primary sources as much as possible, taking into account the different positions of the actors. Ascertaining whether there were impacts and what they were, however, is only a first step in the process of accounting for the pattern of influence. I also seek out empirical situations in which the parts of the explanation vary—places, times, and circumstances in which political contexts were varied as well as how the Townsend Plan or other challengers approached them. I find these situations in analyses of the dynamics of the Townsend Plan and the pension movement through comparisons over time, across policies, across states of the union, and with other contemporary challengers. The story of the Townsend Plan is one of abrupt reversals, paradoxical outcomes, and unrealized possibilities that pose analytical puzzles.

The Townsend Plan provides many advantages in trying to solve these puzzles because its challenge extended over a long period, and it employed many different strategies under varied circumstances. At the national level, the Townsend Plan engaged in strategies that ranged from writing letters to members of Congress to trying to unseat the president. There were many different campaigns and periods in which old-age policy was altered. Aid to Dependent Children (ADC) also provides a useful comparison because it was constructed similarly to Old-Age Assistance—both were grant-in-aid programs for a needy constituency that was similar in size—but had no challenger pushing for it. In addition, the Townsendites and other pension organizations contested OAA in the states, where political situations varied much more widely than they did at the national level. Finally, I also compare the impact of the Townsend Plan with other challengers seeking redistribution, such as Share Our Wealth and veterans' organizations. These challengers sought to forge more generous relationships between the state and a specific social group portrayed as deserving, but they had limited goals. They did not call for the replacement of a capitalist economic system, as did some socialist movements, the creation of an extensive regulatory bureaucracy, as environmental movements later called for, or constraints against any specific group, as workers demanded with respect to employers. By examining the dynamics of these campaigns and policy-making episodes with these comparisons, I can appraise my arguments.

The Book in Brief

One thing I find is that the Townsend Plan does not easily conform to either of the dominant images of social movements. On the one hand, the Townsend Plan was related to the economic and other frustrations of aged Americans battered by social forces and then rocked by a Depression. The pension proposal had its unrealistic aspects. Some of the Townsend Plan's leaders were corrupt, Townsend's political interventions were often blundering, and he fell briefly under the spell of the hateful demagogue Gerald L. K. Smith. On the other hand, the Townsend Plan confronted short- and long-term economic problems that were certainly real, and the program was far more credible than its opponents made it out to be. Its national focus and earmarked tax foreshadowed what Social Security was to become, its flat grants became policy elsewhere, and its gender neutrality is still ahead of its time. Something like the revolving pension proposal could easily have been converted into a usable old-age policy and almost was in 1941. Under the circumstances, what matters more than casting or recasting the image of the Townsend Plan is to assess its consequences.

You will have to read on to find out what happened, but Townsend was certainly right in saying that the Townsend Plan promoted the idea that the American aged should be aided, and in a way that was not demeaning. The plan induced the administration to propose more substantial old-age benefits than it otherwise would have, including the program now known as Social Security. The Townsend Plan and later additions to the old-age pension movement also helped to influence augmentations in national old-age policy, as well as to promote old-age benefits across the states of the union. The Townsendites did so partly through political action and partly through rallying the aged and parts of the public behind the pension idea: that government-provided benefits to aged Americans should be a right. The Townsend clubs helped the elderly to see themselves as a national political group with legitimate needs and demands. That said, the Townsend Plan's influence was limited in ways other than that no version of pension-recovery plan ever became law. It lost all its membership and went out of existence, and even before that did not go far enough to instill political skills and identities in Townsendites. Opponents of the pension program largely discredited it to the point where the Townsend Plan is now almost forgotten. In addition, Witte was doubtless right that the Townsendites did not do as much as they might have done to advance Social Security.

As for the more general findings, the pattern of influence of the Townsend Plan is not what might be expected from standard perspectives on social movements. Many of the results are puzzling. In the heyday of the Townsend Plan, when it preempted headlines and movie screens, and hundreds of thousands surged into Townsend clubs, its impact on old-age policy was minimal. By contrast, the Townsend Plan had great influence merely by beginning to mobilize people behind the pension proposal, while abstaining from a concerted campaign of collective action. The organization's collective action often proved a waste of time and resources and sometimes seemed to backfire. Although it was mainly nationally focused, the Townsend Plan had some of its greatest effects at the state level. Also, it had little influence when the political alignment in Washington was most suited for social spending gains. Instead the Townsend Plan had its greatest influence when it was able to match its action appropriately to the political situations at hand.

But those are stories for later chapters. In chapter 1, I address ways of understanding the consequences of social movements and set forth the collective benefits criteria by which I gauge them. From there I address prominent explanations of the consequences of challengers, as well as my own political mediation arguments concerning the influence of social movements. Also, I set out my methodological strategies, in which I compare several sequences of collective action taken by the Townsend Plan and some other challengers. This is both to portray the dynamics of these contentious episodes and to provide comparative and sequential evidence for my claims. The Townsend Plan went through four phases, which I address chronologically in the book.

In chapter 2, I introduce Dr. Townsend and his plan, Earl Clements, the cofounder and organizational marvel responsible for the Townsend Plan's innovative recruitment strategies, and the Townsend clubs. The Townsend

TABLE I.2.

The Townsend Plan and the Impact of the Old-Age Pension Movement in Four Phases

Period	Era	Mobilization	Influence
1934–Summer 1935	Getting off the ground: reacting to the Social Security Act.	Forming an innovative organization, thrust onto the national stage.	Influence over the administration's old-age security proposals and support for them.
Fall 1935–37	Heyday and investigation: a national challenger implodes.	Peaking in Townsend clubs, fall from grace, as Townsend takes helm.	Influence over the administration of OAA and state-level OAA programs.
1938–41	Revival and a pension movement: remaking old-age policy.	Townsend Planredux, with state-level challengers.	Remaking old-age policy at the national level, nearly creating universal pensions for senior citizens.
1942–50	The war and postwar periods: rethinking the fundamentals.	Old age off the national agenda, and the ascendance of old-age insurance.	Influencing state OAA programs, trying and failing to regain influence in the postwar era.

Plan went from a letter to the editor to a significant political force in one year—largely on the strength of a new approach to politics and political organizing. Chapter 3 situates these developments in their historical and political context and addresses why the Townsend Plan arose in the first place, as well as its impact on the proposals in the administration's security bill in 1934. Chapter 4 considers the debate over old-age policy during the Great Depression and the initial battles surrounding the old-age components of the Social Security Act. The episode suggests that through its presence and mere mobilization of people behind the idea, the Townsend Plan upped the old-age benefits in the Roosevelt administration's security proposal, but the organization did not have the political strength or know-how to influence Congress, even though the opportunity was there. This chapter also compares the consequences of Share Our Wealth, as well as some other social spending militants of the era.

Chapter 5 addresses the heyday of the Townsend Plan in late 1935 and early 1936, when it reached its peak of mobilization, spreading across the country, gaining congressional followers, and winning tremendous national press coverage. I address why the Townsend Plan took off and where all these new Townsendites and Townsend clubs came from. Despite all this activity, very little happened in old-age policy at the national level. I compare the more productive activities of World War I veterans' organizations to gain the early payment of bonuses and whose strategies were at first imitated by the Townsend Plan. The following chapter addresses these issues as well as the shake-up in leadership and the decline of Townsend Plan in the wake of a congressional investigation, with Dr. Townsend taking the helm of the organization and flirting with presidential politics.

In chapter 7, I address the Townsend Plan's return to health in 1938, accompanied by a nationwide pension movement that sought to turn OAA programs into generous and liberally provided senior citizens' pensions. The chapter also addresses the impact of the Townsend Plan and the wider pension movement on the proposals in 1938 to amend the Social Security Act. The following chapter addresses the congressional debate over these proposals as well as over a new Townsend Plan bill. This episode resulted in a transformation of American old age policy—over which the Townsend Plan had a key influence. The Social Security Act Amendments of 1939 converted the administration's annuity program into a real social insurance program, while paying dividends to a lucky group on the verge of retirement and upgrading Old-Age Assistance. In 1941, moreover, the Townsend Plan brought the administration and Congress to the verge of altering old-age policy to create universal senior citizens' pensions. But before this could happen the nation was at war, and the Townsend Plan was unable to gain much influence at the national level. Instead it pressed for "Sixty-at-Sixty" pensions in individual states. Chapter 9 takes up this story. None of these state-level campaigns succeeded, but gains were registered in a relatively hostile political climate for old-age policy. This chapter concludes with the story of the Townsend Plan's loss of influence after the war. When the Social Security Act was amended again in 1950, creating the basis for Social Security as we know it today, the Townsend Plan had little to say about it. Yet the pension movement had an influence over the triumph of Social Security all the same. The conclusion summarizes my arguments and the evidence for them and discusses the legacy of the Townsend Plan and the old-age pension movement.

ONE _____

Success or Consequences, and U.S. Social Movements

ALL SOCIAL MOVEMENTS ARE born seeking social change, often through state action. Yet only recently have scholars sought to move beyond examining mobilization to address the political consequences of social movements and the conceptual, theoretical, and methodological issues the subject poses.[1] What does it mean for a movement to have an impact? Does it mean that a social movement organization achieved its stated goals? Or can social movements have other important macrosocial influences? In addition, challengers do not directly control state actions, unlike choosing strategies, organizing and mobilizing people, and defining collective identities. Mobilizing people and resources and making plausible claims are probably necessary to influence states, but what else matters? Also, it can be difficult to identify what consequences movements have, let alone to appraise arguments about them. Scholars of social movements often engage in case studies, and in such research settings many arguments may seem plausible.

In this chapter I offer ways through these conceptual, theoretical, and methodological difficulties. I argue first that we need to end our attachment to notions of success and failure in thinking about the consequences of social movements and instead think in terms of the collective benefits that might flow to a challenger's constituency. To address the theoretical issues I propose a political mediation theory of social movement consequences. Challengers' collective action is mediated by political contexts and actors. To be influential, challengers need not always employ some specific strategy of action or hope for the right political conditions, but they must match mobilization and strategy to specific political contexts. The argument goes against the grain of conventional social movement thinking, which focuses on the influence of specific forms of organization, strategies, and contexts. Also, unlike other scholars I argue that U.S. political institutions mainly have provided obstacles to the influence of challengers. To address the methodological issues, I devise empirical strategies involving comparisons of movement campaigns across places and over time, as well as comparisons of the results of this movement with similar ones.

Success or Consequences?

Most scholars who study the impact of challengers follow William Gamson's study of challengers across American history. He posits two forms of success—the realization of new advantages for the challenging organization and the acceptance of the organization as a legitimate mouthpiece for a constituency. For Gamson, success in gaining new advantages, the more important of the two for political challengers, means the degree to which a challenger's stated *program* was realized. A challenger whose program or demands were not mainly realized would be considered a failure. Examining success and defining it by way of the challenger's program provides a sharp focus, but that approach limits thinking about the possible impacts of challenges. One key possibility is that a challenging organization or group may fail to achieve its aims, and thus be deemed a failure, but still win substantial advantages.[2] For this and other reasons, it is more useful to think in terms of challengers' influence, impacts, or consequences.

To understand these consequences I begin with the idea of collective goods: groupwise advantages or disadvantages from which nonparticipants in a challenge cannot be easily excluded. Social movement organizations almost always claim to represent a group extending beyond the leaders and adherents of the organization. Leaders and organizers of movements claim to act not selfishly for themselves or for organization members but for larger things, such as the worthiness of the group and the cause, and for justice generally. Collective goods are commonly thought of as material, such as categorical social spending programs or wage increases for large groups. They can also be less tangible, such as cleaner air or dignified ways to refer to members of a group.[3] Some advantages of this approach can be illuminated by the Townsend Plan, whose pension proposal failed. If some scholars are right and the Townsendites were largely responsible for the collective benefits for the aged in the Social Security Act, the Townsend Plan would have to be considered extremely influential. As Sidney Tarrow points out, radical movements in Western democracies invariably fall short of their goals, but a standard analysis would consider them all failures—even when they effect transformations of political, economic, social, or cultural institutions. Recent prominent U.S. challengers, such as for the equal rights amendment and the nuclear freeze, would have to be judged failures under the standard definition, despite their considerable influence.[4] A focus on collective benefits makes it possible to gain a more balanced assessment.

There are two other problems with the success standard. One is that aspects of a challenger's program may not provide collective benefits to a constituency. Often important parts of a challenger's program would aid only the leaders or participants in a challenge, and the program in some instances may incur costs for the beneficiary group. Another problem is that challengers may do worse than merely fail to achieve goals. Their collective action can backfire, resulting in negative consequences.[5] The Townsend Plan provides potential examples. In 1934, the organization opposed Upton Sinclair, a candidate for governor and the founder of End Poverty in California (EPIC), partly by way of $50 per month old-age pensions. The Townsend Plan

opposed Sinclair because he had failed to endorse the doctor's pension proposal and supported Sinclair's expedient opponent, a conservative Republican whose support for the national pension program obligated him to do
nothing for the aged in California. The Townsend Plan may have reduced
collective benefits for the aged in California without greatly advancing the
cause of national pensions. What is more, Townsend's pension proposal had a
requirement for the aged to retire. Winning that goal might be plausibly
viewed as a collective cost to the aged.[6]

Using the collective goods standard requires specifying the constituency or
potential beneficiary group, as John D. McCarthy and Mayer N. Zald would
put it, for any given challenger or social movement. It also means choosing
among the possible collective benefits to study and positing that something is
in a group's interest—always a contentious business. In the debate over the relative importance of subjective and objective interests, however, there is no
reason to take strong sides.[7] I start with the programs and demands of challengers and analyze the collective benefits in them, but also consider potential
concessions other than the challenger's program that might be beneficial to its
constituency. For the Townsend Plan and the old-age pension movement, the
main beneficiary group was the American aged. The next step is to examine
the revolving pension plan for the collective benefits in it—the main one being the large, equal, and relatively unrestricted pension. From there it is a matter of considering other potential collective benefits for the aged, such as
higher pensions or even other types, such as a better representation through
official statements or public opinion to a useful and durable collective identity.

States are often the main source or guarantor of collective benefits sought
by movements. Following Weber, I see states as sets of political, military, police, judicial, and bureaucratic organizations and officials that exert political
authority and coercive control over the people living within the borders of
well-defined territories. States engage in action and enact policies that are
binding on citizens and subjects and backed by the aforementioned organizations. Democratic states are those whose leaders, forms, and policies are decided with key participation and input from everyday people—citizens. In a
democratic state suffrage is relatively inclusive, citizens have freedom to assemble and speak out, and the state is significantly responsive to the actions
of elected officials.[8] State officials can be broken down into the government
and other elected political officials, administrative officials, including political appointees and long-standing bureaucrats, military and police officials,
and judicial authorities. In a democratic polity, the coercive authorities tend
to be under the control of political authorities. These officials are engaged in
ongoing political projects and thus may be predisposed or, more likely, not, to
favor the claims of a given challenger. Elected officials, and those out of
power, but seeking it, may be attempting to appeal to supporters of the challenger or to its claimed constituency.

I see challengers or political social movements as politically disadvantaged groups engaged in sustained campaigns of collective action to secure their claims or other concessions. Challengers typically rely on mobilizing people to gain influence more so than on money. In a democratic polity these challengers may appeal to many groups, including their constituency, other supporters, the general public, other organized groups, party leaders, and elected officials. Challengers make demands for specific categories of people as well as claims about justice. In doing so, they seek to develop coherent accounts of the problems their constituents face and the remedies for these problems, and in the process may attempt to redefine a group and its relations with other groups. Challengers have many lines of action available to press their claims and are likely to engage at least occasionally in noninstitutional, disruptive, or unconventional collective action.[9] Some strategies rely on action by the mainstream news media, and others do not. Some lines of action may require extensive organizational or professional skills, such as being able to form a political party, run meetings, make technical arguments, or litigate. Challengers hope to show state officials and others the justice in and worthiness of their cause and the potential political repercussions from supporting it or not and often do so through demonstrations of support. The more unified and organized the challenger and the greater the resources at its disposal, the greater the number and scope of actions that can be taken.[10]

To understand the potential impacts of social movements on democratic states, I adopt a three-level approach, with each level referring ultimately to collective benefits. At the lowest level, challengers may win something specific for their constituency group, ranging from greater respect through governmental representations, such as having the aged officially referred to as "senior citizens," or through insubstantial, short-run pecuniary concessions that imply a limited conception of rights for the beneficiary groups, such as extensions of unemployment insurance benefits.[11] At the highest level, a challenger may gain structural reforms that give a group greater leverage over political processes and augment the impact of future collective action by a group, such as winning suffrage rights, or that advantage a group in its conflicts with other groups, such as labor movements winning rights to organize, picket, and engage in collective bargaining. It is at the middle level, however, where most challenges seek influence. Much of democratic state action concerns what might be called institutionally provided benefits—collective goods granted in a routine fashion to all those meeting specified requirements. The recipients gain rights of entitlement to the benefits by way of law, and the bureaucratic reinforcement of such laws ensures the routine provision and maintenance of the benefits. Once a program becomes institutionalized in this way, the issue is privileged in politics. It was chiefly these sorts of benefits that the Townsend Plan sought, and the Social Security Act provided.

U.S. Political Institutions and Challengers

My arguments about the impact of social movements are rooted in scholarship about the historical development of public policy and state building—key issues for state-oriented movements.[12] Political institutions influence the possibilities of all state-oriented challengers—including which groups are likely to form, their claims, and their lines of action. As Charles Tilly notes, over the last millennium states everywhere have gained greater infrastructural capacities, especially bureaucracies, and many polities have become democratized. As a result, contentious collective action has become more nationalized, proactive, and larger in extent, as formerly disfranchised groups target states rather than local authorities. Modern democratic polities, however, are structured in ways that influence challengers, and scholars of social movements tend to see the American polity as providing many openings for social movements, because the state is relatively "weak"—federal, functionally differentiated, and with an underdeveloped executive bureaucracy.[13] However, in the last century the American polity has been discouraging to challengers, the main culprit being the U.S. state, with the U.S. political party system not far behind. The American polity also has reinforced challengers who form and act in ways that are congruent with the polity and harmed those who do not.

For instance, a dispersion of authority in a polity may provide many sites for mobilization, but it inhibits challengers because opponents have an easier time blocking new state initiatives. Where the executive can thwart the legislature, and vice versa, and both can be thwarted by the judiciary, as Evelyne Huber and John D. Stephens argue, the bias is toward inaction, and routine politics work to the advantage of polity members, to use Tilly's terminology, not challengers. Although Canada, Germany, Australia, and Switzerland are federal, power sharing in the U.S. polity is extreme, with state-level and local governments controlling education and law enforcement and sharing power in social policy. In the United States authority in the central state over the legislative, executive, judicial, and policing missions of the state is also greatly divided. Unlike parliamentary political systems, presidential systems keep legislative and executive functions separate. U.S. central legislative institutions, with two houses of Congress and their extensive committees, are divided as well. Similarly, the United States stands out in the power of its courts to overturn laws. Divisions in authority in political systems are impervious to rapid change.[14]

Even more important to challengers is the degree to which formally democratic institutions in a polity are bound by democratic procedures. The extension of democratic rights means lowering of legal restrictions on institutional political participation for everyday people. These rights include the ability to assemble and discuss issues, as well as the crucial right to vote for representation. A highly democratized polity is also characterized by meaningful choices among parties or factions. An underdemocratized polity is by contrast one in which political leaders are chosen by way of elections, but in which there are great restrictions on political participation, political assembly and discussion, voting, and choices among leadership groups. The extension of democratic rights influences many aspects of challengers, including their level of mobilization, their choices of collective action, and their political identities. The process of democratization encourages the further mobilization of those who have gained rights to participate but have not yet secured state policies in their favor. By contrast, underdemocratized political institutions mute these political claims. When everyday people cannot vote, political leaders and state officials have no fear of electoral reprisals from them. Doug McAdam argues the propensity of the state to employ repression is an important aspect of political contexts facing challengers, and the more democratized the polity, the lower the propensity to repress.[15] Finally, because the extension of political rights is central to the outcomes of the political process, the configusration and evolution of rights will influence political identification and group formation.

The United States experienced highly uneven historical, geographic, and groupwide patterns of democratization. Suffrage for white males was achieved in the 1830s, and only Switzerland and Australia acted as rapidly. Women won the vote across the country in the early twentieth century. But the enfranchisement of black men immediately after the Civil War was undone by their disenfranchisement in the South by the end of the century. Many of the restrictions also applied to poorer whites, leaving almost a quarter of the U.S. polity highly underdemocratized for most of the twentieth century. There were significant if less dramatic restraints on voting in many states of the North at the turn of the twentieth century, and today restrictions remain on the suffrage of ex-felons. These electoral practices have discouraged social mobilization. For instance, the Populist movement of the 1880s could initially win the votes of southern blacks and lower-class whites, and in the early 1890s was more successful in those states where voting restrictions had not yet taken hold. When barriers to participation became endemic across the South, the movement collapsed.[16] What is more, political identities were influenced by patterns of inclusion and exclusion from the suffrage. Workers in the United States did not have to organize as workers to receive the vote as in many European countries, slowing political mobilization along class lines. By contrast, as Theda Skocpol points out, women were excluded from the franchise and organized as a group in the first part of the twentieth century. African Americans did the same in the middle of the century.[17]

How elected officials are chosen also shapes the prospects of challengers. As Seymour Martin Lipset and colleagues have pointed out, winner-take-all voting systems, such as those in the United States, Australia, Canada, New Zealand, and the United Kingdom, require much steeper electoral support than a proportional-representation system to win legislative seats and diminish the potential of "party movements," to use the term of Mildred Schwartz for challengers that contest elections. In addition, the decentralization of U.S. political authority erects barriers by way of the high costs of securing ballot lines in each state. The Electoral College makes presidential contests even higher mountains to climb by applying winner-take-all rules to the electoral votes of each state. Many party movements with great support, such as Populists, Socialists, and Progressives, as well as parties based on states' rights, prohibition, and the environment, all failed to take root here. Although it has often been possible for a new party to win a few seats in the House, such victories buy much less influence here than they do in a parliamentary system, where small parties are often represented in governments, even in federal and winner-take-all Canada.[18] U.S. electoral rules are particularly punishing to the programs of challengers who test the two major parties. For party movements' electoral gains usually come at the expense of the major party closest in the ideological spectrum. To aid their constituents party challengers have to cut a deal and retire. The 2000 election was a classic example of a new party challenge that backfired. Had the votes of the Green Party presidential candidate Ralph Nader gone to the Democrat Al Gore, he would have been president instead of the Republican George W. Bush, whose policies have been detrimental to the environmental and redistributive goals championed by the Green Party.

U.S. electoral rules thus provide many more reasons for challengers to seek to influence candidates and elected officials of the major parties than to create parties of their own. It is not surprising that at the turn of the twentieth century U.S. women, farmer, and labor organizations abandoned strategies to form parties and instead turned to influencing elections in a nonpartisan way and lobbying, which proved to be more productive.[19] This strategy has become even more important in U.S. politics in the last half century. Congressional campaigns have been controlled by individual candidates, running independently from the major parties, which have been progressively weakened as organizations. Yet this situation does not always aid challengers. Because electing members of Congress has no implications for forming governments on the parliamentary model, promises made to challengers are less likely to be kept. Because of its great expense, lobbying plays to the strength of monied interests.

The U.S. electoral system also provides some direct democratic devices, such as the initiative, referendum, and recall, which enable challengers to attempt to override standard institutional politics, as Hanspeter Kriesi notes. But these options are available in only some parts of the polity and do not outweigh the other electoral disadvantages of the U.S. system. Because canvassers and the publicity to press initiatives and referendums are costly, even direct democratic rules often favor polity members. For instance, California's 1978 Proposition 13 to permanently lower taxes and preempt government activism was orchestrated by real estate interests. Late twentieth-century mobilizations opposing affirmative action and the rights of immigrants worked in the same direction. Probably the main impact that direct democratic procedures have on social mobilization is in inducing challengers to focus on specific issues.[20]

It is sometimes argued, too, that the American party system encourages challengers, for the two major U.S. parties are amorphous, locally autonomous catch-all organizations susceptible to capture. At the turn of the last century, the Populists famously nominated their champion William Jennings Bryan for president on the Democratic ticket, and today the Christian Right bores within the Republican Party. But the U.S. political party system, too, has systemically hindered the claims of challengers. As Martin Shefter has argued, because of America's early democratization and late bureaucratization, its pioneering parties were more oriented toward patronage than programs. Because of America's presidential system, political parties quickly became national in scope. These patronage-oriented parties have been concerned chiefly with their own survival, with party workers involved for material reasons, not to pursue an ideology or program. Granting automatic and long-term entitlement claims to groups of citizens limits the sorts of discretionary spending, such as for government jobs and contracts, that maintains a patronage-oriented political organization. For these reasons, as David Mayhew argues, patronage-oriented parties have been hostile to state-oriented challengers, such as the labor movement.[21]

The partisan orientation of the U.S. party system has harmed left-of-center challengers, too. By the middle of the twentieth century the two major parties had separated themselves ideologically, but less so than elsewhere and leaving the American party system skewed to the right. The Republican Party was transformed in the last half of the twentieth century into a right-wing party backed by business interests, whereas the Democrats became a compromised centrist party—with its northern wing often left in orientation but its underdemocratized southern wing often even further to the right than Republicans. Representatives of the Democratic Party have promoted challengers like the labor movement far more so than the Republican Party, which has mainly posed threats to challengers of the left, including recent ones such as the feminist and environmental movements. Because of the nonparliamentary nature of the American political system, moreover, its parties have no external push toward discipline, with party caucuses mattering increasingly less. In the last quarter of the twentieth century, in the wake of the Voting Rights Act, much of the South has become reliably Republican, pushing the party even further to right. But since the turn of the twentieth century and beyond, the cost of political campaigns has skyrocketed with the corresponding imperative to raise funds from corporations and the well-heeled, and the Democratic Party has not moved far from center. The result has been an increasingly polarized politics of the right against the middle.[22]

TABLE 1.1.

The U.S. Polity at Midcentury, According to Political Rights and Party Systems

Party System Orientation	Political Rights	
	Extensive	Restricted
Program	**Open Polity** 24 Western and Assorted States*	**Underdemocratized Polity** 11 Southern States**
Patronage	**Patronage-based Polity** 13 Eastern and Midwestern States***	**Underdemocratized, patronage-based polity** n/a

Notes: *Arizona, California, Colorado, Idaho, Iowa, Kansas, Maine, Massachusetts, Michigan, Minnesota, Montana, Nebraska, Nevada, New Hampshire, New Mexico, North Dakota, Oklahoma, Oregon, South Dakota, Utah, Vermont, Washington, Wisconsin, and Wyoming.

**Alabama, Arkansas, Florida, Georgia, Louisiana, Mississippi, North Carolina, South Carolina, Tennessee, Texas, and Virginia.

***Connecticut, Delaware, Illinois, Indiana, Kentucky, Maryland, Missouri, New Jersey, New York, Ohio, Pennsylvania, Rhode Island, and West Virginia.

As table 1.1 shows, much of the American polity for most of the twentieth century provided dubious political footing for state-oriented challengers. Most of the former Confederacy was underdemocratized for the bulk of the century. Very few of the less well off, black and white, were able to vote, and those who did vote had their choices restricted to one party. Other parts of the country, too, had their underdemocratized pockets. The American polity also has been characterized by the dominance of patronage-based parties, especially in the Northeast and in parts of the Midwest. Most of the West, by contrast, had neither patronage-oriented political parties nor great restrictions on voting rights through the early twentieth century. These "open" polities were thus the most promising sites for state-oriented challengers. Even in these polities, however, different political circumstances made achieving collective benefits easier or more difficult.

U.S. domestic bureaucracies, organizations within the state executive with domestic missions, may seem likely to aid challengers, as they are more open to influence than their European counterparts. Domestic bureaucracies, typically launched to provide services or payments addressing politically defined problems, or to regulate them, may aid challengers whose goals correspond to the cause of the bureau. But domestic bureaucracies have been fewer in number and more underprofessionalized in the United States in comparison to other rich, democratic polities. Being more poorly staffed, with less well-defined missions and many political appointees, U.S. domestic bureaucracies have been susceptible to the influence of the opponents of movements, including elected officials in congressional committees with oversight authority and interest groups. Even when domestic bureaucracies have missions that are congruent with the goals of challengers, if they are not professionalized they are hampered in promoting shared goals and in implementing legislation.[23] Legislation backed by challengers and passed in 2002 to reform U.S. campaign financing practices was hindered by the Federal Elections Commission, an organization dominated by political appointees of both parties, which is indifferently committed to reform and in any case lacks sufficient staff to monitor campaign activity.

As Theda Skocpol has argued, state policies can reshape politics, including movement politics. These authoritative lines of action, backed by laws and legitimacy, can encourage, discourage, shape, or transform challengers, for state policies influence the flow of collective benefits to identifiable groups. In addition, by designating officially sanctioned and legitimated beneficiaries and by power of categorization, policies also help to define and redefine social groups.[24] Moreover, existing challengers may be encouraged inadvertently by programs that benefit their followers. Spending programs may also aid potential activists by freeing their time for movement work or by providing resources for movement organizations. For instance, labor movements have better withstood right-wing attacks in the last quarter century in places where unions control unemployment insurance funds. Although no challenger demanded Aid to Dependent Children, after a generation of operation the National Welfare Rights Organization mobilized the program's recipients to liberalize it. The overall underdevelopment of these policies in the United States has generally harmed the prospects of challengers.[25]

State-Oriented Challengers and the Political Mediation Model

Despite many discouraging political conditions, it is far from impossible for U.S. challengers to influence states. I see the collective action of state-oriented challengers as often influential but always politically mediated. My political mediation theory builds on arguments by other scholars that resource mobilization, strategies, and political contexts influence the consequences of movements. Mobilizing relatively large numbers of committed people is probably necessary to winning new collective benefits for those otherwise underrepresented in politics So, too, is making claims regarding the worthiness of the group and the plausibility of its program in public discussions. Favorable political contexts, both long- and short-term, are also helpful.[26] However, the political mediation model mainly helps to explain the impact of social movements by examining mobilization and strategies in combination with different sorts of political contexts. In some highly favorable political contexts, all that is required is a threshold of resource mobilization and minimally plausible and directed framing and claims making. In more difficult political contexts, more

assertive strategies of collective action are required. In even more difficult political contexts, where powerful systemic conditions work against challengers,
as in underdemocratized polities, it may be impossible for challengers to exert
much influence. Finally, contexts have to be extremely favorable, and mobilization and action extensive, to achieve the most radical results—such as the
fiscal demands of the Townsend Plan or groups demanding new political rights.

Challengers' action is more likely to produce results when institutional political actors see benefit in aiding the group the challenger represents. And so
challengers need to engage in collective action that changes the thinking of
relevant institutional political actors, who need in turn to see a challenger as
potentially facilitating or disrupting their goals. These might range from augmenting or cementing new electoral coalitions, to gaining in public opinion,
to making good on ideological commitments, to increasing the support for
the missions of governmental bureaus. To secure new benefits, challengers will
typically need complementary action from like-minded institutional actors, or
other movement organizations, or both. According to political mediation theory, the ability of a challenger to win collective benefits depends partly on
conditions it can control, including its ability to mobilize, its goals and program, its form of organization, and its strategies for collective action, including framing and other claims making. However, the impact of well-mobilized
challengers also depends on the political context. This theory holds that political conditions influence the *relationship* between the challenger's mobilization and collective action, on the one hand, and policy outcomes, on the
other. Mobilization and collective action alone are often insufficient to effect
changes in public policy. Different sorts of strategies are likely to be necessary
to win collective benefits in different political circumstances. So what constitutes favorable and unfavorable political situations, and what constitutes
more and less assertive collective action strategies?[27]

A central middle-range aspect of the political context is the orientation of
the regime in power toward the goals of the challenger. A favorable regime is
expected to amplify the impact of a challenger's mobilization and collective
action, while an unfavorable regime would dampen it. For state-oriented
challengers seeking collective benefits through sustained public spending, the
position of the regime on higher taxation is key. In the twentieth century,
U.S. Republican regimes have tended to oppose automatic, programmatic
spending claims because they imply higher taxation. Since Franklin Roosevelt's New Deal, U.S. Democrats outside the South have tended to be "reform
oriented"—more open to taxation and to claims requiring taxation on relatively well-off people. Elsewhere parties can be similarly categorized along
this continuum. Although challengers can sometimes change the views of
parties, and can more easily influence individual members of Congress, often
parties and their representatives have long-standing commitments to ideological positions and other groups whose interests and goals may conflict
with those of challengers.[28]

TABLE 1.2.
Collective Action Strategies Expected to Produce Collective Benefits, Given Specified Political Conditions

	State Bureaucrats	
Elected Officials	*Strong and Aligned with Challenger's Interests*	*Weak and/or Opposed to Challenger's Interests*
Aligned with challenger's constituency	**Sheer mobilization, limited protest**	**Sanction or urge creation of state bureaus**
Opposed or neutral to challenger's constituency	**Sanction or displace elected officials**	**Highly assertive strategies**

Another important part of the political context comprises the missions, activities, and powers of state bureaus in charge of domestic programs related to the challenger's constituency. With Herbert Kitschelt, but more broadly, I am arguing that programs of these kinds will be more easily generated when relevant state actors are present and have initiative, talent, and power. Domestic bureaucrats may see the creation of collective benefits for a group as advancing the mission of their bureau and may intensify the impact of challengers by their own actions. Conversely, the absence of such proficient state actors may make the public believe that new programs, especially those that involve public spending, will waste money. If important and powerful state bureaus have missions that oppose the claims of a challenger, however, I would expect them to diminish the impact of a challenger's collective action, as in the case of military bureaucracies and peace movements.[29]

I expect different sorts of strategies to work best in these different contexts. If the political regime is supportive and the domestic bureaucrats are professionalized and supportive, limited protest based mainly on the evidence of mobilization is likely to be sufficient to provide increased collective benefits (see table 1.2). The challenger needs merely to demonstrate that it has support. Organizing additional members might serve this purpose. So would time-honored activities such as letter writing, rallies, or petitioning, as well as public awareness campaigns. The sequence of thinking and action is likely to work something like this: Members of a reform-oriented regime are likely to use the evidence of mobilization as a confirmation of the beneficiary group's relative importance in an electoral coalition. Domestic bureaucrats are likely to portray the mobilization as indicating the need for the augmentation of its program. If the regime hopes to add to its coalition or if domestic bureaucrats have a mission that is not yet realized, those groups best mobilized are likely to win the greatest benefits in public policy for their constituencies.

By contrast, achieving collective benefits through public policy is likely to be more difficult if neither a supportive regime nor administrative authority exists, a situation depicted in the bottom right-hand box of table 1.2. When

the regime is opposed to the challenger or sees no benefit in adding its beneficiary group to its coalition, and when state bureaucracies in the area are hostile or absent, the sorts of limited action listed here are likely to be ignored or
have a limited effect. Some political actors may dust off old proposals or think
about new ones. This, however, may be solely a tactical maneuver to delay action until the challenge dwindles. But given the circumstances, a challenger
engaged in only limited protest would seem unlikely to influence the content
of legislation or its passage and thus have a minimal impact on the provision
of collective benefits.

As political circumstances become more difficult, represented by movement from the upper left-hand corner to the bottom right-hand corner of
table 1.2, more assertive or bolder collective action is required to produce collective benefits. By more assertive I mean the use of increasingly strong sanctions, something akin to Gamson's "constraints." Sanctions in assertive institutional collective action threaten to increase or decrease the likelihood of
gaining or keeping something valuable to political actors—often positions—
or to take over their functions or prerogatives. The institutional collective
action of challengers works largely by mobilizing a lot of people behind a line
of action, often one with electoral implications. This collective action may
be designed to convince the general public of the justice of the cause and to
influence elected and appointed officials in that manner, but it may also
demonstrate to these officials that a large segment of the electorate is willing
to vote or engage in other political activity mainly on the basis of a single
key issue.

I refer specifically to assertiveness, rather than usual distinctions between
"assimilative" and "disruptive" strategies or "institutional" and "noninstitutional" ones.[30] These categories are of limited use for analyzing challengers in
democratic polities and suggest that challengers must choose between something like cajoling political actors or shutting down the state. The assimilative or institutional category is usually stretched to include all manner of collective action that engages institutional politics. Yet in democratic polities,
there is a wide repertoire of collective action that falls within the rules of the
political game, including many aggressive and innovative activities that can
vary greatly in terms of sanctions. The disruptive side of the analytical coin
is misleading, too. As Jeff Goodwin argues, revolutionary movements never
flourish in minimally democratic polities. In them, collective action harming
persons or destroying property will usually provide openings for challengers'
opponents to discredit them.[31]

The following examples give a sense of variations in sanctions and assertiveness in political institutional action by challengers. Engaging in educational
campaigns and promoting a specific proposal or group is minimally assertive,
though probably necessary to have an impact. Similarly less assertive is merely
mobilizing support behind a program, though gaining commitments of time

from participating members is more assertive than merely compiling mailing lists of like-minded donors, as the potential for more far-reaching action is greater in the former. Letter-writing campaigns to incumbents can be fairly assertive, though the boldness of these actions can vary depending on what the letter writers demand and say they will do. More assertive than that is engaging in protest campaigns targeting programs or administrators. Engaging in public campaigns to replace administrators subject to election or to prevent the appointment of others is more assertive still, though not always possible. Making public statements of endorsement for individual legislators or proposals goes further than educational campaigns but remains only somewhat assertive. Contesting the electoral prospects of individual legislators who oppose specific action or aiding the electoral prospects of those legislators who support it is on the more assertive side. These moves apply a key sanction to legislators. Campaigns that result in the replacement of recalcitrant legislators and administrators would alter political contexts in favor of challengers. Also, merely applying these sanctions may lead administrators or legislators to change their views. The most assertive lines of action require extensive organization and mobilization.

Some extremely assertive lines of institutional action have a systemic bent to them. In some polities, institutional actors can be bypassed by way of institutional options, such as initiatives and referendums. Pursuing these measures can be more assertive than contesting elections. With initiatives, a challenger can potentially put its issue on the agenda, specify the proposal, and lead the campaign to have it voted into law. Challenger-led initiatives may not only produce collective benefits but also greatly alter the political context in favor of the challenger by promoting the challenger in the future. Equally assertive but more systemic is for a challenger to elect its own leaders or adherents to these offices by way of a new party. However, only in a few U.S. polities are direct democratic devices available, and these strategies can also be employed by opponents of challengers, who may be better suited in many instances to using them. Also, creating new parties usually backfires in a political context that is tilted against them, such as the U.S. one.

Challengers benefit, too, by targeting their actions to fit the administrative or legislative context. If the relevant state bureaucratic actors are present and either supportive or neutral, and the political regime is not supportive of the challenger's group, collective action will be most productive if it focuses on elected officials. Such action might induce those who would otherwise be indifferent or hostile to legislation to support it or at least not to challenge it. If the political regime is supportive or neutral, and domestic bureaucrats are either absent or hostile to the challenger's constituency, bureaucratic capabilities must be created or existing bureaucratic actors must be sanctioned to induce them to aid the group represented by the challenger.

When both the political regime and the relevant state bureaucracy are unfavorably disposed to the challenger's constituency, only the most assertive strategies will be likely to win collective benefits. The most direct way to overcome these circumstances is for challengers to take political power through democratic processes, as through initiatives or new parties. Though not optimal, less assertive electoral strategies would work better than limited protest, which in turn would be better than minor educational or informational campaigns. Assertive collective action that does not meet its ostensible goals, however, can also often lead to some benefits for a challenger's constituency in unfavorable political circumstances. A vigorous if failed bid to unseat a legislator may soften his or her views against the program or other programs benefiting the constituency of a challenger. A well-supported initiative effort that fails of passage demonstrates to legislators that the issue is of great significance and may lead to concessions for the constituency. Protests against the actions of administrators may lead to their eventual replacement, for legislation to alter the practices of administrators, or for preemptive alterations in the practices of administrators. Although failed third-party bids, if the threat is fully carried out, will backfire, the process can work by the new party candidate winning support and gaining concessions in exchange for withdrawing.

The policy situation facing the challenger is also an important part of the political context. It is worth dividing the process of creating new laws containing collective benefits into the agenda setting, content, passage, and implementation of legislation.[32] Mobilized challengers will have to do far less work to be influential if their issue is already on the political agenda. A challenger may need to do little more than mobilize to keep its issue from leaving the agenda and can act to bid up the benefits in legislation at issue, as well as induce legislators to back the legislation. A social issue's appearance on the political agenda is usually connected to political alignments. An anti–social policy political alignment will generally prevent augmentations in social policy from getting on to the political agenda. However, a pro–social spending alignment will not ensure that the issue will come up. Similarly, a mobilized challenger has an easier time influencing the implementation of legislation that has been recently enacted but may have a more difficult time influencing it once the program becomes institutionalized. The policy process is a moving target that challengers cannot control but need to pursue as possibilities arise to exert influence. Once an issue comes on the agenda, it is incumbent on a challenger to attempt to influence its content and support. Once a program has been passed, issues of implementation take precedence.

It is easiest for challengers to influence policy in its earliest phases, before a program or policy becomes highly institutionalized. The best case is for movement actors to be installed in a bureaucracy implementing policy chosen by the challenger, affording it great leverage over current and future policy.

Somewhat less advantageous, but more common, are well-run domestic bureaucracies with firm missions, committed experts, and a strong esprit de corps. In such instances, the bureau will press for the mission, which will often, but not always, run in the same direction as the interests of a constituency of a challenger. Worse for movements pushing change is when domestic bureaus' missions are subverted by being captured by political operatives, as when patronage political parties fill bureaucratic positions with nonexpert appointees or, worse, when domestic bureaucracies are captured by opposing interest groups. These groups may also cultivate ties with key members of Congress and form "iron triangles" or "policy monopolies" that become more difficult over time for challengers to influence.[33] A challenger hoping to influence policy often faces a target that is both moving and becoming better fortified against it.

For the most radical results, challengers have to do everything in their power and be fairly lucky. For improving existing programs, merely mobilizing under favorable contexts, or employing assertive action when conditions are structurally favorable but short-term unfavorable, will be enough to exert influence. The more radical and far-reaching the outcome, the greater the favorable conditions required and the more the movement may have to do. Since controlling the government through a party is rarely an option in the U.S. setting, and initiatives and referendums are available only in some states, a U.S. challenger with far-reaching goals is likely to need to have several things, many of them outside the challenger's control, happen at the same time to exert a major influence: a favorable political context, its issue on the agenda, high challenger organization and mobilization, credible claims making directed at elites and the general public, and productive assertive action. The same is likely to be true for bids to transform the structural position of groups, such as through voting or civil rights. As we shall see, these things almost all came together for the Townsend Plan and the pension movement at the end of the 1930s.

Challengers with greater strategic capacities and the most flexible forms are best suited to matching strategy and situation. The best case is to have many activists ready and able to pursue different sorts of strategies and be open to tactical innovations as situations develop. Having access to the services of many talented, skilled, and committed people will help.[34] Yet even the canniest challengers need to make decisions quickly and with limited information and thus will not usually make optimal matches of strategy and situation. As James M. Jasper argued, some challengers may employ some strategies and rule out others as matters of moral commitment, taste, or identity. Others may grow attached to strategies that match the political situation of their founding. National or international challengers working in several polities at once may employ a standard strategy appropriate only to some polities.[35]

The literature suggests centralized challengers are likely to take more coherent strategic action and make decisions quickly, and that democracy within movements provides endless meetings when rapid action is called for. Yet no one form of organization seems likely to produce matches of strategy and situation. Democratic processes in movements may also lead to useful experimentation and avoid calcification in strategic thinking, and centralization will work only to the degree those in charge know what they are doing. In the case of the Townsend Plan, decision making was mainly centralized, but the leaders were only sometimes able to figure out what was best to do.[36]

My arguments contrast in important ways with some prominent ones in the literature. Like John D. McCarthy and Mayer N. Zald, I argue that mobilization matters, and like Theda Skocpol I argue that widespread, participatory organization across classes is best able to win influence in a fragmented polity like America's. But widespread organization and mobilization are not enough. Because of other differences in how polities are structured and different strategies of collective action, simple organization and mobilization are likely to be more effective in some contexts than others. Like William Gamson, I believe that challengers often require help to achieve state-oriented goals. However, I try to specify this sort of help and disagree with Gamson's negative views on challengers with far-reaching goals. Like Herbert Kitschelt, I argue that a state's implementation capacities matter, but a lack of such capacities does not necessarily doom challengers to ineffectiveness.[37]

Establishing Challengers' Impacts and Appraising Arguments

To assess any arguments about the impact of challengers means to determine first whether they had any impact. The methodological challenge is to demonstrate that specific consequences would not have happened in the absence of the challenger and its collective action. Addressing these counterfactual questions is complex, and scholars sometimes simply assume that challengers cause outcomes they seek. But often other actors and conditions may also influence outcomes beneficial to the constituencies of challengers, or even the rise of challengers themselves. For instance, U.S. programs benefiting the aged may have come as a result of the Depression or the rise to power of the Democratic Party rather than the Townsend Plan. Scholars' inability to demonstrate the efficacy of movements may also be due to the fact they are usually engaged in case studies, which are beset by the problem of too many potential explanations chasing too few pieces of information.[38]

To assess the historical impact of a challenger, scholars can survey the views of participants, contemporary observers, and historians. The key primary sources include congressional debates over the Social Security Act and its amendments; congressional committee minutes on the investigation of the Townsend Plan; contemporaneous reports of key actors; their published recollections; congressional testimony by Townsend Plan leaders; governmental statistics; archived traces of Townsend Plan activity; the Townsend Plan newspapers, the *Modern Crusader* and the *Townsend Weekly*; and the national press. These sources also provide background evidence concerning the Townsend Plan's strategies and fund-raising activities, as well as the Townsend clubs. The mainstream press is a somewhat neglected source, but it closely covered the activities of the organization. Going down these paper trails helps to address the counterfactual question in several ways. Policy makers often indicated what they were planning before the Townsend Plan existed and before it had engaged in various actions. Even in the face of denials it is possible to get a sense of whether the Townsend organization induced a change in plans and in what directions. It is also feasible to see whether such strategies as the organization's efforts to endorse congressional candidates influenced members of Congress to act differently from what partisan or regional affiliations would imply. I also juxtapose the trajectory of the challenger's mobilization and action to outcomes of interest, but a positive correlation would not necessarily mean causation.

So I focus on the many campaigns of the Townsend Plan and the old-age pension movement and the many episodes of old-age policy making in its formative years.[39] The Townsend Plan contended for an extended period of time and employed almost every strategy short of armed revolt—from letter-writing and educational campaigns to initiative drives and the launching of a new political party—at different levels of mobilization in many different political contexts. At the national level, the political context was especially favorable in the middle 1930s and quite unfavorable at other times, especially during the middle 1940s. In the late 1930s, the Townsend Plan was joined by several mass mobilizing groups in states demanding old-age pensions with assertive strategies. Political contexts in states varied even more widely—some polities had structural hindrances, but those that did not often varied greatly in their partisanship. These results of these different campaigns can help to sift arguments about the impact of state-oriented challengers.

Analyses of the political process in the development of legislation can help in ascertaining whether a challenger had an impact. Dividing the process of creating new laws containing collective benefits into the agenda setting, legislative content, passage, and implementation makes it easier to judge the impact of challengers. It is possible to trace whether a challenger altered the plans and agendas of political leaders; influenced the content of the proposals as devised by executives, legislators, or administrators; influenced the votes of representatives key to the passage of proposed legislation; or influenced the speed or nature of the implementation of legislation. If a challenger has an impact on any one of these processes, it would increase the expected value of collective benefits for the beneficiary group. But unless placing the issue on the agenda, writing a bill with collective benefits, *and* passing the bill are negotiated successfully, no collective benefits will result. Influence in implementation depends on successfully negotiating these other steps.

I address the Townsend Plan's influence over policy-making processes also by way of selected comparisons. One is between the pension movement and other social spending challengers. Huey Long's Share Our Wealth, like the Townsend Plan, contended during the middle 1930s, recruited from the lower middle and working classes, urban and rural, espoused community control and safeguards against modern capitalism, and promoted a program in opposition to the Roosevelt administration's that aided specific groups and was supposed to end the Depression. Veterans' groups sought the early payment of "bonuses" enacted for World War I veterans, and unemployed workers sought jobs and wages. Another way to ascertain the impact of the Townsend Plan and the pension movement is to compare Old-Age Assistance with Aid to Dependent Children, a similarly structured program created in the Social Security Act. There was great mass pressure for OAA, whereas ADC was advanced mainly by groups within the Roosevelt administration and the executive bureaucracy. In my bid to uncover the reasons behind the pattern of impacts of the pension movement, I occasionally examine members of the House and Senate on key old-age votes. I also examine differences in OAA policies across states to ascertain the influence of the pension movement and its various strategies.[40]

If there is one thing that historical institutionalists and scholars of contentious politics agree on, it is that the mobilizations and campaigns of challengers need to be understood and analyzed dynamically.[41] The Townsend Plan mobilized and tried different strategies and forms of organization in response to its perceived influence and setbacks over a long period. Sometimes the leadership learned valuable lessons and changed its mobilization and strategies to increase its influence. Sometimes it did not. And the policy-making process is a moving target that changes the possibilities for challengers' influence as it develops. I trace these changing efforts to turn policy into senior citizens' pensions over multiple rounds of the policy process, as old-age policy was altered over time and thus changed the possibilities for further influence. The Townsend Plan and the pension movement almost turned U.S. old-age policy into senior citizens pensions, but they failed to do so. Had they done so, most likely the pension movement would have remained influential. The fact that old-age policy developed in a different direction influenced the types of groups and mobilizations that could exert influence for the second half of the twentieth century to the present day.

Conclusion

Trying to understand and explain the macrosocial consequences of a challenger poses difficult issues. One is whether to analyze success or consequences. Considering the collective benefits that it may achieve for its constituency is a more flexible standard than considering the success or failure of a challenger's program, because social movements may have many influences, tangible and intangible, beyond their stated goals. In the case of the Townsend Plan and the pension movement, I see them as representing the aged, the group that stood to benefit most from their campaigns. The pension movement sought to advance the status of the aged in a modernizing industrial capitalist society.

Most arguments about the impact of state-oriented challengers focus on their form and actions or the contexts in which they contend. I think we need to go beyond arguing that a challenger organized in one way is more likely to succeed than one organized differently, or that some specific strategy is always preferable to another, regardless of the situation. The same is true for claims that challengers will have effects if and only if political contexts are favorable. In democratized polities, it is worth thinking about strategies beyond the standard distinction between assimilative and disruptive, focusing on the various constraints that challengers can employ that fall within the rules of the game. And so I think through how different strategies might work in different political contexts facing challengers.

The American political context has been far more hostile than others in the West for the claims of challengers. But I suggest it is possible for challengers to have impacts sometimes even in unfavorable contexts, just as some strategies may backfire in favorable ones. The political mediation argument I present suggests that strategies must match contexts to be effective. It is key to target action where and when it is likely to work and to modulate strategies according to the degree that the contexts are likely to oppose or support the challenge. This approach suggests that sometimes challengers may miss opportunities to have an impact as well as realize them.

Assessing the impacts of challengers presents a double problem—to ascertain whether a challenger had any impact whatsoever and to appraise explanations for influence when there are few empirical observations and many plausible explanations. I employ historical materials and comparisons to assess the influence of the Townsend Plan and the pension movement. But I also trace their influence through the phases of the policy-making process and compare campaigns by the Townsendites and policy-making episodes. The Townsend Plan tried many different strategies and faced as many different political contexts as there were in the United States and across individual states in the 1930 and 1940s. By no means are these analyses static comparisons. The Townsend Plan and the pension movement reacted to the results of these various campaigns and evolved as they tried to turn the moving target of old-age policy into senior citizens' pensions. I turn now to the rise of the Townsend Plan and the Townsend clubs.

TWO

How the West Was Won Over

SOCIAL MOVEMENT ORGANIZATIONS often generate policy proposals and public figures, but the Townsend Plan was built upon an idea and its author. Recently fired from his position as the city's medical officer, Dr. Francis E. Townsend published on September 30, 1933, a letter to the editor of the *Long Beach (Calif.) Press-Telegram*. In it he proposed a just and simple way to restore the economy. Give Americans over sixty years of age $150 every month, on the condition that they refrain from employment and spend the money by the end of the month. Aged Americans would get their just deserts for lifelong social contributions, and the transfer of jobs from old to young and the enforced spending would halt the Great Depression, which had left more than a quarter of the labor force jobless. A national sales tax would fund the pensions. The letter sparked an extensive debate in the *Press-Telegram*'s letters to the editor page. Soon Townsend placed an ad in the paper to solicit volunteers to help promote his idea.[1]

His most important recruit was someone he already knew well: the real estate agent and entrepreneur Robert Earl Clements, who was employing Townsend part-time. The doctor thought Clements had the organizational and promotional skills to "put over" the pension plan—to generate enthusiasm among the aged and support from the general public and political leaders to convert the plan into law. Clements agreed to spearhead the effort, and in January he and Townsend created a not-for-profit organization to pursue the mission.[2] Despite the fact that both the organization and the pension-recovery program were named Old Age Revolving Pensions, by the summer Clements convinced Townsend to call both simply the Townsend Plan. At that time, they hit on the idea of creating Townsend clubs, membership groups in local communities, to unleash the energy of volunteers and open their pocketbooks. By the end of 1934, the Townsend Plan would sweep California and make inroads elsewhere in the West and parts of the Midwest, generating an outpouring of working- and middle-class support among the aged. Although other large-scale membership groups such as the Fraternal Order of Eagles and organized labor had made demands for means-tested old-age benefits in some states and localities, the Townsend Plan became the first organization that mobilized large numbers of the American aged for the sole purpose of demanding equal, widespread, and nationally provided old-age benefits—senior citizens' pensions.

This outpouring of support suggests questions. What was Townsend's pension plan, and how did it stand out from the dozens of other proposals to end the Depression and aid deserving groups? What was its appeal? How and why was the Townsend Plan able to mobilize such great support among the aged so quickly, given the tremendous competition in recovery plans? What was so special about the pension-recovery program or the Townsend Plan that generated this much support? How much support and of what sort did the Townsend Plan gain in its first year? Was the organization really on the verge of attracting anything like the huge share of the American public that Townsend claimed? How the Townsend Plan took off is partly a story about the origins of an interesting program, but mainly about the building of an unusual social movement organization with an innovative application of sales techniques to a social campaign. It is also a story of two unlikely newcomers to movement politics.

Townsend and His Plan, Explained

Meet Doctor Townsend

There was no hint in Francis Townsend's long life that he was destined for greatness. Born in 1867, he was the second of six children of homesteaders, who had settled near Fairbury, Illinois, and a sickly boy, having contracted swamp malaria as an infant. He moved with his family to Nebraska and gained two years of a rudimentary high school education in a Congregational academy but quit well before finishing. At age twenty Townsend was lent $1,000 by his father and set out for southern California with his younger brother George to make a fortune in hay farming, but he quickly lost his stake. Townsend roamed the West working as a ranch hand, teacher, homesteader, miner, and stove salesman before deciding to enroll in Omaha Medical College. The oldest in his class at thirty-one years, he supported himself in part with a newspaper route and was taken under the wing of an instructor who was also an ardent socialist. Upon graduation Townsend eked out a living in Belle Fourche, South Dakota, a Black Hills cattle town, ministering to the rough-and-tumble ailments of cowboys, miners, and prostitutes, while treating his own digestive problems. There he met a widow, Wilhelmina "Minnie" Bogue, who was a nurse and soon became Townsend's wife. The doctor wrote for a local paper and served on the town council, but local political bosses objected to his good-government designs and ran him out of town. He stayed in the state and at age fifty enlisted in the army during the Great War. Instead of fighting Germans in Europe, he fought the influenza epidemic in Vermillion. He achieved good results with his patients by starving them.[3]

After the war, in search of better health and fortune, Townsend moved to Long Beach. But despite the salubrious climate, he was still dogged by illness, and despite the postwar boom his dry ice factory failed. He tried his hand at real estate and could talk up the property but had trouble closing the deal. As the Depression began, Townsend caught a break. A medical school classmate landed Townsend a job as the city's public health officer. In that capacity he witnessed firsthand the effects of poverty on the aged and was able to empathize all the more when in June 1933, after a change of political administrations, the city council pink-slipped him.[4] Minnie was forced to take nursing work to support them, while the sixty-six-year-old doctor went back to real estate.

Nor did Townsend's physical appearance or manner suggest that he was on the verge of stirring masses. He was unassuming and inconspicuous, the kind of person one might see in the back of the church on Sunday. People called him "Doctor" more as a courtesy than through experience of his medical treatment, and he called his wife "Mother." Although he had a full head of white hair and a sporty salt-and-pepper mustache in a contemporary style soon to be discredited by Hitler, his face was gaunt and inexpressive, and he blinked behind standard-issue, horn-rimmed glasses. His stomach ailments had left him a little stooped.

California Dreaming: The Pension-Recovery Program in Brief

How Townsend came up with his idea is unknown. The often-recounted official story is apocryphal and serves largely as a myth of origins. According to this tale, one day Townsend looked out his window and saw three aged women sifting his trash for edibles. He unleashed a barrage of curses, frightening his wife, who shushed him out of concern for the neighbors. But Townsend told her that he wanted to yell until God and the whole country heard him. His head cleared, he drafted his letter.[5] Despair and injustice brought outrage and inspiration. However it happened, sometime that September Dr. Townsend wrote a letter to the editor and began his career in old-age activism.

The doctor's proposal had all the basic components of the framing theory of social movements propounded by David Snow and others and indeed fit well with the metaphors of the main concepts.[6] According to this line of argument, to be successful challengers need to interpret grievances in preassembled ways that diagnose problems, prescribe plausible solutions, and mobilize support to act on these interpretations. The framing worked in two main directions. Townsend saw poverty among the aged and declared it unjust that the people who built the country's prosperity were so insecure in their final years. He had a simple prescription—to give them cash. The $150-per-month guaranteed pension, far more than the median family income of the day, would empty the poorhouses, where in California alone approximately 5,000 of the aged were institutionalized in 1929. The high pension would also end any dependency of older Americans on their children, elevate the status of the aged, and validate their lives. The pension would not be charity but a right of all Americans, aside from habitual criminals, for a life of service rendered to the nation.[7]

Townsend, however, saw his proposal mainly as a recovery program. The doctor also had a diagnosis for the Depression. Technology was simultaneously producing many goods and reducing jobs, leading to a lack of purchasing power, which artificially dampened economic activity, leading to the tragedy of poverty among plenty. What was needed was to increase both employment and purchasing power. Townsend's prescription here was for older employed Americans to relinquish their jobs for the pension.[8] But the pensions would improve employment mainly indirectly, by stimulating the economy with enforced spending. Doctor's orders were "starve a flu, feed a Depression." This is where the "revolving" aspect came in. The mandatory monthly spending would achieve a significantly greater velocity than money handled by others because, supposedly, money spent by the government tended to collect in banks. Pension money would thus spur production more than would alternative uses and result in superior tax collections that would fund the next round of pensions and so on. Aside from ending joblessness, the pensions would arrest a host of social evils related to unemployment—juvenile delinquency, since younger men would have jobs to look forward to, and crime, since habitual criminals would be denied pensions.[9]

Many ideas like Townsend's were being aired as the Depression dragged on. In Britain, a "revolving" recovery proposal had been advanced in the 1920s by Major C. M. Douglas, and his former follower William Aberhart and his Social Credit Party promoted a version of the plan in western Canada. A $30 monthly old-age proposal was pressed in 1932 by Dr. J. E. Pope, an Oklahoma chiropodist whose operation dissolved in disgrace after a congressional investigation exposed him as a con man. Economists like John Maynard Keynes and Irving Fisher and popular economic writers like Stuart Chase advanced more reputable proposals for massive government spending. And although there is no reason to believe that Townsend had heard of him, C. Stewart McCord, a Seattle dentist, developed an old-age pension-recovery plan in 1931 that anticipated Dr. Townsend's. As the slump deepened, concocting anti-Depression remedies was becoming a national pastime—especially on the West Coast. Some twenty groups in San Francisco alone were devoted to this pursuit.[10]

Townsend was well suited to develop such a proposal. His political and journalism background, his experience with the destitute aged, the time he had to reflect on his situation, and his need for attention—all these played a part in his developing the idea and sending it to the newspaper. Townsend later called himself "a persistent cuss" and had the tenacity to pursue his idea. For all his failures, he maintained an outsized belief in himself. He also had

a saving ignorance of economics and plans similar to his own and no distract-
ing moneymaking opportunities. That fall Townsend moved to press his plan
beyond the editorial pages, having material printed up and gathering some
volunteers to help distribute it, solicit contributions, and gain signatures on
petitions in support.

Birth of a Sales Staff

The Original Movement Entrepreneur

But the Townsend's pension-recovery proposal would not have captured the
imaginations of so many strictly on its intellectual merits or on Townsend's
meager organizational and persuasive skills. The program's fate depended instead on the Townsend Plan's mastermind, a thirty-nine-year-old real estate
agent named Robert Earl Clements. Earl Clements was an even more unlikely
aspirant to old-age activism than Townsend. Born in Amarillo, Texas, the son
of a cattleman, Clements bounced around with his family to Roswell, New
Mexico, and El Paso before graduating from high school in Fort Worth. Like
Townsend, as a young man Clements migrated to California, joining his father, who had taken up the real estate business in Long Beach, in search of
fortune. Unlike Townsend, Clements made one, by addressing the desire of
migrants, often refugees from the Midwest, to invest their life savings in or-
ange groves and other agricultural property.[11]

A tall, angular man with thinning blond hair, Clements had bland man-
ners and a stylish wardrobe that telegraphed his considerable shrewdness. In
the years just before the stock market crashed, Clements served as the sales
manager for a settlement halfway between Long Beach and Santa Ana named
Midway City. Clements, who hired Townsend as a salesman on the project,
had a knack for promotion, was a good judge of sales talent, could seal a deal,
and was said to have amassed $750,000 by 1929. During the Depression,
however, the bottom dropped out of the real estate market, and the value
of Clements's holdings shriveled.[12] Clements allowed his former underling
Townsend to use his office to work on his new interest, as well as to attempt
to sell real estate.

In perhaps the biggest closing of his career, Townsend sold Clements's
thirty-two-year-old fiancée, Thelma Morris, on the pension-recovery idea. A
vivacious, determined, and skilled career woman with striking red hair, Morris had served as Clements's stenographer before attracting his romantic attention. She saw tremendous promise in the doctor's idea and had witnessed
firsthand the lack of an immediate future in real estate.[13] And she knew that
Clements had already built one career relying on the savings of the aged. Once
Clements started to think about it, he also perceived potential in the venture.
The Depression would provide volunteers and induce printers and building

owners to provide services and space on speculation. Clements customized Townsend's proposal to ensure that it was consistent with basic demographic and fiscal statistics, on which Townsend was a little shaky. Clements probably also learned that California law regarding nonprofit corporations paradoxically allowed them to make a profit—to be remitted to the corporation's "members" upon its dissolution—so long as the profit was incidental to its main activities. He found himself with Townsend on New Year's Day on hands and knees painting the floor of the organization's new office, or so legend has it. In any case, Clements incorporated Old Age Revolving Pensions (OARP), Ltd. with himself and Townsend as members on January 24, 1934. Its mission was "to promote and secure by means of education and every other means, the adoption of the United States government . . . of plans and laws providing for the pensioning of its citizens." In a seemingly trivial move made to comply with California law, Townsend's brother Walter, a Hollywood hotel porter, was added as the corporation's third member.[14]

Clements began to refer to himself as the Townsend Plan's "cofounder"—a title that greatly understated his contributions to the cause. As secretary and treasurer, Clements plotted the venture's organizational, sales, and political strategies, advised by his new bride, Thelma, as much as by Townsend. The "cofounder" would be the driving force behind the organization for more than two years, a period in which it would rise to national prominence. A quiet man who liked to work behind the scenes, Clements claimed once that he had a voice that did not carry. But Clements was determined that the whole country would hear the doctor's voice.[15] In February they hired their first canvasser, who went door-to-door soliciting collections and signatures. There were also volunteers, some of whom hoped eventually to be paid. Meanwhile, Clements and Townsend traveled around the area arranging meetings, talking up the pension-recovery idea, and soliciting donations. By the end of the month the Townsend Plan had brought in enough money to allow Townsend to retire some of his personal debts.[16] By the end of March, things were going so well that Townsend and Clements issued themselves a salary of $50 per week. They could take all to the bank, too, because they had allocated themselves a similar amount in expenses. With the organization also providing employment for Clements's wife, he decided to devote his full attention to the Townsend Plan.[17]

According to John McCarthy, Mayer Zald, and others, all successful movement organizations need coherent mobilization "structures" to secure resources and commitment from adherents.[18] Clements's innovation along these lines was to apply the organizational forms and techniques of real estate salesmanship to a political challenger. He assembled a hierarchical but loosely connected sales staff of people who were also speakers and solicitors for the Townsend Plan. In May, Clements and Townsend hired Pierre Tomlinson, a former patient of Townsend's from South Dakota who had also relocated to

Long Beach, and Clyde E. Smith. They were to be paid on a commission basis for any publications and paraphernalia they might sell and any donations they could generate. They in turn subcontracted out to other representatives, who were also placed on a commission basis, dividing California into sales territories. The idea was to win converts among the aged, create favorable public opinion surrounding the pension-recovery plan, and generate revenue for the organization. A speaker for the Townsend Plan, Chester J. MacDonald, in June started to publish a sixteen-page newsletter, the *Modern Crusader*.[19]

The organization that emerged from this process brought together people of vastly different motivation and outlook. Typically one expects movement organizers to sacrifice income to convictions, but most Townsend Plan sales reps sought mainly to advance their own welfare. The mixing of political program and career advancement in one political concern was far from new to America, where patronage-oriented political parties in the Northeast had long combined a desire to win elections and jobs for party workers, but the Townsend Plan salespeople did not have to win office to earn, and some of them were so mercenary as to make the lowliest ward heeler seem like an ideologue by comparison. The Townsend Plan anticipated the techniques of Tupperware and Amway, and the pension organization's sales force accumulated many unemployed salesmen, clergymen, and politicians ready for a price to lend their persuasive talents to the cause. Their belief was that the pension-recovery program was plausible and attractive enough to be sold. By contrast, their customers were not merely bodies to mobilize to the polls every few years or to supply with handy plastic containers. Most volunteers and the Townsend Plan–supporting rank and file were true believers in the pension idea. These supporters were willing to take on for free any number of lower-level and unpaid organizing tasks.

Twilight Nation

The intensity of support for Townsend's pension-recovery program had to do in part with what Townsend and Clements were selling and in part with how they sold it. The Townsend Plan reps flogged the pension-recovery program as if it were insurance, Bibles, or real estate. The program had some resemblance to each. As elaborated in the early Townsend Plan booklet *Old Age Revolving Pensions*, Clements's column "Your Questions Answered" in the *Modern Crusader*, and talks given by the organization's approved speakers, the pension plan was more than a technical treatise. Clements had sold real estate, which was like selling people hopes and dreams—a vision of the future. In their contemporaneous account of California recovery ideas and organizations, *Glory Roads*, Luther Whiteman and Samuel L. Lewis called the Townsend Plan's product "mental real estate."[20] The organization's representatives were

YOUR QUESTIONS ANSWERED

By The National Secretary

Q.—Would it help if I were to make a personal call on my Congressman when he returns from Washington and try to get his pledge to support the Townsend Old Age Revolving Pension Bill?

A.—YES INDEED and several more yeses. That would not only help, it would do a lot of good and if you keep after him hard enough and often enough it will probably pass the bill. A million like you calling on their Congressmen is just what we need to get the O. A. R. P. bill passed.

Q.—If I were to visit a foreign country would my pension be cancelled?

A.—Not permanently, but you could not receive any pension while outside the United States as the bill will call for your entire $200 to be spent within the confines of the United States within 30 days.

Q.—What is the status of a child born in the United States whose father is a U. S. citizen but whose mother is foreign born?

A.—Children whose father is a U. S. citizen are citizens wherever born.

Q.—What about children living off the old folks?—Stanley C. S.

R. E.
CLEMENTS

Q.—I lived in the U. S. twenty-one years, and am a property owner in Iowa and Long Beach. Was born in Sweden, but have never taken out naturalization papers. Can I get the pension?

A.—No. Only naturalized citizens of the United States will receive the pension. We would suggest you take out your naturalization papers at once.

Q.—Would the pension be payable to a child born in Canada of American parents?

A.—Yes, the child is an American born on foreign soil.

Q.—Could I give part of my pension to my children?

A.—No. But you could purchase articles or merchandise needed and give that.

Q.—About how many persons in Long Beach would receive the pension, and what payroll would it mean to the merchants?—M. M.

A.—It is estimated that there are 15,000 persons in the city of Long Beach over 60 years of age. At $200 per month the payroll for Long Beach would be more than $3,000,000 each month. If you compare this amount with the Navy payroll you find that the Navy pay is less than one-half this amount, and if you will talk to the business men as to what the Navy payroll means to Long Beach, you will realize what a wonderfully fine proposition a $3,000,000 payroll will be to Long Beach business.

Figure 2.1: Your Questions Answered. Robert E. Clements, the national secretary of the Townsend Plan, was its early guiding light. He wrote a column in the first Townsend Plan newspaper, the *Modern Crusader*, called "Your Questions Answered," which explained the details of Dr. Townsend's pension-recovery proposal. Source: *Modern Crusader*, June 13, 1934, p. 14.

peddling a retrofitted version of the future and a happy vision of America—an imaginary community that Clements might have named Twilight Nation.

This vision of the future superimposed a distant or, to be precise, never-existent image of American history onto a snapshot of the recent past. America would once again, or for the first time, be a place where men were breadwinners and women worked in the home, and where the eldest members of families were truly revered. Townsend Plan publicists situated these idealized traditional social relations in up-to-date settings, with a certain equality granted to the sexes, despite the different roles accorded them. Both men and women needed to be better educated to meet technological advances in the workplace and home, as well as to act politically, according to the vision, as political rights and responsibilities were to be exercised equally in the wake of women's suffrage. No matter what they did for work during their adulthood, men and women would be remunerated for it in old age at an equal rate, and no distinctions were made by race either. Recipients needed only to be American citizens in good standing. The aged's great new spending power and their officially recognized role in ensuring continued economic prosperity would earn the respect of younger generations. Not much thought, however, was given to anything outside this vision—such as the trends of more women working outside the home, families being spread across the country, and family forms spilling outside traditional boundaries. Then again, it was not as if the revolving pension proposal would legislate against these developments.

Although the pension plan studiously avoided reference to any seemingly radical notions, it drew more on Marx than on Keynes, perhaps because of Townsend's socialist background. Without discussing constant or variable capital, the revolving pension plan held that less and less labor power would be needed to run the machines of modern business, opening up possibilities for greater freedom. There was no point in fighting such forces, according to both Marxian and Townsend Plan thinking, but for the Townsend Plan, there was no need for a worker takeover. Good old-fashioned American business know-how could be made to serve all and provide economic security.[21] Instead of introducing more freedom into workaday lives across generations as Marx imagined, however, these grants of security and freedom were to start first with those Americans who had devoted their lives to work. The Townsend Plan would have everyone doing the industrial or domestic equivalent of hunting and fishing before age sixty and becoming full-time critical critics, or whatever they wanted, in the twilight of their lives. Or as the Townsend Plan slogan put it: "Youth for Work, Age for Leisure."[22]

Townsend, Clements, and Townsend Plan representatives also developed a vision of the life course that was not entirely out of step with twenty-first-century thinking and practices. Young people would go to school until age twenty. This was far longer than the average for the day, as the modal education was some high school. This view was consistent with the idea, also in the air, that the overflowing labor market should not be flooded with youthful applicants. "Youth for Work" was somewhat misleading; under the pension plan the youngest were to be schooled and to experience a more extended adolescence and young adulthood unburdened by financial or family responsibility. Their work was to come over their next forty years—in the paid labor force or at home. For the most part the Townsend Plan saw women as "help makers in

Figure 2.2: The Span of Life from Birth to Death. The Townsend Plan proposed a surprisingly up-to-date version of the life course. Education would last until age twenty, closer to today's modal "some college" than the Depression's "some high school." And the retirement age would be closer to today's median of sixty-two years than the sixty-eight years of the era. Source: J. W. Brinton, *The Townsend National Recovery Plan: The Solution of Your Problem* (Chicago: Townsend National Weekly, 1936), pp. 48–49.

the home." But whatever they did for work, men and women were to be treated the same way in their final twenty years, or however many were left after sixty. It would be "Age for Leisure," which would be enjoyed rather than endured in fear of economic insecurity.[23] The only remaining chore would be deciding how to spend the well-earned money, whether to cultivate hobbies, take trips to the theater, purchase automobiles, radios, or refrigerators, or secure better health care.

Although it provided a future that was portrayed as a restoration of old-time family relations, the Townsend Plan displayed no coherent or easily identifiable ideology. Townsend Plan speakers did attack some specific efforts of government and business and sometimes used the rhetoric of populism. Townsend and Clements saw ordinary people of all ages and classes being harmed by forces outside their control. The Townsend Plan relied more on the Christian version of this style of argumentation and tended to criticize government more than business. Whenever possible the Townsend Plan wrapped the pension plan in Old Glory as well as Christianity. An official banner incorporated a Stars and Stripes motif and declared: "God Bless America—with the Townsend Plan." If the plan was God's plan, it was 100-percent American, too. The program also resonated with nineteenth-century republican ideology. All aged people were seen as lifelong producers, whose labor was no longer needed. Yet the Townsend Plan identified no major non-producer groups, aside from habitual criminals. To sell its image of the future, the Townsend Plan amassed Americanism, Protestant religiosity, received economic wisdom, California utopianism, mass consumption, and populist appeals. It was a lot like taking the average person's view of what he would like to see in an oil painting—gathering disparate animal species and having them all peacefully drinking from a lake at sunset. Ideological coherence was sacrificed to the greater good of appealing to the least common denominator and avoiding the ire of any potential opponents.[24]

Townsend and Clements certainly did not tilt at the windmills of capitalist industrialization and socioeconomic modernization as did the latter-day populists Senator Huey Long and Father Charles Coughlin, both of whom led challengers at around the same time and identified distinctive enemies and scapegoats. The Townsend Plan assailed neither chain stores nor banks, neither monopolies nor millionaires, each of which had been claimed by Long and Coughlin to undermine local communities. Banks were a problem for the Townsend Plan only because money tended to gather there, thus hindering its circulation and economic activity, not because bankers were evil and conspiratorial, as others suggested. Millionaires would be granted pensions, too, if they would agree to retire. Nor did the Townsend Plan find fundamental problems with the workings of capitalism, as did the production-for-use plans of Upton Sinclair's End Poverty in California and the resurgent socialists and

Figure 2.3: God Bless America—with the Townsend Plan. The Townsend Plan employed both patriotic and Christian rhetoric in its appeals, as in this slogan. Source: author's collection, photographer unknown.

A BUSINESS THAT
HELPS *all* CALIFORNIA

**CHAIN STORES
HELP ME?**

Yes, Plenty!

MODERN *Independent*
MERCHANTS SAY

Of the 89,000 retail stores in the
state, only 6,500 are chain stores.
Yet, those relatively few chain
stores have set the pace — have
taught independent merchants
how to make a better living
by group buying and efficient
selling.

CALIFORNIA
CHAIN STORES HELP
ALL MERCHANTS

Figure 2.4: Chain Stores Help Me? Yes, Plenty! The Townsend Plan avoided the common scapegoats identified by the neopopulists Huey Long and Father Coughlin, such as chain stores. Dr. Townsend thought small businesses were largely doomed and that that was not a bad thing. Source: *National Townsend Weekly*, July 6, 1935, p. 10.

communists.[25] The threat to local communities came from the loss of work due to the advance of technique, but the lessening of needed work time was simultaneously an opportunity to pension off unnecessary workers. If capitalist industrialization was also fundamentally changing relationships within families or communities, Townsend and Clements preferred not to notice. All that was needed to restore a simpler era of social relations, albeit stocked with state-of-the-art consumer goods, was to rout old-age poverty with pensions and provide jobs to younger men.

The increasing size and role of government was also of no great concern to the Townsend Plan. Like Long and Coughlin, Townsend and Clements wanted to use the government to restore and ensure prosperity. They also expected that a relatively simple governmental intervention would do the job better than Roosevelt's many new alphabet agencies. Like the others, the Townsend Plan's founders were skeptical of Roosevelt's efforts to provide work through such temporary agencies as the Federal Emergency Relief Administration, the Civil Works Administration, or the work camps for youth of the Civilian Conservation Corps. Townsend Plan literature and speakers at-

tacked the New Deal as sometimes wasteful, especially programs that destroyed crops and livestock to raise prices. But Townsend and Clements did
not deride the experimental spirit and social concern of the New Deal. Nor
did they denounce government bureaucracy in general, as Long and Coughlin
often did. The Townsend Plan's founders portrayed the pension-recovery plan
as being complementary to the highly bureaucratic National Recovery
Administration and initially hoped the president could be won over to the
pension-recovery plan. If it took some bureaucratic authority to collect
the taxes and monitor the monthly spending of the pensions, so be it.[26] The
Townsend Plan's desire to refashion government was wrapped in a rhetoric of
hope and faith in representative democracy in the American mode.

The Townsend Plan leaders advanced their fictive, restoration vision with
a kind of neopopulism lite: seemingly minor democratic action was needed to
save ordinary Americans from forces for the good that had veered temporarily
out of control. But there was nothing to blame but bad luck; neither democracy nor capitalism required fundamental change. The pensions that would
restore things would come at the expense of no one and would help everyone.
If anything was to blame, it was a failure of common sense. There was too
much imagination in current counterintuitive, scarcity-producing programs,
like crop and livestock destruction; the solution was right in front of one's
nose. Roosevelt later famously denounced the Townsend's and other pension
ideas as "shortcuts to utopia." But the view of the Townsend's Plan was that if
there were such a path, what was the harm in taking it? The only enemies of
the organization were those who sought to defame the doctor's revolving
pension-recovery idea.

Appealing to the Aged

It was key that this vision was seen as being conjured by someone with whom
older Americans could identify. The Townsend Plan was also selling the man
apparently behind the plan, Dr. Townsend. In this it relied on state-of-the-art
marketing techniques. Clements and Townsend hired a public relations agent
from Los Angeles, Frank Peterson, and designed a marketing campaign, as
the organizer Tomlinson put it, to "build up Dr. Townsend and set him on a
pedestal as a man capable of leadership." Townsend Plan writers and speakers
burnished Townsend's image as that of a wise doctor, someone who had taken
some hard knocks in life, sure, but had distilled from them a vital prescription
for an economy whose ills had been poorly diagnosed and treated by businessmen, politicians, and economists.[27]

Dr. Townsend was made to symbolize the Townsend Plan, not unlike his
contemporary marketing counterparts Uncle Ben, Betty Crocker, and the Gerber baby. Although he was not fictional, no precursor of Ronald McDonald,

Townsend fell short of being like Dave Thomas, the founder of the Wendy's hamburger chain, who created a successful company and then lent his personage to advertising campaigns. Perhaps the most analogous corporate personification to Townsend, to stick to fast food, would be Colonel Harland Sanders, who also came to his calling in his sixties when he devised the special blend of eleven herbs and spices and the cooking technique for Kentucky Fried Chicken. The colonel founded restaurants for more than a decade afterward, but real franchising success came only after he sold the company and its new corporate owners began to exploit his image in an advertising campaign so successful that it has continued long after Sanders's death.[28] The relative contributions of Townsend's original recipe for recovery and the organizational legwork and appeals behind selling it were not immediately apparent, however, to the adherents to the Townsend Plan, or for that matter to the press, once it noticed.

The aged were drawn mainly because of the pensions and the Townsend Plan's justifications for them. The main ingredient was, of course, the generous, equal, and readily available pension. It would dissolve the economic problems of the aged, keeping the poorhouse at bay. The pension-recovery proposal imagined a kind of up-to-date continued dependence of adult children on their parents. The generous monthly benefits not only would prevent them from beseeching their children for help but also ensured that the children of the aged would be more inclined to look to their parents for economic support and would live longer under their parents' roofs. And the homes beneath them would still be there for the parents to bequeath to the children, rather than having to be sold off to pay for the parents' upkeep. In short, the pension would remove the main pecuniary and social fears behind growing old in an economy in which people mainly worked for wages and salaries, and in a society in which families increasingly assumed the nuclear form. It is no surprise that the adherents to the Townsend Plan were almost always aged.

People who are fortunate also want to appear deserving, and the Townsend Plan had this requirement doubly covered. On the one hand, the aged deserved the big pensions because of their years of hard work and virtuous lives. According to Townsend Plan literature, almost all wealth that currently existed was produced in the last forty years. Who else but those over age sixty could have produced it? On the other hand, in taking and spending the money, the aged were being more selfless than selfish, for many of them would relinquish scarce jobs to the young. Townsend and Clements liked to paint the image of a small businessmen taking a pension and turning the company over to his sons. Those with no job to give up would create one and ensure prosperity for all by spending their monthly benefits. Townsend Plan literature was calling prospective pensioners "prosperity agents." If the sums seemed radically

Figure 2.5: "Prosperity Agents." The Townsend Plan encouraged potential pensioners to think of themselves as prosperity agents, whose rapid spending would accelerate the wheels of industry and create jobs. Source: Dr. Francis E. Townsend, *The Townsend National Recovery Plan: New Reference Book* (Chicago: Townsend National Weekly, 1941), p. 10.

large, that circumstance would be moderated by the fact that their results would be so beneficial and conservative in every respect.[29]

Although scholars often claim that the pension-recovery plan's attraction was its extreme simplicity, its appeal to the aged lay in its mix of simplicity and complexity, practicality and utopianism, rights and responsibilities.[30] It is true that the proposal's basics could be readily understood by anyone and were simple enough that they could be printed on the front cover of the Townsend Plan booklet. A government provides pensions through an earmarked tax, and the aged retire, spend the money, and rejuvenate the economy. The pension-recovery plan was often portrayed as common sense, too, combining economic and moral aphorisms. Elders should be respected, youth should be employed, retirements would free up jobs, and circulating money would spur economic activity. The proposal was utopian, but its vision relied safely on many elements of the past and present. What is more, as utopias went, it would be simple to get from here to there. No eggs would need to be broken to make this omelet.

But the pension-recovery plan was also complex enough in its details that it gave many adherents confidence that it would work. Although the proposal did not change much after Townsend's first letters, Clements and various consultants and employees provided increasingly complicated economic justifications for it, especially regarding the taxes to be levied and how the enforced spending would spur economic activity.[31] These claims were backed up with hard and extensive, if often misleading and confusing, data. For those not inclined to examine the fine print, the pension plan seemed to have a solid backing that could withstand the scrutiny of experts. Those so inclined could study the proposal and debate its merits and tinker with it, becoming something like experts themselves, feeling as though possessed of a special knowledge, probably not unlike that of lay socialists and communists mastering the magic of historical materialism and dialectical thinking.

Changes in Plan

There were two significant changes in the pension-recovery plan in its first year. Although technical justifications were provided, both amendments were politically motivated, to gain aged adherents and to avoid opposition among the general public. The first was to up the monthly ante from $150 to $200. The technical justification was that this was the amount deemed sufficient, supposedly after further study, to generate enough economic activity to create one job at decent wages. The sum was also claimed to be necessary for the elderly to exercise their rights as American citizens and enjoy retirement to its fullest. More telling reasons, however, were provided in Townsend's authorized hagiography, *That Man Townsend* (1935): that $200 per month was a glamorous figure and no competing plan could plausibly offer pensioners more.[32]

The second change concerned the taxation provisions. The Townsend Plan's leadership, especially Clements, quickly became dissatisfied with the sales tax as a way to fund the pensions. For one thing, as more and more states engaged in political battles over sales taxes—some eighteen states passed them by the end of 1934—their regressiveness was becoming common knowledge, and the political left and organized labor criticized them.[33] Having the national government gain a monopoly in sales taxation, as Townsend and Clements first proposed, also seemed unlikely now. For another, to pay for the large pensions, a sales tax would have to be set at an extremely high rate, far more than the 10 percent initially suggested by Townsend and perhaps as high as 50 percent. This would make the proposal seem far from costless. Also, it would be easy for opponents to identify a sales tax rate that was set too low to finance the pensions.

To address these problems, Clements turned to a tax on business transactions. A transactions tax is a kind of cascading or pyramiding sales tax—levied on goods whenever they are sold in the production process, not just at the end point like a sales tax. It would produce more revenues than a value-added tax because the entire value of a good would be taxed at each stage, but would ultimately fall on the consumer. All the same, the transactions tax provided political cover. The tax was on "business" transactions—not on consumers or "sales." The leadership focused attention on the transactions between businesses and the stock transactions of the wealthy. The transactions tax also had the rhetorical advantage that its rate could be set low because the tax was collected at multiple places. It was decided eventually that a rate of 2 percent would be sufficient to pay for the pensions.[34] This allowed Townsend Plan speakers to score telling political points by suggesting disingenuously that a mere two cents on the dollar would be needed to save the economy and end old-age poverty. It helped, too, that no one knew for certain the value of business transactions, which were far less easily tracked than end sales.[35]

The Townsend Plan was a going concern by the summer. The organization's income was more than $6,000 for the first half of the year, mainly from individual contributions, collections, and through the sales of literature, mainly the booklet entitled *Old Age Revolving Pensions*, and paraphernalia, including windshield decals and buttons with the slogan "Youth for Work, Age for Leisure" with the organization's triangle insignia.[36] In his real estate business unregulated growth was not something that greatly concerned Clements, but given the less tangible nature of his new product, the rapid rise of interest in the pension-recovery plan was causing him problems. He needed to ensure that Townsend Plan speakers and representatives were on the same page. Many approved speakers were fine orators and had little reason to adhere to the specifics of the pension-recovery plan. More important, Clements needed to make sure that the representatives remitted their full percentage back to the organization. Most Townsend Plan reps all took relatively unmonitored collections, which tempted them to cheat, and some sold their own revolving-pension material. The problem of control over message and revenues was aggravated by the expanding number of subcontractors, who were sometimes more than two steps removed from the control of national headquarters. And once the idea was out there, freebooting speakers would act as if they were Townsend Plan–approved and help themselves to collections.[37]

A Challenger of Fan Clubs

In the summer of 1934, Clements and Townsend hit upon an organizational form—Townsend clubs—which became the Townsend Plan's underpinning. Officially, the clubs were charged with keeping alive interest in the doctor's pension-recovery plan, reporting anti–Townsend Plan activity, and submitting questions to the national headquarters. More generally, the clubs were the first line of fiscal defense against Townsend Plan representatives and crucibles in which new political identities were forged. They were designed to raise revenue and consciousness, as well as to provide a direct line of communication between the founders and their most fervent supporters. The clubs helped to address the problem of message control. The national headquarters could dispatch weekly bulletins directly to Townsendites. The clubs also gave true believers a greater role in handling money—which they would remit directly to national headquarters. The clubs also provided a ready market for authorized Townsend products and a steady source of contributions. And so the sales representatives of the Townsend Plan were converted into club "organizers." The first Townsend club was founded on August 23 in Huntington, California, and Townsend clubs soon spread throughout California and surrounding areas.[38]

Generating Revenue

Townsend clubs were organized on an entrepreneurial basis by way of the sales staff. The yearly membership "contribution" or fee was a quarter, which was the price of the Townsend Plan booklet. The term "contribution" was used because voluntary remittances required less accountability than fees.[39] California's regional and local organizers received commissions for their work. At the top of the organizational chart, Tomlinson and Smith were receiving 2.5 cents per member and 1 cent per booklet.[40] Commission-earning Townsend Plan representatives often organized clubs, but local club officers were mainly drawn from the ranks of volunteers. According to the official procedure, anyone interested in starting a club would contact the national headquarters, receive the contact information of a local organizer as well as a membership form, draft a temporary list of officers, recruit at least 100 members, and secure their membership fees. At that point this person, designated the club secretary, was supposed to turn in the form and at least $25 to the national headquarters. In turn, the secretary would receive membership cards, Townsend Plan booklets, a weekly bulletin, 100 blank petition sheets, and a year's subscription to the newspaper. The clubs would then meet weekly or biweekly and submit occasional donations to the national headquarters.[41]

Often clubs developed in many other ways than the official manner, however. Sometimes potential local club secretaries would hear a speech from a Townsend Plan organizer and agree to start a club, purchasing $25 worth of literature. Or they might cut out the middleman, as the official form was printed in the Townsend Plan booklet. In such instances the club secretary could pocket $7.50 of the $25 collected. To start a club, the secretary-hopeful might make a telephone call to a friend in a neighboring town. These "live

wires," usually among the better-off members, since most Americans did
not yet own telephones, would encourage friends to form new clubs, perhaps
by helping them organize a mass meeting or putting them in touch with a
Townsend organizer. New club secretaries sometimes paid the bulk of the initial $25 fee or even the entire sum with the expectation of signing up mem-
bers and collecting later, or being willing to eat some or all of the charge. New
recruits at an organizing meeting often would enroll and pay for family members who would never take part in club activities.[42]

There was much to criticize in this strategy of resource mobilization. The
use of commissions was not new to a political reform organization. Almost
two decades previous to the Townsend Plan, North Dakota's Nonpartisan
League had employed commissions to organize farmers for its program of state
ownership of terminal elevators, flour mills, packinghouses, and storage
plants, as well as state inspection of grain. For representatives of a nonprofit
organization, however, many Townsend Plan organizers were disturbingly
cash-conscious, even in comparison to high-salaried executives in today's
corporate-run charitable organizations such as the United Way. The rate of
yield from contributions to honest organizers was substandard, as compared
with mass mailing today. At least half of the revenues generated in the first
year were devoted to organizers, commissions, and salaries. Plenty of people
were getting paid. By December Tomlinson and Smith had contracted out to
approximately 300 representatives. And even with the wildfire growth of
Townsend clubs, Townsend Plan organizers continued to have a troubling leeway in handling contributions.[43]

But joining the profit motive of paid organizers with the enthusiasm of volunteers generated a great deal of revenue quickly, far more than could have
been amassed otherwise. High as the overhead was, whatever monies found
their way back to the central headquarters had none of the strings often attached to contributions to charitable organizations. Also, large contributions
from the rich were discouraged, and so the founders were not beholden to any
wealthy interests. The funds came largely from the Townsend Plan's indigenous and sometimes impoverished base—the aged, who liked the idea of
clubs and joined them in droves, especially in Townsend's southern California
and other parts of the West.[44]

Creating Townsendites

Townsend clubs usually met weekly, anywhere from the halls of fraternal organizations to churches to members' homes to rented spaces devoted solely to
club activities. They listened to speakers, shared refreshments and other enter-
tainments, and discussed the revolving pension plan. Unlike other large American membership organizations, which tended to segregate men and women,
in Townsend clubs men and women met together. Although many clubs were

small and often had a certain social homogeneity to them in the manner of fraternal organizations, other clubs were large and diverse. Clubs began meetings by reciting the Pledge of Allegiance, singing "America, the Beautiful," and sometimes praying, and frequently concluded meetings by pledging allegiance to the Townsend Plan.[45] There was an increasing stream of literature to attend to, as well, including bulletins, newsletters, and a weekly newspaper. Townsend called the clubs "debating societies," though no one was taking the negative side of "Should Townsend's Pension Plan Be Enacted?" The first rule of any Townsend club was that you were never to speak against Townsend's pension-recovery plan.[46] Townsend clubs were largely fan clubs.

Like other movement organizations, the Townsend Plan faced the so-called free rider problem: how to induce people to join Townsend clubs, despite the fact that the pension-recovery plan would aid all of the aged, club members or not. Part of the solution was to offer something to club members only. These selective incentives were not mainly material. To use the other categories of James Q. Wilson, as with most social movement organizations, most Townsend club members had nothing to gain materially, and the incentives to join were mainly purposive—to earn the gratification one receives from contributing to a worthy cause.[47] Yet the benefits of Townsend's proposal were multiple. It was to help all, particularly the unemployed, by ending the Depression, but it would greatly aid the deserving aged. To put it another way, club members were to be the direct beneficiaries of the Townsend Plan, but they also were led to see themselves as "conscience constituents," to use the terms of McCarthy and Zald. Townsendites considered themselves to be acting on behalf of the unemployed and youth, as well as the impoverished aged. It was a clever way to appeal to a group that had been circumspect about making demands in its own behalf.[48]

The Townsend clubs also offered solidary incentives—the benefits of being in enjoyable company and from group activities—through a politically inflected sociability, amusement with a higher purpose. Clubs engaged in skits, musical performances, and group sing-alongs, all designed to heighten members' interest and commitment to the pension-recovery plan. Fun was fused with fund-raising, as through picnics, bake sales, and bazaars. The benefits of club membership also included a version of group hero worship typical of fan clubs or modern-day presidential campaigns. Lauded in publications and made famous by radio performances, Townsend was achieving celebrity status. There were also incentives for the specific individuals; in addition to the four officers, Townsend clubs had a mandatory advisory board of ten; many club members were thus also club officials. And the material disincentives to joining were minimized. The fee was not high, considerably lower than the $8 per year paid by Nonpartisan League members, and a certain amount of free riding with respect to dues was allowed, so long as club members remained active and someone picked up the fiscal slack.

The Townsend clubs also forged new political identities among their aged participants. As Elisabeth S. Clemens and other new institutionalists have argued, political interests do not simply emerge from social commonalities and categories, but political organizations play a central role in constructing them. The aged had existed as a demographic group with generic problems and issues well before the Townsend Plan came on the scene, but not until its appearance was there a mass organizational vehicle that identified injustices, expressed specific grievances, and made demands for the group as a whole. The Townsend Plan induced Townsend club members to think of themselves as a distinct group with a separate identity and interests, including the right to an unconditional, government-granted pension. The official identity promoted by national headquarters was, however, an unusually narrow one. Townsend clubbers were encouraged to be enthusiasts of the pension-recovery program and discouraged from thinking about the interests of the aged beyond pensions, ignoring other political projects and policies of potentially great consequence to the aged, such as health care or housing. In short, the clubs were designed to create Townsendites, older Americans who believed in the rightness of large pensions for their service and the validity of the doctor's prescription for the economy.[49]

Challengers engaging in democratic experiments, as Francesca Polletta has shown, can generate innovative ideas and develop political skills in people previously uninvolved in politics. The Townsend Plan headquarters gave the clubs a great amount of autonomy in their weekly activities. Club officers had to shift for themselves in figuring out what the clubs would do each week, after the various pledges and bulletins were dispensed with, and the officers and the members had to figure out how to get through to the public in order to generate resources and support. But the national headquarters placed constraints on the clubs and the political development of Townsendites. Their energies were rarely channeled into directions that would help them learn to become highly skilled political actors. The national Townsend Plan was interested in ideas from the clubs only to the extent that they aided in generating resources or spreading the word. The national headquarters discouraged clubs from taking initiative in local politics, fearing that Townsendites would be swayed by politicians with agendas that ran outside Townsend's proposal. Clubs that defied the national headquarters were subject to having their permits revoked.[50] For all their autonomy, Townsend clubs had no more control over the Townsend Plan's decision making than New York Yankees fan clubs have over whom to sign, trade, or play in the field.[51]

These arrangements allowed Clements and Townsend to enjoy strategic freedom that would be the envy of leaders of any organization, let alone a social movement organization, whose leaders are often highly constrained by their membership. The clubs promised to generate a consistent and growing stream of revenues to finance political projects, but they did not need much supervision. Club members were far more involved than today's standard of occasional check writers or demonstration participants, but Clements and Townsend could make strategic decisions unconstrained, and their decisions were unlikely to seem illegitimate. Townsendites believed in Townsend and, to a lesser extent, Clements, who in any case gave Townsend his marching orders. Thus Townsend and Clements could seize opportunities to advance their cause, if they could identify them.

Organizational Purification

As they planned to take the national stage, Clements and Townsend, however, feared losing control of their creation to rival leaders. The official newspaper exemplified some of the problems Clements and Townsend faced in the latter part of the year. Edited and financed by Chester J. MacDonald, the *Modern Crusader* had been up and running since June. The sixteen-page paper was a useful means to spread the word, answer questions, counter criticisms, and buff Townsend's image. By the summer, though, there was a dispute over the paper's content and ownership, with Townsend and Clements forcing MacDonald out.[52] Townsend and Clements also had financial reasons to take over the newspaper. To run the newspaper Clements and Townsend created another corporation that fall—this time definitely not a nonprofit one—which they called the Prosperity Publishing Company. By the end of the year Townsend and Clements hired their own editor and changed the name to the *Townsend Weekly*.[53]

Also crucial were the forced retirements of Pierre Tomlinson and C. E. Smith. These two had sub-subcontracted out California and some other states to approximately 300 organizers, some regional, others local, most of whom were being paid commissions. Once the network of organizers was out there and it was clear that the Townsend Plan was a going concern, Clements viewed Tomlinson and Smith as a drain on the organization's revenue, approximately 3.5 cents per every new member. Together they probably cleared about $5,000—far more than Clements and Townsend were making. At the end of November, Tomlinson and Smith were induced by Clements to sign an agreement to sever their relationship with the Townsend Plan, each taking severance payments of $500 in addition to the balance of their commissions.[54]

Taking Stock of the Townsend Plan's Support in 1934

By the end of 1934 the Townsend Plan was generating great support in California and other parts of the West, but it varied greatly in its intensity. At the highest level were those militant Townsendites, usually club secretaries and other officers, who volunteered their time, effort, and money to organize clubs and events. Club officers also often subscribed to the Townsend Plan newspaper and would be likely to vote according to the national headquarters' suggestions. Close to them in devotion and militancy were regular club members who made contributions, bought publications and paraphernalia, and regularly attended club meetings and other Townsend gatherings. Next were occasional participants in gatherings or meetings who may have been inducted as club members but who had only sporadic connections to clubs. At about the same level were those who participated only in mass events, such as the so-called world's largest outdoor meeting, orchestrated by the *Modern Crusader*, which was held simultaneously in a number of western communities in October. Below these Townsendites in terms of support were those who were favorably disposed to the pension idea but were not candidates to join clubs. The more committed of this group were those who signed a petition in favor of old-age revolving pensions, with the stronger supporters among them also making a small donation. Although the founders sometimes portrayed the numerous petition signers to be just as devoted as the far fewer militant Townsendites and greatly inflated the signers' numbers in the hope that newspapers would report them, many may have merely acquiesced to an adamant Townsendite. At the lowest level the Townsend Plan's supporters might include all those who would respond positively to a public opinion survey question about old-age pensions.

By the end of the year, Townsend claimed 15 million "supporters." But how much support was there for the Townsend Plan, and how many people were at each level of support? Unfortunately, there are no lists of club members and no petitions on file anywhere. Although there was eventually a list of clubs, it did not indicate when clubs were formed. No polls would be taken for another year.[55] However, there are sources—financial records, testimony under oath, and Clement's statements, which were not as exaggerated as Townsend's— from which it is possible to get an outline of the amount of different sorts of backing for the Townsend Plan. At the lower levels of support, the petition signers numbered far fewer than Townsend claimed, probably only about 1 million. Most signers attended no club meetings or activities and were usually not aged.[56]

More indicative of strong Townsend Plan support were the clubs and club members, especially their unpaid officers and other highly committed supporters. In December 1934 Townsend claimed that there were 2,000 clubs, and a little later he said there were 300,000 club members.[57] These estimates are at least twice as large as the real numbers of clubs and members, as the Townsend Plan's financial records suggest. The amount spent on books and Clements's reliable claims of how much they cost to print indicate that about 158,000 pension booklets were sold in 1934. Probably two-thirds of these represented club members in good standing, as books were often bought

Figure 2.6: Weighed in the Balance. This cartoon from the *Townsend Weekly* exemplified the Townsend Plan's early form of action—hoping to show political leaders that the pension-recovery proposal was supported in public opinion by gathering signatures on petitions. Source: *National Townsend Weekly*, February 25, 1935, p. 6.

in the name of people who did not participate. There may have been another 25,000 to 50,000 who were significant supporters but who did not buy books, making a total in the range of 125,000 to 150,000. If Townsend and Clements's claims concerning the number of members per club, approximately 150, are only slightly overstated, this would mean there were about a thousand clubs. There were about ten to twelve officers per club, making for at least 10,000 committed Townsendites, probably more, as the *Modern Crusader*'s circulation was around 50,000, and only true believers would subscribe or buy it regularly.[58]

The mobilization was highly regional, however. Of the approximately 1,000 clubs, probably around 200 were in California alone. Most of the other clubs were located in the states of the West, although clubs existed as far east as Florida. The regional concentration, however, seemed more promising than limiting, as the Townsend Plan had made only the barest efforts to organize outside the region.[59] Of the $60,000 the organization generated in 1934, two-thirds came in the last quarter of the year, mainly from the initiation of clubs. Also, the organization had printed and in the hands of organizers another

100,000 booklets, suggesting it was confident that it could nearly double its growth in the near future.[60] The Townsend Plan was poised to spread the word and its unique form of political organization to the rest of the country.

Conclusion

The Townsend Plan became a thriving challenger because it was innovative. What was new was not Townsend's pension-recovery proposal, which had been anticipated by others, but the plan's form of organization, which was devised chiefly by Clements, and how the pension program was sold. Clements and Townsend ran their nonprofit company on an entrepreneurial basis, by subcontracting out sales business. To jump-start the mobilization for the pension program, the founders took on representatives who worked for commissions and sold the plan mainly to make a living, while their aged targets really believed in it.

Clements's operatives offered an enticing image of a better world that the plan's enactment would bring—a utopian future that would be easy to achieve. It relied on both romanticized conceptions of extended family life and the consumer goods produced by U.S. industry in mass quantities just before the Depression. As redesigned by Clements and other Townsend Plan publicists, the pension program was simple enough to be understood by many, chock-full of home truths and moral maxims, but complicated enough to engage those who were interested in the details. The Townsend Plan drew in the aged by portraying them not merely as deserving recipients of stipends as reward for their life's work but also as agents of economic recovery. Despite being the main direct beneficiaries of the pensions, the aged were encouraged to see themselves as conscience constituents, working in behalf of the unemployed and the more desperate among the elderly. Townsend Plan operatives also sold an appealing image of the plan's aged founder, Dr. Townsend, a man whose difficult life story much of the American aged could identify with and whose recent financial success and leap in prestige they hoped to emulate.

The other organizational innovation was the Townsend club. These membership organizations provided some of the sociability of fraternal organizations, but they were more egalitarian and far more politically charged, relying largely on the purposive incentives in the pension-recovery plan. Based in localities and meeting weekly, Townsend clubs provided continuous support and publicity for the pension plan. They were also a means to check the more mercenary impulses of Townsend Plan organizers and to provide unmediated communications from the national headquarters. Although the clubs were more fan clubs than democratic devices to decide the organization's direction, they did impart some political skills to their overwhelmingly elderly membership. And although they sought to create a new identity for the aged as

"Townsendites," or believers in the doctor's economic thinking and program, they also could not help making Townsend club members start to see their old-age group as one suffering from specific injustices and requiring special remedies. The Townsend clubs took the first big steps to constituting the aged as a political group.

At the end of 1934, less than a year from its inception, the Townsend Plan was drawing great support among the aged, as 1,000 Townsend clubs arose, mainly in California and other parts of the West. On December 1 the "national" headquarters moved from Long Beach to Los Angeles, and it now had twenty employees to coordinate its operations. Clements had taken charge of the organization's subcontractors, and he could communicate directly with club leaders and members. Having been built up through the Townsend Plan literature, Dr. Townsend was drawing large crowds as a speaker around the West. Having wrested control of the newspaper and its mailing list, Clements and Townsend prepared for a press run of the new *Townsend Weekly*. Everything about the operation was now being linked to its symbol Dr. Townsend. The cofounders had stopped talking about Old Age Revolving Pensions and now referred exclusively to "the Townsend Plan"—a shorthand for the organization as well as the pension-recovery proposal. If the program was going to win the support of Americans beyond the aged, it was going to have to focus more on its economic stimulant qualities and less on its benefits to the elderly. In the wake of their successful year, the cofounders doubled their salaries to $100 per week.[61] It now was up to them to prove that they were earning it.

THREE

Behind the Townsend Plan's Rise and Initial Impact

THE TOWNSEND PLAN made great strides in its first year, but it was just one of many mass-based organizations and groups making demands on the American state in 1934. Some of these others, which included veterans and the unemployed, also promoted state-oriented proposals to boost the economy and aid deserving categories of citizens. All this suggests that partly similar circumstances helped to spark the Townsend Plan and the other state-oriented mobilizations and raises a question that social movement scholars have long debated: What accounts for the rise of challengers? And so what accounts for the rise of the Townsend Plan and these other social spending challengers?

Answering this question, however, does not get at all the issues of interest surrounding the Townsend Plan's rise, notably the extensive mobilization of everyday people behind old-age policy. After all, there were other issues, such as racial discrimination, health coverage, or child dependency, to name a few, around which there were compelling and extensive grievances but far less political organization. Another question is why the Townsend Plan took the form that it did, a social movement organization based on membership and meant to influence the major political parties and individual legislators on a single issue, rather than becoming a party itself or an interest group. Canada's Social Credit Party was founded on similar ideas as Townsend's pension plan, yet it assumed a far different form. The Townsend Plan could have easily dispensed with its novel modes of participation and stuck to lobbying for old-age pensions, as did membership groups like the Fraternal Order of Eagles and expert organizations like the American Association for Old-Age Security.

As the Townsend Plan blossomed, the Roosevelt administration was already planning for social reform. The Committee on Economic Security (CES), a cabinet-level group, was appointed in June, before the existence of the first Townsend club, and charged with making recommendation for the whole of U.S. social policy, which was something of a blank slate. By the end of 1934, the committee weighed in with many proposals, most of which had been previously expected. However, the committee proposed old-age benefits that were more extensive than first imagined. Did the Townsend Plan induce the Roosevelt administration to place old-age policy on the political agenda or augment its old-age proposals in response to the Townsend Plan? I will argue that the issue was already there, but the Townsend Plan helped to move up its priority and induced an augmentation in the proposals. The puzzle is why the Townsend Plan was able to have an impact with a political strategy that mainly involved building a national organization and enlisting older Americans in its fan clubs, primarily in the West, without engaging in sustained collective action targeted at the national government. But first I step back to address the political processes and programs that spurred the Townsend Plan.

Pensions in the News

By the 1930s, the United States was backward among capitalist democracies in the development of modern social policy. It had workers' compensation programs in almost all states but no unemployment insurance or health insurance, and only halting state-level initiatives in "mothers' pensions"—meager benefits that went mainly to select white widows—and in old-age benefits. These state and local efforts were not backed in any way by the national government, despite its greater ability to tax, and provided aid to very few. Yet this backwardness in social policy was something that had developed only in the twentieth century, for the United States had been a leader in a version of national old-age pensions.

Pensions' Progress before the Townsend Plan

This leadership came through veterans' benefits. Civil War veterans' pensions were designed initially for war widows and veterans with war-related disabilities, but legislation in 1879 upgraded these benefits, and soon a veterans' organization, the Grand Army of the Republic, joined with the Republican Party to press for further liberalizations. In 1890, a law made eligible anyone who could demonstrate that he had served and who could not perform manual labor, and, administratively, it was ruled that old age in itself precluded manual labor. Thus all aged veterans, and eventually their widows, became eligible. More than half a million elderly men were on the rolls in 1910, 29 percent of American men sixty-five years of age and older. The average pension was about 30 percent of average earnings, significantly higher than old-age benefits in Britain or Germany. Needless to say, veterans' pensions were restricted to certain groups of northerners, mainly male, native born, and white. As veterans died off, the government did not step in with pensions for the aged who had not served.[1]

A mix of experts and membership organizations pressed for old-age benefits in the first third of the twentieth century. Social insurance advocate Isaac Rubinow promoted the cause in a series of lectures beginning in 1912. The American Association for Labor Legislation (AALL), an expert organization led by John Commons of the University of Wisconsin, also called for social legislation, mainly unemployment compensation, but also for old age. In the 1920s the Fraternal Order of Eagles, a cross-class membership organization founded in 1898, began a mass campaign to demand old-age pensions through state general revenues for the worthy indigent. They were joined in various states by state federations of labor and different labor unions. In 1923 the Eagles and the AALL teamed to draft model state-level legislation. In 1927 Abraham Epstein began the American Association for Old-Age Security, another expert organization, relying mainly on its leader's expertise, fund-raising, and publicity, and pressed for old-age benefits. By 1929 the national American Federation of Labor endorsed old-age benefits. Still, only seven states passed laws in the 1920s, and very few people were receiving payments.[2] America fell well behind most industrial countries in providing aid in old age.

During the early years of the Depression, while Dr. Townsend labored away as a medical officer in Long Beach, the Fraternal Order of Eagles and the California State Federation of Labor promoted means-tested old-age benefits in Sacramento. A bill sponsored by William B. Hornblower, a prominent member of the Eagles, passed in 1929, making California the first state with "mandatory" old-age benefits. Hornblower had the act amended in 1931 to liberalize eligibility requirements, notably by allowing inmates of poorhouses to apply for old-age benefits. As a result of these changes, by 1933 the number of old-age beneficiaries in California quadrupled. By the end of 1934 some twenty-eight states had followed California's lead, with a dozen states enacting mandatory laws in 1933 alone. Many of the states with old-age benefit legislation were in the West. In the three large, industrial states of Massachusetts, New York, and California the average benefits were $20 per month or greater.[3]

Despite all this legislative activity and some promising state plans, old-age benefit programs were pitifully inadequate. Most states paid less than $10 per month, and in three states the laws were inoperative. In most instances counties were designated to provide the benefits but were too constrained by their property-tax bases to pay much. Where benefits were available, a gauntlet of restrictions stood between the aged and checks. All state laws had long residency requirements, and few states provided grants if relatives could be located. Standard clauses denied aid to applicants for reasons ranging from criminal records to spouse abandonment. Almost all laws had strict "lien on estate" provisions, meaning that beneficiaries would forfeit their property rather than bequeath it. Of the more than 6.5 million people over sixty-five years of age in the United States in 1934, fewer than a quarter of a million, or less than 4 percent, were receiving public old-age benefits.[4] Even in California, with its relatively high grants and mandates on counties, the old-age benefits were tightly means- and property-tested and restricted to those seventy years and older, longtime state residents, with a strict "relative responsibility" clause. California covered only about 9 percent of all those aged sixty-five and older. The lesson seemed to be that states and counties could not provide anything like old-age "pensions" on their own, especially during the Depression.

Old-Age Politics at the National Level

The national government was showing signs of weighing in on the old-age question. The most promising development here was the pink slip given in 1932 to President Herbert Hoover. The third Republican president elected in the 1920s, Hoover had dragged his heels on providing relief during the Depression, wedded as he and his party were to policies of low taxation and to industrial and financial interest groups. Hoover was replaced by Franklin Delano Roosevelt, the governor of New York and a Democrat with a strong impulse to social policy reform. His party background mattered. Democrats had led the fight for emergency relief during Hoover's presidency, and the nation's strongest social policy advocate, Senator Robert Wagner, was a New York Democratic leader. The party supported unemployment insurance and old-age pensions in its 1932 platform. What is more, Roosevelt did not rely on the support of the conservative, business-dominated wing of the party, led by Jouett Shouse and John J. Raskob.[5] Roosevelt amassed 57.4 percent of the two-party vote, losing only six states, giving him a mandate to act on his pro–social policy views.[6]

Well before Clements and Townsend had begun to imagine their old-age insurgency, politics had already defined Roosevelt's life. He was born to a wealthy landowning family in Hyde Park, New York, in 1882 and, after graduating from Groton, Harvard, and Columbia Law School, held a series of elected and appointed offices. An indifferent student, Roosevelt was a genius in politics. Despite his patrician background and accent, he could think along with his constituents, imagine their reactions, and win their allegiances. Roosevelt was elected governor of New York in 1928 and again in 1930. That year Roosevelt presided over the passage of New York's breakthrough old-age benefits legislation. As president, Roosevelt's idea was to achieve economic recovery first and social policy reform second. Unlike Townsend and Clements, Roosevelt thought that it would take different sorts of programs to achieve these goals, but he provided immediate relief for those most harmed by the Depression through the Federal Emergency Relief Administration (FERA) in May 1933. The FERA distributed the unprecedented sum of $3.25 billion in less than three years, including payments to the needy aged.[7]

At the same time, more long-term social policy reforms began to surface in Congress, including for old age. In 1932, a proposal known as the Dill-Connery bill appropriated $10 million in federal matching aid to states with old-age benefits programs, at the ratio of two state dollars for every national dollar. It was strongly backed by the American Federation of Labor (AFL). This bill passed the House in 1933 and 1934 and very nearly passed the Senate that year. In response to this legislation and two months before the first Townsend club, Roosevelt announced with fanfare on June 8 the creation of the CES and charged it with constructing a comprehensive economic security policy. Led by Secretary of Labor Frances Perkins and overseen by Harry Hopkins, head of the FERA, the CES was to address unemployment insurance and old-age benefits, as well as public employment and a host of other issues.[8] Edwin Witte, a University of Wisconsin public policy expert, was appointed executive secretary of the CES at the end of July. He hoped to generate a report and the administration's security bill before the end of the year.

Some Other State-Oriented Movements

Roosevelt's administration was also spurring all manner of movement activity. Especially active was labor, which had suffered losses due to the Depression and pro-business Republican rule. Union members had dropped to about 2.7 million in 1933 and were isolated in large cities and in the railroad, printing, building, coal, and clothing industries. Boosting labor became New Deal policy. Roosevelt thought that unions would be organizational bulwarks for the administration, its policies, and northern Democrats and sought a political economy that would be more balanced between business and labor. Section 7a of Roosevelt's National Industrial Recovery Act, adopted in 1933, gave symbolic governmental sanction for unionization and collective bargaining, cementing an alliance between labor and the national Democratic Party. Partly as a result of this alliance, unionization jumped over the next six years from 11.3 percent of the nonagricultural labor force to 28.6 percent. Organized labor's goals with respect to the state chiefly concerned the rights to organize and to bargain with employers, and the administration's action made labor more likely to support the administration's social policy proposals. It helped, too, that these proposals were cleared with labor's champion, Senator Wagner.[9]

More inadvertently, Roosevelt's policies inspired other savvy political operators seeking to promote more radical social spending programs than the president's. In 1934, Huey Long, the junior Democratic senator from Louisiana, began to press his Share Our Wealth plan and organization in earnest. Like Roosevelt, Long was born to a father who owned some land, but his family had to live off what they produced. Long enhanced his rhetorical endowments pitching cooking oil to pay for law school and upon passing the bar won attention in arguing workmen's compensation cases. His political rise in Louisiana was even more rapid than Roosevelt's New York ascension. In 1918, at age twenty-five, Long won a position on the Railroad Commission, and ten years later he was elected governor. Running in 1930 on a record of building highways and improving education, he won the race for Senate and gained total political control in Louisiana and a reputation for ruthlessness. He attacked his opponents with everything from slander to the National Guard, passed reams of legislation without debate, and traveled with armed guards. The *New York Times* referred to him simply as the "dictator" of Louisiana. In Washington Long sought to appear an irreverent champion of the people, receiving a German diplomatic delegation in his pajamas, engaging in barroom fisticuffs, and calling himself the Kingfish, after a character in the popular radio program *Amos and Andy*. In 1932 Long supported Roosevelt for president, but the two soon had a falling-out. It was hard to say whether it was over policy, personality, or the fact that there could be only one president at a time.[10]

Share Our Wealth was Long's bid to gain greater national attention. The program had taxing and spending provisions like the revolving pension plan, but on a larger scale and with a much more left-wing slant to it. Long would tax wealth beyond $3 million and use the revenues to stake every family to a "homestead": about $5,000 to purchase a house, car, and radio. Long's plan guaranteed an annual income of $2,000 to $3,000 for those who worked and also had a program for the aged: they would receive pensions of $30 a month or more. Long was able to finance this campaign and spread his message through mandatory "deducts" from Louisiana employees, kickbacks from state contracts, the senatorial frank, radio speeches, and the road trips of his confederate the Reverend Gerald L. K. Smith.[11]

Unlike the Townsend Plan, Share Our Wealth did not have a sales organizing staff or much control over its local affiliates, which Long called Share Our Wealth societies. Any two people could begin a "society," and members paid no dues and received for free the movement newspaper, the *American Progress*. Long did not see these groups as resource generators, and all he sought was a group of potential voters to prefer him and his plan to Roosevelt and his New Deal. Given the minimal membership requirements and Long's wide net, it was possible for him to claim a great deal of support and support of a purer kind. His membership drive was, however, relatively hampered by its lack of a profit motive. He relied on Louisiana operatives and local volunteers, losing out on the energetic organizers that spread the message for the Townsend Plan. In addition, the fund-raising of the Townsend clubs helped to keep Townsendites active—something that was often lacking in Share Our Wealth societies. It was unclear what Long was planning to do with his amorphous organization. Most political journalists suspected that he was either trying to push Roosevelt's policies leftward or preparing to force Roosevelt from office by way of a third-party challenge, or maybe both. Long may not have been sure himself. There is no doubt that the administration was watching Long very closely, as he claimed that more than 7.5 million individuals had joined more than 27,000 Share Our Wealth societies by the end of 1934.[12]

In its first year, the Townsend Plan did not even receive the greatest attention among redistributive challengers in its home state. That honor went to
End Poverty in California, led by Upton Sinclair, the muckraking novelist.
Among EPIC's twelve points were proposals to put to use idle factories and
farmland, the adoption of progressive taxes, the repeal of the sales tax, and
high old-age, disability, and mothers' pensions. Having switched in 1933 his
registration from Socialist, Sinclair ran for the Democratic nomination for
governor in 1934 behind his EPIC platform and beat the regular Democrat
George Creel. Sinclair went on to construct the California Democratic platform with EPIC planks and promoted "production for use" in the campaign.
The government would take possession of idle factories and allow workers to
occupy them to make goods for their own use.[13]

There were other mass mobilizations and organizations of importance, as
different groups made claims on the state. From his weekly radio pulpit in
Royal Oak, Michigan, Father Charles Coughlin was organizing the National
Union for Social Justice from among his 10 million regular radio listeners.
The union had sixteen principles but was especially concerned with banking
reforms that Coughlin deemed essential to recovery. He was a Canadian by
birth as well as a Catholic priest and thus doubly implausible as a presidential
candidate, and through 1934 he mainly backed Roosevelt, but soon Coughlin's support for the president began to waver.[14] World War I veterans formed
the Bonus Expeditionary Force in 1932 to demand the early payment of Adjusted Compensation certificates, which were passed in 1924 and due to be
paid in 1945. This so-called Bonus Army, which included many veterans'
families, was routed by the army under the command of Douglas MacArthur.
The Bonus Army massed again the next year and was rebuffed more gently by
Roosevelt, who sent his wife as an emissary. But backed by other veterans'
groups, including the American Legion, the bonus issue remained alive in
Congress.[15] Less organized were unemployed workers. Several groups demanded
work or relief, and although they had largely demobilized in the wake of Roosevelt's relief policies, it seemed likely that they would return in force unless
the Depression ended.[16]

What Accounts for the Rise of the Townsend Plan?

One of the most pressing questions in the literature on social movements is
what accounts for their origins or emergence. Two main answers have been
advanced. One is the old-school idea that new grievances prompted by structural changes spur movements, implying that movements are more indicators
of needed social change than instigators of change. From this point of view,
the Townsend Plan and other state-oriented challengers arising around the
same time would be considered a response to new economic and social prob-

lems caused by the Depression, but unlikely to address either effectively. The second view, more favored nowadays, is that state-oriented social movements result from favorable political circumstances and conditions. This view sees movements as rational responses to new possibilities to effect change and win gains and is more optimistic about movements' potential efficacy. From this point of view the Townsend Plan and the other challengers that appeared around the same time were responding to new possibilities in altered political circumstances.[17]

The Impact of the Depression

The influence of the Depression on the Townsend Plan—and on many of the protest groups that developed after 1933—is difficult to deny. The revolving-pension proposal was meant mainly to end the Depression; without it, the Townsend Plan may not have happened. The Townsend Plan also was buoyed by the advance of poverty in old age, which was aggravated by the Depression. Almost 10 million people lost their savings accounts when banks failed, and real estate values dropped precipitously. The retirement plans and prospects of many of the aged changed dramatically for the worse. Very few of the aged were receiving old-age benefits, public or private, to soften these losses. There can be no doubt that the Depression also intensified the grievances of other challengers in the Depression, such as veterans and the unemployed.

It seems unlikely, however, that the Townsend Plan and these other challengers were caused entirely or even mainly by the Depression and its effects, as the old-school theoretical precepts would suggest. The slump had already passed its low point when Townsend penned his letter to the editor. Unemployment was dropping below its peak of more than 25 percent of the labor force in 1933 and was heading down to 14 percent in 1937.[18] And although there are no hard data on Townsend club members, the Townsend Plan's greatest support did not come from the poorest among the aged, as we shall see, but from those who had something to lose economically. In addition, the Depression cannot account for which groups were mobilized. The slump was worldwide, and the demographic presence of the aged was rising across all industrialized countries, but only here was there a mass-based old-age pension movement. Most of all, the Townsend Plan itself has to be given some credit for the appealing way it explained the connection between economic relations, the forms of loss suffered by the aged, and the possibilities for relief.

The Political Context and the Challengers

Arguments about the short-term changes in the political context also help to explain the timing of the rise of the Townsend Plan and other state-oriented challengers. One argument is that the rise of new political governments and regimes can aid challengers if they are favorably disposed toward their issue.[19] The Townsend Plan did not emerge until after Roosevelt's victory in 1932, which brought with him to Washington many progressive congressional Democrats from the North. This change in political alignment signaled that the state might be more receptive to social spending and other state-oriented demands and would be able to do something about them.

A key precept of historical institutionalism is that policies change politics and influence the possibilities for the mobilization of specific groups. New regimes may influence movement activity by formulating state policies that encourage it.[20] The Roosevelt administration immediately altered legal possibilities in favor of challengers. The Townsend Plan did not start until after the National Industrial Recovery Act (1933), which encouraged workers to form collective bargaining units. The organization of workers encouraged the organization of the aged and other groups. It is also consistent with this line of thinking that the Townsend Plan arose in the context of gains in old-age policy. The drive for state-level, compulsory, means-tested old-age benefits had been active in the late 1920s and had its biggest year in 1933, just before the rise of the Townsend Plan. What is more, California, the birthplace of the Townsend Plan, was a leader in providing old-age benefits. The Townsend Plan took off after the creation of the Federal Emergency Relief Administration, which took national responsibility for relief, including aid for many of the aged. There was also activity surrounding old-age legislation at the national level, keeping the subject in the news and making new advances seem likely. New policies can promote specific forms of organization, and groups seek to take advantage of them, as was the case when the Grand Army of the Republic was spurred by the enactment of Civil War veterans' benefits and then acted to extend them.[21]

However, U.S. old-age programs were still too underdeveloped to provide incentives to advance a specific form of organization and provided only diffuse encouragement to the mobilization of the aged. The state was recognizing the right of the aged to benefits. All state laws and proposed national legislation had preambles stating that the welfare of the aged was a legitimate concern and a suitable object of state action. At the same time, the benefits granted were few and meager—far from the "pensions" that were sometimes claimed to have been enacted by politicians. Governments were saying that adequate old-age benefits ought to be provided, but they balked at granting them. Possibly, too, the grievances of the aged and the impulse to organize around old age were policy related in a more indirect way. Because the standard forces for policy change were less evident in the United States and its polity was structurally geared against policy reform, the United States was lagging in the development of old-age policy—which became increasingly apparent to the American aged.[22]

New grievances, new encouraging regimes, and new policies all helped to spur the mobilization of the aged behind pensions, but they were not the whole story. These conditions do not always distinguish the aged from other groups that might have mobilized but did not. African Americans suffered from greater economic deprivations but did not mobilize to the same degree. Family separations were endemic in the Depression, and programs for mothers without breadwinners existed and were funded in a similarly meager manner, but there was no significant mobilization over this issue. The aged were in a far better political situation than American blacks, most of whom lived in polities where they were disenfranchised. Because of their lifelong political skills and engagement, the aged were also better prepared for political mobilization than were mothers with dependent children, whose political prowess was not nearly as well developed and whose previous gains in policy were mainly the result of middle-class women's mobilization.

Arguments about grievances, governments, and policies also fail to account for why this organization of the aged took the form of a pressure group with delimited concerns attempting to influence political parties rather than creating one. Most claims in the literature concerning the influence of political contexts on social movements suggest that the U.S. political system is "open" to challenges or promotes them. This is mainly because the different parts of the state, its courts and legislatures, have more autonomy than elsewhere and thus might be subject to influence.[23] Although the U.S. state and polity have systemic effects on social movements, they more likely influence the form of challenges, rather than encouraging them overall. In particular, the "winner-take-all" electoral system, the presidential system, and the Electoral College discourage new national political parties, because they make them less likely to achieve national influence. This discouraging effect was aggravated by the dominance of long-standing patronage-based party organizations in the East and Midwest, and the elite-run Democratic Party of the South, which made it difficult even for new parties beginning outside their areas of influence to contend for national power.

Because the Townsend Plan had a national focus, it is no surprise that it did not attempt to form a new political party. National "pressure" groups, combining mass mobilization with lobbying and other means of influence over parties in legislators, had already formed around veterans', farmer, labor, and women's issues, as well as the prohibition of alcohol, whereas Prohibition parties had become marginalized in politics. By contrast, in western Canada a party known as Social Credit formed with a Townsend-like tax-and-spend recovery program, made tremendous gains in the provincial legislature in Alberta in 1935, and immediately established a legislative presence. In the United States new parties had been able to take hold only at the state level and only in a few states. In California, Sinclair's EPIC sought to take over the

Democratic Party rather than form its own party. And although the Farmer-Labor Party in Minnesota was new, the Wisconsin Progressive Party was formed by dissidents from the state's Republican Party. Neither of these new parties had much prospect of growing into a national party.[24] Most of the new American challengers did not seek to form parties but tried to influence the existing ones and individual legislators from both parties.

A Plan in Search of a Plan of Action

The Townsend Plan had a great chance to influence old-age politics and win benefits for its aged constituency. Its form of organization, a pressure group hoping to pick off supporters from both parties, was one that had proved influential in the past in American politics. The organization certainly was growing. There was little indication throughout 1934, however, that Clements and Townsend's ideas about putting Townsend's pension proposal into effect extended much beyond getting people to sign petitions, join clubs, and write letters. The Townsend Plan's other main line of action was product definition and differentiation. Its leaders fine-tuned the plan, while avoiding entangling public alliances with groups like Sinclair's EPIC in order to win primary political allegiances from their aged followers. The Townsend Plan organization's not-for-profit status made it questionably legal for it to get involved directly in political activity such as campaigning and lobbying.[25] During the 1934 fall congressional campaigns, Townsend Plan leaders found themselves engaged more in organizational housekeeping than in political action.

The time and effort it took to establish the Townsend Plan as a going organizational concern largely account for its small political presence in fall 1934, but the failure to act forcefully was also due to disagreements between the founders. Clements put organizing first and thought that the Townsend Plan should concentrate on spreading the message and building clubs. Clements estimated that inducing Congress to pass the proposal would be a long-term process akin to forging the coalition that had formed behind the early payment of the soldier's bonus, and so his top priority was to create more loyal Townsendites, which meant to organize Townsend clubs. As more of the aged joined clubs, as more people were induced to sign petitions, and as more clubs were organized across the country, politicians would be forced to take notice. An aggressive strategy of intervening in political campaigns, lobbying, and legislative maneuvering would be premature and come at the expense of building the organization.[26]

Townsend was less patient. The fact that the revolving-pension plan was sweeping California and parts of the West convinced him all the more of his idea's correctness. It would be simply a matter of getting elected officials to see what he and his followers saw in it. If he could meet with the president,

Townsend thought he might be able to persuade him on the spot. If the major parties would not agree to adopt Townsend's plan, the wildfire spread of his fan clubs suggested to the doctor that he himself could lead a third party that would quickly enact revolving pensions.[27] If one believed wholeheartedly in the plan, as Townsend did, it would be unconscionable not to do everything possible to effect it immediately. Whatever qualms Townsend may have had were being dispelled by the fulsome praise of Townsend Plan publicists and the increasingly vocal support of loyal Townsendites.

Given their disagreements, Clements and Townsend relied at first on an unassertive strategy. They merely encouraged candidates for office to announce whether they were for or against revolving pensions. The Townsend Plan would in this way be able to identify friends and enemies without resorting to an elaborate questionnaire and thus an explicit political engagement in the manner of the state federations of labor and other groups. Also, Clements especially did not wish to take sides, hoping that even opposing candidates might endorse the plan. Candidates would often literally advertise their support for the Townsend Plan in the *Modern Crusader*, killing two birds with one stone as far as the founders were concerned. Townsend was more eager to jump on bandwagons than Clements, but the official policy was neutral.[28]

Nonetheless, the Townsend Plan became embroiled in California's gubernatorial race, in which EPIC's Sinclair faced the conservative Republican governor Frank Merriam. William Randolph Hearst's conservative *San Francisco Examiner*, the fiercely antilabor *Los Angeles Times*, and the radio jeremiads of Aimee Semple McPherson were joined in their assault on Sinclair by innovative short subjects produced by MGM. The latter depicted California under Sinclair rule as a jamboree for the nation's hoboes. Sinclair demanded $50 pensions per month from the California treasury for everyone over sixty years old, a tremendous commitment to the aged, but publicly doubted that Townsend's plan was workable and thus drew Townsend's opposition. In contrast, Merriam played to the Townsendites, pledging his support—a move that would cost California nothing and thus not upset Merriam's conservative supporters. Although there was no explicit organizational endorsement, Townsend criticized Sinclair and praised Merriam. Sinclair was beaten by 250,000 votes in the general election. Although Roosevelt withheld his endorsement when Sinclair would not back down from his "production for use" platform, Sinclair attributed his loss to the Townsend Plan. The EPIC nominee for lieutenant governor, Sheridan Downey, supported revolving pensions and almost won.[29]

The strategy of the Townsend Plan in California underscored its emerging approach to state-level politics. It was going to steer clear of developments in California's trendsetting but still quite meager Old-Age Security law and other state-level old-age initiatives. Instead the Townsend Plan wanted state governments to ask the national Congress to enact the pension-recovery program, in the hope that this would win publicity and provide pressure for state congressional delegations to follow suit in Washington. The Arizona legislature quickly passed one of these memorials.[30] The gambit of ignoring old-age programs in the states depended crucially on whether the Townsend Plan would be influential in Congress in the upcoming debate over old-age policy.

In the 1934 congressional campaigns, many candidates from Southern California advertised their support for revolving pensions. In four California districts, both major-party candidates were backers, and in four other races the Townsend Plan had one supporter. The organization also had a few self-declared supporters in other western states. In California's Eleventh District, including Long Beach, the Townsend Plan took a special interest in the race between the Democrat John Steven McGroarty and the Republican incumbent, William Evans. McGroarty was a columnist for the *Los Angeles Times*, as well as an author of a California history and a poet laureate of the state. He praised the plan in print in December 1933, and his column was reprinted in the *Old Age Revolving Pensions* booklet. At age seventy-two McGroarty decided to quit the newspaper and run for Congress, partly to advance the Townsend Plan. Returning the favor, Townsend praised McGroarty, though elliptically by promoting his age and characteristics rather than his name in order to stay within the bounds of the nonendorsement policy. In California, advanced age in a politician was not entirely a disadvantage. Because of the influx of retirees, California was the oldest state, demographically speaking, and Townsend's congressional district was older than the state as a whole. McGroarty and a few of the others who endorsed Townsend's pension plan won their elections, sending the revolving-pension plan into the next Congress with a handful of supporters.[31]

But the political story in that election was chiefly about President Roosevelt, whose activist and wide-ranging approach to the Depression had been decisively endorsed by the electorate in November. Typically the party of a sitting president in midterm elections can count on dropping about twenty-five seats in the House of Representatives. On Election Day 1934, however, the Democrats made dramatic gains, winning twenty-three additional seats in the House and nineteen in the Senate. Included among the victorious were another ten leftward-leaning representatives, seven from the Wisconsin Progressive Party and three from the Minnesota Farmer-Labor Party. On the front page of the *New York Times*, Arthur Krock called the congressional results "the most overwhelming victory in the history of modern politics" for a sitting president. *Time* magazine named Roosevelt "Man of the Year" for the second time in three years. Most political observers read the results as evidence that Roosevelt would be able to have his way on reform issues in the new Congress.[32]

Old-Age and Social Legislation in 1934

That fall Roosevelt's Committee on Economic Security had been working to devise an omnibus security program for the attention of the next Congress. The committee had many issues and voices to consider. It had to contend first with congressional preferences. There was the Dill-Connery bill, which called for aid to states and localities for means-tested old-age benefit programs and had great support. Also well supported was the Wagner-Lewis bill, which provided powerful tax incentives for states to enact their own unemployment compensation legislation.[33] The committee was constrained as well by the administration's social policy bureaucrats and political officials from the various cabinet-level departments. There was the Children's Bureau of the Department of Labor, which wanted to reinstate the federal support that had lapsed in 1929 for maternal and child health services, and to address the failure of county-optional mothers' pension laws by providing a national commitment to families without male breadwinners. Most important of all, there was the Federal Emergency Relief Administration, which was providing cash relief to 5 million recipients, including 736,000 among the impoverished aged.[34]

The proposals also had to please the president. This was no easy task because often Roosevelt had an image of how he wanted things to work but could not articulate his vision or provide much guidance on how to link it to policy. Several things were clear, however, about Roosevelt's preferences for economic security: he did not want to continue a "dole," or cash and in-kind relief for the able-bodied, and wanted to provide employment instead. Under the circumstances of high deficits, moreover, it would be best if social programs would pay for themselves, or at least appear to do so. For this reason, Roosevelt was drawn to social insurance, with its promise to pay its way through "contributions" or taxes on payrolls, and public works, which might somehow become "self-liquidating." Most important, he wanted in some manner to preserve economic security for all. With his patrician background Roosevelt saw people as a kind of exhaustible natural resource, whose preservation was his duty.[35]

The committee decided what it would propose far before its study groups could weigh in. Indeed, the so-called technical board, which was constituted of political officials with decision-making power, chose study groups according to whether they were likely to concur with the board's views. Similarly, the committee appointed an Advisory Council, nominally representing business, labor, and the public but stacked to include members expected to be supporters of the proposals. The technical board's recommendations were made on October 9, well before the completion of the research or the compiling of advice that was supposed to guide them. The committee proposed that old-age security be addressed by national aid for means-tested old-age assistance, in the manner of the Dill-Connery bill, as well as through a national old-age annuity or insurance program that was to be wage related and financed by payroll taxes.[36]

Washington Takes Note of the Townsend Plan

The Committee on Economic Security paid close attention to the Townsend Plan. In September the *New York Times* ran an article very favorable to the challenger, and mail about the Townsend Plan to the administration was being forwarded to the committee, at one point reaching 1,500 pieces in one day, almost all of it demanding the passage of Townsend's proposal. The CES had to develop a form letter to respond. Edwin Witte, the executive secretary of the committee, began denouncing the Townsend Plan through press releases and assigned a staffer to follow it. He began to worry that the revolving pension plan might draw support away from the CES's old-age proposals.[37]

The highest-profile attack on the Townsend Plan was a statement by President Roosevelt before the National Conference on Economic Security. This group convened on November 13 to discuss the issues being addressed by the security committee, whose hope was that the conferees would endorse the administration's approaches. The president shocked the conference, however, by stating that he feared the time was not right for action on old-age benefits. He referred to "organizations prompting fantastic schemes," which "have aroused hopes which cannot possibly be filled," an obvious if unacknowledged slap at the Townsend Plan. By the end of the next week, however, the administration was backtracking and announcing a "correction" to its previous statement. Old age would indeed be addressed in the comprehensive security proposal.[38]

It has been argued that the Townsend Plan motivated this turn of events. After the statement, Townsendites wrote en masse to Washington in protest, and the president seemed to have a change in heart.[39] These events may not have been cause and effect, however. For just after Roosevelt's initial statement, conference members and allied politicians said if the president were not going to act, they would seek passage of the Dill-Connery old-age benefits bill; in addition, the day after the president's statement, before the pro–Townsend Plan letters could have made it to Washington, Secretary of Labor Perkins charged that Roosevelt had been misinterpreted and confirmed that the committee was likely to make recommendations on old-age policy, which had in any case been decided the previous month.[40] The Townsend Plan's impact came instead behind the scenes, during the committee's deliberations and the recommendations for legislation that were produced by them.

The Administration's Approach to Security

The committee finally reported to the president on Christmas Eve, taking a far more variegated approach to economic security and social reform than did the Townsend Plan. The administration's plan divided the population into those deemed "employable" and those deemed "unemployable" and provided separate help for the two groups. The employable were the top priority; they were to be aided to gain or maintain incomes to support their families. The administration wanted to provide this group "employment assurance," by the stimulation of private employment and by direct governmental action—short-term unemployment compensation and work for wages provided by the federal government where needed. The hope was that the government jobs would sustain workers' morale and skills, and eventually they would receive suitable employment through private industry.[41]

Most of the rest of the adult population was deemed "unemployable," but with a right, too, to economic security. One group included families without male breadwinners. The other main unemployable group was the aged. Most economists and administration officials thought that the economy of the future would need fewer workers than in the past and that retirement from the labor force with an income would be a good thing for many of the aged. The current generation of the needy aged was to get means-tested support, in the manner of the Dill-Connery bill. However, the administration also thought that among current workers the loss of income and work due to old age was a risk that could be insured. It proposed a program of compulsory old-age annuities that would tax wage earners during their working careers in order to pay for their retirements.

To address these security issues, the administration was prepared to propose two major pieces of social legislation in the new year. The first was audacious, calling for $4.9 billion to create some 3.5 million work relief jobs. The work projects were to be under the control of the president, would pay a security wage, and through the purchase of materials the administration hoped, would bring the employment of another 3.5 million.[42] The Economic Security Act, the second bill, was an omnibus measure combining the rest of the committee's proposals. It included an unemployment compensation measure, which provided for a 3 percent tax on payrolls and was to provide fifteen weeks of benefits at about half a worker's wages. The bill also dealt with the largest identifiable groups of the "unemployables" through grants-in-aid to the states for means-tested Aid to Dependent Children and Old-Age Assistance. To get the national money, states had, among other things, to provide these benefits throughout the state—"county optional" programs would not do—and at a level to ensure the "decency and health" of their recipients. There was also to be a second old-age program, funded by payroll taxes on the first $3,000 per year of wages, divided equally between employers and employees. These taxes, or "contributions," as the committee called them, were to start at 1 percent and increase over time until they reached 5 percent in 1957, although benefits were not to be paid until 1942. The administration called them "annuities" because the payments were based on the employees' cumulative wages and did not take dependents into account or pool risks.[43]

Slouching toward the Townsend Plan

The importance of reducing the labor force was an idea that had much currency, as did employing government spending to spur employment indirectly. There is some evidence, however, that the Townsend Plan had an impact on the specific old-age provisions, which is evident by comparing the proposal with what Congress had been considering for old age and the administration's proposals. In its proposed OAA program the administration called for one-to-one national matching payments, with the other half being funded by state and local taxes. The Dill-Connery bill had the national government picking up only one-third of the cost, as did the administration's proposal for Aid to Dependent Children. In addition, the amount being requested for OAA was increased from the $10 million envisioned in the Dill-Connery bill to $50 million in the first year and $125 million in the second year for OAA. There were also stronger national standards in the administration's proposal.

The proposed old-age annuity program was also influenced by the pressure of the Townsendites. It was spurred in part by the need to fund the new Old-Age Assistance program, and at a higher level than previously expected. The annuity program was initially called "federal old-age benefits" and had a separate title in the security legislation from that of the payroll tax, mainly to lower the probability that the Supreme Court would find the bill unconstitutional. But the annuity program was to pay no benefits for years, and the administration saw the payroll tax also as a means to fund OAA.[44] The old-age annuity program also advanced somewhat at the expense of the unemployment compensation proposal, another change that seemed to come as a result of the Townsend Plan. A payroll tax of 5 percent from the previous Wagner-Lewis bill for unemployment compensation was reduced to 3 percent. Plans for health insurance were also scrapped. In short, to pay for OAA into the foreseeable future, the administration upgraded its old-age annuity proposal, despite likely employer opposition to the taxes for it.

It has been argued that the administration responded cautiously to the Townsend Plan, countering its pension proposal, and the likelihood it would be bid up by Congress in the manner Civil War pensions, with a fiscally conservative old-age annuity program.[45] But the administration was providing only the appearance of fiscal responsibility. Most of the taxation for this new annuity program would not come due until much later, and there was a great deal of uncertainty as to what might happen in the interim. Also, the administration's projections through 1980 turned out to be wildly off target. Not only was it unable to project, understandably, the influence of the war, the postwar economic expansion, and baby boom, but even its short-term projections about tax revenues were way off. And the new setup did not protect the annuity program from expansion by way of pressure, and greater taxes for old-age programs meant a stronger commitment to old-age policy and thus a higher base from which to start the bidding.

The Townsend Plan influenced the old-age proposals, but the sociological puzzle concerns why. After all, the organization had made few inroads outside the West, had only a few potential congressional proponents, and had yet to present a Townsend bill, much less agitate and lobby for it. It was not a matter of a group organizing, mobilizing resources, using its resources to engage in collective action, and then seeing its collective action being converted into collective benefits. There was little in the way of resources or energy being devoted to collective action. The Townsend Plan mainly sought to make the aged pension-conscious by getting them to join and participate in Townsend clubs. It was largely a strategy of organization and mobilization without collective action, which was to wait for the future, when the organization was better prepared to act.

The favorable political situation for old-age policy was the key to the influence that the Townsend Plan had over old-age policy in 1934. Organizing many of the aged quickly behind the idea of generous and national old-age pensions was influential at a time when an overall security program was being constructed. There was no reaction to a similar mobilization of the aged earlier by Dr. Pope, a chiropodist with a budding pension organization in 1932. In 1933, the administration had not yet turned its attention to permanent social policy reform. The initial mobilization of Townsendites worked mainly by strengthening the hand of the CES officials working on the issue of old-age security, heightening the political salience of old-age proposals relative to others that were being considered, such as those for unemployment insurance and health insurance. Partly because of the Townsend Plan, it was important for the administration to have an impressive approach to old age, even if it fell short of coherence.

Conclusion

The Townsend Plan arose in the context of other challengers attempting to influence the relationships between the state and groups of citizens. Both old-school and new-school perspectives have a line on why the groups arose, and both have something to be said for them. The first would argue for the influence of the Depression and other social dislocations associated with it. The second would argue for the influence of changes in the political context that would increase the probability and degree to which collective action might be productive. The Townsend Plan was aided in part by grievances due to the Depression that made its claims more plausible. However, the plan was spurred in part by changed political circumstances that made mobilization and collective action more likely to be productive. A new regime came into power with a strong commitment to social policy reform, and other groups had been pressing the old-age issue at the state level. Both arguments, however, leave important issues unaddressed—such as why the aged rather than other aggrieved categories of citizens organized, and why the Townsend Plan took the form that it did—a nonpartisan, mass-pressure organization rather than a new political party.

The structure of the American polity and long-standing policies, as well as recent changes, influenced the form of the Townsend Plan and the lines of action that it took. The American polity encourages political groups to form around single issues and organizations seeking influence over the major political parties and individual legislators and candidates. Organizing around old-age programs was also spurred by short-term changes in state action on old age. These changes in policy legitimated both the political identity of the aged as a group and demands for old-age pensions. These new political conditions also aided the mobilization of veterans, who, like the aged, had among their numbers many with extensive political experience, which separated these groups from others with grievances that might have mobilized.

As the Townsend Plan was organizing the West, the Roosevelt administration was already making its plans for permanent reform through the Committee on Economic Security. It seems highly likely that without the Townsend Plan these plans would have proceeded, but also that the administration altered its proposals in favor of old age. It proposed two old-age programs, one of which came at the expense of a greater commitment to unemployment compensation. The Townsend Plan's influence on these moves was not due to any directed strategy of collective action, however. Instead, its influence was largely due to its rapid success of organizing and mobilizing the resources of many of the aged under political circumstances favorable to the development of social policy. The sweetening of the package for the aged was designed in part to win the allegiances of Townsendites. But the Townsend Plan leadership headed to Washington that winter, seeking more.

FOUR

The Townsend Plan versus Social Security

IN DECEMBER 1934, less than two years after being fired, Dr. Francis Townsend arrived in Washington as a nascent national figure. Hoping for an audience with President Franklin Roosevelt to convince him to adopt the doctor's pension-recovery program, Townsend was denied. Aggravating his feeling of disrespect, eastern newspapers poked fun. If pensioning off people was so economically beneficial, the *New York Times* mused, why not provide pensions for everyone? On January 17, the president's security legislation was announced to great fanfare. The Old-Age Assistance program imagined benefits of $30 per month for the indigent aged, far less than the $200 demanded by the Townsendites but more than all but a few states were paying. Led by its secretary-treasurer, Earl Clements, the Townsend Plan tried to steal some of the limelight. The day before, new Long Beach congressman John S. McGroarty had submitted a Townsend bill. Though eclipsed in most print media by the administration's program, the bid for attention was not in vain: Dr. Townsend found himself pictured on the cover of the January 26 issue of *Newsweek*, theatrically smacking his fist in his palm.[1]

The battle over security was on—under circumstances favorable for the advocates of new social spending. Roosevelt was backing a variety of proposals, his hand strengthened by his unprecedented victory in the midterm congressional elections, which were perceived as an endorsement of his "bold and persistent experimentation" and more generous approach to relief. There were now enough northern Democrats and left-wing third-party representatives in Congress, if need be, to outvote the Republicans and conservative southern Democrats. And there was a national bureaucracy, the Federal Emergency Relief Administration, providing cash benefits of extraordinary sums to those harmed by the Depression. Townsend and Clements sought to exploit the situation by substituting the Townsend bill for the old-age portion of the security bill. They called on the approximately 1,000 Townsend clubs for donations to allow them to educate Congress about the program and induce its support. The leaders were also planning to use pressure from 100,000 club members.[2] The Townsend Plan might also aid its constituents by inducing Congress to make the administration's old-age programs more generous. But not only did few members of Congress back McGroarty's bill. Congress rolled back the old-age benefits in the administration's security bill. The issue is why the Townsend Plan had so little impact on old-age policy, even though the political situation was so favorable, there were more clubs, and for the first time the Townsend Plan engaged in sustained collective action.

Dr. Townsend Goes to Washington

The president had much more on his mind than Dr. Townsend. On January 4 Roosevelt proposed that Congress grant him $4.9 billion in a new work relief program. The cost of the work program was greater than the rest of the budget combined—more than 10 percent of national income in 1934—and Roosevelt was asking Congress to grant him complete authority over the appropriation.[3] And there was more substantial opposition. Financed by the du Ponts, a membership-seeking organization calling itself the American Liberty League was fighting the entire New Deal from the political right, as were, increasingly, business organizations such as the National Association of Manufacturers and Chambers of Commerce. The governmental agency in charge of ensuring economic recovery, the National Recovery Administration (NRA), was having trouble establishing codes of competition across industries, and organized labor was demanding a separate law to enforce the collective bargaining rights promised by the NRA. Other alternative programs were on the political horizon, too, including a bill for the immediate payment of the World War I veterans' bonus, with an estimated cost of $2 billion, and Huey Long's Share Our Wealth program, with its stipends for all and taxes on the rich.[4]

Roosevelt had his own security legislation. Sponsored by Senator Robert Wagner of New York, the so-called Economic Security Act complemented the work program and took a multifaceted approach. Although the committee and the bill were called "economic security," the newspapers merged that term with "social legislation" and were calling the result "social security." A political cartoon that ran in the New York Times soon after the introduction of the bill illustrated the conventional Washington wisdom. Sitting in the Oval Office, Roosevelt gazes with fatherly concern at a framed picture of his youthful "social program," with the dome of the Capitol in view. "He'll be a changed boy when he returns," says the caption.[5] Aside from demanding that the program remain largely recognizable, Roosevelt was expecting and even encouraging Congress to alter it, in order to address its objections and gain its support. The Townsend Plan was the largest mass-based group hoping to influence this process.

Security Concerns

After the security and McGroarty bills were introduced, newspapers were suggesting that Congress might sweeten the grants for OAA because of the

The Father—"He'll Be a Changed Boy When He Comes Back."

Figure 4.1: "He'll Be a Changed Boy . . ." This cartoon reflected the conventional political wisdom that Congress would greatly revise the administration's proposed security legislation. There was no consensus, however, as to whether its programs would be augmented or cut back. Source: *New York Times*, January 27, 1935, p. E9. Cartoon by Edwin Marcus, courtesy of Donald Marcus.

pressure of the Townsendites, Long, and others on the left. It was also possible, though, that Congress might lower the grants for OAA and place other restrictions on the program, given the conservative leadership of the House Ways and Means Committee and Senate Finance Committee, which had jurisdiction over the security bill. It was deemed plausible, too, that the

proposed old-age annuity program might be eliminated because it had little
support in Congress. The new payroll taxes, which constituted Title VIII of
the bill, were certain to draw vigorous opposition from business groups, and
organized labor was not entirely happy with compulsory employee taxes, either. Business groups were arguing for dividing the legislation into individual
bills, hoping to forestall the passage of some of them.[6]

The economic security bill also had to wait for the works bill to pass. The
Republicans were seeking to cut the appropriation in half and were likely to
gain support from some southern Democrats, who preferred grants through
the FERA. More ominously, organized labor opposed Roosevelt's "security"
wage for work relief and demanded that project work be remunerated at the
higher rate of wages "prevailing" for the type of work in the area. Congress as
a body bridled at the president's proposal to control the money. It was asking
him in so many words: Where's the pork? Radicals were pushing for an unemployment insurance bill sponsored by Ernest Lundeen, a Farmer-Labor
representative from Minnesota. It was to replace the wages of the unemployed at the rate of at least $10 per week and $3 per dependent, benefits to
be administered by committees of unemployed workers. A group of radical
members of the House formed, naming themselves after their only southern
member, Maury Maverick of Texas, and planning to vote as a bloc. Congress
was also rallying around a version of the $2 billion veterans bonus bill,
which might derail the work and security proposals. Although most of the
left sincerely wanted to pass legislation, Huey Long, Louisiana senator and
leader of Share Our Wealth, was thought to be working mainly for Roosevelt's failure in order to replace him. The administration feared that a coalition of animosity on the right and indifference on the left would defeat its
bills.[7]

Townsend and Clements were pressing for the McGroarty bill, HR 3977,
which called for $200 per month for anyone over sixty years of age, with re-
strictions to spend the pension every month and that the recipient refrain
from gainful employment. The pensions were to be paid for by a 2 percent
tax on business transactions. To deflect possible criticisms, the bill also included some restrictions on donations of pensions and on receiving benefits
from other levels of government and exempted personal services from the
transactions tax. The bill asked for $2 billion to get the program started and
was seen as a possible substitute for Roosevelt's security measure.[8] The
Townsend Plan's lobbyist team numbered ten and was led by Frank Peterson,
the Townsend Plan's publicist, who helped to draft the McGroarty bill.
Townsend Plan leaders deemed House representatives the most vulnerable
to appeals because they all faced reelection in two years. A Townsend Plan
meeting in January sponsored by Congressman Benjamin Ekwall of Washington drew approximately fifty House members. Clements and Townsend

took up a special collection for the Washington effort and generated more than $20,000. Townsend Plan experts, including Dr. Townsend himself, stood ready to testify.[9]

In their bids to gain congressional support, however, the Townsend Plan leaders mainly employed outsider strategies, some of which were fairly assertive. They claimed that a large and growing club membership backed the pension-recovery plan unconditionally, based their political allegiances on it, and would cashier politicians who opposed the bill. The founders also threatened to bring petitions with some 30 million signatures to Washington. The leadership urged club members to write letters to demand that Congress support the McGroarty bill. The addresses of all members of Congress were published in the *Townsend Weekly*. The *Weekly* targeted members of the Ways and Means Committee and those who publicly criticized Townsend's idea. Some members supposedly received 3,500 letters per day, and the Townsend Plan dispatched an organizer to Abilene, Texas, to silence Congressman Thomas Blanton, a vociferous critic. The plan was also pressing state legislatures in the West to follow Arizona's lead in "memorializing" or instructing Congress to adopt Townsend's pension-recovery program. Some clubs proposed to march on Washington.[10]

Congress Goes to Town

Although Townsend's proposal had been attacked before, for the first time professionals went to the task, training their criticism on the hastily drafted McGroarty bill. Called first before the Ways and Means Committee in late January, Roosevelt administration witnesses were able to eviscerate the McGroarty bill without being countered for days. Members of Congress were lying in wait as well, having been supplied arguments and statistical ammunition by Edwin Witte, the executive secretary of the security committee, who notably drafted a detailed memo titled "Why the Townsend Old-Age Revolving Pension Plan Is Impossible."[11] Witte aired for the Ways and Means Committee, and the newly attentive national press, criticisms he had been making of the Townsend's pension recovery plan since last fall. He estimated that 10 million of those Americans over sixty years would take pensions at a yearly cost of $24 billion, half the previous year's national income. He also argued that the tax would not pay for the pensions, leading to the prospect of severe inflation on the order of Weimar Germany. Secretary of Labor Frances Perkins denounced Townsend's idea as "fantastic," and Harry Hopkins, the Federal Emergency Relief administrator, called it "cock-eyed."[12]

The McGroarty bill was opposed from all political directions. The political left supported the Lundeen bill, feeling that the generous unemployment insurance payments in it were fairer than giving the bulk of government aid to

Figure 4.2: Ants in His Pants. The cartoon showed that the organization hoped its letter-writing campaign would irritate members of Congress into favorable action on the Townsend Plan–sponsored McGroarty bill. Source: *National Townsend Weekly,* April 1, 1935, p. 5.

the aged, and also disliked the regressiveness of the McGroarty bill's tax. Organized labor opposed sales taxes as hurting workers.[13] The pension-recovery plan had the additional disadvantage to some on the left of promoting monopoly, since vertically integrated businesses would be subject to fewer rounds of taxes. Abraham Epstein, the director of the American Association of Social Security and an administration witness, also called for a congressional investigation into the operations of the Townsend Plan.[14] The right objected to the great size of the spending and the accompanying growth of government that it would imply. The $18 billion in yearly outlays expected by Townsend Plan publicists was more than one-third of national income and three to four times as large as the sum Roosevelt was requesting for his work program. For all Townsend and Clements's praise of capitalism and businessmen and their criticism of socialism and "production for use," there were few on the right who wanted the government taxing so much. Business organizations mainly ignored the McGroarty bill, however, saving their fire for the security bill and its new payroll taxes for unemployment compensation and old-age annuities.[15]

The doctor and other Townsend Plan witnesses won no new support with their testimony before hostile congressional committees. The trouble began at the top. Although Townsend Plan expert witnesses were supposed to testify on February 4, Dr. Townsend was present and was goaded into taking questions, stumbling through his answers as committee members poked fun at him. Townsend was not alone, though, in being tripped up by the committee. The Townsend Plan's experts, Glen Hudson, an actuarial consultant, and O. Otto Moore, a lawyer representing Denver Townsend clubs, also found it rough going.[16] Among the more grandstanding points scored by the Ways and Means Committee members were that Rockefeller and Morgan could take revolving pensions, that pensions could be spent on luxuries, and that respectable older people would not know how to spend so much money. The committee members also noted that unscrupulous oldsters might hoard rather than spend the money, sign up for multiple pensions, or pay their children living wages to do chores.[17] On the more technical side, the members exposed flaws in the bill's language, including hopelessly vague definitions of "financial transactions" and "gainful competitive pursuits." Committee members hammered home the point that collecting taxes from so many different people, including farmers, would be far more difficult than collecting payroll taxes from relatively large employers or sales taxes from merchants.[18] The main line of attack, though, was that the taxes would not pay for such large pensions. Townsend was claiming that 7.5 to 8 million would take pensions, rather than the 10 million of the 11 million Americans sixty years old or older estimated by Witte. But even Hudson, the Townsend Plan–affiliated statistical expert and actuary, estimated that a 2 percent transactions tax would have garnered only between $6 billion and $8 billion in 1934, not the necessary $18 billion.[19]

By the time the Ways and Means Committee hearings ended on February 12, the McGroarty bill had been fatally wounded. Neither Townsend, nor Hudson, nor Moore could testify that he would vote for the bill as it was written, and none of them could supply appropriate amendments. When Townsend suggested that the Ways and Means Committee could make the necessary changes, the chairman, Robert Doughton of North Carolina, twitted him that only the auteur of such an intricate plan could be trusted to undertake so important a task. In the end Townsend conceded that $200 per month for everyone over sixty was more than the tax would immediately bear and suggested that the pensions start at age seventy-five instead. The newspaper headlines referred to Townsend in terms of the "humor" and "mirth" he lent the proceedings, with only the unsmiling doctor not appreciating the joke.[20]

The *Townsend Weekly*, which published its first issue simultaneously with the submission of the security and McGroarty bills, was placed on the defensive and was harshly critical of the Roosevelt administration. The first headline suggested that Dr. Witte's "fallacy"—that the transactions tax would not pay for the pensions—had been exposed. The *Weekly* was quick to predict the success of the McGroarty bill and to blame the criticisms of administration spokespersons on Roosevelt personally. The president was also criticized for the Post Office's investigation of the Townsend Plan—which had apparently turned up little of use. Nowhere was it mentioned how poorly Townsend's testimony went over, and he was forced to sign off on a front-page disclaimer that he was not compromising on either the age limit or the amount of the pension. Angered, he asked Townsendites to write to committee members in the tone of employers commanding their servants.[21]

When Townsend testified before the Senate Finance Committee on February 16, he came more well prepared to explain the bill, but the results were no better. Under the hostile questioning of Alben Barkley of Kentucky, Townsend admitted that the transactions tax was really a sales tax, and that it would fall mainly on poorer people. Townsend also agreed that all farmers would need to be licensed to pay the tax. Pat Harrison, the Mississippi chairman of the committee, whose balance of power was held by southern Democrats, worried out loud about the disincentives to work the pensions would provide for the extended families of aged black sharecroppers and tenant farmers.[22] The senators also followed Abraham Epstein's suggestion to begin questioning how the Townsend Plan generated and used its funds. Clements detailed the growth in receipts for the organization as well as subscriptions for the *Townsend Weekly*, but the committee cast doubt on the founders' motives and the doctor's working knowledge of an organization that was being referred to by his name.[23]

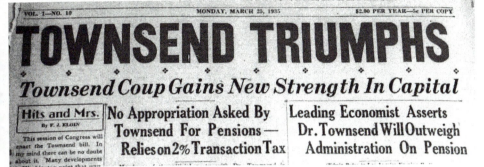

VOL. 1—NO. 10   MONDAY, MARCH 25, 1935   **$2.00 PER YEAR—5c PER COPY**

TOWNSEND TRIUMPHS

Townsend Coup Gains New Strength In Capital

Hits and Mrs.	No Appropriation Asked By	Leading Economist Asserts
By F. J. ELGIN	Townsend For Pensions —	Dr. Townsend Will Outweigh
This session of Congress will enact the Townsend bill. In my mind there can be no doubt about it. Many developments	Relies on 2% Transaction Tax	Administration On Pension

Figure 4.3: Townsend Triumphs? Despite the fact that Townsend Plan representatives performed ineptly before congressional committee, the *Townsend Weekly* portrayed their efforts, including Dr. Townsend's, as effective. Source: *National Townsend Weekly*, March 25, 1935, p. 1.

The Security Debate: Round Two

Senior Discounts in the House and the Townsend Plan's New Bill

As Townsend was occupied in the Senate, the House Ways and Means Committee was amending the security bill in ways disadvantageous to potential old-age beneficiaries. First, it removed administrative control over Old-Age Assistance from Harry Hopkins's Federal Emergency Relief Administration. Some members feared that the FERA, which had a strong sense of fair play and a reputation for acting on it, would withhold grants from states that did not provide adequate benefits.[24] In addition, the language regarding the administration of the program was altered so as not to force states to hire personnel according to merit standards. In the initial OAA provisions, moreover, states would not receive funding if they placed property and income restrictions on beneficiaries and the aged needed to receive an income providing "reasonable subsistence compatible with decency and health." But the committee changed the bill so that states could add any restrictions and provide any income to recipients, no matter how low. The committee also made it difficult to suspend payments to state programs if violations of the federal law were found.[25] Instead of a guaranteed and generous pension as demanded by the Townsend Plan, Ways and Means began to alter OAA in the direction of contingent and stingy benefits, loosely administered.

Meanwhile, Congresswoman Isabella Greenway sought to amend the administration's bill to include only old-age benefits. A society girl turned cattle queen and Democratic committeewoman, Greenway had been a schoolmate of Eleanor Roosevelt and a bridesmaid at the Roosevelts' wedding. Greenway, a strong advocate for old-age benefits, surmised that better benefits could be expected if the bill focused only on this issue, and some of the business opposition would likely disappear, making for a quick and relatively easy passage. Otherwise the old-age provisions might go down with the rest of the security bill, once opposition mobilized. Greenway secured twenty-five signatures from Democrats, which was sufficient to force a caucus meeting on the matter. But the president insisted on keeping all parts of the security bill, and Greenway withdrew without demanding the meeting.[26]

To effect the changes previously agreed upon and to make others, the Ways and Means Committee turned over the security bill to its own legislative draftsman. One set of amendments involved the payroll taxes designed to pay for the old-age programs. These changes were animated in part by the president's dislike of the administration's projections that the programs' benefits would require outlays from other federal taxes beginning in 1965 and reaching $1.4 billion per year by 1980. Roosevelt thought instead that the programs should be paid for entirely by the new payroll taxes, or "contributions," as he euphemistically called them. The Ways and Means Committee also accelerated the schedule by which automatic increases in the payroll tax would take place. For constitutional reasons the committee also dropped all references to an insurance fund, separating the new old-age annuity benefits further from the taxation revenues generated.[27] In addition to these changes, the Ways and Means Committee moved to exempt a number of groups from paying the taxes and their employees from receiving benefits from the program. Notable among these were farm owners and employers of domestic servants and their employees.[28]

As this went on, the Townsend Plan was otherwise occupied, regrouping to rewrite its own bill. The hope was that there was still time to substitute another version of the pension plan for the administration's old-age provisions. Its bid to convince the California legislature to memorialize Congress was meeting with success. Under great pressure from Governor Frank Merriam, the Senate agreed on March 19 to the measure, which the governor gladly signed as an inexpensive way to retire his electoral debt to the Townsend Plan. Townsend clubs in Oregon, an emerging hotbed of pension activity, signed enough petitions to force a recall election of a state legislator who opposed a memorial and threatened to recall the governor as well. The Townsend Plan also encouraged additional letter writing and petitions, while deciding against having club members march on Washington, perhaps fearing the fate suffered by World War I veterans' "bonus marches" in 1932, 1933, and 1934, which dwindled yearly in support.[29]

A new version of the McGroarty bill was introduced on April 1. In it, the $200-per-month figure was demoted from a right to a maximum. Those over the age of sixty and otherwise qualified for a pension would divide among themselves the proceeds of whatever the taxation provisions yielded, after a decent interval of tax collection. In addition to the transactions tax, there were supplementary increases in the income tax and the inheritance and gifts taxes. "Transactions," and other technical terms, were now defined precisely. Although the spending requirement remained, several clauses now restricted potential forms of employment that congressmen considered dubious, such as maintaining an able-bodied person in "idleness." A very forgiving means test was adopted, excluding those with incomes greater than $200 per month and thus ensuring that Rockefeller and Morgan would not take pensions. The Veterans Bureau and the Treasury Department were to share administrative chores.[30] The pensions were expected to be initially on the order of $40 to $60 per month. In short, Townsend and Clements were now willing to try out the revolving pension plan on a more limited basis, with the hope that $200 pensions for everyone over sixty would eventually be sustainable by the taxes.

As amended, the bill was no longer untenable. It was far from outlandish to propose that the federal government pay a relatively generous flat-sum pension to old people with little regard to need and the pension funded by an earmarked tax. This sort of pension would have been far simpler to administer than the two-part system that the Roosevelt administration was proposing. A flat plan would have avoided the often demeaning, intrusive, and costly welfare casework necessary for assistance programs and the elaborate wage records needed to administer social insurance. Indeed, a flat-pension proposal became a cornerstone of the wartime British Beveridge Report. Representatives from the Fraternal Order of Eagles, which had been fighting uphill for old-age benefits for more than a decade, argued to the committee that flat pensions would be the easiest to administer and fairest.[31] The taxation provisions of the bill were not far-fetched either. A transactions tax in some form would have been workable. Even if this tax and the others would have brought in only $6 billion per year, such a sum would have provided for pensions of approximately $50 per month to 10 million of the aged and was similar to the amount that Roosevelt was asking for for work programs. A $50 pension was still more generous than the $30-per-month maximum benefit envisioned by the administration's bill, which was in any case a red herring. Most states were unlikely to offer $30 per month. As we shall see, the provisions of the new McGroarty bill were not far out of line with what the public seemed to want in the way of old-age benefits. And although a national sales tax would be regressive, it was not as if the administration's proposals were going to be financed progressively. If sales taxes were a bad idea, their time had come in America, as they were being adopted in state after state. The United States now stands out for not having consumption taxes at the national level of government—which constitute one reason for lower social spending efforts here.[32]

It was also far from crazy to suggest that the spending in the new McGroarty bill would stimulate the economy. Although the "revolving" aspect of the Townsendites' economic thinking was implausible, the stimulating effect of government spending was already becoming orthodoxy within the Roosevelt administration. The president was arguing that his new work program would employ 3.5 million directly and that many again indirectly. It is generally agreed nowadays that the Depression was ended only by enormous government outlays for World War II. Sizable pensions likely would have had a stimulating effect. If the 1981 Reagan-Kemp-Roth tax cut, which brought a decade of record deficits, and the 2001 Bush tax cuts, which ended record surpluses, provide any lesson, it is that it is unwise to laugh off as irrational, or at least impossible to enact, an expensive proposal combining large benefits for a specific group with dubious declarations about economic gain for all. This second McGroarty bill did not gain nearly as much press attention as the first one, however, and when it did, reporters played up the fact that it no longer guaranteed the $200 per month promised by Townsend.[33]

Security Clearance

Far greater attention was trained on the Ways and Means Committee's rewritten security bill, which was introduced on April 2 with a new and catchier name, the Social Security Act. When the second round of McGroarty and security bills were juxtaposed, it became obvious that there was considerably more backing for the committee's bill. On April 11, test votes on procedural issues indicated the favorable lay of the land for the committee's bill, and McGroarty conceded defeat, only ten days into the life of his bill.[34] The only question was whether it would be possible to amend the new security bill on the floor of the House.

It was not. On April 18, a Townsend Plan amendment to the old-age portion of the social security bill was rejected on the House floor by a standing vote, 206 to 56. Those standing up for the amendment included the few diehard supporters, such as Joseph Monaghan of Montana, who proposed it, and James Mott of Oregon, as well as McGroarty. Also included in the Townsend total, however, were members who mainly opposed the administration's bill. Although some scholars have suggested that the low number of "no" votes indicated congressional fear to be counted against the Townsend amendment, it seems doubtful. For there were twenty-four other defeated amendments, and the 206 voting against the Townsend amendment was a relatively high number. Only 126 votes, for instance, were needed to stop an amendment to drop old-age annuity benefits. Congresswoman Greenway's amendment proposed to alter the matching basis of OAA to five national dollars for each state dollar, with the federal government thus providing a $25 monthly benefit, and she secured the support of her friend Eleanor Roosevelt. But her husband held firm, and the amendment lost, 87 to 165. The committee's bill passed the House overwhelmingly the next day, and the Townsend Plan's Washington contingent decamped.[35] In the Senate, the Finance Committee almost deleted the old-age annuity provisions and almost adopted a provision, the Clark amendment, to make them voluntary for companies with their own retirement plans. Both changes were sought by business critics. The bill did not change dramatically from the House's version, however, and although the Clark amendment was adopted on the Senate floor, it was dropped in the conference committee under pressure from the administration, and the conference bill was passed in both houses.[36] On August 14, Roosevelt signed it.

The first set of Townsend Plan bills failed for obvious reasons. Even McGroarty's more plausible and less expensive second bill demanded an enormous new governmental commitment to taxation and support to one group. It was too much even for a Congress that was the most sympathetic to social spending yet in American history. Also, the unconvincing testimony by the Townsend delegation for the first McGroarty bill had lingering effects that harmed the second one. More important than that, the Townsend Plan was still not particularly well organized beyond the West and so far had little experience in politics. It could not plausibly threaten the vast bulk of Congress with electoral retribution, despite its strident letter-writing campaign. For most members of Congress, the Townsend Plan was not an issue, at least not yet. Even if Townsend clubs had been organized across the country, it would have been a tall order to gain sufficient congressional support for the McGroarty bill, given the rudimentary political skills of the Townsend Plan's Washington contingent, the political dominance of the Roosevelt administration, and the relatively long time it took even for bills with extensive pressure-group and congressional backing, like the veterans' bonus, to build sufficient support in Congress. The Roosevelt administration had placed old-age security on the political agenda and was ready to pass a bill before the Townsend Plan was organized enough to exploit the situation.

The administration's proposals for old age were also difficult to defeat. Federal aid for state and local old-age benefits programs had previously been backed by large numbers in both houses. Although the administration added a less well-supported old-age annuity program, for the immediate future its taxes were going to finance the more popular OAA program. The fact that the taxes and benefits for the old-age annuity program were restricted to larger employers and their employees minimized the opposition from agricultural parts of the country, especially the South. Taking no chances, the administration added more conservative congressional support for its bill when it allowed the Ways and Means Committee to tone it down. In any case, far more new members of Congress felt more beholden to Roosevelt than to the Townsend Plan. Even if the revised McGroarty bill were somehow to pass Congress, Roosevelt stood ready to veto it. He dramatically vetoed the veterans' bonus in May with a speech before Congress, contrasting the expensive demands of one group with the needs of all Americans, and the McGroarty bill was far more expensive and implied an endless fiscal commitment.[37] To make it law, Roosevelt would have to be convinced or replaced, or the support in Congress for the bill would have to become so great that his views would not matter.

The Impact of the Townsend Plan on the Social Security Act

There were too many things working against the Townsend Plan's legislation and too many things working for the administration's. The larger question is the impact of the Townsend Plan and its strategies in 1935 on the old-age portions of the security bill. The bulk of the amendments to the old-age programs harmed the interests of the aged, whereas the fact that the bill passed was in their favor. Did the existence or efforts of the Townsend Plan increase the likelihood that the administration's old-age proposals would pass Congress? The Townsend Plan and its actions may have induced members of Congress to support the administration's bill when they might not have otherwise. It may also have had negative consequences; the *Townsend Weekly* routinely criticized the administration's bill as providing "pauper's" benefits, and Townsendites often wrote to members of Congress in opposition to the security bill. The Townsend Plan may have made it easier for Congress to reduce benefits in it. Might something better for the aged have passed if the challenger had employed a different or better-executed set of strategies? After all, before Congress got its hands on the security legislation, the newspapers were reporting that the pressure of the Townsend Plan combined with other left-wing groups might lead to greater federal commitments to old-age benefits.[38] That certainly did not happen. It is possible, however, that the changes may have been even more restrictive had the Townsend Plan not existed or taken the actions that it did.

The Presence of the Townsend Plan

The organized presence of the Townsend Plan and the existence of its alternative were helpful. Merely by staking out a position to the left of the administration on the old-age question, organizing supporters around it, and threatening to mobilize more, the Townsend Plan doubtless made it easier for members who were predisposed to supporting some new old-age benefits to accept the administration's bill. The existence of the alternative posed by the Townsend Plan may have moved some members of Congress to favor the administration's program in hopes of taking the wind from the sails of the Townsend Plan, or to gain some credit from the majority of the aged not already committed to revolving pensions, or both. The threat of widespread, generous, and equal pensions, more eventual than short-term, was probably also useful in persuading more conservative supporters and constituents that the administration's bill was the lesser of evils. Because Roosevelt insisted on pressing the security bill as a package, the mobilization of Townsend clubs probably also helped to secure support for less popular parts of the bill, such as Aid to Dependent Children.

According to Witte, at one point the existence of the Townsend Plan and its support may have saved old-age annuities. As the Senate Finance Committee was in executive session, Witte made a deal with Senator William King of Utah. The senator would support unemployment compensation, but only if Witte would in return secretly supply the senator with Witte's best arguments against the old-age annuity program, the most vulnerable part of the bill. After King made his speech, the chairman asked Witte to provide a brief for old-age annuities. Witte concluded by suggesting that if Congress were to fail to adopt the program, the alternative ultimately would likely be Townsend-style pensions. The chairman called the question, a few key senators who had seemed doubtful supporters of old-age annuities voted in favor, and the provision survived.[39] Had the committee removed annuities, however, Roosevelt most likely would have demanded that they be reinstated in conference. After all, he did successfully eliminate the Clark amendment. That said, the story taps into the concern of Congress that something like the McGroarty bill might eventually pass—in the absence of giving the administration its way on its security bill.

It is difficult to place great blame on the Townsend Plan, too, for the downgrades in the old-age programs. The Ways and Means Committee doubtless would have scaled down the administration's plan regardless of any efforts of the Townsend Plan. The four southern members of the committee, including the chairman Doughton, opposed any sort of national control or standards in any social spending program. They and their planter and other wealthy constituencies preferred flexibility. Southern Democrats and their compatriots in patronage-oriented political parties did not want civil servants running the new programs. And if the Ways and Means Committee had not scaled back the program, the even more conservative Senate Finance Committee most likely would have. Once Roosevelt invited Congress to amend the bill, trimming national and administrative standards was certain.

The Townsend Plan's alternative may have had some inadvertent positive influence. By staking out a fiscally reckless course, the Townsend Plan helped to define down the actuarial deviance of the administration's proposals, which were merely irresponsible. Administration witnesses claimed that Old-Age Assistance would cost the federal government $125 million in its second year of operation and in later years. The witnesses also testified that about 3.5 million of the 7 million Americans sixty-five years of age and older were dependent. But if all the states took the maximum federal matching money, and all aged dependents were to take benefits, the outlay would be $630 million per year—five times the administration's figure—whereas the payroll tax was estimated, generously, to bring in $200 million per year.[40] Roosevelt, too, could be charged with proposing something for nothing. The shoddy construction of the first McGroarty bill also deflected attention from the technical problems in the administration's bill, which had to be completely rewritten. Without the McGroarty bill, the administration's bill would likely have taken greater heat, possibly leading up to a successful attack on old-age annuities. Instead, problems were quietly addressed outside the media spotlight.

The Townsend Plan's Failed Strategy

The academic literature on the Townsend Plan and Social Security often suggests that though the organization performed miserably its first time on the national stage, the Townsend Plan nonetheless spurred old-age benefits and the cause of the security legislation.[41] Yet it is difficult to identify anything the Townsend Plan did in Washington that buoyed old-age benefits. Almost all the beneficial effects of the Townsend Plan on old-age policy would doubtless have materialized regardless of whether its leaders had drafted the McGroarty bill, come to Washington to testify and lobby for it, induced Townsendites to threaten legislators to pass it, to amend it, and to attack the security bill and support no alternatives, as they did. The Townsend Plan mishandled its own bill, allowing the administration to measure its strength, place it on the defensive, and quickly neutralize it. The organization also failed to engage the security bill in more than a dismissive way, reducing the potential impact of its critique. In addition, the Townsend Plan took too hard a line both for its bill and against the security bill, using aggressive tactics that were unsuited to the favorable situation for old-age policy and to the Townsend Plan's undermobilized status. Finally, the Townsend Plan avoided any alliance with others who might have successfully upgraded old-age policy.

The key lever the Townsend Plan held over old-age policy was the threat that some bill or amendment based on Townsend's idea might be substituted for the old-age provisions of the administration's bill. Any actions that undercut the plausibility of pension-recovery legislation also reduced the Townsend Plan's potential influence over the content of old-age policy and its prospects for enactment. Having made Townsend's pension-recovery idea immediately manifest in a specific bill had its disadvantages. It was quickly subject to attacks and compounded its troubles by the fact that the first McGroarty bill was so poorly written. The resulting wave of bad publicity helped to discredit the alternative early in the process. Townsend Plan leaders found themselves on the defensive, trying to explain technical details of their legislation, and missed opportunities to influence the discourse surrounding old-age policy, as well as the possibility of gaining allies in Congress.

Some of the disadvantages of the Townsend Plan's strategy are evident by comparing it with the strategies of other groups, as well as with the Townsend

Plan's later strategies. The supporters of the Lundeen bill avoided the hostile Ways and Means Committee and instead used the hearings on the security bill to criticize the administration's bill. They shepherded their bill through the friendlier Labor Committee, which was possible because their bill was crafted not to include taxes. This modified outsider strategy allowed the bill's supporters to criticize the benefits in the administration's bill in Ways and Means but without being held to the details. The Ways and Means Committee's ability to focus attention on problems in the McGroarty bill preempted the Townsend Plan's critique of the administration's proposals. The critique would have carried weight and might have led to improvements in the old-age programs in the security bill, given the greater public support behind the Townsend Plan than the Lundeen bill.

What is more, the Townsend Plan's unwillingness to engage the administration's proposals was a lost opportunity to shift the security debate in the direction of the universal and generous pensions. There was ample room in the hearings to disrupt the discourse surrounding the administration's program, especially the old-age annuity proposal, by articulating the more progressive thinking behind senior citizens' pensions. The president and his committee insisted on calling the payroll taxes for its old-age insurance or annuity proposal "contributions." Yet the new insurance program was compulsory, and the administration's taxes on payrolls were as mandatory as any other government levy, perhaps more so because of the reduced possibilities for evasion.[42] The tax was expected to fall almost entirely on the wage bill and thus be taken from paychecks, and the fact that it applied only to the first $3,000 of income compounded its regressiveness. Perhaps worse, defining contribution to mean to pay a specific tax was a more impoverished understanding of the underpinning of rights and less closely allied to standard ideas of citizenship than the Townsend Plan's alternative: that lifetime societal contributions gave citizens a right to a pension. That point was made by the Eagles, but they did not command the attention the Townsend Plan did. Had the Townsend witnesses not been fending off criticisms about their own tax proposals, they might have been able to make these points stick.[43]

More important, the commitment to old-age benefits also might have been made stronger by the Townsend Plan's contesting the administration's degrading language surrounding Old-Age Assistance. The expected $30-per-month payments were attacked by the Townsend Plan as suitable only for "paupers," but OAA was referred to by some administration witnesses similarly as "gratuitous," versus the "contributory" benefits of old-age annuities. The rhetorical slap at Old-Age Assistance was gratuitous in itself. Once OAA became law and states conformed with their own legislation, the benefits would be allocated to recipients as their right under the law. And although "needy" was in the preamble of the title, there was no guarantee that the benefits would be strictly means-tested. No Townsend witnesses pointed this out, and they could have spoken against the pauperization of OAA recipients in a preventive way, possibly deflecting the Ways and Means Committee's bid to make it easier for states to add restrictions on accepting OAA benefits. Instead, the Townsend Plan made this move easier.

The Townsend Plan might also have joined others seeking to upgrade the administration's old-age programs. In January, Senator William Borah was hoping to introduce a flat-rate, generous, and universal federal pension, but the Townsend Plan was unwilling to budge from the first McGroarty bill. It also ignored Congresswoman Greenway's amendment for the national government that would pay at least $25 monthly benefits to all qualified OAA recipients, as well as a bid by some Republicans in the House to increase the federal government's maximum matching payment, a goal that later was championed successfully by the Townsend Plan. It missed the opportunity to press plausible alternatives that might have aided the aged—and the Townsend Plan as well.

The problems were aggravated by the aggressive and blunt means employed by the Townsend Plan. The political circumstances were such that some old-age benefits were highly likely to pass for the first time at the national level, and so those in favor of that should have been treated differently from those who opposed old-age benefits altogether. Instead the Townsendites did not distinguish between the potential friends of old-age benefits but not of the McGroarty bill, or not yet, and the enemies of old-age benefits generally. The Townsend Plan's ire was aimed at the administration and its allies, as well as friends of the aged like Congresswoman Greenway. The flood of hectoring letters must have been especially annoying to those who were sticking their necks out to back old-age benefits in districts where public support was not overwhelming. As Witte claimed, these representatives stood little chance of getting any credit from the largest organization devoted solely to old-age pensions. The threats to replace members of Congress who were unlikely ever to have much Townsend club presence in their districts had the further potential drawback of motivating these members of Congress to discredit the Townsend Plan.

Relying on such assertive means may in some circumstances may be productive, but for the Townsend Plan the threatening tone was also somewhat premature given the geographic imbalance in its organizational progress. Margaret Weir, Ann Orloff, and Theda Skocpol argue that the Townsend Plan was effective in Congress because it established clubs in all congressional districts.[44] But in the first half of 1935, the organization had little presence outside the far West and had not yet decided on targeting congressional districts. It thus could not plausibly threaten the electoral prospects of the bulk of Congress. The organizational inroads the Townsend Plan was making in the East and Midwest were being undercut by the revolts it had to put down in these places, such as in Massachusetts. Threatening southern legislators, as the Townsend Plan did in the case of Senator Tom Connally of Texas, was

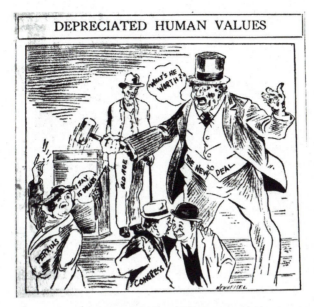

Figure 4.4: Depreciated Human Values. The Townsend Plan was angrily dismissive of the Roosevelt administration's proposal for $15-per-month federal contributions to Old-Age Assistance and failed to join with members of Congress who sought to increase these grants. Source: *National Townsend Weekly*, April 29, 1935, p. 2.

especially implausible. There were few Townsend clubs in the South, outside of southern Florida, and Texas proved inhospitable to Townsend organizers.

The Townsend Plan's moves might be seen as opening gambits—a loss of benefits to the aged and prestige to the organization in the short run in order to gain political advantages to increase the probability of winning the pension-recovery program or other benefits for the aged in the future. And no doubt any initial foray into national politics would have brought setbacks. But the way Townsend and Clements went about it hurt the cause more so than was necessary. The questioning by congressmen was tough and often unfair, but that should have been anticipated given the threatening letters the Townsend Plan had ordered sent to them. The likelihood of harsh criticism put a premium on ensuring that legislation was carefully crafted. If Townsend Plan leaders were certain they needed a bill, they should have waited until they could draft a plausible one. Once the battle was done, moreover, the Townsend Plan made the beginner's error of failing to declare victory. To attract additional support, it helps if an organization can make plausible claims of influence, and the Townsend Plan's leadership could easily have claimed that its efforts had forced the administration to upgrade its initial old-age proposal. In his 1943 autobiography Townsend recognized this and took credit for Roosevelt's programs, but in 1935 he did not, and neither did the more skilled Clements.[45]

The Example of Share Our Wealth

Huey Long's Share Our Wealth shows how the Townsend Plan might have avoided some mistakes. Like the Townsend Plan, Share Our Wealth was threatening to Roosevelt to the extent that it might deny him the political support of groups demanding stronger social policy and lower the chances of his reelection. Unlike the Townsend Plan, though, Long was not defending Share Our Wealth legislation before Congress and was focused on mobilizing people around his ideas and criticizing the Roosevelt administration. He did not give the administration a chance to embarrass him publicly. Indeed, an attack over the airwaves by former National Recovery Administration head Hugh Johnson in March backfired.[46] Worried that Long might enter the presidential race as an independent or support a surrogate and draw off votes, Roosevelt had the Democratic National Committee, whose chairman, James Farley, was also conveniently the postmaster general, conduct the first horse race poll. Roosevelt faced an unnamed Republican and Long. Emil Hurja, the committee's pollster, interpreted his results to give Roosevelt 49 percent of the vote and 305 electoral votes, the Republican 43 percent and 226 electoral votes. But if Long's 7 percent were assumed to be taken from Roosevelt, the results suggested that Long would deliver five states and 122 electoral votes to the Republican candidate. The defection of Michigan, Iowa, and Minnesota—where Roosevelt held slim leads—would swing the election. Long seemed on the verge of holding the balance of power in the presidential election.[47]

Roosevelt could potentially check Long by adopting some parts of Share Our Wealth, which included stiff taxes on income and wealth, bonuses for veterans, benefits for the aged, aid for farmers, and wages and hours legislation for workers. Long and Share Our Wealth did not place the economic security program on the political agenda, though, and had little influence on its content, and Roosevelt was holding fast for now against the veterans' bonus.[48] What is more, Congress had less reason to worry about Long than the president did, and so it seems unlikely that his challenge had much influence there. However, Long did seem to place taxation reform on the political agenda. On June 19, the president unexpectedly demanded the passage of a Treasury Department plan to tax extremely high incomes at a stiff rate, to raise inheritance and gift taxes, to tax undistributed dividends of corporations, and to increase and to make more graduated the corporation income tax. This so-called soak-the-rich tax measure did not threaten the truly wealthy, and the estimated $400 million in revenues from it could not finance a spending program as ambitious as Long's. But the measure broke with the pattern of regressive New Deal taxation initiatives. Long immediately took credit for it.[49]

Long and Share Our Wealth did not have a decisive impact on social policy in the second New Deal, but they had a significant impact and showed how to employ restraint and avoid counterproductive situations. As was the case with the Townsend Plan, the impact of Share Our Wealth depended crucially on the fact that there existed a reform-oriented administration and a pro-spending Congress. Otherwise a president would likely be unwilling or unable to attempt to "steal the thunder" of a challenger bidding for economic redistribution. The fact that his new social legislation required revenue also mattered in the outcome. But Long was amassing political strength rather than squandering it by defending Share Our Wealth legislation and attacking the administration's initiatives when it was bending in his direction. There is no telling what additional influence Share Our Wealth might have had if Long had not been assassinated that summer.

Why the Townsend Plan Chose Unproductive Strategies

The comparison between Share Our Wealth and the Townsend Plan raises the question of why the Townsend Plan focused on the ill-fated McGroarty bill and employed inappropriate and unproductive strategies. The inability of social movement leaders to shift from a hard-line position in demands or tactics can depend on relations within movement organizations. Sometimes the organization cannot veer far from positions, tactics, or ideology that mobilized its supporters, especially if the decision-making process is relatively democratic. Organizations relying on volunteers may lose support if they depart from a popular position, as Jane Mansbridge suggests regarding the campaign for the equal rights amendment.[50] But despite the many Townsend club members, the Townsend Plan leaders' hands were far from tied. Clements and Townsend had the authority to call the shots, and their legitimacy was bolstered by Townsend's prestige as author of the pension plan. What is more, the leaders could influence the flow of information to its membership, and thus the interpretation of their actions. The *Townsend Weekly*, whose circulation increased to 100,00, was routinely employed to counter the national news media's coverage of the Townsend Plan, as were weekly bulletins. For instance, the second McGroarty bill did not provide for the full $200 pension, a fact repeated in the national press. Yet the *Weekly* claimed that the leadership had not changed the figure, relying on the bill's language to provide pensions *no greater* than $200 per month.[51] It seems certain that the Townsend Plan could have sold the membership on other compromises in the same way—as first steps down the road to the enactment of the complete pension-recovery plan.

Although the ideology of the Townsend Plan was too minimal to be a hindrance, Townsend's idea, with its dual mission of providing old-age pensions and achieving economic recovery, may have constrained the leadership. Its recovery aspects, which Townsend and Clements increasingly emphasized, may have made it difficult for them to declare satisfaction with changes to old-age programs alone. Still, there was plenty of room for interpretation here, too. The leadership could have plausibly claimed that any sort of old-age benefit would have a stimulating effect—merely not as powerful as that from the larger revolving pensions. They could provide discursive cover for seeking half a loaf by insisting that only once Townsend's own pension and recovery measure were enacted would the full economic benefits follow.

Another set of potential reasons for the misguided tactics concern the Townsend Plan's entrepreneurial form of organization and the desire of Clements, and probably Townsend, to do well while doing good. This argument is a version of Michels's so-called iron law of oligarchy, in which the interests of a challenger's leadership supposedly inevitably diverge from those of its constituency. Some reporters and disaffected former Townsendites doubted that Clements wanted to see immediate passage of the McGroarty bill, as it might undermine the impulse of Townsendites to donate cash and to subscribe to the *Townsend Weekly*.[52] But it seems doubtful that Clements was sabotaging the pension-recovery program in order to take salary and profits from the *Weekly*. If the second McGroarty bill had passed, Clements could have found other work for the Townsend clubs. They might police the enforced spending of the pensions and of course continue to press for increases in the tax to gain the promised $200. Even if the first McGroarty bill had somehow immediately passed for the full $200 per month, and the Townsend Plan had disbanded, Clements would still have been able to cash in through the *Townsend Weekly*. What self-respecting recipient of a generous old-age pension would begrudge a subscription to the newspaper that would safeguard the pensions, published by its deliverers? Had either McGroarty bill passed, the *Weekly*'s subscription rate no doubt would have skyrocketed.

Townsend's position was far less mercenary but in the end was the most constraining. Passing his plan and only his plan would vindicate the doctor as genius and hero. He wanted to end the Depression as well as free the aged from insecurity and thus become the Lincolnesque figure he fancied himself. The only way to do this, to his way of thinking, was to pass the plan in almost the exact form that he first imagined it. He was probably the truest believer of them all. The hard-line tone was his as well, his peevishness intensified by his ill-treatment in Congress. The rest was inexperience. With Townsend as one of the key leaders, it was like having both the strategic disadvantages of relying on volunteers and the leadership's interest diverging from that of its constituents. All the same, as we shall see, he saw his program change dramatically over the next several years.

Conclusion

In early 1935, a cabinet-level committee produced an economic security proposal with greater old-age benefits than initially intended—moves that were induced by the Townsend Plan and its action. With a liberal Democratic administration backed by a heavily Democratic Congress, there was little doubt that a new old-age policy would pass. Once the administration brought its proposals to Congress, the Townsend Plan's intense focus on its revolving pension bills, its hardball approach to promoting them, and its animosity toward the security legislation were inappropriate to the favorable political context for old-age policy, as well as the Townsend Plan's limited organizational strength and lack of political skills. Trying to get Congress to substitute the McGroarty bill for the security bill, or even to amend the security bill to make it more like Townsend's idea, was a far more difficult task than to induce a pro–social policy administration to alter its omnibus security proposal as it was devising it. The Townsend Plan had to be able to convince large blocs in Congress to support its bill or to enhance the administration's bill. Yet the McGroarty bill's costs were high, and members of Congress did not believe it would secure economic recovery. The Townsend Plan had few favors to call in, and its highly localized organizing pattern made it unlikely that it could sanction more than a few western House members.

Single-minded and aggressive though they were, the Townsend Plan's actions reduced the threat of a substitute measure based on the concept of generous, equal, and widespread old-age pensions. Yet that possibility was the key to inducing Congress to sweeten old-age benefits in the social security bill. The Townsend Plan's leaders were in any case unwilling to employ the minor leverage it had. Instead, they merely attacked the security bill, rather than joining other supporters of generous old-age policy such as Congresswoman Greenway of Arizona, and sometimes attacked the friends of old-age policy. By the time the Townsend Plan had developed a more plausible bill, old-age programs in the security bill had already been reduced, and the debate was largely over. Congress adopted old-age legislation that was not as beneficial for the aged as what the administration had proposed in January, despite the Townsend Plan's growing number of clubs and its extensive Washington efforts. Its hard-line strategies doubtless would not have panned out even if they had been pursued with more skill than the Townsend Plan possessed. Its misguided tactics did not result directly from its reliance on its aged constituency or from its centralized leadership, but mainly because one of its leaders, Dr. Townsend, was loath to shift quickly away from his pension-recovery idea.

The Townsend Plan leadership took the passage of the security bill as a defeat, and the plan's supporters in Congress were no more numerous than when the doctor had arrived in Washington. Worse still for the future, the Townsend Plan leadership turned on itself. The publicity director Peterson, who had helped to place Townsend on the cover of *Newsweek,* had charged Townsend and Clements with bilking their aged followers and lying about the $200. Otto Moore, one of drafters of the second McGroarty bill, left in a huff over lobbying and fund-raising strategy and founded his own organization.[53] In the wake of these disputes and the triumphant passage of the Social Security Act, the national press, having buoyed the Townsend Plan in the winter, declared that summer that it had sunk for good.

FIVE

A National Challenger

APPARENTLY DEFEATED IN THE SUMMER OF 1935, Earl Clements and Dr. Townsend were far from giving up. They hoped to learn from their mistakes, and Clements would seek to make the Townsend Plan a national challenger. His goal was to show Washington that the organization could do for the rest of the country what it had done for the far West—win the enthusiastic backing of the aged for the doctor's pension-recovery plan. Instead of folding in the face of defeat and the passage of the Social Security Act, the Townsend Plan was on the brink of making its mark on American awareness. Townsend club membership increased almost tenfold from what it was at the end of 1934—reaching almost 2 million. By 1936, a new Townsend club was being inaugurated every two hours. As it became the largest U.S. challenger based on membership, the Townsend Plan also generated unprecedented cash for the cause, at a rate comparable to that of the well-heeled Republican Party and during a presidential election year. As members of Congress signed up in favor of the McGroarty bill, the Townsend Plan broke through into the national consciousness. In the year following the convention the Townsend Plan was mentioned on the front page of the *New York Times* more than sixty times and became a featured subject in movie theaters nationwide. Clements had seen to it that all America would hear the doctor's voice.

These developments suggest several questions. Journalists and average Americans wanted to know why the Townsend Plan was able to rebound from its poor performance and organizational dissension to achieve such impressive levels of support and attention. Political officials during an election year wanted to know how much support there was, and who all these new Townsendites were. They also wanted to know why some parts of the country, especially in the Northwest, proved to be more open to the message than others. What accounted for the differential formation of clubs and support for the Townsend Plan across the country? All these questions were predicated on the fact that the Townsend Plan's leadership reconsidered its strategy in the wake of its debacle in Washington.

Going National

Clements attributed the failure of McGroarty bill to the fact that there were too few Townsend clubs. Townsendism was rampant only in California and the far West; even there the coverage was uneven, with Southern California having far more clubs than Northern California, and some western states being better covered than others. In his analysis of the vote for the defeated Townsend amendment, Clements found that sincere backing for it had come chiefly from congressmen whose districts were blanketed with Townsend clubs. These legislators were convinced perhaps less by Dr. Townsend's brand of economic thinking than by the fact that the organization had the potential to alter their political destinies.[1] The amateurish campaign for the McGroarty bills also revealed that the leadership lacked the expertise needed to influence Congress. With its bad publicity, the campaign also hurt the Townsend Plan in the revenue department. The Townsend Plan organization brought in more than $40,000 in the last quarter of 1934—more than double the amount that it had gained in its first seven months—and revenues jumped to $75,000 in the first quarter of 1935, an increase of about 83 percent. But the second quarter's yield, $94,000, was only 25 percent, and the circulation of the Weekly had similarly flattened.[2] The lesson Clements drew here was similar to one regarding congressional support: only so much revenue could be gained from a mass-pressure organization isolated in the far West with a yearly membership fee of a quarter.

Clements Reveals Policy

Clements's solution was to organize the entire country in the manner of Southern California, and to do so he made several crucial changes in organizational policy. These moves were far from secret, detailed as they were in a front-page article in the May 13 Townsend Weekly under a banner headline declaring "Clements Reveals Policy." His first and most important reform was to organize the Townsend Plan on a national basis. He divided the country into four regions and appointed salaried directors. Regional offices were to handle money, as well as coordinate radio coverage. The efforts in the highly populous East were led by the Reverend Clinton Wunder, a Baptist minister from Rochester whose dramatic sermons had proved so popular that he had taken his act to Hollywood, serving as executive vice president of the Academy of Motion Picture Arts and Science before becoming a radio speaker for the Townsend Plan in early 1935.[3]

Just as important as the organization's new national scope in organizing clubs was *how* it organized them. Clements created a system of commission-earning state and district organizers, focusing on congressional districts, rather than on cities and towns as before. In each state the Townsend Plan appointed an organizer, who was bonded and commissioned to hire organizers for each congressional district in their territory. Of the 25 cents that each Townsend club member provided in an initial contribution or membership fee, the national headquarters would send a dime to the state organizer, who would remit

Figure 5.1: Clements Reveals Policy. After its failure to gain support for the McGroarty bill in Congress, the Townsend Plan, through its leader Robert Clements, sought to organize Townsend clubs throughout the country. Source: *National Townsend Weekly*, April 29, 1935, p. 2.

a nickel to the local organizer. The state organizer's commissions also covered the costs of maintaining an office staff to oversee the district organizers. By targeting congressional districts, the Townsend Plan would be able to enumerate its strength and demonstrate to House candidates its clout in term of clubs and members. It also could use the information to determine where additional organizational efforts were needed.[4]

To run this nationwide operation and to hire the expertise to mount effective publicity and lobbying campaigns, Clements thought it crucial to generate additional revenue. New club membership fees would help, but he also proposed monthly dues for Townsend clubs, which, for legal purposes, he called their "quota." Each club was to remit to the national headquarters a dime each month for every member. It was up to the club as a group to pay its quota, allowing the better-off and less risk-averse Townsendites to pick up the financial slack for poorer or more cautious ones. Clubs could pay their dues by running fund-raisers like raffles, dinners, and bake, quilt, or rummage sales. The quotas provided incentives for organizers to stay in contact with clubs after their founding and to encourage membership and fund-raising drives, for state and district organizers would each gain a penny for every dime remitted to the national headquarters. The resource mobilization strategy was to remain an "indigenous" one. The vast bulk of contributions to the pension insurgency were to come from the purses and exertions of individual Townsend club members—who were mainly older and not well-off.[5] The organization continued to avoid wealthy benefactors.

Clements was not above, however, capitalizing further on differences in incomes among middle-class and working-class Townsendites and called for a new category of membership. Members willing to pay a dollar per month could be inducted into a new organization, the Townsend National Legion, and gain a snazzier lapel pin, signifying greater prestige, and a subscription to the *Townsend Weekly*. These special operations forces of the Townsend Plan had a mission to protect and defend the plan against defamation. Like the quotas, the legion was designed to secure additional funding from Townsendites who could afford it, without losing the support of the more impecunious rank and file. Clements sought to enlist 50,000 legionnaire recruits—who would yield a cool half million every year.[6]

Despite their increased financial responsibilities and growing numbers, Townsend club members old and new, regular and legionnaire, were being given no more say over the Townsend Plan organization and its strategies. Townsend and Clements were adhering to the initial arrangement in which only the board of directors of Old Age Revolving Pensions, Ltd.—Clements, Townsend, and Gomer Smith of Oklahoma—controlled policy. The board in turn was chosen by the "members" of the organization—Clements, Townsend, and, in theory, Townsend's brother Walter, who resigned from the board in July. Townsend and Clements planned a national convention of club representatives from around the country. The First Annual National Convention of Townsend Clubs, to be held in Chicago in October, would provide an opportunity to gain the blessing of the membership for the new organizational and political initiatives. It would also constitute the coming-out party of the Townsend Plan as a national challenger.[7]

As for political strategy, the focus would be on gaining support for the second McGroarty bill in the House of Representatives. Each member would be mailed a questionnaire inquiring respectfully whether he or she would or would not support the new McGroarty bill in the upcoming session of Congress.[8] The results of the survey were to be reported in the *Townsend Weekly*, with the preliminary returns published at the end of the year. The supporters would be held to their word in the 1936 session of Congress, as the organization hoped to have the bill brought up for a vote. If the professed Townsend congressional supporters proved reliable, they would be aided in their bids for reelection in the following November. For others, if they were unfortunate enough to reside in a well-organized district, they might be singled out for electoral elimination.[9]

The House strategy had the advantage of targeting those political officials most susceptible to electoral pressure. To provide the widest maneuverability and to apply the greatest force on incumbents, the policy was to be strictly nonpartisan, treating each legislator or candidate as an individual. The organization was opening its arms to all reasonably competitive Townsend Plan supporters, incumbents or challengers, Democrat or Republican, and third

parties where they were established. It avoided a blanket endorsement or re-
jection of either major party, as well as support for hopeless challengers to the
main parties. The Townsend Plan would pick its fights solely on the question
of the pension-recovery program. This single-issue "friends and enemies"
strategy was reminiscent of the Anti-Saloon League, which employed it successfully to gain a series of restrictions on alcohol, culminating in the Prohibition amendment in 1920, and had been employed to good advantage as
well as by the American Legion in its bid to win the early payment of the
World War I veterans' bonus—which was on the verge of gaining a veto-
proof majority in Congress. This political strategy had been also used at different times by U.S. women's, farmer, and labor organizations. Its application
by the Townsend Plan was quite a step up in assertiveness from the plan's
laid-back political strategy of 1934, which was to wait for candidates to endorse the program.[10]

Winning over President Roosevelt was less important. The hope was that if
Congress voted in favor of the McGroarty bill, Roosevelt, or, possibly, who-
ever replaced him, might eventually accede. And so there was no need to de-
monize him, as the *Townsend Weekly* and Dr. Townsend himself were danger-
ously close to doing in early 1935. For the medium run, the Townsend Plan
would seek to hammer pro-Townsend planks into the platforms of the major
parties, possibly by entering slates of Townsend-pledged delegates in the presidential primaries. Another goal was to win the support of hopefuls for the
Republican nomination. But the Townsend Plan would intervene in the presidential race only if one nominee or party endorsed the pension recovery plan
and the other did not. The best case would be to remove the issue from partisanship by winning the backing of both presidential nominees. Because the
Townsend Plan was focusing its activity on Washington, it moved its headquarters there.[11]

In the summer the *Townsend Weekly* moved to the capital, too, and became
the *National Townsend Weekly*. The tabloid told a story of constant progress. It
provided a mix of news about the Townsend Plan, articles demonstrating the
viability of the plan, letters from Townsendites ("What Our Readers Are
Thinking: Letters from Everywhere"), club news ("News Reports from the
Field"), cartoons, and columns—a cornball one ("Walter's Weekly Windup")
by James Walter and a substantive front-page effort ("Hit and Mrs.") by the
editor, F. J. Elgin. There was a surprisingly sophisticated page ("The Week in
Washington") with reporting and commentary by the observant Franklin
Roudybush.[12] A spread in the middle of the *Weekly* included editorial features, with a cartoon and below it a column by Earl Clements, the chief interpreter of the Townsend Plan. The paper soon ran separate editions for the
East, West, and Northern and Southern California.[13] To spread its message,
the Townsend Plan was transmitting farther over the airwaves. In January
1935, the organization was sponsoring only two weekly broadcasts in the

Figure 5.2: A Friend in Need. In early 1936 the Townsend Plan's political strategy focused on Congress and stopped attacking President Roosevelt. This cartoon from the *Townsend Weekly* portrays him as a friend in need—of help from Dr. Townsend's pension-recovery plan. Source: *National Townsend Weekly*, January 13, 1936, p. 6.

West, but by the end of the year the organization's Radio Extension Division was broadcasting regularly throughout the country. Led initially by Tom Wallace, the division had developed a number of personalities, including Wunder, the eastern regional director, and Jack Kiefer, working out of Chicago. By 1936, the Townsend Plan was frequently broadcasting over national radio hookups.[14]

Clements also made a number of personnel moves. Replacing the publicity director Peterson was the far more able and experienced Boyd Gurley, the former managing editor of the *Indianapolis Times* and the recipient of a Pulitzer Prize. The lobbying group was retooled, with a former senator from Georgia, Thomas W. Hardwick, retained to present the case to his former congressional colleagues.[15] Perhaps most important of all, by early 1936, Clements had appointed area organizers responsible for each state, and the organizers hired by them covered more than 300 congressional districts. The organizing plan and radio campaigns built on each other, as the Townsend organizers increasingly found receptive audiences for their pitches.[16]

The new organizational plan quickly paid off. In the third quarter of 1935, OARP raised about $193,000—or more than twice as much as the previous quarter. The number of clubs approached 4,000, and the number of Townsend club members had surpassed half a million. What is more, there were some 320,000 *Townsend Plan* membership books already in the hands of organizers in anticipation of another growth spurt. Many congressmen had already signed on in support of the McGroarty bill. And that fall Senator William Borah of Idaho, whose name was bandied about as a likely Republican nominee for president, endorsed Townsend's pension-recovery plan.[17]

A National Phenomenon

All this news was highlighted in an event that returned the Townsend Plan to the attention of the mainstream print media and the nation. In late October, the first national convention of Townsend clubs drew almost 7,000 registered Townsendites from across the country to Chicago. The event was innovative politically as it took the form of a political nominating convention, but with a single issue and the enthusiastic participation of everyday people rather than experts, professionals, or elected officials. Clubs elected delegates, and Clements and Townsend promised a different sort of political theater by offering to hear and answer any critics. Dr. Townsend kicked off the carefully scripted convention by proclaiming his pension plan the "sole hope of a confused nation." Others followed with attacks on the inadequacy of the old-age benefits in the Social Security Act and with paeans comparing Townsend to Lincoln and Washington. The latest financial report was read, triumphantly. The convention floor endorsed all the new policy positions outlined by Clements in the *Weekly*—to raise the 10-cent-per-member "quotas" by the clubs, to steer clear of alliances with major political parties, and to vest all authority over congressional endorsements in the national headquarters. None of the Townsend Plan's opponents showed up. A lengthy story with a two-page photo spread appeared in *Time* magazine.[18]

The first test of the new political strategy came less than a month later. In a special election to fill the late Republican Henry Kimball's House seat in Michigan's Third Congressional District, the Republican primary featured a candidate, Verner Main, who endorsed the Townsend Plan. Though Main was not considered a major contender in a field of five, his candidacy was buoyed by 30 Townsend clubs in a district centered in Battle Creek and Kalamazoo—and by personal appearances by Townsend and other speakers. On November 19, Main won the primary with a majority and almost three times as many votes as his nearest competitor. The extensive newspaper coverage gave Clements a forum to announce his latest estimate of Townsend clubs, which he reckoned at 5,000. In the November special election, Senator Arthur Vandenberg, who opposed the pension program as infeasible and unconstitutional, but was also a possible Republican presidential nominee, refused to abandon Main, whose opponent denounced the pension plan. Main won by a two-to-one margin. In the wake of this victory, Clements pressed House members to go on record regarding the McGroarty bill. He wrote each member and promised to publish the results in the *Weekly*'s final issue of the year, declaring that equivocations and no replies would be interpreted as negative responses. Congressmen were squirming. The *New York Times* estimated that the Townsend Plan was already powerful enough to unseat seventy-three members of the House. Arthur Krock of the *Times*, the bearer of the era's Washington conventional wisdom, warned that the pension plan could easily be imposed in the manner of Prohibition.[19]

On the eve of the New Year and the new session of Congress, the Townsend Plan was ascendant. In the last quarter of the year, the national headquarters brought in $350,000, about twice as much as the previous quarter. The number of clubs had reached 5,000, with the total membership in them popping over 1 million. The circulation of the *Weekly* was on its way to 250,000. Some thirty-nine members of Congress, mainly from the West, had promised to support the McGroarty bill. There were also a few from Pennsylvania and Massachusetts, as well as Earl Michener of Michigan, a recently vociferous opponent who was won over by Main's victory. Only five members declared their opposition, with the vast bulk of the House still considering how to respond.[20]

The Townsend Plan was the talk of Washington and increasingly the nation. On December 22, there were no fewer than three stories in the Sunday *New York Times* featuring the Townsend Plan, and three other stories referring to it. In his national radio broadcast that day, Father Charles E. Coughlin devoted his lecture to the Townsend pension-recovery program. The following weekend the *Times* Sunday magazine ran a puff piece on the founder that read

Figure 5.3: On the Cover of *Newsweek*, Again. The second time Dr. Townsend was displayed on the cover of *Newsweek*, on December 28, 1935, the magazine portrayed him as a symbol of a highly organized national phenomenon, rather than a lone man with an idea, as it had done the first time.

as if it were written by Townsend Plan publicists. The doctor was allowed to aw-shucks his way through an interview that portrayed him as virtuous, down-home, and wanting nothing more than a pension so that he could retire from public life. On December 28, Townsend appeared once again on the cover of *Newsweek*. This time the image focused on the organization rather than the leader, with Townsend dwarfed by a huge emblem with the Townsend Plan insignia and slogan—"Youth for Work, Age for Leisure."[21]

Even more impressive to the general public, however, was a March of Time short subject that ran in the nation's movie theaters in December and January and marked the Townsend Plan's arrival as a national phenomenon. Produced monthly by Time, Inc., these brief documentary films had debuted in March 1935 and ran prior to the main features in thousands of theaters around the country. Running for eight minutes, March of Time short subjects addressed controversial topics and dug deeper than the snappy, tabloid-like newsreels, which skimmed across celebrity, entertainment, and the lighter side of current events. It was something like the difference between a segment on *60 Minutes* and the same topic as treated on the local evening news. Produced by Louis de Rochemont, the March of Time interlarded documentary footage with historical reenactments and futuristic sequences, all from an omniscient perspective. The stentorian narrator Westbrook Van Voorhis sent off each segment with his enigmatic coda, "Time marches on!"[22]

The March of Time short *Townsend Plan!* opens with a club meeting in a San Francisco meeting hall. It is called to order with a version of the "Battle Hymn of the Republic," whose chorus resounds, "We shall end all poverty." A speaker then announces Main's victory, to the cheers of scores of Townsendites. One club member asks whether individual pensions will go to both husband and wife (yes, of course), and another inquires when the pensions would be forthcoming (after the 1936 elections, possibly). The questions are staged, but the setting and members are authentic. The life of Townsend is quickly recounted, ending in a reenactment of a fateful if fictional presentation to Clements—who on the spot pronounces the pension program a "great idea" and dubs it "the Townsend plan." The film cuts to the Townsend Plan's Washington operation, buzzing with dozens of workers efficiently routing correspondence, which is often bulging with banknotes. State-of-the-art presses churn out new *Townsend Plan* booklets. Although the film ends with Senator Duncan U. Fletcher of Florida declaring the plan "wild" in its great expense, the climax is Dr. Townsend speaking at a rally, in which he is asked "where he stands" on Roosevelt's reelection. Visibly fighting the impulse to denounce him, Townsend hesitates, as the film cuts to the anticipating faces of an admiring elderly couple. To their delight, the doctor finally offers that he is "going to lie down on it."[23] With Dr. Townsend falling into line and Townsend clubs being organized all across America, time truly seemed to be marching on the side of the Townsend Plan.

Some remarkable public opinion polls that winter confirmed this impression. George Gallup's American Institute for Public Opinion (AIPO), whose polls were beginning to run weekly in the *Washington Post*, reported in December that the Townsend pension plan was the ninth most important political issue in the country. In January, Gallup reported results of a poll on old-age "pensions" that showed that Americans were 89 percent in favor. He also claimed, however, that the poll indicated little support for Townsend's pension-recovery plan and great support for Roosevelt's old-age program. Gallup's interpretation was based on an open-ended question about the monthly sum the aged should be paid. The modal sum was $40, and only about 4 percent of the American public volunteered $200. Gallup concluded that the $40 was close to the $30 promised by the administration's Old-Age Assistance program, and that if respondents did not offer $200, they did not favor the Townsend Plan.[24]

A closer look suggests that the public support for the Townsend Plan was far more substantial than Gallup's lowball appraisal. The $40 selected by the public was far closer to amount the McGroarty bill would be likely to deliver than the sums granted by OAA. As it happened, three years after its passage, OAA would pay less than $20 per month per recipient. Also, those who selected $200 more likely represented die-hard sentiment in favor of the pension program, rather than the far more substantial public opinion favoring senior citizens' pensions on the Townsend model. A great many in the West specified $200-per-month pensions—with 25 percent doing so in Oregon. Because those who volunteered this lofty figure were split almost evenly between Republicans and Democrats, moreover, Gallup wrote that the Townsend Plan already held the balance of political power in Oregon, California, and Washington and was approaching this status in some Rocky Mountain states. What is more, later Gallup polling efforts, which for reasons unknown were not reported in the *Post*, confirmed much greater public support for the Townsend Plan. In a poll taken on March 7, 42 percent of those questioned said they favored the pension-recovery program. In another poll taken a week later, the result jumped to 55 percent in favor! Half of America had been won over.[25]

Why So Much Support for the Townsend Plan?

The American public and political leaders wanted to make sense of the growing public support, intense and diffuse, for the Townsend Plan. The press usually exaggerated in the other direction from Gallup, printing the doctor's outlandish boasts that 1,000 clubs per week were being started and wild conjectures that between 8 and 10 million Americans—or almost the entire U.S. population sixty years old and older—were already members of Townsend clubs. Nevertheless, the growth in support was remarkable. The number of clubs probably reached above 7,000 in the first quarter of 1936, and the number of club members certainly surpassed 1.5 million and probably 2 million. As before, these club members included both the highly committed, including the approximately 100,000 militant club "officers." Probably another million non–club members among the aged had participated in at least one mass meeting. The Gallup results regarding $200 pensions suggested that perhaps 4 million American adults were likely to be active Townsendites or susceptible to recruitment. Additional House members pledged themselves to back the McGroarty bill, which had gained forty-nine backers, with about twenty more converts on the way.[26]

Why the Townsend Plan Flourished

One reason that the Townsend Plan gained so much support is that it still had everything going for it that it had before. It had extended its organization, which was an innovative combination of hungry salespeople with true-believing volunteers and novel membership affiliates. The clubs provided sociability as well as the usual purposive incentives. The program still provided a solution to the economic insecurities of the aged, a blanket affirmation of their social contributions, and an enticing image of a better future for all that could be effected by the aged. Townsendites would help all Americans as they helped themselves. The plan's extravagant fiscal policy was cloaked in socially conservative language and imagery. Its personification and symbol, the hard-luck Dr. Townsend, was back on his feet again, with his program promising the same for all older Americans. It helped, too, that the Townsend Plan launched its national organizing drive when expectations were low and regrouped below the radar of the national news media. Once the news turned positive, after the convention and Main's election, nothing much was happening in Washington to compete with it, with Congress in recess.

More important, however, were systemic political changes that buoyed support. The Townsend Plan's heyday coincided with the rise to power of the progressive wing of the Democratic Party. After the midterm elections in 1934, the Democratic margin in the House was well over 200, and the Democratic margin in the Senate was 44. This political formation spurred reform and reform movements of all sorts. The Townsend Plan was also aided by new national policy that promoted political organization. The labor provisions of the 1933 National Industrial Recovery Act, which in part encouraged workers to form collective bargaining units, had been replaced in 1935 by the more substantial National Labor Relations Act, which guaranteed trade union organization and provided for the enforcement of its provisions. Although these policies did nothing to protect Townsend clubs, they gave considerable encouragement to all manner of political mobilization. The effervescent effect of the new approach was only partly offset by Congress's hard questioning, the postal investigation, and Roosevelt's occasional elliptical put-downs of groups promoting "fantastic schemes." Also, Congress had already approved the social spending programs of the second New Deal, notably almost $5 billion for work projects, and passed about $2 billion in payments for World War I veterans, though Roosevelt had vetoed the bill. All this suggested to challengers that further collective action to promote social spending might be productive.[27]

The political change that boosted the Townsend Plan most, however, was something that newspapers and politicians thought would doom it: the passage of the Social Security Act. The extensive debate surrounding the security legislation and its passage validated claims for old-age pensions. Roosevelt himself used the term "pensions," rather than "public assistance" or "annuities," suggesting that such payments were now a right of aged Americans. But no widespread and generous benefits were forthcoming. The old-age annuity provisions were not scheduled to pay until 1942. The Old-Age Assistance program required states to pass new legislation in order to receive federal matching funds, and no funds were to be released until 1936. The slow progress of old-age programs stood in bold relief to the rapid arrival of and high funding for the Works Progress Administration (WPA), which was employing more than 2 million in the winter of 1935. On old age, the national government did for the country what state governments had done for the West. The Social Security Act validated claims for old-age pensions, without coming close to satisfying them.

All the New Townsendites

The Townsend Plan exploited these circumstances to increase the ranks of Townsend clubbers until they included more than 10 percent of the U.S. aged and almost 2 percent of the population. But who were these new Townsendites? There were no records kept of club members, and the limited information available derives from two sources, both flawed. There was journalism. The Townsend Weekly tended not to focus on the characteristics of participants, and mainstream print media accounts were often skewed toward the particular events that individual journalists covered. Journalists tended to describe Townsend club members as resembling Francis and Minnie Townsend in being mainly older, white, Protestant citizens who had fallen on hard times during the Depression.[28] Then there are Gallup's public opinion polls, which tend to show public approval of Townsend's proposal was inversely related to economic status and positively related to age. These polls, however, do not help to make sense of those who were active participants—the 2 million who joined clubs by the middle of 1936 or the somewhat larger number who participated in Townsend activities like rallies and meetings.[29]

It is possible, however, to piece together information about these commit-

Figure 5.4: Townsend Youth Band. The Townsend Plan continually stressed its support among the young, such as through a "Townsend Youth Band." But for the most part only the elderly engaged regularly in the activities of Townsend clubs, though they sometimes cajoled their grandchildren into participating. Author's collection, photographer unknown.

ted Townsendites from these sources and from surviving archival evidence. As before, it is worth separating the more militant club officers, regular Townsend club members, and others among the aged who came to rallies and other mass events from the many more who might signal support for the Townsend Plan in a public opinion poll or by signing a petition. All evidence indicates that the vast majority of ardent Townsendites were sixty years old or older, with most of the rest approaching that age. This was true despite the fact that most Townsend Plan organizers, like Clements, were mainly of working age. The Townsend Plan was unsuccessful in expanding the club membership to include the "youth" of its slogan. Many attempts to inaugurate youth clubs foundered, despite the constant attention in the Townsend press to the "youngest" members and speakers for the organization. The organization was only marginally more successful in attracting the older adults, less often discussed, who would be relieved of the potential responsibility to support dependent parents. There were few rank-and-file Townsendites under fifty-five.[30]

As the polling figures suggest, Townsend club members also were likely to be economically less well off than the average American. Most older Americans were at least partly dependent, with insufficient private pensions or savings, and had to rely on either their own labor or the help of their children. There is no good evidence about whether Townsend club members were more likely to be newly poor in the manner of Townsend, having lost their jobs or private pensions to the Depression and their savings to the crash of the banking system, whether they still had something to lose, or whether they had never had prospects for savings or pensions before 1929. But Townsend club members were not necessarily poorer than the average older American, and probably the more active Townsendites were slightly better off. Accounts from 1935 and 1936 suggest that those joining clubs and actively participating in events were in direr economic situations than were the members of the earliest clubs. These newer recruits very likely never had much in the way of savings. The "quota" system, in which the clubs were held collectively responsible for paying dues, helped to encourage the participation of less well-off members.[31]

The Townsend Plan was not, however, as old-school theories of social movements would expect, a challenger based on the perpetually disconnected, impoverished, or disgruntled elements of American society. Townsend clubs mainly included "working people," according to the longtime California organizer John C. Cuneo, who did not see themselves as poor. They were mainly middle-class in identity and outlook, as most Americans were in the 1920s, regardless of whether they held working-class employment throughout their lives or had become impoverished in old age. In addition, the club officers and other militant Townsendites were by all accounts more likely to be better off and better connected to their local communities—to have higher amounts of social capital—than the average Townsend club member, as well as to be somewhat younger. To organize or lead a Townsend club required extensive community ties and a willingness and ability to communicate with acquaintances and relative strangers.[32]

As the journalistic accounts suggest, moreover, Townsendites were also more likely to resemble their leader in being white, Protestant, and American citizens. Although older Americans were more than younger Americans likely to be white, Protestant, and citizens, Townsendites probably were more likely to be all these things even in comparison with their old-age peers. The higher representation among citizens was due in part to the fact that the Townsend Plan called for pensions for citizens only, reducing its appeal among noncitizen immigrants. The hyper-Americanism of approved club practices, with their pledges of allegiances and singing of slightly doctored patriotic songs, reinforced this tendency. The singing of hymns and often nonalcoholic picnics also appealed to pietistic Protestants. All the same, the way that clubs were organized partially counteracted the tendencies toward ethnic

or religious homogeneity within the organization as whole. As many clubs
could be set up as desired in any community. Thus there was often a socially
similar membership in a given club, but with the possibility for great diversity
across clubs. Most African Americans in Townsend clubs, for instance, were
apparently members of all-black clubs. On the whole, however, blacks were
less likely than whites to join or form clubs, a situation partly connected to
the dearth of clubs in the South, where most blacks resided in the 1930s, but
also to poverty in black communities in the North.[33]

Townsend activists included both men and women. Spouses often joined,
and for the most part men and women participated together in Townsend
club activities. Journalistic accounts and archival records suggest that men
and women were represented as leaders in Townsend clubs about equally frequently. All this attested to the equality in pensions promised men and
women. There was some evidence, however, of a stereotyped division of labor by gender. Women organized the various picnics and sales, whereas the
Townsend National Legion was made up of men whose duties did not extend
far beyond donating extra money to the cause.[34]

Accounting for the Geographic Dispersion of Townsend Clubs

Another way of making sense of the appeal of the Townsend Plan is to examine the geographic dispersion of Townsend clubs, which are key to understanding Townsend Plan activity. Although the Townsend Plan did not divulge its
lists of clubs, the *Townsend Weekly* reported on club growth and new club
drives, and two extensive enumerations remain: reports from the *Weekly* concerning the best-covered states and a list obtained by Abraham Holtzman of
all the Townsend clubs ever in existence through 1950. Taken together, these
sources give a good idea of club activity during the heyday of the Townsend
Plan in the spring of 1936. There were probably almost 8,000 clubs.[35] Perhaps
the most useful way to examine the dispersion of Townsend clubs is the way
the Townsend Plan leadership viewed it: by way of the number of clubs per a
state's apportioned number of congressional districts. Townsend leaders
thought that about 100 average-sized clubs would provide the organization
the balance of power in any reasonably competitive congressional district.[36]

The West remained the Townsend Plan stronghold. Oregon had the dens-
est concentration of clubs, 415 over three congressional districts, well above
the recommended 100-per-district coverage. Other states in the West also
had relatively large numbers of clubs, though none were at the 100 level.
North Dakota had slightly fewer than 90 clubs per district, and South
Dakota, Arizona, and Washington had about 80 clubs per district. Colorado,
Washington, Arizona, and Wyoming had between 68 and 79 clubs per district. California had only 54 per district, but because it was the first state organized, it had some very large clubs, such as George Highley's Los Angeles

TABLE 5.1.
Townsend Clubs by State per Congressional District, Circa Spring 1936

Ten Highest Ranking			Ten Lowest Ranking		
Rank	State	Clubs per District	Rank	State	Clubs per District
1.	Oregon	138	48.	South Carolina	1
2.	Colorado	79	47.	Virginia	1
3.	Washington	76	46.	Louisiana	2
4.	Arizona	74	45.	Rhode Island	2
5.	Wyoming	68	44.	Mississippi	2
6.	Montana	57	43.	North Carolina	2
7.	New Mexico	56	42.	Alabama	4
8.	California	54	41.	Tennessee	4
9.	South Dakota	53	40.	Georgia	4
10.	Florida	50	39.	Texas	6

Sources: Harry B. Presson, "Tells History of First Townsend Clubs," *National Townsend Weekly*, November 2, 1936, p. 10; Abraham Holtzman, *The Townsend Movement: A Political Study* (New York: Bookman, 1963), pp. 50–51; *Townsend Weekly*.

Note: These figures are based on analyses incorporating both of the above estimates and employing data from the *Townsend Weekly* on membership drives and mentions by state.

club, with 20,000 members. Several others in the West were in the 50s. Although the Midwest did next best as a region, it trailed far behind. Kansas, Wisconsin, Iowa, Nebraska, and Minnesota had only between 25 and 32 clubs per district. Michigan, the site of Main's tremendous victory, had 26. Despite the new national attention in the newspapers and magazines and the efforts of Wunder, regional Townsend organizer, however, the Townsend Plan still was not as well organized in the East. The South also was greatly underorganized, despite the extensive efforts in Texas and the appointment of a regional organizer for the South. Eight of the eleven former states of the Confederacy had fewer than 7 clubs per congressional district.[37]

Nevertheless, the prevalence of Townsend clubs did not always correspond neatly to geographic lines. The northeastern states of Maine and Vermont were just below the top 10 with more than 40 clubs per district each. Florida provided a beachhead of southern Townsend support, with about 50 clubs per district, mostly in the southern part of the state. Nevada had only 8 clubs. Texas, the birthplace of Clements and a state where the Townsend Plan made a concerted organizational effort, including incorporating it into the portfolio of the western regional director, however, could muster only 6 clubs per district. California was unusual in its strong urban representation, for in the East and Midwest, states with large cities did not have proportionate Townsend club strength. New York, for instance, had about 400 clubs, making it the sixth-largest Townsend Plan outpost in raw numbers of clubs, but its coverage was only slight, as the state sent forty-five representatives to the House, making it unlikely that the Townsend Plan would be able to influence the delegation.

What accounts for these differences in Townsend club activity? The geographic pattern may have been due to differences in the severity of the Depression and the economic grievances of the aged, as old-school arguments about social movements might suggest.[38] Dr. Townsend later claimed that Townsend Plan volunteers often relied on "relief" payments for economic support. The differences across states in Townsend clubs might also be due to long-standing differences in civic engagement. In some places the citizenry may have developed the habit of joining voluntary membership organizations, such as religious, fraternal, and political organizations, and these organizations and clubs themselves may have supported a kind of culture of involvement, including the starting and joining of Townsend clubs. Political contexts, which varied in dynamic as well as structural and systemic ways, may have influenced club formation, as newer school theories would predict. This was especially true in terms of democratic practices and political party systems.[39]

There is something to be said for each of these views. In a regression analysis of Townsend clubs per congressional district in 1936, measures from each view are significant. The state's income level is negatively associated with the number of clubs, perhaps indicating that the membership was aggrieved, perhaps indicating that Townsend clubs had somewhat higher support among the less well-off. Some religious organizations, not Methodists like Townsend, but Christian Scientists, are strongly associated with Townsend club formation. So, too, is resource mobilization in the Women's Christian Temperance Union. There is no good measure of those on relief in 1936, but a given state's fiscal capacities in terms of revenues per capita are also positively associated with Townsend club formation.[40]

Structural political conditions also help to explain the differential coverage of the Townsend clubs around the country. The only states in which Townsend clubs were really prominent were those with democratic political systems and non-patronage party systems. The average state in a democratized political system with an open party system had about fifty-two clubs per congressional district. States with dominant patronage-oriented parties had only about 10 clubs per district, and the underdemocratized part of the polity had fewer than 8. The political problems with starting Townsend clubs in the South went beyond racism. After all, Townsend clubs were not expected to be integrated. Within the South, the worst-covered regions were in the "black belts," where voting rights were most fully denied. The South's resistance to Townsend clubs was not due entirely to a lack of effort, as the organization's fruitless campaigns in Texas indicated. Only Florida stood out. Within

Florida, south Florida, whose polity and politics diverged from those in the northern part of the state, was the only southern outpost of the Townsend Plan.[41]

Near the bottom as well were some states with strong patronage-oriented political party systems. The extensive support for the Townsend Plan in Maine, for instance, whose party system was open, was counterbalanced by the lack of support in Rhode Island, whose party system was not. Illinois bordered the relatively well-covered Iowa and was the site of Townsend's birth home but had about half of its population in political machine–run Chicago and fewer than 10 clubs per congressional district. The poor showing in the cities of the Northeast and Midwest had much to do with the dominance of patronage-oriented parties there, in comparison with the more open cities of the West, such as the Townsend Plan strongholds Los Angeles and San Francisco. The Townsend Plan was going to need somehow to devise strategies to overcome these obstacles if it were going to succeed in placing pressure on members of Congress across the country.

The Agony of Dr. Townsend

The forward progress of the Townsend Plan was confronting another, more personal, obstacle. Transformed into a national star, Dr. Townsend was becoming dissatisfied with his role in what he now liked to call the "Townsend movement"—a term that embraced the national headquarters, the field organizers, the Townsend clubs and members, participants in Townsend Plan events, and less vocal supporters. Though he portrayed himself as modest, the doctor shouldered an enormous self-regard, which was further inflated by the proliferation of Townsend clubs, the Townsend Plan publicity machine, and the attention of the news media. He had led a national convention, decided a congressional race, drawn crowds in the tens of thousands, and was the leading man in a film playing in the nation's movie theaters. Townsend believed his press, mainly written though it was by Clements and their employees, and was a proud man, especially of his pension-recovery plan. He was now confirmed in his vision of himself as a prophet, whose revelation was moving masses and, if given a chance, would restore and transform the American way of life. In short, Townsend could no longer disagree with supporters who claimed that he was an American figure on a par with Washington and Lincoln, suitable for having his bust carved onto Mount Rushmore. And despite public demurrals, there is little doubt that the doctor saw himself as made of presidential timber.[42]

Yet Townsend's influence over the Townsend Plan seemed not in keeping with his lofty status in the public eye—and in his own mind's eye. His role within the organization had in some ways shrunk. Under Clements's new pol-

KEYSTONE

Mrs. Clements, F. J. Elgin and R. E.
Clements, 'the Chief' to the Organization

Figure 5.5: "Chief" to the Organization. The national news media recognized that
Earl Clements was the driving force behind the Townsend Plan. Here he is labeled
"chief" to the organization and is pictured with his wife and the editor of the *Weekly*
in a cover story in *Newsweek*. The media's portrayal did not sit well with
Dr. Townsend. Source: *Newsweek*, December 28, 1935, p. 7.

icy, Townsend was being built up as the organization's moral and inspirational
leader, but no longer as its intellectual powerhouse and guiding light.
Clements had the final say on matters of organization and strategy, and he was
duly credited by the national press for the gains made by the Townsend Plan. It
had to rankle the doctor that *Time* referred to Townsend as the organization's
"front" and Clements as its "big guy," and that the cover story in *Newsweek* referred to Townsend as a "figurehead" and Clements as the "chief." For his part,
Townsend discounted the role of organization in the Townsend Plan's rapid
success. As he saw it, after his pension-recovery proposal, the rest of the operation was immaterial.[43]

Although he relished his new role as moral leader, Townsend wanted to be
the intellectual leader again, and the organizational and strategic leader, too,

as he had definite ideas along these lines. He wanted to reform the Townsend Plan, to make the operation worthy of the pension program and his name. Some aspects of the organizational setup disturbed him, especially the opportunities for profits among its leaders and organizers. Townsend did not desire to inflate his bank statement. The firmest believer in his pension plan, he was the embodiment of its recommended lifestyle, spending his salary as soon as he got his hands on it, or probably not even handling it.[44] From Townsend's point of view, it would be better to assign the profits from the *Weekly* to the Townsend Plan organization, as much to keep his reputation pure as to hasten the day when his pension plan would become law.

Townsend also wanted to democratize the Townsend Plan, which he understood largely as granting like-minded leaders in the organization greater influence over policy. Many of them were bridling, as Townsend increasingly did, at Clements's tight control. Most Townsend Plan leaders would gladly align themselves with the doctor for the chance to increase their authority. This was especially true of the regional directors, whose elevated titles did not generate commensurate remuneration and decision-making power. The Reverend Wunder, the eastern regional director, was a case in point. He resigned in reaction to Clements's prohibiting his lucrative sideline in speaking engagements and was looking for a way back in. More substantively, Wunder wanted more emphasis placed on mass-media publicity, personal appearances, and radio speeches, at which he excelled, rather than organizing clubs on the ground. Because Townsend was the organization's top-drawing speaker, these complaints resonated with him. Recruits and revenues would be generated through radio audiences or public appearances. Townsend clubs would spring up through the initiative of community leaders and volunteers, eliminating the need for networks of commission-seeking organizers.[45]

Townsend also wanted to elevate the role of Townsend clubs within the organization. He envisioned the Townsendites as the foot soldiers of a new progressive, issue-oriented political organization that would displace the old parties. The revenue being generated by the clubs lent some plausibility to his vision. In the first two months of 1936, a presidential election year, the Republican Party would raise $260,000, not significantly better than the pace of the Townsend Plan in the last quarter of 1935, and the Republicans were trailing if one adds in the profits from the *Weekly*. In the same two-month period the ruling Democrats had raised only $50,000. Having been long ago ousted from political life by corrupt forces in Belle Fourche, South Dakota, Townsend longed for the day when American politics could be rid of patronage and bossism. Townsend clubs might be the nucleus for a programmatic and issue-oriented mass politics. Townsend's belief in the clubs, however, went only so far. Deciding key policy was to remain in the hands of leaders like himself.[46]

Townsend also had differences with Clements on matters of political strategy. The doctor thought a quick passage of his pension-recovery proposal was possible and thus was dissatisfied with the incremental progress of seeking congressional backing for the McGroarty bill. Townsend had been annoyed by his treatment in Congress and considered dealing with House members beneath him and beside the point. He favored bolder action aimed at higher officials, such as campaigns to recall senators from Arizona and California, designed to frighten the rest of Congress into action. Townsend also thought that a party based on the Townsend clubs and his potential presidential candidacy would be an immediate contender for power in California, just as new parties had taken power in Minnesota and Wisconsin. The Townsend party could then spread to other parts of the West and beyond. Townsend understood nonpartisanship to mean that the Townsend Plan should take on the old parties, not, as Clements did, to work with potential supporters regardless of party.[47]

At the very least Townsend saw the Townsend Plan as a kingmaker in the presidential election. His preferred option was to induce a Republican to endorse the pension-recovery program, aid his nomination bid, and then have him run as the Townsend candidate for president. Townsend had changed his registration to Republican and had already spoken out in favor of Senator Borah, the progressive Republican from Idaho who had endorsed the pension plan. Townsend was sure that he would countenance no compromise with Roosevelt, as the doctor felt himself treated disrespectfully by the president, who had repeatedly rejected Townsend's overtures to meet and smeared his idea with elliptical abuse. Townsend was convinced his plan would never become law with Roosevelt in the White House.[48]

Hitting even closer to home was Townsend's fear of being eclipsed in the eyes of his followers by Congressman McGroarty, whose credibility was strong among Townsendites and whose advanced age made him a plausible substitute as a symbolic leader of an old folks' challenger. The poet McGroarty was also by far a more accomplished wordsmith than Dr. Townsend, and with the focus on Washington the congressman's views often received bigger play than the founder's in the *Weekly*. Townsend's pension plan had congealed into McGroarty's bill, making the doctor feel as though he had lost control over his brainchild. Part of the thinking behind having the congressman out front was that if his bill proved defective, the Townsend Plan leadership could drop or amend it, while the doctor's charisma would remain intact. But Townsend had reservations about the bill. He had never believed in the transactions tax, and the McGroarty bill was not likely soon to generate $200-per-month pensions. But only the full amount would ensure recovery, as Townsend saw it, and in any case that was the sum he had pledged to his followers.[49]

Townsend wanted to transform the Townsend Plan into something like Father Charles E. Coughlin's National Union for Social Justice. Canadian by birth, Coughlin was a Catholic priest with a parish in Royal Oak, Michigan, just outside Detroit, who had been broadcasting a national radio program on the CBS network since 1930. With his appealingly mellow brogue, Coughlin promoted a set of anti-Depression monetary schemes, wrapping them in populist ideology and rhetoric. He was also a fervent supporter of the early policies of the Roosevelt administration, stating the choice as "Roosevelt or ruin." The National Union, begun in the fall of 1934, had sixteen points to it—principles in which the followers were expected to believe. The more concrete among them included the nationalization of banks, the end of the Federal Reserve System, and the control of money by Congress, which presumably would press an inflationary policy. Before 1936, however, Coughlin's National Union was little more than a mailing list of those who wrote to him in support of his broadcasts. There were no local organizations, which were expressly forbidden by Coughlin, who claimed as members the estimated 10 million regular listeners to the *Shrine of the Little Flower Hour*.[50]

In 1936, however, Coughlin moved to transform the National Union for Social Justice into something like the Townsend Plan's form of organization. Perhaps as many as 6,000 local chapters of the organization were founded, mainly in the Midwest, and his goal, too, was to place them in every congressional district. The local chapters were unaided by any sort of organizing network, paid or otherwise, and their leaders were largely self-selected through Coughlin's radio exhortations. Given their lack of direction from above or connection to one another, however, the local units of the union frequently found themselves embroiled in minor political issues far removed from the concerns of Coughlin, who was becoming increasingly critical of Roosevelt's policies. The chapters were often dominated by political hopefuls trying to use Coughlin's popularity to boost their careers.[51] What Townsend noticed about Coughlin's operation, however, was that the headman was on the radio every week, able to criticize Roosevelt at will, spout off on almost any subject, and was seemingly in complete command of a far-flung organization without organizers.

Conclusion

By early 1936, the Townsend Plan had completed perhaps the best six-months' growth spurt of any U.S. challenger ever. As the spring approached, there were about 8,000 Townsend clubs, more than double the number of half a year earlier. These clubs were now organized all across the country, instead of being focused on the West, and membership in them was nearing the 2 million mark. The organization was raising revenue faster than the major political parties were, despite the fact that the Townsend Plan was relying exclusively on small contributions. In part this was due to its new organizational plan of action, which now employed a nationwide network of commission-earning organizers to spur Townsend clubs in each congressional district.

But Clements and Townsend were greatly aided in their efforts, too, by favorable political circumstances. The most important was the passage of the Social Security Act. Far from stealing the thunder of the Townsend Plan, it validated the claims of the Townsendites for old-age pensions, while not yet providing any significant benefits. The Townsend Plan leadership was primed to exploit this political and discursive disjuncture, having just finished testing its organizational prototype on California and the West. In addition, although economic activity was increasing, the Depression was far from over, lending plausibility to the Townsendite critique of the administration's economic policy. The Townsend Plan did its best to turn the political situation further to its advantage. A convention of Townsend clubs in October drew the nation's attention—which was multiplied when the Townsend Plan intervened with spectacular success in an off-year House race in Michigan. As a result of organizing gains, the prospects for more, and the demonstration of political power, Congress began to line up behind the McGroarty bill. Each House member was being asked to put in writing his support for the bill—or face the electoral consequences.

As it spread around the country, the Townsend Plan overwhelming drew its support from the aged. Older Americans constituted almost all the members of Townsend clubs. Townsend club members were also more likely to be white, Protestant, and citizens, but they were not disproportionately impoverished, newly or long-term. There seemed to be little difference between the average Townsendite and the average older American, suggesting that the potential appeal of the Townsend Plan to the rest of the aged might be widespread indeed. Although nonelderly America was not joining Townsend clubs, it was not out of opposition. Opinion polls suggested that almost half of the American public was in favor of Townsend-style old-age pensions. Although support was significantly related to lower incomes and support for the president, the program appealed widely, to adherents of both major political parties.

For all its organizing, political, and publicity successes, however, the Townsend Plan was bumping up against substantial barriers. Its inability to make organizational headway in the South outside southern Florida had to do with the obstacles facing any fiscally demanding challengers in such underdemocratized polities. The Townsend Plan was foundering there, as did Populists and labor union organizers before them. Also, Townsend clubs proved difficult to get off the ground in patronage-oriented polities, especially in the cities of the urban Northeast. If Townsend's pension-recovery plan was going to become law, the organization would have to figure out how to install Townsend clubs in these places or start so many elsewhere that it would not matter. Another potential problem was personal. Dr. Townsend was unhappy with his figurehead status in the burgeoning "Townsend movement." He and cofounder Clements, who remained firmly in control of the organization, would need to resolve their differences if the Townsend Plan were going to realize its potential in national politics. There was no longer any doubt, however, that the Townsend Plan had become a formidable national challenger. If there were limits to its potential influence over old-age policy, they were not obvious.

SIX

Dr. Townsend, Now at the Helm

AT THE START OF 1936 the Townsend Plan was riding high. The March of Time short *Townsend Plan!* was playing in movie theaters all across America, and Townsend clubs were being started at the rate of 500 per month. Dozens of House members had agreed to support the Townsend Plan–sponsored McGroarty bill, and public opinion was coming around, too. As the Congress returned in January, an article in the *Nation* asked what many were wondering, "How Strong Is the Townsend Plan?"[1]

According to all major perspectives on the impact of social movements, there were reasons to believe that the Townsend Plan's influence on old-age policy would be substantial. According to the resource mobilization and bargaining perspectives, the amount and variety of resources a challenger commands are central to its ability to exert influence. The Townsend Plan had about five times as many club members as in the previous year and rivaled the Republican Party in fund-raising. A new organizing infrastructure now extended across the country, and the organization had gained professional help for its lobbying efforts and its newspaper. In terms of the plausibility of its claims-making and framing strategies, the Townsend Plan was also sitting pretty. Its arguments that the aged were worthy were hitting home; almost the entire U.S. public was in favor of old-age "pensions." Its framing strategies were also selling the general public the idea that senior citizens' pensions could be helpful for all. Polls showed that more than half of American adults were in favor of the pension-recovery program. And the political context could not have seemed more favorable. The most pro–social policy administration and Congress in the nation's history were in power in Washington and had brought into being the Works Progress Administration and the Social Security Act. Congress contained the same overwhelming Democratic majorities of 1935 and was ready to add another $2 billion in payments to World War I veterans. Perhaps more important for the cause of senior citizens' pensions, the only off-year election was a dramatic victory for the Townsend Plan, and there were ten times as many Townsend Plan supporters in the new session of Congress as there were in the previous one.

It seemed as though "oldsters," as the aged supporters of the Townsend Plan were frequently called in the news media, were ready to rule in American politics. Yet the Townsend Plan failed to transform old-age policy. Not much happened in Congress. The McGroarty bill unsurprisingly did not pass, but no other bill to improve old-age benefits came up for consideration either. The main action was at the state level, where Old-Age Assistance programs were being enacted rapidly through grants under the Social Security Act. By the end of the year, the Townsend Plan was in disarray, with Dr. Townsend for the first time at its helm. And so the episode also offers a puzzle about theories of the consequences of social movements: Why did such a well-mobilized challenger acting in political circumstances so favorable to social policy have so little impact? And why did it seem to have more influence in the states, where it was paying scant attention, than in Congress? And why was it influential at the national level only in the implementation of programs rather than in the passage of new legislation? And there is a final question: what accounts for the sudden reversal in fortune of the Townsend Plan?

The Impact on Old-Age Policy in the Townsend Plan's Heyday

State governments responded quickly to the old-age provisions of the Social Security Act. To receive federal funding, states had to make old-age benefits available statewide—no more "county-optional" programs—and to designate a single agency to administer the program or to supervise local administration. By New Year's Day, sixteen states had requested approval of OAA programs as compared with eleven for the Aid to the Blind and ten for Aid to Dependent Children. When funds were first released in February for the payments to states, the grants for OAA outpaced those for ADC by more than four to one. After six months, only four states had failed to request approval of an OAA program. It was not a matter of greater need. The now-defunct Federal Emergency Relief Administration had been aiding about 700,000 of the aged, but also about the same number of dependent children, plus their parents. What is more, states with many Townsend clubs were among the first in demanding program approvals, and states with few Townsend clubs were among the last.[2]

The better treatment for the aged was also evident in how old-age programs were handled. Although to gain matching funds all states had to provide payments on the basis of "need," the language was not binding. In many states old-age benefits were administered like pensions; the grants were fairly high, widespread, and unfettered, as the Townsend Plan was demanding, by way of generous income exemptions. This practice contrasted with the intrusive "family budgeting," in which social workers assessed needs and resources on an individual basis and then provided grants to fill the shortfall—a technique that was greatly preferred by the Social Security Board's new Bureau of Public Assistance.[3] California, Washington, Massachusetts, Nevada, and Colorado quickly opted for such "pension" systems, and four of these states harbored quite extensive Townsend clubs. In states where programs were adopted both for the aged and for dependent children, there was usually far less case-work applied to determine eligibility for the aged. And despite the board's qualms about the administration of the new assistance programs, it was eager to approve them in part to forestall the criticisms and slow the growth of the Townsend Plan. Edwin Witte, who had led the Committee on Economic Security, urged the board to take a "nonmeticulous" approach to approving plans.[4]

That said, some opportunities for the Townsend Plan to make gains at the state level were missed. Although old age was forced onto the political agenda of all states, the Townsend Plan was making no efforts to boost OAA programs. A case in point was Colorado, where the Townsend Plan had an extensive following, but one that was fractured as a result of Otto Moore's and the Denver-based Townsend clubs' defection to form the National Annuity League. This breakaway organization called for a guaranteed income in old age of at least $45 per month and sought signatures for a referendum to create a state constitutional amendment for the pensions, as well as specific taxes to pay for them. However, the Townsend Plan fought this initiative, arguing that any attempt to provide old-age pensions at the state level would drain urgency from efforts at the national level and would not provide a sufficient economic stimulus to effect nationwide recovery. The National Annuity League pressed on all the same and by November had its referendum on the ballot. In California, a Townsend Plan stronghold, a Republican state senator who helped secure the passage of the Townsend Plan's "memorial" to Congress in 1935 thwarted a proposal by End Poverty in California's Culbert Olson to increase the average benefit to $50 per month. Instead, the state guaranteed an income of at least $35 per month for the qualified aged.[5]

There is little doubt that the presence of the Townsend Plan stimulated the states to participate in the new national programs—even in Colorado. Had there been no Townsend Plan, there would have been no National Annuity League, and thus no organized effort to alter the state constitution and pressure political leaders on old age. All the same, the political strategy of the Townsend Plan did not much advance the process there or elsewhere. Its policy was not to intervene in these battles or, worse, sometimes to speak out against the insurgents advancing old-age benefits in states. Its efforts to discourage state-level pension activity probably did not greatly hinder these campaigns, and the Townsend Plan's existence no doubt improved the prospects of higher benefits in old-age programs across the country. What was lost were the potential benefits of the Townsend Plan's intervention on the side of advocates to improve OAA programs. The boost would likely have been substantial. Later on the Townsend Plan did join these battles, and with good results.[6]

At the national level, the main story regarding old-age policy had less to do with Congress than with the rapid administrative implementation of the Social Security Act. The fabrication of the Social Security Board had been slowed by Huey Long's final filibuster. Until January, the board was forced to operate by way of WPA funding, FERA personnel, and makeshift space. The board included three members, designated as representatives of political parties, but was controlled largely by the administration. John Winant, a Republican but a member of the CES advisory committee, was named chair, and Arthur Altmeyer, an assistant secretary of labor who was closely connected with the CES, was appointed to the board. Thomas Eliot, who helped to draft the administration's security legislation, served as general counsel. The urgency of the old-age situation, however, spurred the rapid growth of the organization, especially its Bureau of Public Assistance, which had oversight over Old-Age Assistance programs.[7] Otherwise the Roosevelt administration and its congressional allies were sitting tight with their hand on old-age policy, waiting for OAA legislation to go into effect.

In striking contrast to the national legislative inaction on old age was the dogged campaign to provide the early payment of the World War I veterans' bonus. Veterans' groups began demanding this as early as 1930, and after failed attempts by various "Bonus Armies" in Washington in 1932, 1933, and 1934, the cause was being pressed more effectively by the American Legion and Wright Patman, a Texan congressman who wanted to use the bonus payments to inflate the currency. Patman's bill had won out over the Legion's in the 1935 session, but Roosevelt emphatically vetoed it. When a new early-payment bill, without the inflationary measures, passed in January 1936, Roosevelt once again vetoed it but this time indicated that he would not fight a bid to override him. Congress quickly and overwhelmingly did so.[8] The veterans' organizations had won their battle not by attacking the two main parties but through a meticulous process of organization and winning support from individual representatives and despite the vociferous opposition of the president. This episode suggested that the Townsend Plan's congressional endorsement strategy could ultimately win, but might take a while to effect.

The Townsend Plan had great influence at the state level and little influence at the national level largely because of differences in the place of the old-age issue on political agendas. The new national matching payments for OAA, the emerging guidelines necessary to receive the payments, and the end of the Federal Emergency Relief Administration aid to the aged forced the old-age issue onto the political agendas of all states. Because of the strength of the Townsend Plan, old age was the top priority among the new public assistance programs. In states where Townsend clubs were particularly prevalent, state officials were more likely to pay more generous old-age benefits with fewer restrictions and limitations on them, making them more like "pensions." This happened despite the Townsend Plan's lack of engagement in state-level OAA battles. Had the Townsend Plan attempted to exert influence, probably even better results would have followed. A rival organization begun with disaffected Townsend clubs succeeded in pressing a referendum for pensions in Colorado.

At the national level, the administration was not proposing any new legislation, so there was no chance to induce it to alter its proposal, as there had been in 1934. Nor did Congress have an old-age bill in front of it to upgrade as it had in 1935. Had there been such an opportunity in 1936, the Townsend Plan would have been in a far better position to take advantage of it. Well mobilized though the plan was, it did not have nearly a majority in the House, which could have forced old-age policy on the agenda through the discharge-petition process. In any case, the Townsend Plan had to direct its congressional attention elsewhere.

Called on the Carpet

In the wake of the Townsend Plan's tremendous recruiting and publicity successes, opposition began to mobilize. Moderate social scientists were among the first to publish warnings, including a group of University of Chicago economists who claimed that the pension proposal would lead to impossibly high taxes that would be difficult to collect and would devastate the securities industry. Negative, too, were the verdicts of social scientists working for the National Industrial Conference Board and the Committee on Old Age Security of the Twentieth Century Fund. The National Association of Manufacturers and the far-right American Liberty League also joined the fray. The latter claimed, somewhat less thoughtfully, that Townsend's pension-recovery plan was a natural extension of Roosevelt's New Deal.[9]

The House versus the Townsend Plan

A more ominous source of opposition soon appeared. On January 29, C. Jasper Bell, a Democratic congressman from Kansas City, called for an investigation of the Townsend Plan. Bell had statesmen in his lineage but was currently representing the corrupt machine of boss Thomas Pendergast. Perhaps because he was unlikely ever to be unseated by Townsendites, Bell did not mince words: "Several groups of fraudulent promoters are enriching themselves by working the so-called pension racket. . . . The promotional activities . . . falsely and cruelly deluding . . . should be unmasked." He referred to Dr. Townsend as a "charlatan" and a "quack." Bell was hoping to burnish his image and join his forebears in political greatness, perhaps by being promoted to the Senate someday in the manner of the state's junior senator, Harry S Truman, who had made the jump in 1935. Pendergast liked to install men of clean reputation in the Senate to whitewash the machine's lower-level operations.[10] Worse for the Townsend Plan, Bell was acting with the blessing of the House Democratic leadership, which enlisted Republican support for the investigation. Having witnessed the recent election of the pro-Townsend Congressman Main in Michigan, fearing havoc in its upcoming congressional primaries, and remaining unsympathetic to the expensive pension plan, the Republican House leadership agreed.[11]

Before February was out, the special committee's members were named, with Bell installed as chair. A bipartisan group, it had equal representation for each party, despite the Democrats' lopsided margin in the House. Joining Bell was the Republican Clare Hoffman of Michigan, also known to be hostile to the Townsend Plan. Balancing them to some extent were two pro-Townsend members, Democrat John Tolan and Republican Sam Collins, both of California. The committee's two other Democrats, Scott Lucas of Illinois and Joseph Gavagan of New York, and its two other Republicans, John Hollister of Ohio and William Ditter of Pennsylvania, were unknown quantities, but they seemed unlikely to be supporters of the Townsend Plan given that Townsend clubs were underrepresented in these populous states. The committee appointed as its investigator James Sullivan of Kansas City, who began questioning witnesses like Pierre Tomlinson, Otto Moore, and Frank Peterson, each still seething from their ousters from the Townsend Plan. On March 13 the committee won an appropriation of $50,000, beating back a surprisingly strong effort by the Townsend Plan's congressional supporters to reduce the sum to $10,000, by a vote of 240 to 112. More than half of those on the losing side were said by the national press to be part of a pro–Townsend Plan voting bloc.[12]

Calling an investigation was a seemingly bold move by the Democratic and Republican leaderships. There was little evidence of corruption beyond the claims of disaffected former Townsend Plan officials, whose motives and reliability were questionable. The costs were potentially high, given the increased mobilization of the Townsendites, the favorable publicity surrounding the Townsend Plan and its plucky figurehead leader, and gains it made in public opinion polls. Pundits were uncertain whether an investigation would help or hurt the cause. After all, the Townsend Plan had rebounded smartly from the previous year's grilling in Congress. If the investigation uncovered few abuses, it would constitute free and positive publicity—a kind of House bill of good political health. Clements, in the hope of forestalling the investigation, predicted that it would "boomerang" and force Congress to vote on and for the McGroarty bill.[13]

The House pressed ahead nonetheless. Some members, especially on the Ways and Means Committee, remained angered by the heavy-handed tactics of the Townsend Plan in the previous year. But there were cooler-headed reasons for the investigation. The most important was the radical nature of the pension-recovery program. Even the stripped-down model featured in the McGroarty bill promised to cost at least $6 billion per year for as far as the eye could see and would provide enduring rights to pensions to all Americans as they turned sixty. Nothing granted to veterans would be remotely in this fiscal vicinity, even if all were granted pensions on the Civil War model. Besides, members of both parties had already passed the bonus bill to the tune of $2 billion, and Democrats had already rallied around a $5 billion work relief program. The McGroarty bill was far too rich for the blood of almost all Republicans and the majority of Democrats, too.[14] In addition, the Townsend Plan might have a difficult time making its congressional opponents pay electorally for the investigation. It was a major political force only in about a dozen states in the West and upper Midwest. The South, outside south Florida, was not likely ever to host large numbers of Townsend clubs, and the committee's bipartisanship meant that neither party could be singled out for retribution. And the Townsend Plan was already in the news.[15]

Townsend's Opening Moves, Clements's Gambit Accepted

As Congress stonewalled on old-age policy and pressed forward with its investigation, Townsend's disagreements with Clements were breaking into the open. Townsend's view that the Townsend Plan should focus on the presidential election and form its own party brought tension. William Borah, who had previously endorsed the pension plan, embarrassed the organization when he then criticized the McGroarty bill as being both too expensive and too restrictive in its requirement that pensions be spent immediately. Townsend's retorts brought press attention of a sort that Clements considered counterproductive. A cartoon in the *New York Daily Post* showed a dignified Borah on stage behind a podium speaking to an even more dignified-looking audience of Republicans on "liberalism," while brushing off an attention-seeking dog—labeled the "Townsend Plan." Defying Clements and the organization's nonpartisan policy, Dr. Townsend devoted the funds from a Los Angeles rally in February to the exploration of a Townsend political party.[16]

Townsend also was upset that Congressman McGroarty was planning to run, with Clements's blessing, as a favorite son in the California Democratic primary. The Townsend Plan's nonpartisan strategy meant trying to gain a beachhead in each major party, and the idea behind the California campaign was to elect a slate of Townsend Plan delegates to gain leverage over the Democratic platform. Roosevelt's renomination was a foregone conclusion. But Townsend feared that his followers' allegiances might somehow be captured or compromised by his enemy Roosevelt. Townsend's problems with McGroarty also now included the congressman's bill. The standard criticism that it would not provide the full $200 monthly pensions began to rankle. Townsend flirted with an idea put forward by his new personal attorney and former EPIC candidate for lieutenant governor Sheridan Downey—to finance more generous pensions partly by way of bond sales.[17]

With Clements cooperating with congressional investigators, hoping to control the damage, Townsend felt the urgency to act. It was only a matter of time before they unearthed embarrassing details regarding the Prosperity Publishing Company, which was owned by Townsend and Clements and which published the *National Townsend Weekly*, whose circulation had ballooned to more than a quarter million. Although Townsend and Clements could compromise on many issues, one was nonnegotiable. Clements wanted to do good, but he entered movement politics in order to do well. Clements would never agree to turn over his stock in the publishing company to the Townsend Plan organization without considerable compensation. Townsend decided to force the issue. He knew that the clubs were more loyal to him than to Clements, and most of the other leaders would back Townsend in any dispute. Also, when the Townsend Plan organization was incorporated, it had three all-powerful members, and the third was Townsend's brother Walter. Townsend thus had the power at any time to alter the board of directors—and now he had the motivation. Townsend changed the bylaws of the organization in late February, adding two directors to join him, Clements, and the vice president, Gomer Smith, and then called a board meeting for March 9 in Kansas City, which Clements refused to attend. The meeting proceeded all the same, and Townsend released a statement that the new board had taken "under advisement certain important improvements and changes in the organization." On March 24, two days before the congressional hearings were to begin, Clements resigned from the Townsend Plan, taking with him his profits in the Prosperity Publishing Company.[18]

Analysts speculated that Clements's resignation was a ruse. More likely it was a gambit to express his displeasure at Townsend's power play in the hope that the doctor would soon find himself incapable of running the organization and come crawling back to his co-founder. If Clements did not discredit himself before the committee, perhaps he would soon return to head the Townsend Plan.[19] Clements was masterful, praising Townsend as a "brilliant man" and documenting the rapid growth in the organization. Clements even thrust his organizational rival Margett onto the front pages with the suggestion that he was receiving exorbitant commissions. The information blunted the impact of the revelation of Clements's 1935 income of $12,600 in salary from the Townsend Plan and profits from the Prosperity Publishing Company. Although investigators revealed that the Townsend Plan had taken in nearly a million dollars since its inception, a figure that made newspaper headlines, they found nothing inappropriate or illegal in how the money was spent. At the end of the week, Townsend Plan leaders were "openly jubilant," as the *New York Times* put it, for the investigators had taken their best shot and had come up short. McGroarty expressed to reporters the hope that all Townsend leaders could soon convene and clarify Clements's future role in the organization.[20] After the special committee adjourned, Richard Strout in his "TRB"

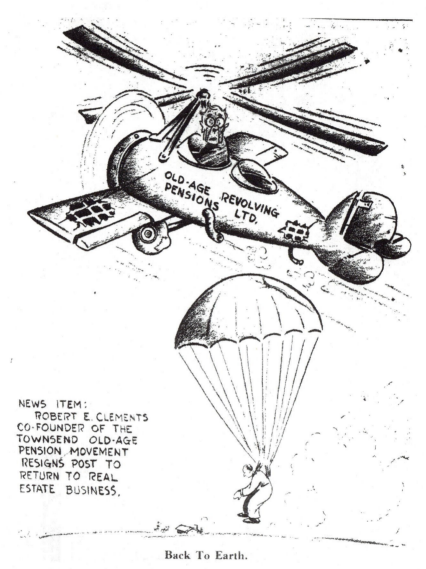

Back To Earth.

Figure 6.1: Back to Earth. This cartoon, printed in the *Washington Post*, illustrates the common view that Dr. Townsend would have a difficult time continuing once his "copilot" Earl Clements had "bailed out" from the organization. Source: *Washington Post*, March 26, 1936, p. 8.

column in the *New Republic* characterized the investigation as operating under "the watchful eye of the man it was chiefly supposed to catch."[21]

Unraveling before the Investigation

The Townsend Plan was at a crossroads. It seemed possible that it was going to
be back to business as usual for the organization—which in the first months of
the year was very good indeed. But first Dr. Townsend had to decide what to
do. He could bring Clements back quickly or appoint a replacement to carry
out his old functions. Margett was hoping to get the call. Townsend also could
try to implement a completely different leadership arrangement, with power
shared by all the major leaders in the organization—or even with the clubs. Or
he could decide to run the organization himself.

Townsend at the Helm, Takes a Walk

The day before Clements's appearance before Congress, Townsend announced
some changes in policy to ensure greater influence for himself and his allies.
The Townsend Plan was now to be led by its board of directors, which was
expanded to include the four regional directors, with Rev. Clinton Wunder
being reinstated as the eastern regional director. Townsend renounced his
salary from the Townsend Plan corporation and announced that henceforth
he would be paid solely from the earnings of the *National Townsend Weekly*.
The state area managers were to be placed on a salaried basis rather than
being paid by commissions.[22]

As the House committee recessed, in nearby Baltimore Townsend and the
new board made the decision to root out dissidents. George Highley, leader of
the largest Townsend club, a Los Angeles club with 22,000 members, was
ousted for allegedly conspiring with Clements. After being dressed down by
Dr. Townsend in the *Weekly* for having "political ambitions," Congressman
McGroarty broke with the Townsend Plan. Clements was charged with having
pressured Walter Townsend to resign as the third member of the Townsend
Plan corporation, a plot allegedly including a Clements confederate imper-
sonating a representative of the investigating committee. Denouncing the
"traitors," the *Weekly* marked Townsend's ascension by a centerfold illustration of a ship's captain complete with tiller. The headline, "Our Leader Now
at the Helm," announced the end of Townsend's figurehead status. A photo
of Townsend's head was attached to the captain's massive torso, as if poking
through a cardboard cutout at a fair. Townsend never again spoke Clements's
name in public.[23]

At the end of April, the committee, smelling blood, renewed its inquiry. In

Figure 6.2: Our Leader *Now* at the Helm. This illustration, which ran in the *Townsend Weekly*, celebrated the ascension of Dr. Townsend to true power within the Townsend Plan, implying of course that he was not "at the helm" previously. Source: *National Townsend Weekly*, April 6, 1936, pp. 8–9.

Washington, Clements returned to the stand to cite the details of the stock transactions that netted him $50,000 from the Prosperity Publishing Company. The committee sent barnstorming teams around the country. In Detroit and Battle Creek, Congressman Hoffman's one-man investigation induced former Townsend Plan organizers there to call the organization a "racket." Out west, Congressmen Gavagan and Collins presided over a parade of former and disgruntled Townsend leaders. Pierre Tomlinson, the Townsend Plan's head organizer in its first year, testified that Townsend maintained they would all make "hatfuls" of money from the Townsend Plan and that Townsend had schemed to sell his 1934 endorsement of Frank Merriam, now the California governor, for $12,000. Otto Moore of the Townsend Plan's 1935 congressional committee and now of the National Annuity League charged that the plan dishonestly solicited more money for its congressional fund after the battle for the McGroarty bill had already been lost.[24]

But the highlight was Dr. Townsend, who took the stand on May 19. To coincide with his arrival in Washington, the Townsend Plan dispatched a national caravan from Los Angeles, bearing a supposed 10 million signatures on pro–Townsend Plan petitions. The committee room was jammed with forty-three Townsendites and even more reporters and photographers. On the first day of testimony Townsend charged President Roosevelt with being responsible for the investigation; when goaded by Congressman Hoffman, Townsend vowed he would lead a third party. The next day the investigators took aim at Townsend's pension-recovery plan. In a reprise of the previous year, they baited the doctor into headline-grabbing statements that he would pension off Morgan, Rockefeller, and so forth, despite the fact that the McGroarty bill now included an income test, and that most farmers would have to be licensed to pay the transactions tax. On the third day, the investigators pressed the charges of Moore that the Townsend Plan's Washington lobby appealed for funds by way of deceptively urgent "Townsendgrams." After an afternoon recess, Townsend demanded to make a statement, and the committee refused him. Announcing that he would return only under arrest, Townsend strode out of the committee room.[25]

The committee soldiered on for another month, but with little attention and few witnesses, as Townsend ordered other Townsend Plan leaders to ignore their subpoenas. The committee never found the smoking gun of illegal activity that it sought, and Townsend's boycott of the proceedings made the committee seem weak. Townsend could defy Congress without fear of serving prison time, for Roosevelt had no need of an old-age martyr in an election year. The committee's lack of prosecutorial glory hurt Chairman Bell, whose audition as a crusader had flopped. Instead of a statesman, he came off as a bully.

All the same, the leaders of each party saw their mission as largely accomplished. The investigation generated much splashy coverage showing that Townsend Plan leaders made a lot of money. Also hurtful were impolitic missives from the founder, indicating that his saintly public image was of recent vintage. The investigation also revealed some leaders as being of dubious morality, including ones who had been recently promoted. The new national director for public relations, Edward Margett, had been indicted for pimping and bootlegging, and several profanity-laced letters from the new board member Rev. Clinton Wunder were read into the record. Wunder and Jack Kiefer, another former radio extension leader who had been elevated to the board,

Nothing To Conceal.

Figure 6.3: Nothing to Conceal. This cartoon pursued the findings of the congressional investigation, which found that the leadership of the Townsend Plan had done nothing strictly illegal but had made a lot of money from the organization and its aged supporters. Source: *Washington Post*, March 28, 1936, p. X6.

were both held in contempt of Congress, and neither had the practical immu-
nity that Townsend enjoyed. Margett discharged his public relations duties
while evading subpoena servers.[26] For a group whose base was more religious
than the general public and which was supposedly on a moral crusade, the
Townsend Plan looked like an organization on the lam.

The Townsend Plan in Disarray

Harmful as the investigation's fallout was, the central problems for the
Townsend Plan were the shake-up in its leadership, a loss of organizational
direction, and poor prospects for regaining its bearings any time soon. Even
without the investigation, there would have been changes. Townsend was
profoundly dissatisfied with his role and with the way the organization oper-
ated. Anxious as he was about the upcoming presidential election, he would
have attempted to alter the policy. Other leaders' opposition to Clements's
control had been growing, too. Townsend always had the legal backing to
make changes and had something on Clements that would ensure the latter's
withdrawal—Townsend's determination to commit the *Weekly*'s profits to the
Townsend Plan.[27]

As a result of Townsend's moves, however, the Townsend Plan became top-
heavy with public speakers and lost valuable experience in its organizing and
political cadres. Many state area organizers, the organization's backbone, were
dropped when they refused to go on salary. The loss of long-standing leaders
also gave credence to the committee's claims that there was trouble at the top
of the organization. It was especially difficult to explain why Clements was
unfit for leadership, central as he had been to interpreting Townsend's idea to
club members and the press. Worse, with much of the new leadership neutral-
ized by contempt charges, the Townsend Plan's course was now being navi-
gated almost entirely by Dr. Townsend, whose inexperience was outstripped
only by his counterproductive impulses.

The distress in the leadership was quickly felt at the club level. To try to
gain reaffirmations from his following, Townsend issued a bulletin to the approximately 7,000 Townsend clubs with an affidavit professing that the club's
contributions had been voluntary and that it remained loyal to the organization's leadership. Only 4,450 were in hand by the end of May. These steadfast
clubs supposedly accounted for 1.5 million members, according to Congressman Tolan, who was receiving the affidavits. But the *total* club membership
prior to the investigation was only slightly higher than that. Loyal clubs constituted less than two-thirds of all clubs, and the largest club, Highley's, had
cut its ties with the Townsend Plan. Probably many members of the loyal
clubs had dropped away, too, and so membership doubtless dipped well below
1 million, and few new clubs were being formed.[28]

The result was a sharp drop in revenues. The $180,000 received in the first quarter of 1936 was only half as much as in the previous quarter. In the second quarter, during the leadership shake-up and investigation, income plummeted to only about $35,000—the worst quarter since the end of 1934. Richard Neuberger reported in the *New York Times* that many clubs in Oregon and probably elsewhere had stopped paying their quotas to the national organization. The profits from the *Weekly* now accrued to the Townsend Plan but did not amount to more than $15,000 per month. In any case, the larger salaries of the new Townsend Plan leadership were to be paid by way of the *Weekly*. The cash on hand dropped from $130,000 in April to $40,000 by July. The transfer of the headquarters to Chicago was admitted to be an economy move.[29]

Washington was being abandoned by the Townsend Plan in more ways than one. Clements's political strategy relied on holding congressmen's feet to the fire of a Townsend bill—by way of written agreement—and then making them take the electoral consequences if they opposed it. But since Townsend had repudiated McGroarty, there was no longer a Townsend-approved bill and no official Townsend Plan leader on Capitol Hill. The key means for the Townsend Plan to upgrade old-age benefits was by threatening to substitute the McGroarty bill for the old-age sections of the Social Security Act, and the plausibility of this threat was now almost nonexistent. A telling sign of the decline in political support for the Townsend Plan was the lopsided vote in June to cite the doctor for contempt of Congress. The House voted 271 to 41, with far fewer on Townsend's side than the more than 112 who voted against the $50,000 to fund the investigation.[30]

Townsend's New Plans

Townsend began to put into practice his new organizational and political strategies. There would be high-profile speaking engagements. There would be a new organizational and revenue-generation plan; clubs would pay higher yearly dues; and recruitment would rely on radio broadcasts and the energy of rank-and-file club members, not commission-earning organizers. There would be a second convention of Townsend clubs, bigger than the first, maybe bigger than the conventions of the major parties. All critics were invited again to attend. And there would be an intervention in the presidential race.

Organizational Changes

One of Townsend's key changes was to shift the Townsend Plan's reliance on commission-based organizing to recruitment of Townsendites through speaking engagements and radio publicity. To this end he launched a highly publicized tour with the Reverend Gerald L. K. Smith, who had become a close adviser to Townsend soon after his walkout. The former aide of Huey Long claimed improbably to command the allegiances of former adherents to Share Our Wealth. Townsend added Smith to the board of directors and charged him with organizing younger people for the Townsend Plan, in the fond hope that he would deliver Long's constituency. As an orator Smith had few peers, but he had more baggage than following and thought that any publicity was good publicity. In his own March of Time segment that summer, filmed with Smith's cooperation and extensive mugging, the thesis was that he openly aspired to be the dictator of America.[31]

In addition to public appearances and radio engagements, the new publicity strategy included "visual education"—through films, graphic art, and photography. These visual projects would provide engaging and informative material for the Townsend clubs, giving them something to do other than invite speakers, who were often off message and sought to win the allegiances of clubs. The *Weekly* adopted a much sharper, streamlined look—once it officially became the *Townsend National Weekly* in November 1936. Otherwise, the visual education project was an uneven success. It produced some awkward films designed to show how technology reduced jobs and how the Townsend-style pensions could remedy the situation. Often the new techniques were devoted to promoting the image of the founder, a process of deification that seemed increasingly central to Townsend Plan policy. But most of all, the project absorbed revenues during a difficult time.[32]

To reverse its flagging fortunes, the Townsend Plan scheduled the second national convention of Townsend clubs for Cleveland in mid-July. The meeting was timed to fall between the two major-party conventions in order to maximize media attention. At the very least the meeting would prove a fiscal shot in the arm. More than 10,000 Townsendites from thirty-eight states attended, jamming the halls that had recently accommodated the more staid Republican National Convention; each paid a dollar fee to listen to speakers and join in the singing of patriotic anthems, Protestant hymns, and American standards whose lyrics had been reworked to glorify the Townsend Plan and its founder.[33]

But this summer's version of the convention was nothing like the previous fall's well-orchestrated display of unity. Townsend opened the convention off message, denouncing President Roosevelt and telling reporters that he supported Gerald Lemke, a congressman from North Dakota and the candidate of the Union Party, backed by Father Coughlin and his National Union for Social Justice. Reverend Smith and Father Coughlin then hijacked the conclave, blasting Roosevelt as a "communist" and a "double-crosser," with the minister gulping water straight from the pitcher and the priest divesting himself of his clerical collar in the summer heat. They also spoke more about their own plans than Townsend's. It was as if the doctor were sponsoring a debating contest for other leaders to win the allegiances of his followers. Nor-

Figure 6.4: The Real Dr. Townsend. The Townsend Visual Education Project was innovative in selling the doctor's pension program but was often used to glorify the doctor in the *Townsend Weekly*, as shown here, rather than advancing his pension-recovery proposal and used up scarce resources during a period of decline. Source: *National Townsend Weekly*, May 25, 1936, pp. 8–9.

man Thomas, the Socialist Party leader, picked up the gauntlet thrown down to Townsend Plan opponents and lectured Townsendites on economics.[34] After Gomer Smith, the Townsend Plan's vice president, gave a pro-Roosevelt speech, the doctor demanded his resignation. But Smith refused to resign, and half of the thirty-eight state delegations signed a petition for him to lead them out of the meeting. The convention passed a resolution to remain neutral in the presidential race. Most Townsendites decamped well before Lemke's closing-day speech at Memorial Stadium. The meeting produced $30,000 in collections, but poor publicity and much dissension for the Townsend Plan.[35]

After the convention, Townsend formed a new nonprofit corporation, the Townsend National Recovery Plan, Inc. (TNRP), employing the name almost everyone had been using. Like its predecessor, the new corporation's mission was to educate and instruct the American people to appreciate the desirability of old-age pensions. Like its predecessor, too, its corporate "membership" had a majority of Townsend family members, this time the founder and his son, Robert. To prevent what the doctor had diagnosed as an illness of the previous corporate entity, however, no employee in the new enterprise could make more than $50 per week.[36] Townsend inaugurated a new plan for Townsend clubs. The large commissions of state area organizers and the smaller ones of congressional district organizers were eliminated. Instead, club members themselves would be made more responsible for recruitment. Those with initiative and moneymaking impulses could earn tiny bonuses for signing up new members. Membership fees were increased to $2 per year, with 40 cents of this fee being remitted to the club for its own activities. Club dues were eliminated, and sales of paraphernalia to clubs were curtailed.[37]

A New Electoral Strategy

Dr. Townsend also reversed the previous official plan of political action. Instead of focusing on congressional races, working with individual candidates from each party, and speaking softly on the presidential contest, Townsend went on a vigorous anti-Roosevelt and pro-Lemke public speaking campaign. A special "victory edition" of the *Townsend National Weekly* that fall declared, "Townsend Millions Can Elect President," claiming that the Townsend Plan commanded the allegiances of at least 10 million voters. In states like California, where Lemke was not on the ballot, the founder called on Townsendites to support Landon, the conservative Republican nominee. The reason for the presidential focus, as Townsend indicated in an article about his support for Lemke, was that various presidents had been able to delay the soldiers' bonus for too many years. The more specific strategy, somewhat difficult to grasp in retrospect, given its implausibility, was for the Townsend and Coughlin forces to deny the major-party candidates a majority in the Electoral College. The Townsend supporters in the House of Representatives would then hold the balance of power and agree to select Landon in exchange for the passage of Townsend's recovery plan.[38]

Townsend sought to solicit more local input in selecting and supporting congressional candidates. State boards were supposed to communicate their selections to the national organization after consulting with congressional district boards, which had club representatives. But little effort was expended in this direction, with the boards being haphazardly constructed and much being lost in the translation among levels. As a result, the primary season came and went without the Townsend Plan developing an organized strategy of engagement. Some primary races pitted as many as four Townsend Plan–endorsed candidates against one another. In the South, where the only real political competition occurred during primaries, the lack of attention meant abandoning electoral politics altogether, such as it was. Although Townsend Plan candidates did surprisingly well in Democratic races in Florida and in Republican races in Maine, they did less well in the West, where the organization was expected to make major gains. The Townsend Plan forces found themselves divided and ineffective in their Oregon and Minnesota strongholds. Joseph Monaghan, a Townsend stalwart in the House, had lost in the Democratic senatorial primary in Montana, as had Gomer Smith, who at the time was still in Townsend's good graces, in Oklahoma. The Townsend primary challengers dispatched to retire the Republican Senators William Borah of Idaho and Charles McNary of Oregon were crushed.[39]

The problems that surfaced in the congressional primaries were not corrected before the general election. The Townsend Plan failed to make endorsements in most races and sometimes endorsed both candidates. The nod often went to overmatched third-party and independent candidates. Worse still, the Townsend Plan failed to aid incumbents who had already agreed in writing to vote for the McGroarty bill. The choices were poorly publicized, with a complete listing appearing in the *Weekly* only the week before the elections. Townsend's attacks on Roosevelt and support for Lemke made life on the stump difficult for Townsend Plan–endorsed Democrats, who sought to wrap their campaigns in the president's popularity.[40]

The final tally of Townsend Plan supporters elected to the House of Representatives fell well short of the predicted 200. Although the postelection Townsend bloc in the House was listed in the *Weekly* at 101, only 61 of the supposed supporters had been previously endorsed. Failures were rampant in the larger states. In New York, 18 candidates were endorsed, and in Illinois 13, but only one in each state was victorious. None of the six members of the House investigating committee targeted for elimination was defeated. The Townsend senatorial candidate in Oregon, the Democrat Willis Mahoney, narrowly lost in a state swept by Roosevelt. And it was uncertain what exactly the 61 elected endorsees were expected to do in exchange for the Townsend seal of approval. Most were able to win with only the most vague declarations of support for the Townsend pension-recovery plan or for changes in current old-age programs. There was still no official Townsend bill to support. Jasper Bell, the Townsend Plan nemesis, was easily reelected, and he only slightly overstated the case when he crowed that the Townsend congressional bloc was "negligible in numbers and utterly impotent."[41]

Among his followers, Townsend made the election a referendum of himself versus Roosevelt. But the president was both hugely popular and taking no chances, having forged alliances with radical third parties, including the Wisconsin Progressive Party and the Minnesota Farmer-Labor Party, and progressive Republicans, such as Mayor Fiorello La Guardia of New York and Senator George Norris of Nebraska. The 9 million votes guaranteed by Father Coughlin for Lemke were off by an order of magnitude. Lemke polled less than a million votes and did not even come close to winning any of the thirty-four states where he had managed to secure a line on the ballot. Roosevelt won every state but Maine and Vermont, with 60 percent of the two-party vote, and the Democratic majority rose to 242 in the House and 60 in the Senate. Even California Townsendites ignored Townsend and voted to re-elect the president. The fact was, like other lower-income groups in the country, Townsend club members were largely Roosevelt supporters. Dr. Townsend had gambled and lost badly.[42]

What augured worse for the future was the organization's failure to learn from its mistakes. Instead of admitting defeat and the corresponding need to alter political and organizational strategies and to bring new blood into the TNRP leadership, however, the *Townsend National Weekly* declared victory. A banner headline and accompanying graphic went so far as to claim that Americans voted with Townsend and not with James Farley, the head of the Democratic National Committee, despite the greatest Democratic party sweep in the history of U.S. politics. Townsend rescinded an offer to Edward Margett to run Townsend Plan operations and instead retained the leadership stalwarts who supported his presidential folly.[43]

Conclusion

The year 1936 began with real promise for the Townsend Plan to alter American old-age policy. From all the main perspectives on the impact of social movements, the Townsend Plan would be expected to exert great influence to transform the policy from restrictive annuities and stingy assistance to generous and equal senior citizens' pensions. Resources were up, its claims were hitting home, its strategies were working, the most pro–social spending political alignment in U.S. history was in place, and the Townsend Plan had signed up many new congressional supporters. Yet Congress did not act on old age, and instead great gains were made in the states, which acted to receive federal Old-Age Assistance funds. By the end of the year all but six states had OAA programs in operation, moving much more rapidly on OAA than on assistance programs for the blind or dependent children. States usually made OAA less restrictive, and in some states the programs were close to being senior citizens' pensions. All that suggested an influence of the Townsend Plan. The need to administer these new OAA programs also kicked the Social Security Board into gear.

The Townsend Plan had more influence on the states chiefly because the old-age issue was already on the political agenda there, just as it had been on the national agenda in 1934 and 1935. Even in the states, however, the challenger's influence was based on its mobilization of Townsendites and a potential for action, not on any specific collective action program. The Townsend Plan mainly ignored the states, focusing on national pensions, and in many states probably the most productive move was not to act but to let New Deal–inspired governments and local pension movements press forward. But the organization sometimes joined the side of the opponents of more generous and less restrictive payments to the aged.

At the national level, the Townsend Plan's lack of influence was due to the radical nature of the changes it sought to make and the fact that it was still just getting started. The challenger wanted to transform old-age policy, as well as to redistribute to the aged resources that were going to all groups through social policy. To effect this sort of change would take commitments from members of Congress on the order of the support won by World War I veterans for the early payment of their bonus. The Townsend Plan was not strongly organized enough across the country and had not influenced enough congressional races to have that sort of sway. The Townsend-sponsored bill probably would not have been considered, even if the major parties had not agreed to investigate the organization.

The inquiry was unfriendly, embarrassing Townsend and shocking socially conservative Townsendites. But the wounds suffered by the Townsend Plan in its aftermath were mainly self-inflicted. Dr. Townsend purged its leadership and for the first time set the course for the Townsend Plan and his "movement." But he dropped the carefully laid plan of organizing clubs by congressional districts to win the written support of the House members for the McGroarty bill. Townsend instead followed Father Coughlin in attacking Roosevelt and supporting Gerald Lemke, the doomed Unionist presidential candidate, hoping that clubs would reorganize themselves. At the helm, Townsend launched the Townsend Plan squarely at Roosevelt, a political suicide mission whose only saving grace was that it was so misguided that it missed its target. Townsend's lack of interest in congressional campaigns resulted in the reduction of the pro–Townsend Plan bloc. With McGroarty out of the picture, there was no Townsend Plan bill to support in any case. Townsend's idea that clubs would organize themselves after hearing radio broadcasts was mistaken. Oldsters who had flocked to Townsend clubs had abandoned the Townsend Plan, whose moment had apparently come and gone.

SEVEN

The Rise of a Pension Movement

THINGS SOON GOT EVEN WORSE for Dr. Townsend and the Townsend Plan in 1937. Another controversy brought the defection of most of the Townsend Plan's leadership, paying Townsendites dropped to their lowest level since the first days of Townsend clubs, and the news media now counted Dr. Townsend, along with his former allies Father Coughlin and the Reverend Gerald L. K. Smith, among the walking political dead. But Townsend, his idea, and his organization were far from finished. The Townsend Plan rebounded in the second half of 1938, and its revival was not even the main story in the old-age pension movement. In state after state, Townsend Plan–like organizations led drives to convert Old-Age Assistance programs into senior citizens' pensions. A group known as Ham and Eggs even briefly overshadowed the Townsend Plan in its home state with an initiative to provide pensions to all over the age of fifty.

The old-age issue also returned to the national political agenda. By the end of 1938, the Roosevelt administration was once again making plans for social policy—this time mainly for old age. The Social Security Board sought to transform a government-run annuity program for individual wage earners in the future into real social insurance for the present. This new program would pool risks, increase benefits, redistribute income, add benefits for wives and dependents, create benefits for survivors, and cover almost all wage earners. The Townsend Plan and other radical advocates sought to substitute equal and generous pensions to all aged Americans. In the end, the Social Security Act was amended to alter old-age policy.

This episode of old-age mobilization and policy making raises two sets of questions. Why did the Townsend Plan suffer the same problems in 1937—conflict among the leadership and then a loss of mass support—it had suffered in 1936? And why, after seemingly fatal wounds, was the Townsend Plan able to rebound? More generally, what accounts for the proliferation of so many other groups pressing for senior citizens' pensions and the development of a wider pension movement? A second set of questions has to do with the impact of the Townsend Plan and other pension groups. What influence did the pension movement and the Townsend Plan have on the agenda for old-age policy making? Also, what influence did the Townsend Plan have on the content of the proposals to transform the American approach to old-age policy?

What was the impact of pension movements in the states, and why were some of these mobilizations more influential than others?

Falling Apart Again

As 1936 ended, the Townsend Plan had been humiliated, and the doctor had been indicted for contempt of Congress. But all was not lost. The organization retained many people of talent. Among the veterans was the vice president, J. W. Brinton, who oversaw the *Townsend National Weekly* and became the chief interpreter of the recovery plan through his "I Was Just Thinking" column and his handy *Townsend Plan Ready Reference*, which sold for a quarter. The secretary of the Townsend Plan remained the experienced Gilmour Young, who was aided by Harry B. Presson, who was in charge of clubs. Dr. Townsend's image was so built up that he remained a bankable star, able to attract talent. A notable new recruit was Arthur M. Johnson, a California lawyer and member of the state's labor commission, who drafted a replacement for the McGroarty bill.[1]

Johnson called the new bill the General Welfare Act, hoping that its abbreviation, the GWA, would have a New Deal ring to it and meet with the approval of President Roosevelt. Appointed the Townsend Plan's legislative representative, Johnson led a staff of seven in Washington to promote it, and, given his young age and lack of elective office, he was not as threatening a figure to Townsend as Congressman McGroarty had been. Like McGroarty's bill, the GWA included a 2 percent transactions tax, with the sums accrued by the taxes to be placed in a special fund and then divided among qualified pensioners. As usual, the recipients would have to be sixty years or older, citizens, not habitual criminals, retired, and willing to spend their entire pension every month. The size of the pension would be determined entirely by the revenues brought in by the taxes and the number of approved applicants. The bill called for a maximum pension of $200, though, like the McGroarty bill, the GWA was estimated initially to provide approximately $50 or $60 per month. If economic activity took off, the stipends would increase. Although only eighteen House members showed up to a Townsend Plan caucus in January 1937, eight supporters saw sufficient political future in the pension-recovery plan to form a bipartisan steering committee. Its leader, Charles Crosby, a Democrat from Ohio, introduced Johnson's bill as HR 4199 on February 2.[2]

To stem the tide in membership declines, several moves were made at the club level. The circulation of the *Townsend National Weekly* by the end of 1936 had dropped to about 50,000, but being a Townsendite in good standing now meant paying a $2 yearly subscription, and its funds, though controlled its owner Dr. Townsend, were being devoted to the promotion of

Figure 7.1: Women's Auxiliary. In the Townsend Plan's time of trials, clubs were encouraged to form women's or ladies' auxiliaries, to tap the fund-raising energy and talents of women members. The Ohio delegation from the Townsend club convention of 1941 is shown here. Author's collection, photographer unknown.

the pension–recovery legislation. Although they were no longer required to pay "quotas," or monthly fees, clubs were encouraged to form "women's auxiliaries"—a seemingly strange recommendation as Townsend club women and men met together and were formally equal. But women usually organized the clubs' various sales and dinners—key fund-raising activities that the Townsend Plan sought to promote. Townsend also made some democratizing reforms. The founder authorized the clubs of each congressional district to hold conventions and form advisory boards. To exert maximum pressure on the new Congress for the welfare bill, Townsend asked Townsendites to lend him $5 million.[3]

Lifting the gloom over the Townsend Plan was also the occasional media spotlight. Although the doctor was convicted in March, fined, and sentenced to thirty days in prison for contempt of Congress, his legal troubles were, paradoxically, producing favorable national publicity. Portrayed in the press as ineffective, stubborn, and a little kooky, the doctor was also often depicted as sincere, good-hearted, and worthy of respect. His impending imprisonment made it appear as though his political enemies were kicking an older man when he was down. Knowing this, Townsend refused to cop a plea. Out on appeal, he went on a nationwide speaking tour, drawing better crowds and publicity than he would have without the conviction hanging over him, and, always good copy, Townsend did not hesitate to express to any reporter within earshot his continued contempt for Congress. The Townsend Plan also was thrust into the news by the efforts of individual clubs, which, unsupported by national headquarters, were conducting tiny social experiments. A well-heeled Townsend booster would donate $200 in marked bills to launch some lucky Townsendite on a monthlong spending spree with local merchants agreeing to pay a 2 percent tax on the money. The hope was that the revenues generated would fund another Townsendite, and so on.[4]

In Washington, President Roosevelt was planning no augmentations to the Social Security Act's two old-age programs—Old-Age Assistance and old-age annuities—waiting to see whether the Social Security Act would pass constitutional muster. Indeed, the president forced the issue by proposing legislation granting him authority to add justices to the Supreme Court, ostensibly to ease the workload of its aged members, but transparently to prevent the invalidation of any further New Deal legislation, including the Social Security Act. In any case, again in 1937 there would be no opportunity to attach a Townsend amendment like a tail to the kite of administration-sponsored old-

---

Figures 7.2 and 7.3: Townsend Club Test. Although not officially supported by the Townsend Plan, in 1937 clubs often embarked on "tests" of the doctor's pension-recovery proposal by raffling off $200 to be spent within a month by a lucky Townsend club member, such as Henry Folz, of Eugene, Oregon, in March. These tests provided publicity for the Townsend Plan during a low point. Author's collection, photographer unknown.

age legislation. That spring, the Ways and Means Committee, dominated by Democrats, grounded the General Welfare Act. In response, the Townsend Plan sought 218 House members—one more than half the House—to sign a petition to discharge the bill from committee. By early May, the *Weekly* claimed seventy signatures, and its circulation had climbed back to over 100,000, more than twice as high as it stood just six months before.[5]

But then trouble returned. The proximate cause was Dr. Townsend's response to Roosevelt's Court reorganization plan. Like many opponents of the measure, Townsend thought the president's proposal flouted the Constitution. If Roosevelt wanted to secure New Deal legislation, Townsend thought, he should have sought a constitutional amendment instead of exploiting his dominance in Congress. In a June meeting Townsend threatened his steering committee members with electoral retribution if any of them were to support the Court legislation. The doctor also insisted that the GWA retain the $200 maximum pension figure—despite the fact that Johnson, Crosby, and the steering committee were finding the number a political liability. Opponents were using it to make the GWA seem extreme. It was deceptive to supporters, too, as the bill was expected to bring stipends that initially would be much lower. The bill's handlers also bridled at Townsend's demeaning justification for retaining the maximum, which he had supposedly analogized as being like "a wisp of straw placed in front of an ox" to get him to work.[6]

Angered and confused by Townsend's unwillingness to grant any autonomy to the steering committee, most of the Townsend Plan's leadership bolted. In Chicago, the Townsend Plan lost twelve officials from the national headquarters, including the vice president Brinton, the secretary-treasurer Young, and the club manager Presson. The editor and most of the editorial staff of the *Weekly* also resigned. In Washington, the legislative representative Johnson led the exodus. Joining him were most of the Democrats on the steering committee, including Crosby. The twelve stated that Dr. Townsend had put his personal pique ahead of the legislative cause and was abusing the trust placed in him by the Townsendites, who had signed on to an organization devoted to the pension-recovery program. If they thought that Dr. Townsend would beg forgiveness and ask them to return, as Robert Clements doubtless expected in 1936, they, too, were mistaken. The founder likewise denounced them all as self-serving traitors, with the *Weekly*'s banner proclaiming "Plot against Movement Bared." Johnson and some of the others formed the General Welfare Federation of America, Inc. They pressed for Johnson's bill and proposed also that Congress grant Dr. Townsend a national pension—in return for his retirement from politics.[7]

Things went from bad to weird. Dr. Townsend promulgated six Father Coughlin–like general "principles." Among them were a minimum wage equal to the plan's pension level and the governmental control of credit, hallmarks of the program of the discredited radio priest. Another principle held that there should be "no change in form of government except through constitutional amendment"—a slap at Roosevelt's Court-packing plan. Townsend declared it the official policy of the Townsend Plan to make the pension-recovery program law of the land through a constitutional convention.[8] All aspects of the "Townsend movement" foundered. The Third Annual National Convention of Townsend Clubs, scheduled for July in Washington, D.C., was canceled. The Townsend Plan was again forced to close its Washington office. The *Weekly* missed editions. When it returned, in an abbreviated form, for the first time it printed letters critical of the founder, suggesting that the antipathy toward his moves ran deep. Maude Keller, the secretary of Auburn (Calif.) Club 1, likely spoke for many Townsendites in writing that her club voted to reject "this program of principles. We believe the principles . . . will not further the enactment of HR 4199 into law." When the Townsend Plan began to provide data on its finances again, it revealed that only about $120,000 had been generated for the period including the last quarter of 1936 and the entire year of 1937. Membership doubtless tumbled into the five digits.[9] Why did things go so wrong again for the Townsend Plan?

The precipitants of this second organizational implosion came from the routine workings of U.S. politics, suggesting that the Townsend Plan's problems were intrinsic to it—the structure of the organization, the nature of its leadership, and its mission. In both 1936 and 1937 the administration and congressional Democratic leadership could use American political institutions to prevent old age from arising as a live political issue. That in turn brought to the fore conflict in the Townsend leadership between those seeking fast action—and thus more drastic measures—and those willing to build support gradually. These tensions in turn revealed the inherent shakiness of the Townsend Plan's organization. Although centralized authority in a social movement organization promotes quick decision making and maneuvering, it can also lead to lurching organizational policy and conflict among the leadership group as well as between leaders and supporters. This is especially the case when, as in the case of the Townsend Plan, there is a minimum of democratic or even routinized decision making among its leaders.

A quirk in the Townsend Plan's leadership also helped it to realize its potential for conflict. The Townsend Plan's symbol controlled it. Dr. Townsend was a kind of all-powerful figurehead who did not manage the *Weekly*, the national headquarters, or the Washington lobby but could intervene in them at any time.[10] Townsend owned the Townsend National Recovery Plan, Inc., and the *Townsend National Weekly*, but the primary part of his hold went beyond legalities. Townsend's image and plan had become brand names of considerable power and were not easily transferred, even to those responsible for creating the doctor's image. Townsend was a little like the New York Yankees' owner, George Steinbrenner, during the team's unsuccessful years in the 1980s and early 1990s—able and willing to make erratic leadership changes due to impatience and ignorance. If the Townsend Plan were ever going to sustain its challenge, Townsend would have to cede substantial control over operations to those with requisite political skills and expertise, as Steinbrenner eventually did with his "baseball people"—experts with a deep knowledge of the game.[11]

Another aspect of the organization helped to ensure that the Townsend Plan's leadership conflicts would come at the expense of the organization's following and mission. The Townsend Plan was based on a specific program rather than a more general ideology. This constrained the leadership, even Townsend, in terms of policy advocacy. Father Coughlin had been able to attack Roosevelt's proposal for America to join the World Court and to mobilize followers by connecting the initiative to his vague sixteen principles. Although Dr. Townsend thought that his legal, moral, and celebrity status gave him the right and ability to take the Townsend clubs in any direction he pleased, he could not convince his most loyal followers that the Supreme Court legislation was related to the Townsend Plan's mission. Nor could he, without losing great support, promulgate the sort of Coughlin-like "principles" that might have provided the justification. Dr. Townsend did not perceive that his appeal rested entirely on his claim to be the discoverer of his pension-recovery plan.

Townsend Redux

Yet Townsend's charisma and the power of his brandlike name remained considerable, and he was nothing if not dogged. Townsend was again able to replace much of the lost leadership. This time he installed his son Robert as secretary-treasurer and heir apparent and, more important, L. W. Jeffery as vice president. Having started in the organization as a congressional district organizer in 1935, Jeffery became the Townsend Plan's chief publicist and political strategist. A Republican, Jeffery held political views that were congenial to those of Townsend, who harbored great animosity toward the president and the Democratic Congress. Otis J. Bouma, the business manager of the *Townsend National Weekly*, was pressed into service as the Townsend Plan's legislative representative. A former editor of the *Weekly*, Walter S. Schuck, returned to lead it.[12]

Townsend backed away from his "principles," and the Court battle ended. Disaffected rank-and-file Townsendites were eager to return, and new ones were ready to join. In July 1938, the organization held the Third Annual National Convention of Townsend Clubs. The meeting was only regional in scope, taking place in Los Angeles and drawing largely from California and the West. But it drew thousands of people to its events and helped the Townsend Plan to regain members in its initial stronghold.[13] More important, the Townsend Plan had embarked on a membership drive in April to gain new members in existing clubs, and a push to organize new clubs began in September 1938. The drive's slogan was "Out to Win," as it was timed to finish just before the November elections. But it was so productive it was

Figure 7.4: Townsend Club Convention, 1938. Although the third "annual" Townsend club convention held in Los Angeles at the Shrine Theater in June 1938 was largely regional in scope, it drew thousands and marked the return to health of the Townsend Plan. Author's collection, photographer unknown.

TABLE 7.1.
New Townsend Clubs from "Out to Win" Drive, 1938, by State, per Congressional District

Three or More New Clubs	One to Three New Clubs	Less Than One New Club	No New Clubs
New Hampshire (12)	Illinois (2.7)	Texas (0.9)	Arizona (0)
Montana (7)	Maryland (2.7)	California (0.7)	Delaware (0)
Wisconsin (7)	Ohio (2.4)	New Jersey (0.6)	Georgia (0)
South Dakota (6.5)	Oregon (2.3)	Kentucky (0.6)	New Mexico (0)
Maine (6)	Washington (2.2)	North Carolina (0.6)	Rhode Island (0)
Minnesota (5.7)	Kansas (2.1)	Utah (0.5)	South Carolina (0)
Nebraska (5.6)	North Dakota (2)	Alabama (0.4)	Tennessee (0)
Michigan (4.5)	Pennsylvania (2)	Arkansas (0.4)	Virginia (0)
Florida (4.4)	West Virginia (2)	Oklahoma (0.3)	
Indiana (3.8)	Iowa (1.6)	Louisiana (0.3)	
Colorado (3.5)	Idaho (1.5)	Connecticut (0.2)	
Wyoming (3)	Massachusetts (1.4)	Mississippi (0.1)	
	Mew York (1.4)		
	Missouri (1.3)		
	Nevada (1)		
	Vermont (1)		

extended through the end of the year, netting about a thousand new clubs and 100,000 new members. The Townsend Plan was back in business.[14]

The Townsend clubs recruited in 1938 differed somewhat geographically from the pattern of the heyday of early 1936. Although the Townsend Plan did well in its previous western strongholds, Out to Win made greater inroads in the Midwest and parts of the East. The drive produced 24 new clubs in New Hampshire, which was the largest gain for a state relative to its number of congressional districts, as table 7.1 shows. Also among the top 10 by this yardstick were Maine, Nebraska, Wisconsin, Michigan, and Indiana. Illinois, Pennsylvania, and New York also had strong showings during the drive, accounting for more than 200 of the new clubs. The results of the drive prompt two questions: What explains this turnaround, and why did the recent mobilization take on this new geographic pattern?

Some of the reasons for the comeback were internal to the Townsend Plan. It still had a good product to sell. Townsend's pension-recovery plan remained attractive to the aged, with its generous benefits and its high-minded role for retirees as "prosperity agents." Club activities still provided the same social benefits. Also appealing was the embattled doctor, who remained by far the best symbol of the old-age pension cause. Townsend was winning further sympathetic press coverage as the time neared for him to surrender. But on the recommendation of several members of Congress, including his tormentor

Figure 7.5: Dr. Townsend Is Pardoned. Dr. Townsend was convicted of contempt of Congress and used the publicity from his failed appeals, as pictured here, to gain sympathy and support for his organization. He was hoping to be imprisoned but was pardoned at the eleventh hour by President Roosevelt. Author's collection, photographer unknown.

Jasper Bell of Missouri, who claimed that the doctor had been under the control of "men of stronger will and intelligence than his own," Roosevelt granted him a last-minute pardon on April 18, as well as a brief audience.[15]

The most important reason, however, was that the Townsend Plan returned to its initial emphasis on organizing—and in the way that it had done before. Jeffery, with his background as a congressional district organizer, borrowed liberally from Robert Clements's playbook. The membership drives were led by "national representatives." Like the previous state organizers, whom they resembled in all but name, the national representatives had state territories, worked on a commission basis, and were supported by a "field staff," commission-earning subcontractors like the previous congressional district organizers. The Townsend Plan concentrated its organizing efforts on congressional districts. There were twenty-nine national representatives by the fall of 1938, and they took control over organizing from congressional district boards, which represented clubs. In another back-to-basics move, the Townsend Plan had returned to the 25-cent yearly membership fee. To speed club formation and recruitment, the Townsend Plan also required only 30 members to form a club—far less than the previous 100-member minimum. By summer of 1938, clubs were to remit $1 every month to the national headquarters—much like "quotas" of 1935. It was back to the old system, with the names changed to protect the doctor's innocence.[16]

The Townsend Plan also returned to Clements's political strategy, focusing on congressional endorsements and legislation, and downplaying Dr. Townsend's pipe dreams of a constitutional convention. Providing enough club and membership support to tip elections in a majority of congressional districts was the explicit goal of "Out to Win." In the spring of 1938, Vice President Jeffery took charge of the congressional endorsement policy, traveling around the country, interviewing candidates, and making selections. As with the membership drives, Jeffery wrested power from the congressional district boards. Because the Townsend Plan was in a much weaker condition than it had been in early 1936, Jeffery could not in most cases induce endorsees to agree to vote for the general welfare legislation in exchange, usually settling for a commitment to aid a hearing for and vote on the Townsend Plan's legislation. And in some instances the Townsend Plan merely sought to defeat candidates—especially Democratic members of the House Ways and Means Committee—held responsible for preventing a hearing on its general welfare legislation. Robert Townsend went so far as to rent a sound truck in North Carolina to blast the Ways and Means Committee chairman Robert Doughton, although he faced no real opposition and was easily reelected. Also targeted were the former members of the Townsend Plan steering committee, mainly Democrats, who had gone over to the General Welfare Federation.[17]

Jeffery fought the campaigns from primaries onward. In Florida that spring, each candidate selected by Jeffery, including Senator Claude Pepper, won his Democratic primary contest and thus was a shoo-in for election in the fall. In Ohio, the Townsend Plan claimed responsibility for the primary defeat of the former steering committee leader Crosby. In California, the Townsend Plan endorsed Sheridan Downey, Townsend's former attorney, in his Democratic primary race for Senate against William McAdoo, who was being supported by Roosevelt. By the middle of October, Jeffery and the *Townsend National Weekly* had made endorsements in almost 250 congressional races in the general election. To give the policy a chance to work, Jeffery convinced Dr. Townsend to visit Hawaii to study the territory's gross income tax. This time, too, the selections were far better publicized in the *Weekly*—with photos and bios of most of the candidates appearing well before the election. It was not always clear, however, that the vendetta against former friends, who remained staunch old-age pension supporters, and Jeffery's predilection for Republicans were going to work to the advantage of old-age policy. In Indiana, the Townsend Plan endorsed six candidates, each one a Republican facing a first-term New Deal Democrat.[18]

The claims of the Townsend Plan again began to resonate. It was not that it altered its appeals. Economic and political conditions combined to lend renewed plausibility to well-worn themes regarding the need for economic recovery through spending and the unfairness of the Social Security Act. The sharp economic decline that began at the end of 1937 halted a four-year recovery. The administration's opponents were referring to the "Roosevelt Depression." The administration countered with the term "recession," but no matter what it was called, it was severe. Unemployment rose almost 5 percentage points to 19 percent in 1938, and national income declined by 3.4 percent.[19] The recession indicated the failure of New Deal recovery programs, providing new credence to the Townsend Plan's standard attacks on counterintuitive crop-control programs and the poor career opportunities provided by the WPA.

What is more, something like the Townsend Plan's economic thinking was being echoed from a far more legitimate source. In the spring of 1938, the president, running out of recovery-plan options, was allowing administration spokesmen to propound a "spending solution" to the recession. Although the secondary economic benefits of government spending had always been part of the justification for New Deal programs like the WPA, now the approved thinking was that the government should self-consciously run budgetary deficits to increase purchasing power and bring recovery. The *Townsend National Weekly* was soon quoting with approval the pro–deficit spending pronouncements of Lauchlin Currie of the Treasury Department and Mariner Eccles, the chairman of the Federal Reserve. No administration official came close to endorsing the Townsend Plan, but the *Weekly* suggested that it would be consistent with the administration's forward economic thinking to deputize 8 million aged "prosperity agents" to do the job.[20]

More important still in intensifying the grievances of the aged and the plausibility of the Townsend Plan's anti–Social Security Act rhetoric were the design and operation of the security legislation itself. For all the activity of its first few years, the fact remained that neither new old-age program was paying much or could be anticipated to do so any time soon. Old-Age Assistance relied on the political action of states to make good on the $30 per month promised by the administration. But southern states with their underdemocratized polities averaged less than $10 per beneficiary per month, and many richer states in the Northeast and Midwest dominated by patronage-oriented

parties fell far short of the maximum. The average old-age benefit across the
United States at the end of 1938 remained under $20 per month—
significantly less than the promised $30 or the $40 that Gallup polls had
shown to be desired by the public. And the national old-age annuity program,
known nowadays as Social Security, was not scheduled to pay out regular benefits until 1942. Even then, the minimum benefit was going to be only $10 per
month and the average benefit about $20. For now, the old-age annuity pro-
gram paid only tiny lump-sum retirement or death benefits. For the Townsend
Plan's publicity purposes, these pittances were far better than nothing, for the
Weekly routinely ran photos mocking them. A typical depiction involved one
William Stanley, who posed ruefully with his lump-sum payment check of
$43.31, with the cutline "Gets His First and Last Social Security Check"—
which would barely get him through the month.[21]

Most of all, the Social Security Act supported the Townsend Plan's critique
by seeming to shortchange the aged. By the end of 1938, $868 million had
been collected from the legislation's Title VIII payroll taxes. But OAA programs had received only $250 million from national sources. And the admin-
istrative costs of getting the annuity program off the ground had reached
$43 million, far more than the $10 million that had been paid out in lump-
sum benefits. The old-age annuity program was theoretically developing a
trust fund, but the U.S. government of the late 1930s, like today, was running
a deficit. And so, also like today, Social Security payroll taxes were financing
current government expenditures, and the trust fund was chiefly an accounting device. The main difference, though, between then and now was that old-
age insurance was paying no regular benefits. The Townsend Plan pounded
away at this disparity, often with cartoons depicting social security funds
being wasted on congressional pork as impoverished elders look on in dis-
belief.[22]

Shortcuts to Utopia?

Another development greatly aided the Townsend Plan and helped to press
forward old-age policy. The Townsend Plan had throughout its existence
largely dominated the senior citizens' pension movement. By mid-1938, this
was no longer true. Other old-age pension mobilizations, some of them off-
shoots of the Townsend Plan, were spreading around the country. Like the
Townsend Plan, these new challengers demanded that the government provide pensions—generous and uniform benefits based on a political entitlement for all aged Americans. Unlike the Townsend Plan, however, these pension mobilizations focused on specific states, and only some made major
claims about the economic benefits of old-age benefits.

No bid for pensions in any state was more dramatic than that of Ham and

Eggs, an organization whose program drew from Dr. Townsend and whose name anticipated Drs. Seuss and Atkins. Initially the idea was promoted by Robert Nobel, a real estate salesman and radio announcer who had also been ousted from the Townsend Plan organization in 1936. He was further inspired by the writings of the economist Irving Fisher, who argued that as part of a larger effort to fight the Depression, self-liquidating and stamped scrip might boost the velocity of money and thereby reinflate the economy. Dumbed down by Nobel, Fisher's program was converted into an economic cure-all, whose selling point was that it supposedly could provide $25 every Monday for Californians aged fifty or older. In 1937, Nobel propounded this idea in California mainly through radio broadcasts. As with the Townsend Plan, he formed an organization and requested that individuals join.[23] But Noble was soon ousted by the brothers Lawrence and Willis Allen, a lawyer and a salesman of hair tonic, respectively. They outbid Nobel by offering "$30 every Thursday"—which also provided a catchy slogan. Officially named the Retirement Life Payments Association, the organization's board consisted largely of ex-members of the Townsend Plan and EPIC. But soon the program and organization were dubbed "Ham and Eggs," a chant that had caught fire at rallies and apparently expressed the pensioner hopefuls' preferred but unaffordable breakfast.[24]

Ham and Eggs leaders claimed by the end of 1938 to have 270,000 members, who were expected to pay a penny a day in membership fees. With many other means of generating income previously perfected by the Townsend Plan, including pamphlets and lapel pins, $332,000 was supposedly generated that year. Despite its California-only base, Ham and Eggs now rivaled the national Townsend Plan in membership and outstripped it in revenue. Ham and Eggs leaders were able to secure a record-breaking number of signatures, some 789,000, on a petition to place a pension proposition on the November ballot. Sheridan Downey won the Democratic senatorial primary partly by jumping on the Ham and Eggs bandwagon. Culbert Olson, a state senator and former leader of End Poverty in California, won the Democratic nomination for governor with more equivocal support.[25]

Pension issues were thrust onto the ballots of eight states west of the Mississippi. In Oregon, for instance, Elbert Eastman, a former Townsendite, led a group that won a ballot line for the Citizens Retirement Annuity Bill, providing a maximum pension of $100 per month and financed by a 2 percent transactions tax. In Oklahoma, there was an initiative for $100 maximum pensions. In Arkansas, a group called the Old Age Security League placed on the ballot a proposal to pay up to $50 per month to all persons over age sixty with less than $50 per month of income, to be financed by sales and sin taxes. In other states, politicians rather than pension organizations led the drive for old-age benefits. In North Dakota, an initiative placed on the ballot by the Democratic and Nonpartisan League candidate for the Senate, Governor

William E. Langer, called for old-age pensions of $40 minimum per month. In Kansas, a Democrat was basing his gubernatorial campaign largely on pensions of $400 per year to anyone sixty years and older. In neighboring Nebraska, politicians were pressing a similar plan. In Minnesota, the Democratic nominee for governor was running partly on the basis of his support for a $40 pension. In Colorado, the National Annuity League, led by ex-Townsendite Otto Moore, was fighting a ballot initiative to repeal the state's generous old-age statute, which guaranteed an income of $45 per month and had been written into the state's constitution in 1936.[26]

The state-level pension challenges were spurred in 1938 for many of the same reasons the Townsend Plan was aided that year, but also by the fact that Old Age Assistance, the only program granting regular old-age benefits, had its parameters determined state by state. All states had programs, and almost all had unused capacity in their federal matching payments—giving pension proponents something tangible to fight for. Also, since the National Annuity League's victory in Colorado in 1936, it was clear that mobilizing in states could pay off—and very quickly in states with direct democratic devices like the initiative and the referendum.[27] Ham and Eggs and some of the other pension mobilizations were likely aided, too, by the setbacks of the Townsend Plan and its lack of attention to state-level pension politics. Its only state-level initiative was a quixotic measure on the Oregon ballot calling for a constitutional convention to write Townsend legislation into the Constitution.

Ham and Eggs faced vehement opposition. Business interests in the state did not like Ham and Eggs. Banks declared they would not, could not handle Ham and Eggs warrants. That summer President Roosevelt was aiming squarely at the organization, not the Townsend Plan, when he declared that there could be "no shortcuts to Utopia." Probably this was the first time the doctor agreed with the president. Townsend derided Ham and Eggs, arguing that only a national pension program would bring economic recovery. But Townsendites were often fervent supporters of Ham and Eggs, and on the ground in California, national representative John C. Cuneo counseled cooperation between the groups. The campaign was filled with bizarre incidents, including a bribery scandal exposed by a former Los Angeles police captain, a silent partner of the Allen brothers who had been convicted for an attempted car bombing. There were also curious moves, such as the Allen brothers' failure to secure an endorsement at the Democratic gubernatorial convention and their flirtation with the incumbent governor, Frank Merriam, who publicly opposed the initiative. These missteps invited speculation that the brothers were sabotaging the measure in order to squeeze more cash from their supporters in future campaigns. The Ham and Eggs measure fell short by only about 250,000 votes of about 2.5 million cast.[28]

There were some bright spots in the state-level pension campaigns. North Dakota's modest bid for $40 old-age pensions met with the approval of voters.

In Missouri the pension age was lowered from seventy years to sixty-five. The efforts of the National Annuity League to prevent the repeal of Colorado's pension law also proved successful. However, in Oregon, strong business opposition, aided by the Townsend Plan, brought a narrow defeat for its $100-per-month initiative. By contrast, the Townsend Plan–sponsored initiative in that state demanding a constitutional convention drew few opponents and passed. These contrasting results suggested that if the Townsend Plan had joined the effort for pension initiatives, they would have had a better chance of carrying.[29]

The congressional elections brought very good news for the Townsend Plan. About 60 percent of the approximately 250 House candidates it endorsed were victorious, and 14 endorsed senators were elected, too. Townsend Plan endorsees constituted the entire incoming House delegations of the states of Florida, Maine, Oregon, Arizona, Wyoming, North Dakota, South Dakota, Montana, and New Hampshire. Impressively large numbers of Townsend Plan–approved candidates were elected in Pennsylvania, Wisconsin, and Ohio. In Indiana, all six endorsed Republicans who opposed incumbent New Deal Democrats were victorious. Two targeted members of the House Ways and Means Committee also went down to defeat, and three Townsend-approved members of the committee were reelected.[30]

The Townsend Plan's responsibility for these victories is not obvious, however. Outside the South, the electorate swung to the Republicans, with about 100 new Republicans winning House races. This number was four times as large as the standard midterm loss of seats by the presidential party and was attributed mainly to the "recession," for which Democrats were blamed, and the party's dominance of House, which had put so many Democratic seats in play. Jeffery's Republican sympathies and Townsend's anger at the ruling Democrats meant that the endorsements that year mainly went to Republicans. And the Townsend Plan had fallen far short of gaining 20,000 Townsendites per congressional district, its goal in the Out to Win campaign, but the results appeared favorable and could be plausibly claimed as victories to the constituency and the press.

Open Season on "Social Security"

The new congressional pension advocates were not going to have the old-age policy stage entirely to themselves. One of the main outside spurs to the Townsend Plan and the pension movement in the states was that a debate on old age had already begun at the national level, mainly about the old-age annuity program. Known today simply as Social Security and revered as America's most popular and successful social program, in its first two years this program had become controversial. It was not really even a program in the standard sense. The term was the Social Security Board's way of linking the Social Security Act's Titles II and VIII, which dealt respectively with "federal old-age benefits" and employer and employee payroll taxes. These titles were separated at birth in the hope of preventing their nullification by the Supreme Court, and Congress repeatedly tried to delete both titles. The Republican Alf Landon had made them an issue in his 1936 presidential campaign, and Republicans saw political traction in denouncing the program. They sought to link the phrase "social security" with these unpopular provisions and hoped to convert it into a pejorative term, something like "welfare" today.[31]

Taking especially great heat were the payroll taxes—mainly from the political right. Organized business saw the tax as offensive chiefly because it was a big tax on businesses, and its rate was scheduled to increase automatically every three years. Despite the recession, on New Year's Day 1940 the tax rate would jump from 2 to 3 percent of payrolls. The Chamber of Commerce and the National Association of Manufacturers preferred that the tax be rolled back but demanded that the automatic increase be stopped. Republicans in both the House and Senate took up the cause, with Senator Arthur Vandenberg of Michigan turning the issue into a personal crusade. In February 1937 he introduced a resolution condemning the reserve fund. Vandenberg had some unlikely allies. Most New Deal liberals, organized labor, and others on the left criticized the payroll taxes because they were regressive. They took equally from low and high incomes, and there was a cap on the amount of income subject to the tax. Many pro–social insurance reformers also wanted old-age insurance to gain a third of its funding from general revenues, whose sources were more progressive and stable.[32]

Moderate social policy advocates and others more influential than the Townsend Plan on the political left had problems with the annuity program, too. One was that it was currently paying nothing. The most emphatic critics among Roosevelt administration officials were "spenders" advocating government deficits to end the recession; a program that might be putting money in the hands of consumers was doing the opposite. Moderate social insurance experts had concerns, too. Once benefits had begun, very modest checks would go only to individuals, and then only according to their previous incomes. Most potential beneficiaries, mainly men, thus faced the prospects of meager benefits and unmet family needs—especially aged wives and future widows—because the benefits did not take them into account. Abraham Epstein of the American Association for Social Security (AASS), whose flair for publicity and fund-raising gave his organization influence far out of proportion to its mom-and-pop nature, was demanding that the program be turned into social insurance, with adequate benefits for the lowest paid and the needs of families met.[33]

Other complaints, from all political directions, were due to the federal old-age program's peculiar combination of taxation and spending and how it was implicated in budgetary processes. In theory, the program was supposed to be generating a reserve fund, one that its critics often overestimated as reaching in 1980 the enormous sum of $47 billion, which was the entire national income of 1934 and a number that the press could not help reporting. Critics from the right feared that the prospects of such a surplus would spur further government expenditures, such as work projects, which had been stepped up during the recession. Yet the payroll tax revenues of Title VIII were being used to pay for current government expenditures, and so they were generating only IOUs. Herbert Hoover called the Roosevelt administration "immoral" for taxing workmen supposedly to secure their futures, while spending the revenue on current "extravagances." To the *New York Times* editorial page the whole process smacked of dishonesty, as administrators spoke as though the funds were being saved, even earning interest. Advocates for old-age insurance feared that spending the revenues might create pressure to reduce benefits in the future. Many, including Epstein's AASS and the Social Science Research Council, suggested that old-age insurance be put on something closer to a "pay-as-you-go" basis, with only a contingency reserve fund. One way to move in this direction was to advance the starting date for regular benefits.[34]

Remaking "Social Security"

The Social Security Board, the independent agency charged with administering the legislation, was hoping to convert the annuity program into a social insurance program and then make it the cornerstone of U.S. social policy. It was the best building block because, unlike unemployment compensation, the annuity program was wholly under the control of the national government. The board had been gathering payroll information on the 42 million employees taxed by the program; once these data were in hand, it would be relatively simple to provide coverage for additional risks to income, such as permanent disability, ill health, and outliving a breadwinning annuity recipient. And the board was in a position to do something about it, as it was also charged with suggesting improvements to the Social Security Act. But to turn the debate around, board members knew they would need to transform the old-age annuity program into something far more appealing.

The Social Security Board's planning for amendments began in earnest in 1937, once the Social Security Act was found constitutional by the Supreme Court. That fall Arthur Altmeyer, who had become chairman of the board, wrote a memo to the president suggesting the next steps. Partly in response to Senator Vandenberg's criticisms, however, the Senate Finance Committee had also appointed an Advisory Council on Social Security to address the federal old-age benefits and taxation titles of the act, and Altmeyer scrambled to gain control over it. The Advisory Council was to have twenty-five representatives of business, labor, and the public, and Altmeyer stacked the committee to be dominated by its thirteen "public" members, who mainly consisted of pro-administration social insurance experts. The public members included Edwin Witte, who had managed the deliberations of the Committee on Economic Security, and J. Douglas Brown, a Princeton economist, social insurance expert, and member of the original staff committee on old-age security, who served as chairman. This council was to receive technical support and recommendations from the board—whose representatives sat in on all the council's meetings.[35]

Altmeyer thought that old-age annuities might be improved in ways that would address the friendly criticisms and also wanted extensions of social insurance. He was hoping especially to add permanent disability as well as survivors' insurance. He also wanted to see a number of improvements in unemployment compensation, a program that was drifting out of the board's control, as it was being administered state by state. The boldest advance, not suggested by Altmeyer, would be to demand health insurance, which had been discussed but put aside by the Committee on Economic Security. Now the Interdepartmental Committee to Coordinate Health and Welfare Activities, a group set up by the CES, recommended health insurance. That summer the president also suggested that it was an idea whose time had come for the United States.[36]

When the Advisory Council reported on December 10, 1938, it followed the lead of the Social Security Board. It proposed to convert the annuity program into social insurance by increasing payments for retirees at the lowest end of the economic spectrum. Qualified retirees would also be provided a supplement, equal to half of the benefit, for wives reaching sixty-five years. In addition, survivors' insurance was proposed. Benefits would be added for the dependents of a qualified worker and to widows without dependent children upon their becoming sixty-five. In other ways, however, the council called for converting the program into something like an old-age pension—disconnected from payroll tax contributions. Retirement payments to "primary insurance beneficiaries" were proposed to begin in 1940 rather than 1942. The key change, however, was in the amounts they were to be paid. Benefits would be calculated by way of average earnings rather than cumulative earnings. The earliest cohorts of retirees would thus receive benefits based on what they made in the final years of paid work. The council justified these moves by saying they would improve the "public understanding" of social insurance. They would certainly increase public support—especially among those in their sixties and late fifties who would receive monthly checks for the rest of their lives in exchange for a few years' worth of nominal "contributions."[37]

The council also toed the Social Security Board's line on coverage and taxes. The 42 million being covered by Titles II and VIII constituted less than half of U.S. workers. To afford a firmer footing for the growth of social insurance, the council proposed that eventually all industries and workers be covered. For now it suggested that Congress act to include 12 million agricultural workers and domestic workers. Although there is no evidence that the council was paying attention to the National Urban League, this move was something that it had been advocating, as most African Americans were working in these fields.[38] The Advisory Council also agreed with moderate social insurance advocates that the program eventually should be funded in part by general revenues and with a contingency fund, but it argued that the next tax increase go forward, in opposition to demands by business organizations. The council dismissed the more heavy-handed critiques of the trust fund; even if the government were someday to run a surplus, the taxes would not linger in an account but would pay down the national debt.[39]

In short, the council advocated transforming a poorly supported government annuity program for individual wage earners into a social insurance program that would pool risks, provide more adequate payments for those with lower incomes, and address family needs. The shift was away from what feminist scholars of the welfare state would call an "individual" model, in which benefits went to those qualified through payroll taxes without regard to family situations, toward a "breadwinner" model, which addressed the entire family and assumed a traditional family division of labor with a male breadwinner. Under the employment circumstances of the era, however, the individual model was highly disadvantageous to women, as it was overwhelmingly men who were qualifying for public annuities. To help win support for the makeover, the council was willing to provide "unearned" pensionlike support to the first several cohorts of recipients.[40]

The Social Security Board followed three weeks later with its own recommendations, which unsurprisingly resembled the Advisory Council's on old-age and survivors' insurance. The board did not, however, make recommendations for disability insurance, and the speculation in the press that health insurance might be added proved unfounded. Despite the recent national agitation surrounding Old-Age Assistance, the board had little to say about it. It was mainly concerned that advances in OAA would come at the expense of social insurance and instead suggested greater support for poorer states, especially those in the South, to make more adequate OAA payments. This could be done through "variable" grants: higher federal payments for the first increments of benefits provided for OAA and smaller ones for higher benefits.[41] In the board's view, moreover, assistance programs were supposed to be for the needy only and proposed stricter means-testing regulations. It wanted to require states to consider all of an applicant's income and assets when determining eligibility for assistance.[42] When the president released the report in January, he referred front and center to the immediate "desirability of affording greater old-age security." He urged Congress to adopt the recommendations and to reject "untried and demonstrably unsound panaceas"—a slap at the resurgent Townsend Plan.[43]

Accounting for the Old-Age Proposals

A Senate study group and the Roosevelt administration had proposed major changes to America's approach to old-age security. But what accounts for the appearance and content of these proposals and their high place on the nation's political agenda? How much did pension mobilizations and the Townsend Plan have to do with all this? In what ways did their mobilization, collective action, or both, contribute to the rise of old age on the political agenda and the specific proposals? To answer these questions means surmising first what the administration would likely have done in the absence of the pension movement and its activities.

There seems little doubt that left to its own devices the Roosevelt administration in 1938 would have proposed some advances in social policy. Its programs had been ruled constitutional, the president retained overwhelming support in Congress, and his social policy still had many gaps. Without outside pressure the proposals doubtless would not have been confined to old-age security. The Social Security Board wanted disability insurance. Health insurance was being promoted by a cabinet-level committee and was desired by Roosevelt. Although this suggests strong influence by pension challengers, other political forces were demanding change in old-age policy. The Senate committee and Altmeyer's initial recommendations had been prompted by Republicans and organized business, which had been attacking the scheduled payroll tax increase well before the revival of the Townsend Plan and the rise of state-level pension challengers. The pressure from the right was augmented by administration "spenders." There seems little doubt, too, that old age was boosted farther up the administration's list of priorities by the results of the November elections. The Democrats suffered a loss of more than 100 seats in the House. Defeated, too, were most of the radical third-party House members. With this congressional alignment the administration could not plausibly set off in new directions on social policy, ruling out health or disability insurance.[44]

But had the Republicans, organized businesses, and administration critics been the only influential voices, it seems doubtful that there would have been as great an impetus toward improving the benefits in old-age annuities. Simply reducing the payroll tax would have served most of these groups well. Also, the one pro-spending result from the election had to do with the issue of old age. Pension advocates were pressing everywhere, and the Townsend Plan had committed many new House members, including Republicans, to enhance old-age benefits. And if augmenting established programs were the only possible way to go in social policy, the administration might have turned toward unemployment compensation, which was seen as a programmatic jumping-off point for temporary disability insurance. The fact that old-age benefits were so prominently on the table owed much to the pension movement.

As for the specifics, Altmeyer had written his memo at a time when the Townsend Plan was presumed dead and Ham and Eggs had not yet been hatched, so it is not surprising that the old-age proposals reflected the Social Security Board preference's for advancing social insurance and keeping assistance programs in their place. The proposals, however, were at least partly influenced by the Townsend Plan and other pension challengers—especially the provision of extensive "unearned" benefits, essentially senior citizens' pensions for covered workers closing in on sixty-five years. All old-age insurance programs tend to aid the earliest generations more, but this proposal erred far on the generous side for a cautious board that would have preferred to use the tax dollars for groups other than the aged. The board's proposing benefits for survivors happened before the pension movement revival and fell well short of the movement's demands. But the fact that adding survivors' benefits became politically viable was probably due to the pension movement with its call for benefits for both sexes. It seems likely, too, that the movement's influence was felt on the increase of the lowest insurance benefits. Although the administration's old-age proposal was closer in content to the demands of pro–social insurance critics like Abraham Epstein than those of the pension radicals, Epstein and others had made the same complaints during the deliberations over the Social Security Act and afterward, but they were ignored then. And the board was hoping to *reduce* the percentage the federal government paid in matching payments for OAA—to discourage high benefits—but the pension movement in the states made that politically impossible.[45]

If the old-age pension challengers helped to keep old-age benefits on the political agenda, move it to a top priority, and sweeten the proposals, what was it about these challengers that was influential? Was it their specific lines of political action or merely their large presence and potential for further action? Might they have done other things that were more influential? It seems clear that the sheer size and vigor of the organizing and mobilization was important. When Roosevelt declared that summer there could be no "shortcuts to Utopia," he was referring to Ham and Eggs and probably pension advocates in Oregon. Also, in the second half of 1938 the Townsend Plan broke new organizing ground in the Midwest and East, areas of the country that had not seen intense pension activity previously. As in 1934, when the Townsend Plan first appeared on the scene and pushed the security legislation in the direction of old age, it was the mobilization of the pension challengers in 1938 and the potential for yet greater mobilization and later electoral influence that mainly altered the administration's plans. The pension advocates demonstrated that the old-age issue remained of intense importance to a significant part of the electorate, one that the administration hoped to keep voting Democratic. One further question is why state-level mobilizations would prompt national legislation. The reason lay in the threat pension advocates posed in transforming Old-Age Assistance into something that the administration did not want: a plausible alternative, more liberal and generous, to social insurance for old age.

The Townsend Plan also played an important role in forcing the issue at the national level. Its aggressive electioneering probably did not swing many races, and some of its campaigns were counterproductive attacks on "traitors," like Crosby of Ohio, who remained advocates of senior citizens' pensions. But it put a great deal of effort in congressional campaigns, and a lot of the endorsed candidates won, making it seem as though old age was the one area of social policy with great prospects for advancement. The many new Republicans elected to the House at least partly beholden to the Townsend Plan provided more material to fashion a coalition behind old-age policy, which would not be the case for other existing programs, such as Aid to Dependent Children or unemployment compensation.[46]

In influencing the specifics of the administration proposals, the pension challengers as a group achieved what the Townsend Plan had done in 1934, when old age was previously on the political agenda. They induced the administration to press further ahead than it otherwise would have done with an alternative to pensions for all aged Americans. Because of the swing against Roosevelt and the Democrats and the establishment of the WPA, however, this time old age was going to be the focal point of social policy proposals. The social insurance approach was the preference of both the president and the administrative body that was running social insurance and assistance programs. Partly as a result of movement pressure, the administration planners sought the sort of advances and improvements long advocated by moderate social insurance advocates such as Abraham Epstein. In 1938, the pension challengers were not strong enough to get the administration to propose senior citizens' pensions—at least not yet.

Conclusion

The Townsend Plan was back, and as during its heyday the old-age pension movement was based mainly in the West. This time, however, the Townsend Plan did not dominate the pension movement, which included a variety of organizations and groups, most of which targeted state-level OAA programs. Ham and Eggs, led in part by former members of the Townsend Plan, was only the most notable. As these challengers emerged, the Townsend Plan was reborn, lifted by a back-to-basics organizing program that brought great gains in membership as well as a surprisingly effective campaign in the midterm elections.

The Townsend Plan and the pension mobilizations were spurred by the recession, which intensified the grievances of the aged and lent plausibility to pension-recovery programs as it discredited the New Deal. But the pension movement was also boosted greatly by the Roosevelt administration's approach to old-age security and the national debate that had broken out over it. Both the form of the programs and the disparity between the claims for the programs and their meager delivery mattered. State-level OAA programs gave challengers something to fight about. Most of them did not pay nearly the full $30 per month that the administration had advertised. The national old-age annuity program was criticized by Republicans, business organizations, and administration spenders for its high and routinely increasing payroll taxes. Business interests found the taxes to be excessive, and administration spenders considered them counterproductive. Moderate expert advocates like Epstein pointed out the gaps in the annuity-like nature of the program and demanded that it be converted to social insurance.

The old-age challengers advanced the issue. Radical critics, like the Townsend Plan, pointed out that much money was being collected for old age, but little was being paid to few. In response to the challengers, Washington old-age proposals became as focused on benefits as on taxes. And if the Roosevelt administration had any doubts about whether to address old age in the new Congress, they were dispelled as state-level challengers pressed initiative campaigns in the West, and the Townsend Plan made membership inroads in the East and Midwest. Once again, as in 1934, the old-age issue was already on the political agenda, and the administration turned to increased old-age benefits in the face of a powerful mobilization by groups demanding a radical alternative.

That the new Congress would have old-age programs as its highest social policy priority was due in large part to the fall campaigns by the pension movement. The state-level pension organizations upgraded OAA in a few states and came close to changing the nature of old-age support in a few others. The Townsend Plan had its first successful legislative campaign, as many of its endorsed members were elected to Congress. Most of these were Republicans, who might be subject to breaking their political party's usually negative line on social spending, but only on old age. Indeed, the Republican resurgence ensured that 1939 would not be like 1935, as reform opportunities would be narrowed. The administration demanded to convert its old-age annuity program into old-age insurance and to improve funding for states with the poorest OAA programs, but it had to put on the back burner other social policy reforms, such as for health insurance. What Congress would do with the administration's proposals and the radical alternatives posed by the Townsend Plan and others remained to be seen.

EIGHT

The Townsend Plan versus Social Security, Part 2

IN 1939, THE OLD-AGE issue moved from state capitals to the nation's capital, and the first order of business for the new Congress was to amend the Social Security Act. Attention returned to the Townsend Plan. The *New York Times Magazine* ran a story marking the rejuvenated organization's fifth anniversary and the doctor's seventy-second birthday.[1] Reporting the results of a public opinion poll taken on the eve of the congressional hearings, George Gallup declared that the Townsend Plan and the old-age pension movement were winning over the general public. In round two of its battle to transform the Social Security Act, the Townsend Plan would be far better prepared and have far more congressional support.

This time the Ways and Means Committee respectfully considered extensive testimony regarding the doctor's pension-recovery bill and similar proposals, rather than making fun of them. The committee even allowed a vote on the Townsend Plan–sponsored bill, and another pension proposal was voted on in the Senate. This time, moreover, Congress did not reduce what the administration proposed in the way of old-age benefits. Instead, Congress eagerly transformed old-age annuities into old-age and survivors' insurance—the precursor to Social Security as we know it today—and provided something like senior citizens' pensions for a group of retiring wage earners. Congress also boosted the amount that the federal government would match for Old-Age Assistance—despite the administration's resistance. But the Townsend pension bill did not pass.

These events suggest several questions. Why did the Townsend Plan's pension legislation, or something like it, again fail to become law? After all, the challenger had a great deal of support in Congress, other groups and individuals were also pushing for guaranteed pensions for all aged Americans, and the administration's old-age program was taking great heat from every political direction. As for what did become law, why did Congress this time go beyond what the administration requested in old-age benefits? To what extent were these legislative changes the result of the Townsend Plan and other old-age pension challengers? If the pension movement did influence the newly enacted increases in old-age benefits, what accounts for its effectiveness?

Open Hearings

Despite the loss of seats in Congress and an increasing concern with defense issues, as war brewed in Europe, the Roosevelt administration began 1939 with an active domestic agenda. It sought action on its so-called spend-lend bill, the centerpiece of its latest economic recovery efforts, which would have made $3 billion available for public works projects. The administration was fighting as well for full funding for its main social program, the Works Progress Administration. The administration also sought congressional support for a housing bill pushed by organized labor. Roosevelt's message to Congress on old age—in which he railed against "unsound panaceas"—was quickly followed by hearings in the House Ways and Means Committee. The Townsend Plan legislation—the bill written in 1936 by Arthur Johnson, now the head of the rival General Welfare Federation of America—was entered early. Johnson's organization had its own pension bill, as did some members of Congress.[2] All were to receive a hearing.

The Townsend legislation kept the committee busy for much of February. The Townsend Plan–sponsored expert witnesses included the credible Louis C. Silva, a former deputy tax commissioner of Hawaii, whom Townsend had recruited during the previous fall's fact-finding trip. But the other witnesses for HR 2 wilted under the interrogations of the Massachusetts congressmen John W. McCormack, a Democrat, and Allen T. Treadway, a Republican. The Townsend Plan's legislative representative, Otis J. Bouma, was unable to provide ballpark estimates of the revenues to be generated by the transactions taxes, was unaware whom exactly would be taxed, and was unsure even whether the bill upheld "Townsend-Plan principles." Dr. Townsend talked himself in circles explaining why he sought a constitutional convention if his legislation were already constitutional. He was goaded into agreeing that the transactions tax would eliminate the small businessman, dismissing him as "a useless appendage in the profit scheme."[3] Several unfriendly witnesses, including a series of economists, cast further doubt on HR 2. Although they testified that the bill's transactions tax might fund pensions of $30 to $60 per month for all Americans over sixty, they agreed that the transaction taxes were regressive, and that the amount of taxes required to provide $200 per month for 10 to 12 million aged Americans would slow economic activity. Abraham Epstein, of the American Association for Social Security, argued that if social spending were devoted mainly to the aged, they would suffer a backlash in public opinion. Arthur Johnson, of the General Welfare Federation of America, attacked Dr. Townsend as deceiving his followers with his promise of $200.[4]

Still, the Townsend Plan did not suffer the sort of overwhelming negative publicity that it had in 1935 and 1936—just the opposite. Townsend Plan witnesses were handled courteously by Democratic committee leaders. Bending over backward to aid them were the Minnesota Republican Harold Knut-son and Bertrand W. Gearhart, a California Republican and a Townsend club member representing the district of the state's national representative, John C. Cuneo. At the end of his appearance before the committee on February 17, Dr. Townsend for the first time expressed himself satisfied with his treatment by Congress. And before the hearings were finished, almost forty members of Congress had spoken in favor of the bill.[5]

The Ways and Means Committee entertained several other old-age proposals, including Johnson's HR 11. Since 1937, he had amended his bill, addressing many of the issues Congress found problematic. Johnson's bill employed a gross income tax and called for a minimum pension of $30 per month and a maximum of $60—much lower than the incendiary Townsend Plan maximum of $200. The tax was projected to generate enough revenue to provide pensions in the targeted range. Also, the bill provided no requirement to spend the money. The spending clause fired up die-hard Townsendites, as it partially justified the high pensions and granted them a key social role as re-covery agents, but it had been attacked by congressional opponents as being unenforceable and coercive. Like most others, Johnson estimated that pensioners would spend most of their money anyway, but Johnson made no extravagant claims guaranteeing economic recovery. The gross income tax also included a number of exemptions for small businesses. Johnson performed well, reassuring the committee that his legislation was moderate and work-able, that his organization was upstanding and accountable, and that he was no crackpot.[6]

Others offered different forms of old-age benefits or made other proposals to amend the Social Security Act. Wright Patman, the congressman who had led the charge for the early payment of the World War I veterans' bonus, was promoting a bill to provide a federal pension of $30 for almost all Americans sixty-five years of age and older—with no taxes offered. David Lasser of the Workers Alliance of America, an organization representing WPA workers, offered his own Sixty-at-Sixty pension plan—$60 per month for all over sixty years of age—also with no specific taxes. Epstein of the American Association for Social Security volunteered suggestions, including confining old-age insurance benefits only to those in need, but largely hailed the proposals of the Social Security Board. The board had finally come around to his way of thinking—to convert the old-age annuity program into a social insurance program, with higher minimum payments and support for dependents.[7]

One result of the intensified political attention to old age was that the general public was again quizzed about its views on the subject. Unlike the model proposed by the theorists of democratic representation, in which politicians take public opinion polls to find out what their constituents want and then act on it, in the 1930s polls were taken episodically, largely by private pollsters at the request of newspapers, and only when issues were already being considered.

In February, George Gallup published the results of a new poll on old-age policy—and, as always, his idiosyncratic interpretation of them. Sampling likely voters, Gallup found they favored governmental old-age benefits even more strongly than three years previously, with 94 percent indicating that they "believe in pensions," up from 89 percent in 1936. Gallup also found that the public's view of adequate old-age benefits remained similar to what it had been in 1936. The median desirable amounts named again were $40 for a single person and $60 for a couple. Unlike in 1936, however, this time Gallup noted that the Social Security Act fell far short of this aspiration. The desired sums were far larger than was currently being paid out by the most generous state OAA programs and about double the amounts that average wage earners were slated to gain through old-age insurance, even with the proposed upgrades.[8]

More surprising yet were Gallup's conclusions regarding the Townsend Plan and the pension movement. The headline in the *Sunday Washington Post*, which ran Gallup's syndicated column, spelled out his interpretation: "Political Strength of Pension Movement Growing." Having grossly underestimated the support for the Townsend-style pensions in 1936, Gallup now reported that one-fifth of the public favored the $200-per-month pensions of the Townsend Plan, dwarfing the 4 percent of 1936. This supposed leap in support was due chiefly to differences in question wording and estimation techniques, but Gallup's column gave the impression that many more Americans had come to support the Townsend Plan. Moreover, 87 percent of those naming the median $40 pension sum also said they were willing to pay a sales or income tax to fund those benefits—a result that suggested underlying support for pension legislation of the Townsend Plan and the General Welfare Federation. The pollster concluded that the pension issue would be "red hot" for the 1940 campaign.[9]

Having finished testifying, Townsend leaders pressed ahead with recruitment. With the New Year, the Townsend Plan had launched a new membership drive with the hypnotic slogan "Every Town a Townsend Town." Moreover, for the first time since the reorganization, Townsend Plan leaders mapped existing clubs by congressional district, attempting to pinpoint where the organization needed to fill gaps. The congressional hearings aided organizing efforts. The *Townsend National Weekly* ran extensive glowing testimony from the congressional supporters of HR 2 and eagerly reported Gallup's results. Its optimistic headlines—"Telling Blows Are Scored by All Witnesses" and "Expect Vote on HR 2 within 90 Days"—gave the impression that a successful recruitment drive would ensure the bill's passage. During the Every Town drive, new clubs formed at approximately the same rate as during Out to Win the previous fall, and the new drive produced more new clubs, about 1,000 with about 50,000 members in them. The existing clubs likely added a similar number of new members during the drive. Townsendites were encouraged to write the Ways and Means Committee to demand a vote on HR 2.[10]

Figure 8.1: Every Town a Townsend Town, Honor Club. The
Townsend Plan embarked on a successful recruitment drive in 1939
and awarded banners to clubs that had been instrumental in the drive,
such as the one pictured here. Author's collection, photographer
unknown.

In March the Ways and Means Committee turned to the proposals of the
Advisory Council on Social Security and the Social Security Board. J. Douglas Brown of the council made the case in favor but was quickly countered by
business interest groups concerned about increased coverage and the rise in
the payroll taxes. The Ways and Means Committee summarily dismissed the
proposal to cover farmers and domestic workers, with Congressman McCormack remarking that registering these workers would be excessively cumber-
some.[11] Mainly, however, business groups requested relief from the payroll tax
schedule. Walter D. Fuller, the representative of the National Association of
Manufacturers and a member of the Advisory Council, argued that they
should be frozen permanently, while Edwin Witte, a public representative of
the council, argued against delays, asserting that the costs of old-age insur-

ance were going to be far higher than initially anticipated and that there
would be less than half the $47 billion reserve fund claimed by critics.[12]

Before the committee could sort this out, Secretary of the Treasury Henry
Morgenthau preempted the debate, as he had during the deliberations over
the security act in 1935. In his first intervention, Morgenthau had demanded
a payroll tax schedule sufficiently steep to fund old-age insurance through
1980. This time he retreated on payroll taxes, making nice with organized
business and taking the advice of the deficit-spending advocates in his department. He proposed options to reduce or postpone the payroll tax increase
scheduled to take effect in 1940. Morgenthau was again backed by Roosevelt,
who also had changed his tune on payroll taxation, stating that only a contingency reserve fund of about $4 billion was necessary for old-age benefits. And
so reduced payroll taxes were going to be part of any administration-supported
bill.[13]

In April, Altmeyer tried to sell the Ways and Means Committee on the
board's recommended tranformations in old-age benefits. These proposals included the speeding up of payments, the addition of wives' and dependents'
benefits and survivors' insurance, and upping the minimum benefit from $10
per month to slightly more than $20. But the big winners would be the first
wave of retirees, whose monthly benefits would be greatly increased, as they
would now be calculated according to workers' average wages rather than their
cumulative wages. By the time he had stepped down, he and the Social Security Board were batting .333 with the Ways and Means Committee, which
seemed amenable to the proposed enhancements. However, it was not tipping
its hand on the board's proposal for Old-Age Assistance to be funded by "variable grants," which were designed for poorer and largely southern state governments to offer higher OAA benefits without increasing their contributions.[14]

Security Debate, Part II, Endgame

As the Ways and Means Committee spent the spring writing the provisions
of the Social Security Act amendments, the Democratic leadership in the
House devised a plan to smooth their passage. It would hold a record vote
on the Townsend Plan's HR 2.[15] The logic behind the gambit was compelling. The Democrats would meet the organization's demands and would
turn some of the heat of the Townsendites away from the Democrats. Some
25,000 letters had requested a vote on HR 2, and most were addressed to the
Ways and Means Committee chair. The Democrats would also be calling the
bluff of Townsend-endorsed Republicans. Many of them had agreed only to
demand a vote on the Townsend measure and would likely vote against such
an expensive bill if forced to show their cards. After the bill's likely overwhelming defeat, it would be implausible for Townsend Plan leaders to say,

Figure 8.2: "Hell, We Haven't Even Started Yet." The Townsend Plan viewed the House vote on its legislation as a positive sign and was defiant in the face of critics who claimed Congress had killed the legislation. A homemade sign over a feed store indicates the organization's line on the vote. Author's collection, photographer unknown.

as they had in 1935, that Congress did not consider a "true" Townsend bill. A big defeat would also disprove their overblown claims of support. Afterward, the Townsend-endorsed members of Congress would have to do something for their aged constituents—which is where the Democratic-led committee's amendments would come in.[16]

On June 1, the Ways and Means Committee took the unprecedented step of reporting out a Townsend bill without a recommendation, and the Rules Committee placed it on the calendar for debate. The House leaders agreed to a no-amendment rule requested by the Townsend Plan and four hours of debate. After two rewrites, Congressman Hendricks introduced the final version. Although some forty-three House members spoke in favor, others harshly attacked the bill. And because the debate was controlled by the chair of Ways and Means and its ranking Republican member, the concluding speeches were both negative. When roll was called, the bill went down 306 to 101, garnering about 50 fewer votes than knowledgeable insiders in the Townsend Plan leadership had hoped for. Townsend watched from the gallery, dejectedly, according to the newspapers. But the doctor expressed satisfaction with the result, declaring that the vote was the culmination of his challenge, and that the Townsend Plan had "just begun to fight"—a battle cry that soon echoed through the Townsend clubs.[17]

One reason the Townsend Plan leadership wanted a vote on the record was to separate the sincere Townsend-endorsed House members from the deceitful. The bill received most of its votes, fifty-five altogether, from Republicans, capturing more than a third of their House delegation. Most of the Democratic support came from "left-wing New Dealers," according to Arthur Krock of the New York Times. Some eighteen unendorsed Democrats supported the bill, as opposed to eight unendorsed Republicans, with these accounting for more than one-fourth of the bill's supporters. But the Townsend Plan had endorsed many more Republicans than Democrats, and the Townsend-endorsed Republicans voted in favor of the bill at a lower rate than did Townsend-endorsed Democrats. Given the Townsend tilt toward Republicans, they accounted for more than three-fourths of the fifty-nine "betrayers," "turncoats," "traitors," and "double-crossers," as the Townsend Plan was now denouncing them.[18]

Those who won with Townsend support but who could not bring themselves to vote for the Townsend bill were now looking to do something to repay their electoral debts to the aged. The Democratic leaders were eager to help. The Ways and Means Committee placed its bill before the House, with all the new benefits suggested by the Social Security Board. On Old-Age Assistance, however, the committee had gone its own way, rejecting the board's proposed "variable grants" to aid the poorer and less generous states. Instead it opted to raise the federal matching payment to $20, a provision of interest chiefly to the more generous states. Washington observers attributed this move to the committee's desire to redirect pressure from pension groups from itself to the states. In a less publicized move, however, the committee agreed to new Social Security Board–proposed means-testing requirements designed to rein in the liberality of some OAA programs, such as California's, which had allowed the aged to keep up to $15 per month of income in addition to OAA benefits. The committee also opted for the most forgiving of Morgenthau's options for payroll taxes, a rate freeze until 1943. This move was voted unanimously, with the Republicans on the committee pointing to this as the signal achievement of the bill, and the House passed it overwhelmingly. The Senate Finance Committee largely concurred with the House's handiwork.[19]

On the Senate floor, battles were rejoined. With the support of majority leader Alben Barkley of Kentucky, Senator Tom Connally of Texas proposed both a variable grant and a higher matching limit: the federal government would pay a two-to-one match for the first $15 of monthly benefits for an OAA recipient, and a one-to-one match up to $40 in benefits after that. It passed, 43 to 35, largely along party lines. The Townsend Plan's point of view was represented mainly by Senators Sheridan Downey of California and Claude Pepper of Florida, both of whom proposed pension amendments. Pepper's proposal seemed as if it were taken straight from Gallup's opinion poll: a $40 federal pension for individuals and $60 for couples, based on need. Because it was expected to go down to an overwhelming defeat, however, Pepper dropped it. An amendment by Senator Josh Lee of Oklahoma for $40 pensions for all over sixty failed 56 to 17. Downey made a motion to recommit the legislation so that the Finance Committee might write a pension bill on the Townsend Plan model, but he lost 47 to 18, and the Senate agreed to the bill by the lopsided margin of 56 to 8. After much squabbling Connally's amendment was quashed by House conferees. The conference committee's bill passed on the last day of the session, and President Roosevelt signed it on August 10.[20]

The legislation provided a much greater commitment to old-age benefits. The old-age annuity program was transformed into a fledgling old-age and survivors' insurance program, and the individual wage earner model was replaced with a family breadwinner model. Yet the way benefits were upgraded also meant that the program would stray far from insurance for the earliest cohorts of new beneficiaries. They would gain benefits not because they had "earned" them through payroll tax "contributions" but because they were sixty-five years old or close to it and fortunate enough to have worked in a covered industry. The sums were not nearly the $40 per month or more demanded by pension advocates, but the checks would be pensionlike in their automatic delivery to recipients because they were American citizens who had reached retirement age. Their good luck would be passed along to their dependents and survivors.

The Impact of the Townsend Plan and the Pension Movement

With this background I can better specify the questions from the beginning of the chapter. Why did the Ways and Means Committee legislation, with its emphasis on old-age insurance, its tax cuts, and its continued encouragement of Old-Age Assistance, pass instead of the Townsend Plan bill? After all, perhaps a million Americans were mobilized behind the pension idea, and $40 pensions were supported by the general public, but very few Americans even understood old-age insurance. Did the Townsend Plan and other old-age pension mobilizations influence the content of the new old-age legislation and its adoption? If so, what parts of the process were influenced? And what was it about the mobilization or collective action of these groups that proved influential? Can this episode of policy making help sort out debates about why social movements have impacts on social policy?

To take the easiest question first, the Townsend legislation lost in 1939 for some of the same reasons that Townsend legislation lost in 1935. It was not, as we have seen, that public opinion was dead set against the latest Townsend bill. Still, the pension legislation remained expensive. According to most reliable estimates, it would have almost doubled the amount of revenue being brought in by the national government. To pass such a fiscally consequential program would have required far greater congressional backing than the Townsend Plan had thus far rallied behind it. Despite gains in organizing and breakthroughs in the Midwest and East, the Townsend Plan was not represented well enough in these regions to influence their representatives. Even if the proponents of the General Welfare Federation and the Townsend Plan had been able to join forces, it remains doubtful that any pension bill would have passed. Members of Congress in favor of old-age pensions had formed something of an alliance without them. Many spoke in favor of each group's legislation, and many General Welfare Federation supporters, such as Voorhis of California, voted for the Townsend legislation anyway. But there were not enough of them.

The U.S. political system is an imposing gauntlet to run for any legislative initiative, like the Townsend Plan's, not approved by the administration or the party holding congressional power. The pension bill needed to pass the Democratic-dominated Ways and Means Committee, gain a favorable rule from the Democratic-dominated Rules Committee, and then pass the Democratic-dominated House. It was able to negotiate these first two obstacles only because the Democratic leadership gave the legislation a courtesy pass for strategic reasons, knowing that it had no chance to get past the third. Had the Townsend legislation somehow been adopted by the House, it would in any case have encountered the Senate, which had its own committees. Had it got past them, the bill would have to accumulate so much support on the Senate floor that it could overcome a possible filibuster. Then there was the likelihood of a veto from the president—and the two-third majorities in Congress needed to override. The Townsend Plan would need to generate far more support than it had thus far gained to clear all these hurdles.

Another reason for the failure of the legislation had to do with the party in power and its policies. Under Roosevelt, the Democratic Party, outside the South, had adopted a far more favorable approach to social spending. But the Roosevelt administration had developed both a distinctive approach to old-age benefits and a disinclination to alter it radically. Its policy, which now had four years under its belt, had achieved significant bureaucratic and political momentum. More important, the Democrats' approach to old age had a saving if inadvertent flexibility that advantaged it over the pension alternatives. The program's relentless schedule of payroll tax increases through Title VIII of the Social Security Act and its confusing reserve fund provided extensive fiscal and discursive resources that could be exploited by both the opponents of the taxes and the supporters of social insurance. Because the program could be portrayed as "running a surplus"—the only real possibility in its first years—and because tax increases would have happened without new legislation, businesses could be granted a tax delay that had the political impact of a tax cut. Also, because of this accounting surplus, old-age benefits could be speeded up, increased, and extended to new groups of recipients without the standard negative fiscal ramifications, despite current budgetary deficits. Old-Age Assistance also had a formula that was easy to manipulate and could be used as a political safety valve. Pressure for greater benefits could be released by allocating additional money to the states, dispersing the force of pension groups.

To address the issue of influence, it is worth dividing the legislative process into agenda setting, the content of proposals, and their passage into law. As we have seen, the old-age issue was placed back on the political agenda mainly by the administration and other political forces, which were especially interested in slowing the payroll tax for the old-age annuity program. Still, the mobilization of pension challengers around the country and the Townsend Plan revival ensured that old age would remain on the agenda and that the discussion would be a wider one that would address benefits as well as taxes. Also, the administration's decision to speed and raise the benefits through old-age insurance, providing windfalls for "covered" workers on the verge of retirement, seemed to have been proposed with the pension movement in mind, as this move worked against all ideas of insurance previously promoted by the administration. The fact that old age was being addressed rather than health or disability suggested the further impact of the pension movement.

The Townsend Plan and other old-age pension challengers had only minor influence over some of the changes by the administration and Congress in the content of the old-age proposals of the Social Security Board. The board was undercut by the Treasury Department and the president, both of whom called for payroll tax relief, and Congress dismissed the board's suggestion for greater coverage. The Townsend Plan may have also stiffened the resolve of the committee not to cover farmworkers under old-age insurance, as the administrative difficulty of taxing farmers seemed to be one of the rhetorical blows easily landed against wider pension legislation. Claims by congressional proponents of old-age pensions that sales taxes might just as easily as payroll taxes be understood as "contributions" giving citizens an earned right to pensions in their old age may have weakened the rhetorical link posited by the security board and their allies between payroll taxes and insurance benefits and reduced committee support for the payroll taxes. But their efforts here probably did not have nearly as much influence as the pounding of business groups and the inside critiques of administration spenders against the automatic extension of payroll taxes.

On benefits, the pension movement had greater influence. Although the hearings over pension alternatives served mainly as a warm-up act for the advisory council's and Social Security Board's proposals, the threat that the pension movement's expensive bills posed to members of Congress had some impact. Many members of the House expressed support for senior citizens' pensions. This in turn likely softened up the Ways and Means Committee, making it more receptive to the new, responsible-seeming benefits proposed by the board and moderate social insurance experts. In 1935, when pension alternatives had little congressional support, the committee had reduced the administration's proposed old-age benefits. In 1939, the committee also upped the matching payments for Old-Age Assistance, something the administration and the Social Security Board did not want. Journalists attributed that to the influence of pension movements in general and the Townsend Plan in particular, and there seems little reason to dispute them. Attempting to convince the Senate to drop the increase to $20 per month per OAA beneficiary in the matching payment, Abraham Epstein underscored this interpretation and argued that the move would not buy off the pension movement: "If you . . . raise the Federal grant to $20 . . . they will say 'It is Dr. Townsend that did the job,' and the Dr. Townsend movement will grow." But the Senate kept the increase just the same.[21]

It seems likely that the Townsend Plan and pension mobilizations aided the passage of the old-age legislation, too, for the old-age amendments passed very easily while other administration-proposed advances in social policy struggled or failed. Roosevelt's $3 billion spending-lending bill was killed in the House along with his $800 million housing bill. Both had been labeled "must" legislation by the administration. During the first session of the Seventy-sixth Congress, the legislative balance sheet for the administration was equally weighted with wins and losses, a fine record when taken in historical perspective, but Roosevelt's worst according to the *New York Times*. The old-age bill had the advantage of including a large tax cut. But without the Townsend Plan and the other pension challengers, it is likely that the benefits part of the old-age legislation would have stalled, given the Republican resurgence and their alliances with southern Democrats against social policy advances in the House, which was becoming a graveyard for social legislation.[22]

If the pension movement had these effects, what about it made it so influential? The old-age issue's presence on the political agenda was important, for in the previous three years Congress and the Roosevelt administration had refused to budge on old age, and the Townsend Plan and other pension advocates got nowhere despite sometimes great support. Now the Townsend Plan and other pension challengers did not have to do much aside from mobilizing to exert additional influence. Some of the influence of the pension movement as a whole had to do with the geographic pattern of organization and mobilization. There was division of organizing labor. The newer pension challengers were rekindling interest in areas of the West that the Townsend Plan had already shown to be susceptible to pension activism. In the meantime, Townsend organizers made some inroads in the more treacherous political terrain of the Midwest and East, where pension support had never been strong. Congress in 1939 thus had to contend with a pension movement that was better mobilized than in 1935 and more widespread.

A more difficult task is to sort out the influence of the Townsend Plan from other pension challengers and what the Townsend Plan did, aside from running club and membership drives, that influenced the policy-making process. Unlike the pension challengers in the states, the Townsend Plan was active in national politics, being the only mass-based national pension organization in the field. And there is evidence that the actions of national pension organizations influenced how the old-age issue was handled in Congress. If the administration and Congress were reacting to the mobilization alone, however, one would have expected results similar to the cutbacks of 1935—which may have been more even likely in 1939 given all the new Republicans in Congress and their dislike of the New Deal and its social policy initiatives. The Townsend Plan's testimony during the hearings probably had little impact on old-age benefit, as it again failed in defending its legislation. And the Townsend Plan again remained aloof to the administration's and Ways and Means Committee's legislation.

But the Townsend Plan's approach did have indirect results on the content of legislation this round. On the negative side, the Social Security Board managed to slip greater means-testing regulations for OAA through Congress—which might have been stopped by the Townsend Plan, if it had it cared, or, say, by the Colorado-based National Annuity League, if it had a national presence. On the positive side, for all their scrambling to write a bill, there was no question that this time the Townsend legislation was much better drafted and posed a far more plausible alternative than the McGroarty bill of 1935. Here, too, there was a wider effect of the pension challenge, as the expert-based General Welfare Federation had an even more plausible bill and witnesses. And despite the bad blood between the groups, the Townsend Plan leadership did not revisit its scorched-earth policy toward other old-age proposals and their supporters. So if the Townsend Plan ignored the negotiations over the improvements in administration-proposed old-age programs, it did not undermine the pressure that it was turning in that direction.

More important to boosting benefits, however, was the Townsend Plan's aggressive action in the previous congressional elections. Although victorious Townsend Plan endorsees constituted only about a third of the new House, and when push came to shove many of them defected from voting for the Townsend Plan's legislation, there were plenty of representatives available to provide credible witnesses for the Ways and Means Committee and a baseline of support for pension legislation. A large group of legislators felt in debt to the Townsend Plan and saw it, or at least the politically active aged, as crucial to their futures. This not only helped to move old age up on the administration's social policy agenda but also helped to induce the Ways and Means Committee to sweeten old-age benefits.

Taken together, mobilizing membership, having made extensive successful congressional endorsements, and providing a plausible legislative alternative also pushed the administration's old-age proposals toward final passage. Because the Townsend bill was workable, many members of Congress were ready from the start to support it. The organization's letter-writing campaign for a record vote, a more respectful approach than was taken in 1935, made the Ways and Means Committee more accepting of the tactic to report out the legislation. Being implicated in these maneuvers was not a sign of weakness for the Townsend Plan, for the Democrats helped to crystallize the bloc of support for the pension legislation and increased the chance that it might substitute for the administration-supported old-age programs. The failure of the Townsend bill also left the Townsend-endorsed House members seeking to do something to aid their aged constituencies. Also, to redirect the political heat of the pension movement, Congress became more eager to upgrade Old-Age Assistance. Even if the Democrats had not called for a vote on the Townsend bill, the campaign that brought congressional support for it would have remained a buoyant force. The number of Republicans needing to do something for their aged constituencies was great, and the Democratic legislation was the only bill with a chance to pass. But had the expert-heavy General Welfare Federation been working alone, in the absence of a wider pension movement, it seems doubtful that there would have been a vote on a pension bill or much advancement of administration proposals.

As before, however, the impact of the Townsend Plan was partly predicated on the political situation. Two aspects of it were crucial. The administration and other forces had placed the old-age issue on the agenda—making it possible for the challenger to press its alternative and in that way to exert influence. Also, there was the overall favorable alignment for social policy change. Although the Democratic forces in Congress had taken a blow in the previous election, and conservatives of both parties were beginning to coordinate their efforts against the New Deal, the Democratic margin was still high there, and it remained overwhelming in the Senate. In a more closely divided Congress, a bloc of pro-old-age Republicans mattered, providing a potential swing vote for old-age benefits that was not available for other social initiatives, such as disability insurance, new housing projects, or the spend-lend bill.

Great as the changes in old-age policy were, the Townsend Plan, along with the General Welfare Federation of America and sympathetic legislators, was going to continue to demand that Old-Age Assistance and Old-Age and Survivors Insurance (OASI) be transformed again—into senior citizens' pensions. It was no pipe dream. Edwin Witte, a champion of the old-age insurance program, warned in the *New York Times* that the administration's approach to old age was "still in very grave danger of being scrapped within the next few years" in favor of pensions on the Townsend model.[23]

Townsend Plan Resurgence

While Congress was completing its business, the Townsend Plan was making the final preparations for its first truly national meeting in three years, the Fourth Annual National Convention of Townsend Clubs, scheduled for late June in Indianapolis and with the catchy if overoptimistic slogan "It's Townsend Time in '39." More important, right after the convention the Townsend Plan initiated its Townsend Trailblazer League campaign, an organizing spree targeted at the congressional double-crossers. In an analysis of the vote for its pension bill, Jeffery noted that many of the betrayers came from the Midwest and Northeast. Pennsylvania, Michigan, and Illinois alone accounted for twenty-four of them. His view was that these states and others were not covered well enough with Townsend clubs, and that endorsements in these sections ran somewhat ahead of the plan's organizing achievements in them.[24] Organizer posses were dispatched. One district each was targeted in Illinois, Ohio, and Pennsylvania—the states with the most betrayers—as well as in Indiana, Wisconsin, New York, and Vermont.[25]

The Townsend Plan was verifying Epstein's prophecy that the new old-age benefits would give it a boost. This time, too, the Townsend Plan took credit for them, while insisting they were not nearly generous enough. The Trailblazer campaign was very productive and even more successful than the Every Town a Townsend Town campaign that it replaced. The organizing gains were almost a replay of 1935, when the Townsend Plan took off after the passage of the Social Security Act. The publicity over the new old-age programs and their continued inability quickly to make good on their promises once again helped to drive the elderly into Townsend clubs. Once again there were "national representatives," similar to the state area organizers of four years earlier, covering all states but four southern ones. The Townsend Plan was finally making great inroads in the Northeast and the eastern part of the Midwest. In September the leaders in the formation of new clubs were, respectively, Pennsylvania, Indiana, Illinois, New York, and Michigan. According to Baxter Rankine, the new director of organization, in July and August as many clubs were organized as during the six months of the Every Town campaign. The pace of organization was quickening as the year ended. In the second half of the year almost 2,500 new Townsend clubs had been organized, increasing the number of Townsendites by more than 100,000.[26]

Unfortunately for the Townsend Plan, 1940 was also starting as something

Figure 8.3: Trailblazers League Speakers. The Townsend Plan created the Trailblazers League in 1939 to sanction those members of the House who had run with the support of the organization, but who voted against its legislation, by organizing clubs in their districts and supporting their opponents. Author's collection, photographer unknown.

like a replay of 1936, though without the congressional investigation. Old age was again off the political agenda, as the Roosevelt administration and Democratic leaders decided to wait for the reaction to its latest old-age legislation. They hoped that the immediate provision of old-age "insurance" benefits to some new retirees would take a little of the steam out of the old-age issue and that the new matching limit for OAA would redirect pressure for adequate benefits to the state level. The Townsend Plan had a new, revised bill. Based on its experiences in the previous Congress, this effort now included a gross income tax with generous exemptions for small businesses. But this time it was unable to get the committee to report it out. In response the Townsend Plan sought the signatures of House members on a discharge petition, which required a majority of the House, to release the bill to the floor.

As the year went on, approximately 175 members of the House signed, but the petition still came up short.[27]

In 1940, Townsend still despised Roosevelt and wanted to stop his bid for a third term, flirting again with a third party before calling on Townsendites to support Roosevelt's Republican opponent, Wendell Willkie. However, the Townsend Plan managed to avoid the worst of its mistakes in the 1936 campaign, with Townsend being talked down from going on a vendetta. Instead, the organization sought to build on its congressional support for pensions and focused largely on races in the House of Representatives. For legal purposes the Townsend Plan created the Townsend Legislative League,[28] which sought to gain commitments from incumbents and candidates for the new Townsend pension bill, and Jeffery once again handled the selections. He tapped the vast majority of the 101 "immortals," in the glorifying words of the *Weekly*, who had voted for the 1939 Townsend legislation. Targeted for defeat were many of the "double-crossers" and "traitors." As in 1938, most of Jeffery's selections were Republicans, given his and the doctor's preferences and the fact that Republicans constituted a majority of the supporters of the bill. But the Democratic backers of the bill were also being supported, as were some new Democratic challengers. Jeffery had noted that one-third of the votes in favor of the bill had come from first-term House members endorsed by the Townsend Plan, making him think it was worth the risk to back challengers regardless of party affiliation. In the end, the Townsend-endorsed House members that were elected numbered 132, slightly fewer than for the previous Congress. But fewer had been endorsed, and the winners would likely be more reliable.[29]

The Impact of Pension Movements in the States

Not all legislative action on old-age policy was taking place in Washington. State-level initiatives by pension advocates in 1938 forced the issue onto the legislative agenda of state after state, including the entire Northwest, during the 1939 sessions. Nowhere was the activity greater than in California, where the recently failed Ham and Eggs initiative helped to restart the legislative process. Although the legislature rejected a bid to increase old-age benefits from $40 to $50, it authorized counties to drop liens on beneficiaries' property and reduced the conditions under which relatives would be held financially responsible for the aged. The legislation, signed by the Democrat and former EPIC leader Culbert Olson, who had beaten the Republican Frank Merriam in the 1938 race for governor, brought greater liberality to a law that was already paying out more in benefits than the federal government would match. The legislature also passed two memorials demanding national old-age pensions.[30]

Ham and Eggs also was on the move, having forged an agreement with Governor Olson, who was supported by the group, to have its initiative voted on again in 1939. Its organizational efforts were led by George McLain, who placed Ham and Eggs officials in each precinct. The group gained 1.1 million signatures on a petition for its initiative, a tally that almost equaled the votes it had received the previous year. Ham and Eggs leaders requested a special election for August, and it seemed as though its measure might be approved, after Ham and Eggs packed the Shrine Auditorium with 8,000 supporters that summer. But Olson reneged on the deal to hold an early election, delaying the measure until election day in November and then speaking against the proposal. Moreover, the organization's proposition now incorporated several unappealing features, including sales taxes, a reorganization of the banking system, and an administrator with tremendous powers—to be chosen from among Ham and Eggs leaders. These taxes and the naked power grab drew great opposition across the political spectrum. Furthermore, this time the Ham and Eggs initiative was not accompanied by an antipicketing proposition, further reducing the possibilities for a coalition with labor. In the end, the Thirty Every Thursday proposition won only a third of the votes, losing by nearly a million. Ham and Eggs tried to recall Olson, but it failed in that and in getting another proposition on the ballot for the following year.[31]

Chastened by the dominance of Ham and Eggs in its home state, the Townsend Plan took action in California in 1939. The Townsendites took aim at the enforcement of lien and "encumbrance" provisions for old-age benefits. Under the law, counties could take out liens on the property of old-age beneficiaries, in order to recoup funds from their estates, and now had latitude in making them sign agreements not to encumber or transfer their property. Hundreds of beneficiaries dropped off the OAA rolls to avoid losing control of their homes; other potential beneficiaries chose not to apply. In response, Townsend clubs marched on county boards in Los Angeles and San Francisco, which were enforcing these provisions. This line of collective action was designed to uphold the Townsend Plan's view that old-age benefits should be provided as a right to senior citizens, as pensions, rather than as a pauper's dole. In Los Angeles, the county board relented, but administrative rulings jeopardized the county's funding. The Townsend Plan for the first time dispatched lobbyists, led by the national representative Cuneo, to the state capital, to press on these and other old-age issues.[32]

In 1940, the Townsend Plan sought initiatives to amend the California constitution to release OAA recipients from liens and outlaw encumbrance provisions, as well as to make sweeping changes in California's OAA program. Its initiative for upgrading OAA benefits did not make the ballot, but this campaign and the Townsend Plan's pressure on the county boards helped to gain political support for ballot measures to prevent counties from controlling the property of OAA beneficiaries. At the start of the legislative session

Governor Olson asked for constitutional amendments to repeal the lien and encumbrance provisions—despite the fact that he had previously stated that he was hoping to avoid old-age issues. These measures passed easily, even though almost all of Olson's "New Deal for California," a mix of Rooseveltian reform and EPIC-style production-for-use ideas, was dismissed by a conservative state legislature. Support for the initiatives was mobilized through the *Townsend National Weekly*, and in November two propositions to repeal liens passed by a more than half a million votes each.[33]

California's pension movement activity was unusually extensive, but challenges over the nature of OAA programs across the country continued, and less dramatic changes occurred in a series of states, Ohio being the most publicized, with pension mobilizations. The influence of the failed pension drives and their aftermath often resulted in higher old-age benefits, even among the twenty-four states that were similar in being in the open part of the polity. These states had relatively high benefits, approximately $21 per OAA beneficiary in 1938. By 1940, however, the seven states with pension-related propositions on the ballot had increased their average monthly benefit by $2.34. In the seventeen states without ballot propositions, the average benefit increased only 36 cents. Having a proposition on the ballot was worth about $2 a month for each OAA recipient—about a 10 percent increase.[34]

The increase in the matching amount for OAA approved by Congress placed the old-age issue back on the political agenda of the states with generous programs and strong pension challengers. Pension movements were going to continue to try to up OAA benefits and turn the program into something like an unrestricted pension. They would be up against fiscal conservatives and antitax forces in each state. They also would have to contend with the Social Security Board, which was going to try to enforce the stricter means-testing standards for OAA, in the hope that its new Old-Age and Survivors Insurance program would become the dominant form of public social provision for old age.

Conclusion

As the new decade began, America had intensified its commitment to its elderly. The "federal old-age benefits" program, which had begun life as a public annuity for the distant future, was converted into a combination of a social insurance program and an unrestricted pension to new retirees. This hybrid Old-Age and Survivors Insurance provided a limited version of what the old-age pension movement was calling for: unrestricted old-age pensions. Those who were both soon to be retired and lucky enough to have been working in a covered industry were now receiving benefits because they were aged and retiring, not because they made lifelong "contributions" through payroll taxes.

Although the program's benefits fell far short of providing the generous support demanded by the pension movement, OASI also now provided larger payments to recipients with the lowest incomes, reducing benefits for those at the highest end of the income range. It paid benefits according to a recipient's dependents and to his survivors as well. Congress also added to the matching formula for Old-Age Assistance, the workhorse program that was providing most of America's aid to the aged, allowing the more generous states to pay higher benefits.

Although the Townsend Plan did not get what it wanted—the passage of its pension-recovery legislation—it and the wider pension movement had a key influence on these advances in old-age benefits. The support behind the Townsend Plan and the pension movement helped to influence Congress to augment the administration's proposed old-age benefits and then pass them into law. The Townsend Plan had become the embodiment in Washington of the nationwide pension movement. Its impact came not through its arguments for its legislation, which were mainly unconvincing, or for its engagement with the administration's legislation, which it mainly ignored, but through its organizing, its congressional endorsement strategy, and the live threat that its pension alternative posed to the administration's approach to old-age policy. It helped, too, that other pension groups had plausible bills before Congress. Both the mobilization of the Townsend Plan and the wider pension movement and the Townsend Plan's political action mattered.

The Townsend Plan's mobilization and strategies fit well with the political situation in 1939 for expanding old-age policy—much better than its efforts had in 1935. As in 1935, in 1939 the administration and Congress had placed old age back on the political agenda. This greatly increased the possibilities of exerting influence. Also, this time the political alignment was only marginally favorable for social policy generally, as 100 new Republicans were added to the House. Because of the Townsend Plan's electoral action in 1938, however, a bloc of Republican congressmen were ready to support action on old age, while not being keen to support other parts of the administration's expensive social agenda. Many Townsend-endorsed congressmen reneged on their support for the organization's legislation when it came to a vote, but they needed to do something for their aged constituents. This left the administration's old-age legislation, which passed easily while other New Deal social legislation stalled. The electoral pressure placed by the Townsend Plan induced Congress to add greater benefits to Old-Age Assistance—against the recommendations of the Social Security Board. The fact that old age was on the political agenda mattered. The Townsend Plan was better mobilized after the enactment of the new legislation, and the congressional alignment was the same in 1940, but the old-age issue was back off the national agenda, minimizing the pension movement's possibilities for influence. Nothing happened.

By the end of 1940, U.S. old-age policy remained unsettled. The increase in matching funds for Old Age Assistance ensured that it would remain a programmatic competitor to Old-Age and Survivors Insurance, which the Social Security Board saw as the first line of defense in old-age policy. The fact remained that states with the political will and financial resources could provide OAA payments to the vast majority of the aged who were ineligible for OASI. And these states could provide almost double the payments available to most of the new recipients of OASI benefits. Moreover, Congress also delayed payroll taxes for OASI and refused to cover new classes of wage earners. These moves undercut both the funding and the potential base of support for the program; only half of the workforce was covered, and few were receiving benefits. The increased payments to those who had made minimal "contributions" through payroll taxes similarly undercut the insurance imagery with which the Social Security Board was selling the program.

The Townsend Plan and the pension movement exerted their greatest influence yet over national policy in 1939 and were becoming better organized as the 1940 elections approached. With the pension organizations on the offensive at both the national and state levels of government, it seemed possible that the 1940s would see the replacement of the fledgling U.S. old-age assistance and insurance programs with senior citizens' pensions. But the pension movement was chasing a policy target that was moving away from it and getting stronger, too. Both old-age programs of the Social Security Act were becoming institutionalized and better established. As more and more of the aged received benefits, due in no small part to the efforts of the pension movement, and as more old-age policy supporters in the general public thought that the benefits were approaching adequacy, the more difficult it would be to transform the U.S. approach to old age, with its double base of assistance and social insurance. Aged Americans were having their political interests and allegiances transformed as recipients of one or another old-age program, or both.

NINE

The Elusive Double Victory

AFTER FIVE YEARS OF CONTENTION, the Townsend Plan had finally won a vote on a pension bill. Congress increased the matching amounts for Old-Age Assistance, revamped old-age insurance and sped up the payments for it, and granted pensions to some older Americans by grandfathering them into old-age insurance. Journalists attributed these advances to pressure from the pension movement. Pension activists had even higher hopes for the 1940s. Public opinion polls indicated growing sentiment for universal old-age pensions. President Roosevelt floated the idea of providing a minimum pension for all aged Americans and won an unprecedented third term. The 1940 elections also returned a large Townsend Plan bloc to Congress, and the old-age issue returned to the congressional agenda in 1941. It seemed only a matter of time before pensions for all aged Americans became law.

But then the roof fell in on the senior citizens' pension movement. By the end of the year the United States had been bombed into World War II. The war effort preempted domestic policy, and massive military expenditures apparently accomplished what all the New Deal programs could not. The Great Depression was history. The pension movement focused on old-age poverty that persisted despite the boom. The Townsend Plan called for a "Double Victory," in the war overseas and on the home front for pensions that would go into effect after the war. But few were paying attention to the second part. Then, in 1943, a deeply conservative and anti–social spending Congress came to power and sought to roll back the New Deal.

The Townsend Plan was forced to rethink its fundamentals. Its leaders belatedly recognized that the progressive Democratic left, the labor movement, and even President Roosevelt were its main allies in the fight against poverty in old age. The Townsend Plan also did an about-face on state-level OAA programs, seeking to convert them through initiatives into Sixty-at-Sixty programs, which would pay $60 per month for everyone of age sixty and older. The Townsend Plan expected that World War II's end would bring an economic slump, as the first one did, and recovery and old-age benefits would return to the forefront of American politics. But there was no postwar depression, and the aged found themselves well behind veterans in the line of deserving groups seeking government aid. Townsend clubs were losing a war of attrition, and the Townsend Plan degenerated into an expert advocacy group. In 1949, when the Democrats returned to power and could address social policy, senior citizens' pensions were off the agenda. The Old-Age and Survivors Insurance program was upgraded again, this time to the point where it was in position finally to overtake OAA as the main source of public support for the aged. It could finally become Social Security.

The experience of the pension movement and old-age policy in the 1940s provide several social scientific and historical puzzles. Why did the old-age issue, in the form of flat pensions, return in force to the national political agenda in 1941, and what was the Townsend Plan's and the pension movement's influence on it? Why was not old-age policy transformed again, as it had been in 1935 and 1939, but this time into senior citizens' pensions? Why did the Townsend Plan during the war turn its focus to the states? What accounts for the failure of the Townsend Plan to win referendums? What influence did these campaigns have on state-level OAA programs? What accounts for why an old-age insurance program won out over senior citizens' pensions? Did the pension movement influence the Social Security Act amendments of 1950? Why did the Townsend Plan decline, as did the national pension movement as a whole, while some old-age organizations at the state level continued to flourish?

Old-Age Pensions on the Verge

In the 1940 elections, the old-age issue was indeed hot, as pollster George Gallup had predicted. A universal flat old-age pension was part of the Democratic party platform, and President Roosevelt employed the issue in his re-election campaign. Despite the European war crisis, ostensibly the reason to run for a third term, Roosevelt turned the election into a referendum on the New Deal. Although his victory was not the overwhelming triumph of 1936, Roosevelt captured 55 percent of the two-party vote, trounced the Republican Wendell Willkie by more than 350 electoral votes, and brought additional northern Democrats to Congress. The Townsend Plan had dropped many previously endorsed Republicans who had voted against the Townsend bill, but returned a bipartisan and presumably more reliable 135-member contingent to the House.[1] Against the wishes of the Social Security Board, during the campaign Roosevelt called for modifying the new OASI program. According to this "double-decker" plan, the revamped old-age policy would combine a universal senior citizens' pension with higher social insurance benefits for qualified wage earners. All aged Americans would receive about $30 per month—the initial sum promised by the Roosevelt administration in 1935, but which was being provided only in rare instances through OAA.[2]

At the opening of the new Congress, Roosevelt's first order of business was to generate revenue for defense, but the old-age issue persisted all the same.

Led by the Townsend-endorsed senators Claude Pepper of Florida and Sheridan Downey of California, both New Dealers and Roosevelt supporters, too, a special Senate committee on old-age pensions was convened. The committee heard expert testimony from many sources, including from the Townsend Plan and its founder. Its deliberations helped to convince George Gallup to commission another poll on the subject. The results indicated that the average American thought that a $42 monthly stipend was fair for a needy aged person. That summer the Senate committee called for the immediate payment of pensions of at least $30 per month for almost all Americans over sixty years of age. The Senate Finance Committee, which had been addressing new taxes for military readiness, was scheduled to pick up the issue in the fall. Roosevelt was not supporting the old-age proposal but was also signaling that he would not veto any bill that Congress might want to pass.[3]

The Townsend Plan continued to demand that its own, more generous and expensive, pension recovery bill be passed. The bill had dropped the complicated transactions tax and now relied for funding on a simpler and more progressive gross income tax, along the lines proposed by the General Welfare Federation of America. The Townsend Plan version exempted $100 per month, avoiding those targeted by social insurance, which taxed low-wage earners only. The bill was bottled up in the House Ways and Means Committee, and so the Townsend Plan began another discharge petition drive, relying on endorsed House members and others, too. As the signatures mounted, the organization flooded the office of the Ways and Means chair, Robert Doughton of North Carolina, with letters demanding that he hold hearings. The Townsend Plan leadership was asserting that both the economic upswing and increased taxes for defense purposes were vindications. The partial recovery indicated that extensive government spending would be stimulating to the economy. The new taxes showed that Townsend-sized pensions would be fiscally affordable. The organization was generating new clubs with its latest drive, called "Victory in '41" and convened another successful convention, this time in Buffalo, having made further organizing inroads in the East.[4]

It seemed as though 1941 was going to be something of a replay of 1939, when old-age benefits had been upgraded and partially transformed in the direction of senior citizens' pensions. The situation was in some ways better. Democrats had increased their margin to 106 in the House, while holding a 38-seat majority in the Senate, though the fact that southern Democrats and Republicans slightly outnumbered northern Democrats made it more likely that existing programs would be advanced rather than entirely new programs, such as health insurance, adopted. And old age had a comparative advantage over other domestic issues. As in 1939, the Townsend Plan's congressional contingent still tilted toward Republicans, and if they had to provide public funds to any disadvantaged group, Republicans generally preferred the aged.

They were relatively demographically contained, socially conservative in out-look, and politically adept. The aged compared favorably to larger and, given the Republicans' business allies, politically more problematic groups, notably workers, the unemployed, and citizens as a whole.[5]

This time around, however, the administration's hand was being forced al-most entirely by the Townsend Plan and the pension movement. Business groups had already won their payroll tax freeze. The Social Security Board did not want to add a floor of pensions to Old-Age and Survivors Insurance. With the new incentives in the federal legislation for OAA, the old-age issue was again being taken up in state after state, with a new string of initiatives to transform OAA programs into senior citizens' pensions. In the recent elec-tion, pension advocates had brought home the point that the new OASI pro-gram and revamped OAA programs were insufficient. The Townsend Plan had retained a large base of support in Congress and had crafted a plausible alternative. With the Democratic congressional majorities, the fact that so many Republicans had gone on record in support of old-age policy ensured that it would jump to the head of the domestic agenda. The Townsend Plan also had high-profile allies in Congress in Senators Downey and Pepper, who could cut deals, while giving Dr. Townsend the political cover he needed to keep the faith among his following. Downey's $30-per-month pension was a figure that newspaper columnists said Roosevelt would agree to. But this "half a loaf," as the *Townsend Weekly* put it, would have transformed old-age pol-icy and enshrined the pension principle in law. Instead of denouncing the legislation, as Dr. Townsend might have done in the past, he declared it a "step in the right direction" and pronounced himself "gratified" by the low-ering of the age limit, the end of the means test, and the elimination of the matching system. He also claimed that the measure would lend "tremendous new force and vitality to our club activities, for we can all now see clearly that our work is bringing results." He also vowed to press to increase the stipend over time.[6]

But Congress was moving slowly. For most of 1941, the Ways and Means Committee had been addressing an administration-sponsored tax bill. The Treasury Department was hoping to use the crisis to reform the federal tax structure. The 1941 Revenue Act was designed to add about $3.5 billion in revenues and about 5 million people to the income tax rolls. Although the House Ways and Means Committee held firm against reporting out the Townsend pension legislation, once the tax legislation had been addressed, in the late fall, the Senate Finance Committee began hearings on the proposals of Downey's special committee. Many observers thought that it would report out some version of a national pension in the New Year. But on December 7 the news came from Pearl Harbor, and war preempted the political agenda. The Townsend Plan and the pension movement had come within a whisker of creating senior citizens' pensions.[7]

Rethinking the Fundamentals

The war crisis ended the discussion of all domestic reform issues aside from taxation. Any group demanding benefits would be in the politically unsupportable position of putting itself ahead of the national war effort. The logistical problems were also severe. The congressional financing committees, which had jurisdiction over the Social Security Act and Townsend's legislation, were going to be even more consumed with raising revenue, as Roosevelt was asking for more than $7 billion to pay for the first year of war.[8] The war-related economic boom also posed problems. Despite its seeming vindication of the spending thesis, it called into question the Townsend Plan's chief ostensible reason for being—to end the Depression. No recovery program of any sort was going to be needed at least until after the war. But the recovery aspect of Townsend's idea drew the support of the nonaged and fired up Townsend club members, who liked to see themselves as part of something larger than an interest group demanding cash for itself. Under the changed economic circumstances, too, the former "spenders" in the Treasury Department were following their Keynesian principles and, now fearing inflation, sought to dampen consumer demand for the duration. The Social Security Board, which sought to promote social insurance, and the National Resources Planning Board, which hoped to create a guaranteed income through work projects and national public assistance, put aside immediate social policy proposals and began to plan for postwar social policy.[9]

The Townsend Plan did not have the luxury to wait for the war to end. It would lose membership, revenues, and potential influence. To make matters worse, at the outset of the war Dr. Townsend attacked President Roosevelt for issuing war bonds, inducing many Townsendites, who were intensely patriotic, to jump ship.[10] Addressing the new circumstances, the Townsend Plan called for a "Double Victory," seeking to win the war and pensions for senior citizens. Dr. Townsend proposed that Congress enact a gross income tax with generous exemptions for workers. Some of the proceeds would fund $30 minimum pensions, with the bulk of the revenues devoted to the war effort. After the war, the entire proceeds of the tax would pay for old-age pensions. To fire up the base and win the support of the general public, the group focused on the most destitute of aged Americans and also would provide pensions to the permanently disabled and families with dependent children. Moreover, according to the doctor's new thinking, war was a result of poverty, and in attacking poverty his pension program would prevent war. However, the Townsend Plan's campaign to induce House members to sign a discharge petition to release the Townsend bill faltered. Although only fifty-two additional signatures were needed at the beginning of 1942, only about half were secured before the next election rolled around.[11]

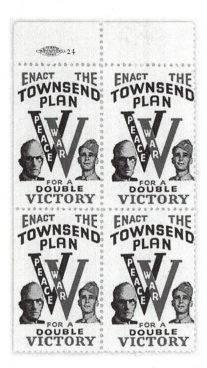

Figure 9.1: Double Victory. The Townsend Plan called for a double victory in the war and for prosperity, but no one was paying much attention. Dr. Townsend's son Robert, pictured on this stamp with his father, joined the war effort and Townsend Plan publicity. Author's collection.

Soon the pension movement was facing worse problems. In the 1942 elections, Republicans captured fifty additional House seats, placing Congress under the control of a conservative coalition of Republicans and southern Democrats. Moreover, Roosevelt almost entirely ceded domestic policy to Congress, transforming himself, as he famously put it, from Dr. New Deal into Dr. Win the War. Although the Townsend Plan had on paper its most successful election yet, with 187 Townsend-endorsed supporters elected to the House, they were largely incumbents approved because they signed the discharge petition, not because of a commitment to senior citizens' pensions. In any case, old age was so far off the political agenda that it was not worth mounting a new petition drive. Instead, Congress sought to roll back New Deal social policy. With a conservative Congress and a liberal president focused on a war, extensive organization and mobilization and successful congressional endorsements were not nearly enough to advance social policy.[12]

Facing this right-wing political formation, the Townsend Plan turned left. In a changing of the guard, L. W. Jeffery, the registered Republican who had been running the Townsend Plan, was replaced in 1941 by Sherman J. Bainbridge, the editor of the *Townsend Weekly*. Bainbridge had migrated to the

Townsend Plan from Ham and Eggs, after being ousted in a power struggle with the Allen brothers. Bainbridge's sympathies were with the left wing of the New Deal, and he was closely allied with Senator Downey, a California Democrat who had made his peace with Roosevelt. The other high-profile supporter of the Townsend Plan was Senator Pepper of Florida, also a rabid New Dealer. Even Dr. Townsend was starting to perceive that the social policy of the New Deal, now that it was under attack, was a substantial achievement.[13]

Stymied on senior citizens' pensions, the Townsend Plan struck out in new political directions. It joined efforts to end the poll tax in the nine southern states that still had them, claiming that restrictions on the franchise explained why these states and their representatives rarely supported the organization and its pension legislation. The Townsend Plan also fought corporate profiteering from the war effort and allied itself with the watchdog efforts of Senator Robert La Follette Jr. of Wisconsin. The Townsend Plan backed Roosevelt's demands for progressive taxes and fought proposals to fund the war by sales taxes, as was being demanded by the National Association of Manufacturers and other groups on the right. The Townsend Plan pledged allegiance to the administration's left-wing Keynesians, like the economist Alvin Hansen, who had been commissioned by the National Resources Planning Board and whose "underconsumptionist" thesis held that extensive domestic spending would be needed to avoid a second depression after the war. The *Townsend Weekly* even put in a good word for the WPA, the program that had aided so many unemployed Americans during the Depression, but had been criticized by the doctor as a mere palliative.[14]

It was too little too late. No real ground was made on poll tax legislation, and the conservative coalition in Congress gained considerable traction in its rollback efforts. The WPA was given its "honorable discharge" and put out of service in 1943. The National Resources Planning Board, which had commissioned a comprehensive report that proposed that all Americans should have a guaranteed income, had its funding zeroed out and its report brushed off; it was ordered to pack up its stuff and ship everything to the National Archives. Congress then passed a regressive revenue bill over Roosevelt's veto.[15]

Sixty-at-Sixty

Making no progress on the national level, the Townsend Plan made a radical strategic shift in late 1943 and addressed state-level OAA programs. Dr. Townsend had always insisted that his pension-recovery program would never provide sufficient stimulus if confined to a few states. Now Townsend invoked the need to fight old-age poverty and his prerogative to change his mind.[16] But there was a powerful if unstated political logic behind the switch to pen-

Figure 9.2: Seeking Support. The Townsend Plan turned left and continued its congressional endorsement policy in the 1940s, but endorsees had to agree only to support the discharge of a Townsend bill from committee. Here an Austin, Texas, Townsend club greets Congressman Lyndon Johnson (second from right). At right is the national representative for Texas Glen S. Wilson, and second from left is Claudia "Lady Bird" Johnson. Photographer unknown, photo courtesy of Richard Christy.

sion small ball. The Townsend Plan was predicated on the support of its aged club members, but there was nothing at the national level the Townsend Plan could plausibly do for them. With restrictions on travel, it was no longer feasible to hold national conventions of Townsend clubs. States were inviting targets. They set their own OAA policies, including the generosity and extension of benefits to the aged, and could go beyond the federal matching limits to pay benefits of beyond $40 or $45 per recipient. What is more, states were not being pressed into fiscal service for the war effort, and in their budgets domestic policy still reigned supreme. Especially inviting were western states with direct democratic devices like the initiative and the referendum, which were well suited to the strengths of the organization.[17]

California, the home state of the Townsend Plan, was a natural. After losing its initiative in 1939, Ham and Eggs had flown the coop, and in Bainbridge the Townsend organization had a veteran campaigner in California initiative politics with a familiar radio voice. So the Townsend Plan pressed petitions to put a Sixty-at-Sixty measure on the ballot in November 1944.

The measure called for stipends of $60 for the nonemployed older than sixty years funded by a gross income tax of 2 percent. In three other states, including Washington and Oregon, which retained the greatest per capita concentration of Townsend clubs, Sixty-at-Sixty campaigns were also mounted.[18] The initiatives lost in each state. In California, the margin was about 2 million opposed to 1 million in favor. All the same, the drives were not in vain. The Townsend Plan had given its members something to fight for. California managed to maintain its club membership levels, despite the fact that they were dropping off elsewhere.[19]

The drives also promoted old-age policy. Among states with extensive Townsend club presence in open political systems, those states with Sixty-at-Sixty drives (California, Oregon, and Washington) saw their OAA benefits rise as compared with those (Colorado, Maine, Minnesota, Montana, New Hampshire, South Dakota, and Wyoming) with no drives. In 1941–42, the average OAA pension was 35.6 percent of per capita income in the seven states without drives, but after five years the sum held steady, at 35.5 percent of per capita income by 1946. In the three states with initiative drives, the average pension stood at 31.7 percent of per capita income in 1940–41, but this figure shot up to 42.4 percent by 1946—more than a 10 percentage point increase. California provides a positive case in point. In the elections of 1940 and 1942, a Republican was elected governor, and Democratic representation in the legislature dropped. All the same, in 1943, as the drive began, California adopted legislation that raised the maximum OAA grant from $40 to $50, further reduced the responsibility of relatives to support the aged, increased the amount of personal property a recipient could own, and provided that the state pay a greater portion of nonfederal costs.[20]

The Failure of the Townsend Plan Revival

As the war wound down, the Townsend Plan was hoping to pick up where things had left off before the attack on Pearl Harbor. Some signs were encouraging. President Roosevelt was elected a fourth time in 1944 and brought with him an increased Democratic majority. But several things happened that helped to undermine the cause of old-age pensions. Economic activity remained high, and the healthy economy drained the urgency from Townsend's pension recovery program and its supporters. Also, World War II was replaced almost immediately by a cold war with the Soviet Union, deflecting attention from social policy and eliminating the possibility of any great peace dividend. With organized business also demanding tax cuts, there was little government revenue available for new domestic programs.[21]

What is more, another group had jumped well ahead of the aged in terms of political favor. In the wake of the Allied victory, returning soldiers were viewed as being deserving in a way that was never true for their counterparts

from the brief and ambiguous World War I. Benefits for veterans also had substantial Republican and southern Democratic support for reasons other than
the wartime sacrifices and the flush of victory. World War II veterans were far
fewer in number and unable to replenish their ranks, thus posing nothing like
the continuing fiscal burden that would be required to support the aged. Conservatives in Congress engaged in a rearguard action by rejecting New Deal
proposals for general benefits for all Americans, while giving veterans' organizations almost anything they requested through the GI Bill of Rights and
other legislation.[22]

Other obstacles were internal to the Townsend Plan, which suffered yet another schism. In the 1940s, with the doctor's backing, the organization was
creating a council form of government based in the Townsend clubs. By way
of indirect elections, club representatives formed congressional district, state,
and regional councils. Once all the regions were organized, there was to be an
election for a National Advisory Council. In 1945, Dr. Townsend was on the
verge of realizing what he claimed to be his democratic dream, to vest the authority of the Townsend National Recovery Plan, Inc., in a council rooted in
Townsend clubs. But when the time came, the doctor was reluctant to let go,
retaining control of the *Townsend National Weekly*, which he used to undermine and second-guess the council. A power struggle ensued, with Robert
Townsend squeezing the council through his control of the Townsend Foundation. Predictably, many council members bolted, forming the American
Pension Committee, Inc., and taking their clubs' allegiances with them.[23]

Then the 1946 elections brought a Republican House of Representatives for
the first time since the 1920s. It seemed to some that it would open the way for
the Townsend Plan. In the House Ways and Means Committee, the southern
Democrat Doughton was replaced by the Townsend-endorsed Harold Knutson
of Minnesota. The Townsend Plan saw seated in Congress its largest contingent ever of endorsed representatives, some 182. But the conservative Republican leadership had no intention of reporting out the expensive Townsend
Plan bill, and Ways and Means saw its mission as ushering tax cuts to the
House floor. With the slippage in Townsend club membership, the Townsend
Plan–endorsed representatives, who were committed at best to signing a discharge petition, were not keen on forcing the issue. Allying with southern
Democrats, the Republican leadership was also able to roll back labor's rights
to organize workers with the Taft-Hartley Act of 1947. The episode showed
again that social policy gains for groups like the aged were possible only with
substantial Democratic majorities. The Townsend Plan's bipartisan endorsement strategy proved useless in the context of a Republican majority.[24]

Worse, the Townsend Plan had fallen into a new and less influential mobilization pattern. It remained able to raise money, but its funds were no longer
being generated from the nickels and dimes of hundreds of thousands of
Townsendites. No new clubs were being formed, no one was joining the clubs

Figure 9.3: Townsend Club Convention, 1947. The Townsend Plan held its Seventh Convention of Townsend Clubs in 1947 in Washington, D.C., but membership had so declined that the attendees could be counted in the tens rather than the thousands, as in the past. Author's collection, photographer unknown.

that existed, and Townsendites were dying. Far fewer members gave larger sums, bequests to the Townsend Foundation were increasingly important to the revenue stream, and more money was raised from the general public. An increasingly large proportion of the revenues of the Townsend Plan, Inc., as the main organization was called in 1948, came from sales of "Dr. Townsend's Own Formula" vitamin pills, cashing in on the ageless founder's stamina. Membership had dropped dramatically, back into the five digits. The Townsend Plan held its 1948 convention in Washington to maximize a show of force on Congress, but attendance was sparse, and a brief *New York Times Magazine* article that spring read like an elegy.[25]

The decline of the Townsend Plan did not mean the end of the old-age pension movement. Mass-based groups remained active in the states. In California, an organization led by the former Ham and Eggs official George McLain was mobilizing in force. McLain's organization went by many names but by the late 1940s was known as the California Institute of Social Welfare. McLain's institute differed from the Townsend Plan in making no claims for the wider economic benefits of old-age pensions and was constituted instead as a welfare-rights organization with a membership base of OAA recipients, interceding with county authorities and demanding greater generosity and liberality in the provision of benefits. It organized clubs on the Townsend Plan model in each California assembly district. The National Annuity League remained prominent in Colorado, where old-age benefits were now central to the state government's mission. In Oregon, where Townsend clubs still flourished and met regularly, another initiative, the "Little Townsend Plan," calling for pensions of about $100 per month, was added to the ballot in 1946, and Townsend clubs were also active on OAA in some other western strongholds.[26] McLain's organization gained 250,00 signatures on a petition in 1948 to place on the November ballot a proposition calling for OAA stipends of $75 per month at age sixty, liberalizing eligibility requirements, and placing control of the program in a new state agency headed by one of McLain's lieutenants. The proposition narrowly carried. Although it was repealed the following year, the end result was a permanent upgrade in California's OAA program.[27]

Boring from Within

The decline of the national old-age pension movement did not mean the end of national action on old-age benefits. The Democratic Party and the Social Security Board, led by its chairman, Arthur Altmeyer, continued to seek improvements. The board was not greatly concerned with the aged, whom it saw as being relatively privileged in public policy. All the same, it focused on improving Old-Age and Survivors Insurance, for it was the only national social insurance program and thus the foundation for other types of protection from the loss of income. The board wanted greater coverage across both groups and risks. Farm workers and operators, the self-employed, and domestics, among others, were without coverage. The board also hoped to aid disability, health, and hospitalization insurance to the package of protections. The low benefits were also a concern. The formula had not changed since 1939, yet inflation had cut well into the value of the grants.

During the war and immediately afterward, the Social Security Board had little luck in its initiatives. It called for payroll taxes to increase to 10 percent without any corresponding benefit increases, and the administration proposed more moderately that these taxes be increased by $1 billion.[28] But these bids failed. The board then placed its hopes in the Wagner-Murray-Dingell bills, which called for steeply increased payroll taxes to fund health and disability insurance as well as higher old-age insurance benefits. The first was introduced to no great effect in 1943. A second version was introduced in 1945, a seemingly somewhat more hopeful time in Congress for social policy advocates, but was rejected, too.[29] Worse, Congress, led by Senator Vandenburg, continued to freeze scheduled increases in the payroll tax, preventing about $1.4 billion from accruing to the trust fund. By 1944 the board had to drop the fiction that the OASI program was self-financing. It cooperated with Vandenberg on an amendment to back the program with general revenues if the trust fund were to come up short—a scenario that now seemed likely. Under the Republican Congress elected in 1946, Senator Vandenburg won another freeze of the payroll tax, and the coverage of OASI was restricted.[30]

Meanwhile, old-age insurance's programmatic competitor, Old-Age Assistance, advanced. In 1946 Congress changed the reimbursement formula to one that benefited states that paid low amounts per recipient, a move that won the support of southern Democrats. The federal government would pay two-thirds of the first $15 in monthly assistance grants. As a sop to the more generous states, the federal government would reimburse half of the next $30, increasing the maximum subject to reimbursement up to $45 per month. Two years later another congressional deal upgraded the formula, reimbursing states three-fourths of the first $20 per month per recipient and upping the maximum monthly payments subject to 50 percent matching from $45 to $50 per month.[31]

There is no shortage of scholarly books that portray the executives of the Social Security Board as dominating the politics of U.S. social policy, but anyone looking forward from the immediate postwar period would be hard-pressed to see it that way. The board's claims that the old-age insurance program was the mainstay of U.S. social policy and public assistance programs like OAA were a safety net were so much graveyard whistling. More than a dozen years after the passage of the Social Security Act, there was little sign that the public truly supported or understood the OASI program, with its complicated payroll taxes, trust fund, and benefit schedules. All the high-profile political battles over U.S. social policy had been over public assistance, notably the WPA and Old-Age Assistance, and OAA remained by far the superior old-age program. By 1949, the average OAA benefit was about $45 per month, dwarfing the $25 received by the average individual OASI recipient. About 2.7 million were receiving OAA benefits, as compared with only 1.6 million aged recipients of OASI, and only about a million of them were receiving the more generous "retirement" benefits. As for OAA being the safety net to catch those not fortunate enough to qualify for OASI, it was just the opposite. About 12 percent of OASI recipients were forced to top off their grants with OAA benefits. In the states with generous OAA programs, this figure was as large as one-third.[32]

The Triumph of Old-Age and Survivors Insurance

Undaunted, the Social Security Administration (SSA), as the board was renamed in 1946, when it lost its status as an independent agency reporting directly to the president, pressed on. Its Old-Age and Survivors Insurance program managed to survive despite its meager benefits, its tattered insurance imagery, its whipping boy status in Congress, its lack of even lukewarm support by the public, and its program executives having been no more than bit players in the New Deal. Not only that, after the 1948 elections, the program was on the verge of a major upgrade. The turnabout was due to a lot of good fortune, with several things having to happen at once.

The first was the bad fortune of the SSA's programmatic and institutional competitors. The war whisked old-age policy off the political agenda just as the Roosevelt administration was conceding to add a universal pension as a "floor" to the OASI program. Had such a minimum pension been enacted, however, its many beneficiaries would have placed it at the center of the politics of old-age policy in the postwar period and overshadowed OASI. The conservative Congress that gained power after 1942 froze OASI payroll taxes but also destroyed the National Resources Planning Board and the WPA. These agencies were central to the New Deal, and their visions of social policy diverged from that of the Social Security Board. The left-wing Keynesians of the NRPB viewed the OASI payroll tax as both regressive and inimical to economic growth. It wanted to center U.S. social policy on nationalized public assistance programs and, like WPA officials, wanted to keep work projects at the head of U.S. social policy. By 1944, both agencies were out of existence, clearing the way for the board to press its proposals on the administration.

Another key change was that organized labor, assiduously courted by the Social Security Board, had come to back extensions of the OASI program.

Both the AFL and the Congress of Industrial Organizations (CIO) had rallied around the failed Wagner-Murray-Dingell bills, which would have provided comprehensive social insurance. The CIO had moderated its views partly because it was now being led by Philip Murray of the United Steel Workers, a longtime supporter of Roosevelt and the New Deal, rather than Roosevelt's obstreperous nemesis John L. Lewis of the United Mine Workers. Also, some of its union affiliates were seeking even greater pension benefits from their employers through collective bargaining. As a result, the CIO was dropping its demand for Sixty-at-Sixty pensions at the national level. This position of labor was key because the war had greatly strengthened its organizational capacity and political power. In return for agreeing not to hold up war production through strikes, labor was being granted a freer hand in organizing, and workers had streamed into AFL and CIO unions. By 1947, there were 15 million union members, up from 9 million in 1939, accounting for more than a third of the nonagricultural labor force. The CIO had vigorously supported Democrats in elections starting in 1944 and was foursquare behind President Truman's 1948 bid as he vowed to repeal Taft-Hartley.[33]

For reasons having little to do with the Social Security Administration, organized business and Republicans, which had opposed OASI because of its payroll taxes and its potentially massive trust fund, started to soften on the program. Workers had begun bargaining for fringe benefits, for which the government was now providing tax relief, and businesses were generally willing to grant them in order to reduce their wage bills. Central among them were old-age benefits. Prior to the war only the most well-paid employees had any significant old-age coverage from their employers. But now private pensions for industrial workers were considered beneficial by both conservatives, who wanted to forestall government efforts along these lines, and liberals, who wanted workers to have retirement protection in the face of indifference by the national government. The United Auto Workers notably bargained for $100 monthly pensions, with the provision that the company's contribution would be reduced by the amount the retired worker gained in Social Security Act benefits. These pensions helped to deflect big business hostility from OASI, since increases in its benefits would result in savings for the parent corporations.[34]

Southern Democratic opposition to the extension of OASI benefits to agricultural workers also started to wane. The representatives of these states remained opposed to major federal spending programs with national control. But the OASI program was starting to look better to them. With the mechanization of agriculture, New Deal policies moving tenants off the land, and the draw of war industries, there were far fewer tenant farmers. In any case, OASI benefits were not so high that they would pose a major threat to the economy. Given the relatively generous eligibility requirements being considered, the newly enrolled would not have to pay much in order to receive benefits, thus making it possible for many southerners to gain in essence small old-age pensions and redirect national spending to the region.[35]

OASI was also favored due to program characteristics that had little to do with the imagery of social insurance, which had never taken hold in the public mind, or with the fact that the program "covered" 35 million Americans. After all, being covered was not nearly as compelling as receiving benefits, and few did. But one advantage of OASI was that Congress controlled its parameters and could legislate in minute detail benefit levels and who would receive them. There was no executive discretion, as with the WPA, opening the way to winning favor with southern legislators. What is more, OASI was well designed to take advantage of prosperity. The trust fund grew from about $2 billion in 1940 to about $12 billion in 1949, from about 1 percent of GNP to about 4 percent, despite the tax freeze and 1.6 million recipients. The programs structure made it possible to give away much to many without apparent great cost. Members of Congress could grant the newly aged and soon-to-become retired among their constituents far more in benefits than what recipients could have expected given the payroll tax "contributions" made by them or on their behalf. As in 1939, OASI again offered a responsible-seeming way for Congress to spend irresponsibly without having to increase taxes very much.[36]

Ever hopeful, the Social Security Administration had maintained good, almost masochistic, relations with unhelpful Congresses and their taxation committees. Another Senate Finance Committee Advisory Council had been formed to consider alterations in the Social Security Act programs in 1947, as part of a compromise in which the SSA would support another Vandenburg-proposed payroll tax freeze. Like its predecessor of the late 1930s, the new advisory council was to include representatives of business, labor, and the public, but it was again dominated by pro–social insurance members. Notable among its returning "public" members was J. Douglas Brown, the Princeton economist whose interest in and commitment to social insurance was long-standing and substantial. Included among the business representatives were previous council members and social insurance supporters Marion Folsom of Eastman Kodak and M. Albert Linton of Provident Mutual Insurance. Among the labor representatives was Nelson Cruikshank, the head of the AFL's social security department and a firm supporter of the Wagner-Murray-Dingell bills. The staff director was Robert Ball, a former field worker for the Social Security Administration deeply committed to social insurance. Altmeyer and SSA employees were allowed to funnel information and ideas to the council, while the Townsend Plan and other advocates of senior citizens' pensions were shut out. When the council reported in 1948, it focused on the OASI program, and, unsurprisingly, its twenty-two recommendations regarding it called for increasing coverage, payroll taxes, and benefits. By contrast, its report regarding public assistance began with the claim that it would eventually be rendered superfluous by improved social insurance.[37]

The elections of 1948 also provided a political opening for a move on OASI. Running against the conservative Republican Congress more so than his opponent Thomas Dewey, President Truman called for greatly increased benefits for OASI as well as a national health program and the repeal of Taft-Hartley. He had to contend with the States' Rights Democratic Party candidacy of Strom Thurmond, the South Carolina governor, who was popular in the Deep South states, as well as a challenge from the left by Henry Wallace, who ran on the Progressive Party ticket and backed $100 per month universal old-age pensions. Truman won a surprising victory and turned a 57-seat Democratic deficit in the House into a 92-seat majority, with an 18-seat swing in the Senate. This mandate made it possible for him to gain ground on the more moderate parts of his extensive Fair Deal and to fight off a southern Democratic and Republican coalition that was plotting to preempt old-age reform by granting expensive pensions to veterans only. But the Democratic congressional contingent was not of the enormous size of its counterparts of the mid-1930s, making it impossible to achieve the Fair Deal's more radical parts, notably the repeal of the Taft-Hartley Act and the enactment of health insurance.[38]

In October 1949, the House passed a bill to upgrade OASI, ensuring that some benefits would be enacted once the Senate, bogged down by a civil rights filibuster, could address the subject. In January 1950, a 1 percentage point increase in the Social Security Act payroll tax, enacted so long ago, was finally allowed by Congress to go into effect and foreshadowed the passage of the bulk of the House's legislation. In August 1950, the OASI program was significantly expanded. Eligibility and coverage were increased by approximately 10 million, reaching about three-fourths of the labor force. Benefits were increased by 80 percent, to the point where they were competitive with the average OAA program. As before, very generous eligibility provisions made it possible to provide unearned benefits to many aged Americans. Those aged sixty-one or older could qualify for benefits with eighteen months of covered employment. Many others who had paid taxes but had not been able to qualify under the old rules were grandfathered into program. Congress had granted pensions to another large segment of the populace, while calling it something else. By the end of 1950, aged OASI beneficiaries had increased to 2.6 million, about the same number as OAA, and OASI retirement beneficiaries increased to 1.7 million. OASI retirement beneficiaries surpassed OAA recipients by 1953, and the growth in OAA recipients was halted for good.[39]

The Social Security Administration did not get everything it wanted. Disability insurance was conspicuously rejected, along with the president's highly publicized national health initiative. But the Social Security Act Amendments of 1950 were a turning point for the program and social insurance in the United States. The administration and its reformers had induced Congress to turn back bids to starve OASI, by defrosting the payroll tax and by preventing the program's conversion into a flat benefit, as demanded by the pension movement. The OASI program was placed in a position from which it could be improved in the future. The programmatic victory also presaged the victory of the reasoning for old-age benefits. Benefits would be granted not because the elderly had made lifelong contributions to society, as the senior citizens' pension movement was arguing, but because that they had paid a compulsory payroll tax. It did not matter that it would be decades before these taxes would even come close to matching the benefits paid out by the program. Social Security as we would soon know it was born.

The Impact of the Pension Movement

As the pension movement had done before, it used the occasion of congressional hearings for administration-sponsored legislation to introduce and testify in favor of universal, flat, and generous benefits to the aged. The latest version of Townsend's own pension-prosperity program was contained in two bills, one regarding taxation and the other spending. A gross income tax of 3 percent was expected to generate an eye-popping $35 billion per year, or about 15 percent of the national income in 1948. These revenues would have provided pensions to the approximately 18.5 million aged, permanently disabled, and widows with children of about $156 per month, the program having advanced during the war from its focus only on the aged. Several members of the House testified in favor, including its sponsor, Homer Angell, an Oregon Democrat who had lined up forty cosponsors.[40] The General Welfare Federation and the American Pension Committee joined forces behind a more moderate Sixty-at-Sixty universal pension bill. The coalition, led by Townsend-endorsed Congressman Toby Morris of Oklahoma, left it up to the Ways and Means Committee to devise a means of generating the necessary revenue. Morris estimated that the bill would have a net cost of about $7.2 billion per year. The measure won the backing of many congressmen who declared themselves backers of Townsendism in principle, but not the Townsend Plan's expensive bill. A witness from the Fraternal Order of Eagles also came out in favor of generous and universal flat pensions.[41]

However, as Stephen Young, a Democrat from Ohio, pointed out, in the past when Dr. Townsend testified, the chamber was crowded with supporters, but in 1949 attendance was sparse. His testimony went unnoticed by the national news media. Even less attention, if possible, attended other pension advocates, whose less expensive bill was still far too pricey to be reported favor-

ably from committee. With old age in the news, there was a minor uptick in
Townsend Plan activity after the House passed its bill that fall, but the boost
was nothing like in 1935 or 1939. When the Senate held hearings in 1950,
Dr. Townsend drew only polite attention and then almost as a journalistic re-
flex.[42] Before the Ways and Means Committee's bill could be passed, it under-
went a series of House floor votes, any of which could have tripped it up. Did
the Townsend-endorsed members of the House help the bill along in the
spirit of doing something for their aged constituency? On votes regarding gag
rules, which the bill's supporters favored to ensure that it was not crippled by
unfriendly amendments, Townsend-endorsed Republicans were indeed more
likely to cross party lines to join Democratic proponents. But on no vote were
these representatives numerous enough to hold the balance of power.[43]

The upgrading of OASI thus seemed to have little to do with the efforts of
the pension movement in Congress. The movement clearly did not force the
issue onto the political agenda, as it had in 1941. The Democratic Party had a
social policy agenda that had been delayed since before the war. Presenting a
more radical alternative with political support was helpful, as always, in providing the majority the opportunity to demonstrate its relative moderation in
enacting new social benefits. On the House floor, as a scare tactic Congressman Wilbur Mills of the Ways and Means Committee declared that a rejec-
tion of the committee's handiwork might mean the enactment of a flat pension.[44] But the threat of a national and universal senior citizens' pension was
not nearly what it had been before the war, and there was nothing like the
partisan maneuvering of 1939. The Townsend Plan was no longer seen as
politically consequential. The Truman administration and the Social Security
Administration much more greatly feared that veterans groups' demands for
pensions would upset the plans.

Nonetheless, the pension movement had a substantial influence on the
old-age legislation, though indirect and a result of the pension mobilizations
of the previous fifteen years. The pension movement had provided support for
a radical alternative to OASI that was frightening enough to opponents that
they were willing to support augmentations of old-age insurance—the consistent advance of state Old-Age Assistance programs. Providing more matching funds to the more generous OAA programs had been viewed by Congress
as a means to preempt the pension movement at the national level and redirect its attention to the states. Congress had developed a formula to ensure
that the stingier and more generous states would share in federal largesse. In
the more radical states in the West, average OAA benefits were more than
$70 per month. In the more liberal southern states, such as Louisiana and Ok-
lahoma, the vast majority of the aged were receiving benefits.[45]

The expansion of OAA programs and the potential for further upgrades
in them were far more important in softening business groups' opposition to
OASI than were the fact that Ford Motors and a few other companies had

agreed to pay some of their workers old-age annuities someday. For more than a decade, business groups had been fighting pension movements in Washington and out west. In the states where initiatives were on the ballot, the opposition coalition almost always included the Chamber of Commerce and other prominent business organizations. The national pension movement had induced Congress to pass the issue to the states through OAA, and there it advanced. These business organizations saw OASI, with its lower benefits, as less dangerous than OAA. What is more, increases could be granted without significantly higher payroll taxes. Presumably it would be possible to prevent greater advances in benefits by holding down this tax in the future. Needless to say, since most of the major corporations were already paying the payroll tax, they did not have strong objections to extending it to those not paying.[46]

The position of organized business on OASI was a strategy to limit the growth in OAA benefits. In their testimony before Congress, the main concern of representatives of peak business associations was for the federal government to drop all support for means-tested aid. They wanted such aid to be funded entirely by the cash-poor states and counties in order to starve OAA. Although these groups provided lukewarm support for OASI upgrades, they were adamant against any further support of public assistance programs, including a proposed grant-in-aid for general assistance. And although they were in favor of extensions in coverage for OASI, it was not as if they embraced the social insurance principle. The U.S. Chamber of Commerce was part of the successful coalition against insurance for the permanently disabled—not to mention health insurance, which was vehemently fought. As a representative of the chamber saw it, the "greatest challenge facing our citizens in social security is to deflate old-age assistance."[47]

More evidence for the role of high OAA payments in increasing the appeal of OASI upgrades comes from the testimony of a group of witnesses who were definitive in their demands. Although they were supposed to be weighing in on a new grant-in-aid for general assistance and about the federal reimbursement formula, state directors of welfare from all across the country, from the generous Colorado to the stingy South Carolina, stood before the House Ways and Means Committee and demanded relief from their high Old-Age Assistance payments. In each case the directors called for the federal government to pick up more of the burden. They disagreed among themselves over whether the committee should adopt a variable grant formula, with matching payments according to a state's income, or whether there should be a higher matching limit for OAA. But they all favored increased coverage through OASI. Because in the current bill only a very minor amount of credit would be needed for covered workers to qualify for OASI benefits, which would be greatly increased, these directors all saw the program as relieving them of their top public aid burden and making it possible to address other needs. Although many felt it was unfair that workers in the more industrialized states were disproportionately reaping the benefits from the OASI program, even the New Jersey commissioner saw an advantage to increasing its coverage and benefits.[48]

All this was testimony to the importance of OAA in shaping the debate over social insurance. But if there had been no pension movement, OAA would never have posed the threat that it did to businesses and state budgets and welfare departments across the country. And despite the decline of the national pension movement, without it, OAA would be what ADC was, no major fiscal burden. And if OAA were not the fiscal threat that it was, OASI would not have been seen as a feasible alternative for conservatives. Unfortunately for them, but fortunately for the aged, the Social Security Administration was determined to use all its analytical and political skills to advance the program. It retained all its expansionary advantages—especially the ever-increasing trust fund, which took off during the economic boom of the 1950s and 1960s—and was picking up more and more recipients as time passed, all of whom were convinced they had earned their benefits. Social Security was on its way.

The Decline of the Townsend Plan

In the 1950s, the Townsend Plan was a spent force. Over the course of its career it had transmogrified in the way that Theda Skocpol identifies the overall transformation of American voluntary organizations in the second half of the twentieth century. The Townsend Plan was inaugurated as a grassroots membership organization, relying on the participation of masses of Americans. Now it was an advocacy and lobbyist organization, relying on outside funding and deploying expert testimony. Its past influence, however, had been based not by convincing politicians of the workability of its pension recovery program but by its ability to move masses and its potential to affect politician's electoral futures. The organization, now led by Townsend's son Robert, continued its quest and pressed on even when Dr. Townsend's twenty-seven-year career as a pension crusader ended with his death in 1960 at age ninety-three. The Townsend Plan still called for universal pensions financed by a gross income tax but was no longer even an afterthought in policy debates. Having long been eclipsed by the American Association for Retired Persons as the main national organizational spokesperson for the aged, the Townsend Plan closed up shop for good in 1980.[49]

The question is not so much why the Townsend Plan lingered for so long, but why it had been banished to the outskirts of national politics by 1950, after being a dominant force less than a decade earlier. Two potential answers—that it was too successful or that political opportunities had closed—seem unpersuasive. The Townsend Plan's most notable impact was to spur politicians into action on Old-Age Assistance, and Congress had figured out that sweetening the matching formula was an easy way to redirect the attention of the pension movement to the state level. But the Townsend Plan's pension legislation never came close to becoming law, and its bids to convert old-age policy into flat and generous universal pensions never came to pass. The main success of Old-Age and Survivors Insurance did not happen until the 1970s. Indeed, had Townsend-style legislation passed, the Townsend Plan probably would have been more prominent than ever in attempting to improve its handiwork. The dominance of war issues and conservatism in Congress from 1942 through 1948 was far more harmful to the Townsend Plan. War took its issue off the agenda just when senior citizens' pensions were on the verge of breaking through, and being frozen out of national policy debates for seven years is difficult. But even during the war there were some gains in old-age policy. And in 1950, great strides were made in national old-age policy. Given the great support behind the Townsend Plan, it should have been able to ride out the storm.

That the Townsend Plan foundered instead was due partly to how it was organized. Centralized organizations can strategize rapidly, maneuver nimbly, cut deals, and find compromises. But the Townsend Plan gained few of the advantages of centralization because it was controlled by one very flawed man, who was so invested in the details of his idea that it hindered his maneuverability. The end of the Depression and the advent of war posed discursive and political challenges, but Townsend was slow to change course. Although few aged leaders were developed through Townsend clubs, the organization attracted much middle-aged talent, and Townsend usually adopted the ideas of his smarter associates. He had returned to Clements's organizational and political strategies, had agreed with Johnson to allow his congressional allies autonomy and to dump the complicated transactions tax for the simpler gross income tax, and had taken Bainbridge's suggestion to stop fighting the president and to take advantage of state-level politics. But Townsend always first resisted and dismissed key leaders, leaving the organization rudderless at crucial moments. The Townsend Plan's implosion over democratization in 1945 was just another in a series of damaging leadership shake-ups. Under the circumstances, that one was impossible to survive.

Conclusion

The 1940s were the best of times and the worst of times for the Townsend Plan. It began the decade with such great influence that it and the pension movement were poised to force the Roosevelt administration and Congress to adopt universal senior citizens' pensions. It ended the decade in irrelevance, despite its founder's good health and congressional interest in old-age policy.

What lessons do these episodes of social movement activity and old-age policy provide for theories about the consequences of social movements and the development of social policy?

One lesson is that under a series of favorable circumstances, it is possible to jar the balky American political system into extensive action on social spending policy. After 1940, a reform-oriented president had been reelected with a substantial congressional Democratic majority. He had a Treasury Department, a Works Progress Administration, and a National Resources Planning Board all in favor of a spending solution to the Depression. He also faced an old-age pension movement that was well mobilized across the country and was contending on both state and national issues. This movement was politically engaged, having influenced congressional elections and winning over a significant number of Republicans to the cause. The rank-and-file members of the movement generally supported the president. Under these circumstances, the president came to support pensions for all senior citizens, reversing his previous position. Pensions most likely would have become the law of the land had war not intervened.

Another lesson is that it is almost impossible to make major social spending gains when political conditions are highly unfavorable, whether or not there is a well-mobilized social movement. Old-age pensions had no chance while there was a war on. The only area where reform was possible at the national level was in taxation policy. And, worse, once the political alignment turned highly conservative, with Republicans and southern Democrats dominating Congress and a Democratic administration focused on war, there was little chance to make gains even in taxation. The Townsend Plan had to adapt to these new circumstances, and it eventually moved to the only game in town, the states and their Old-Age Assistance programs.

The war and postwar period also demonstrated how hard it is for a national social movement organization based on mass membership to survive a long period in the political wilderness. The Townsend Plan, on the verge of transforming old-age policy in 1941, was listing by the time the war ended. A period of Republican dominance of Congress after the war was another blow. The Townsend Plan had little to show for its constituency except in some western states. A nimbler social movement organization could have sustained itself. In California, George McLain and associates were able to drop the political baggage of Ham and Eggs and form an organization based on OAA recipients pressing for improvements in that program. The Townsend Plan, with its commitment to senior citizens' pensions and unusual leadership structure, could not adapt.

The episode also suggests that it is possible for policy gains to be made for a group in the absence of sustained and effective social movement activity. With war and international issues on the back burner and with the election of a reform-oriented Democrat and a moderately large congressional majority in 1948, social policy was back in play. Advances were possible, however, only where previous policies had already been developed and in the directions in which administrative authorities were pointing. By 1949, the WPA was long off the scene. So was the National Resources Planning Board, with its desire to advance public assistance. Remaining was the highly motivated and savvy Social Security Administration, with a vision of U.S. social policy based on social insurance and a national OASI program to build. It had a proposal to advance old-age policy without significantly raising taxes and with the promise of reducing increasingly onerous public assistance burdens. Given the choice between that and enacting national health insurance, Congress jumped at old-age improvements.

In the historical institutionalist literature on social policy, it is a commonplace that new policies influence politics. From this point of view, social movements can have an influence on politics by way of their previous influence on policies. The pension movement was in the doldrums in late 1940s and was little more than a sideshow in the debate over the Social Security Act amendments. Yet the pension movement cast a large shadow over the proceedings through its previous impact on Old-Age Assistance. Through a series of political moves designed to forestall universal and more expensive old-age pensions at the national level, and through a series of mobilizations at the state level, the OAA programs in the states had grown tremendously. They had become a bugaboo for the business community, which began to see upgrading Old-Age and Survivors Insurance as a safer and cheaper option. This impression turned out to be mistaken, and the Chamber of Commerce later backtracked and sought a small, flat national pension to replace the OASI program. But it was too late. All the same, having had a long-term expansive influence on OAA had something like the impact of a pension movement being highly mobilized once old age returned to the agenda. The pension movement indirectly did its part to bring about Social Security.

CONCLUSION _____

A Hero for the Aged?

In the dispute that began this book, Dr. Francis Townsend claimed that the Townsend Plan was responsible for U.S. old-age benefits. Edwin Witte, the executive secretary of President Roosevelt's Committee on Economic Security, charged that the Townsend Plan hindered the cause by its attacks on the administration's old-age programs. Was Witte right that the Townsend Plan harmed the aged? Or was Townsend, as he claimed, a hero for the aged? There is no question that Townsend achieved celebrity status among the older Americans who streamed into Townsend clubs, and most historians concede that the Townsend Plan had some minor positive influence on U.S. old-age policy. A more key question is whether this examination of the Townsend Plan, the pension movement, and Social Security alters the standard account.

Social scientists, however, want to know more than that. We seek to account for the pattern of influence of social movements like the Townsend Plan and the senior citizens' pension movement. Can the experience of the Townsend Plan and the pension movement tell us something about the consequences of challengers aimed at states? Are there lessons to be learned for other U.S. social movements or movements anywhere? In short, when do movements matter? And when do they not? Also, what does this episode tell us about the determinants of public social provision and the development of the U.S. welfare state? Here I draw historical and social science lessons from this episode of contention and conclude with the legacies of the Townsend Plan and the pension movement for American politics.

The Impact of the Townsend Plan

The conventional historical wisdom steers a course between Townsend and Witte. It holds that the support behind the Townsend Plan helped to keep old-age benefits on the political agenda and marginally contributed to the contents of the 1935 Social Security Act, which was devised largely by Roosevelt's cabinet and moderate policy experts hired by it. The Townsend Plan made the aged more politically salient than other needy groups, such as dependent children or people with disabilities, and the security legislation aided the aged with two programs: Old-Age Assistance, which immediately provided funds for state-level programs, and a long-range national annuity program that eventually became Social Security. After the passage of the Social Security Act, according to the conventional wisdom, the Townsend Plan faded into insignificance.[1]

There is something to be said for this account. Old-age security was already in the Roosevelt administration's plans before there was a single Townsend club, and the administration probably could have pushed through its security legislation—Townsend Plan or not—after the unprecedented Democratic electoral triumphs of 1934. And so Dr. Townsend's claim that the pension movement was the source of all old-age policy progress is exaggerated. But the standard story greatly understates the influence of the Townsend Plan. It did indeed help to move up old-age policy in the administration's priorities in 1934, but, more important, it influenced the administration to propose more substantial old-age benefits. The fledgling old-age insurance program and its payroll tax—the basis of Social Security today—doubtless would not have been added to the initial legislation without the rapid mobilization behind the Townsend Plan, which also induced the administration to upgrade its proposal for Old-Age Assistance. If the Townsend Plan representatives were unhelpful during the congressional debates over the legislation, as Witte rightly suggests, they did not induce members of Congress to reject it.

But far from fading away after the passage of the Social Security Act, the Townsend Plan took off, becoming a national phenomenon that would influence old-age politics for years. In the late 1930s, it notably led a wider old-age pension movement that boosted the 1939 amendments to the Social Security Act. Under pressure from the pension movement, Congress increased aid for Old-Age Assistance, which provided the bulk of aid to the American aged during the 1930s and 1940s, agreed to abandoning the conservative annuity model for the national old-age program, and provided many pensions through it to older Americans. In 1941, the Townsend Plan was on the verge of inducing Congress to enact universal senior citizens' pensions, when World War II intervened. Although the Townsend Plan and the pension movement exerted little influence after the war, in advancing Old-Age Assistance, the pension movement further aided the cause of upgrading Old-Age and Survivors Insurance in the late 1940s by making it seem like a conservative alternative. Instead, this program became the basis of Social Security. More than that, the Townsend Plan's influence on social policy during its formative years combined with the difficulty of adopting new social programs in the U.S. political context gave the American welfare state an old-age slant that it retains today. Reformers were never able to pass national health insurance, but it was possible to add old-age health and hospitalization insurance, Medicare, to the existing old-age insurance program. These two programs make up more than a third of today's budget, and that is not counting substantial old-age benefits through Medicaid.[2] So score one for Dr. Townsend.

Witte has a point, however, in suggesting that the Townsendites were not as helpful to the cause of old-age security as they might have been. In 1935, the Townsend Plan leaders failed to join with congressional proponents of old-age policy hoping to improve the legislation. That the old-age annuity program was not eliminated from the legislation owed nothing to the Townsend Plan and everything to the efforts of the administration. In later years the Townsend Plan also frittered away chances to aid the aged. When it reached its peak of mobilization in 1936, the Townsend Plan had little impact and was bogged down in internecine strife due largely to the doctor's ego and his great control over his organization. It could have done much more than it did to advance Old-Age Assistance at the state level and sometimes even opposed efforts there by others in the pension movement. At the national level, the Townsend Plan often threw its electoral power behind Republicans who were less friends of the aged than enemies of Roosevelt—whom Townsend engaged for far too long in a quixotic political vendetta.

The Inadequacy of Standard Explanations

The checkered historical pattern of influence of the Townsend Plan provides a starting point for social science. This literature on the consequences of state-oriented movements provides four main explanations that could illuminate the uneven influence. These explanations focus on support and resource mobilization, the amount and types of collective action, strategic choices, including claims making, and the receptivity of political contexts.[3]

According to the resource mobilization hypothesis, the Townsend Plan's impact should be directly related to its support, especially in club members and financial resources. Gains in committed Townsendites would indicate to politicians the degree of intense interest in old-age pensions, as would increases in financial resources generated by the organization. Both members and money would make it easier to get out the message and engage in influential collective action. And since the money was generated from aged followers, there would be few strings attached to it. From this point of view, as figures C.1 and C.2 suggest, the expectation would be that the influence of the Townsend Plan would grow rapidly in the second half of 1935 and peak in 1936; it would fall off greatly over the next two years, but rise again in 1939 and 1940, before gradually slowing during the war and afterward. There is some evidence in favor of this explanation. The Townsend Plan had little influence in 1937, as clubs broke up and most sources of revenue withered. Also in favor is the fact that the Townsend Plan and the pension movement generally were influential in 1939, when the Townsend Plan regrouped and won new club members and resources, along with the rise of other pension

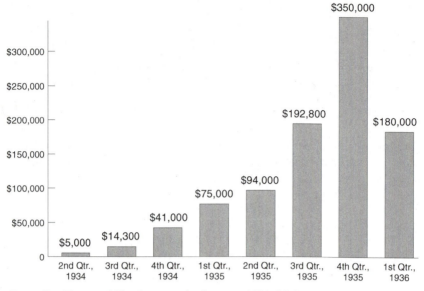

Figure C.1: Townsend Plan Revenues by Quarters, 1934–36. *Sources: Modern Crusader, Townsend Weekly.*

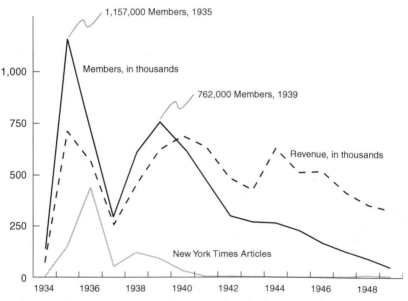

Figure C.2: Membership, Revenues, and *New York Times* Articles for the Townsend Plan, 1934–49. Membership is in 1,000s and revenues are in $1,000s. *Sources: Townsend Weekly*; Abraham Holtzman, *The Townsend Movement*, pp. 49, 80; ProQuest Historical Newspapers.

organizations. Another piece of corroborating evidence is the fact that the Townsend Plan was no longer directly influential once it lost its membership base for good in the late 1940s.

But there are some key anomalies for the resource mobilization explanation. In the heyday of the Townsend Plan, in early 1936 when it commanded the attention of the American public and new clubs were springing up hourly, its impact on old-age policy was minimal. By contrast, the Townsend Plan helped to improve the proposals for the aged in the administration's Economic Security Act in 1934 even though it had only begun to mobilize and had accumulated less than one-tenth of its peak membership. When in the first half of 1935 the Townsend Plan was somewhat better organized and had amassed a congressional fund, Congress taunted the Townsendites and reduced the old-age benefits in the administration's legislation. Also, membership seemed to matter more than resources, as the Townsend Plan was able to continue to generate revenues in the postwar period after membership had declined. There is no escaping the fact that the Townsend Plan had influence at wildly different levels of support.

A second line of argument is that the Townsend Plan's influence should be related to the amount or type of collective action it engaged in. In the now-standard view of social movements, collective action is rational and should bring collective benefits. It is also sometimes argued that noninstitutional or more assertive action will have the most influence. These arguments are not easy to appraise because the Townsend Plan engaged in so much collective action of many different sorts across numerous polities. But there are many inconvenient facts for most versions of the argument. The Townsend Plan and the pension movement, with their aged supporters, engaged in little noninstitutional action. To counter the 1936 investigation, the Townsend Plan led a car caravan to the capital and later protested outside county board offices in California, but that is about it. Its mass events were usually more on the order of picnics. More important, the Townsend Plan had an influence in 1934—before it engaged in any action targeting the state and before its action became even mildly assertive. The organization's collective action often proved a waste of time and resources, as during the congressional debate over the Social Security Act in 1935. Moreover, in 1936 the Townsend Plan aimed almost exclusively at the national government and had almost no impact there, but exerted influence in the states, which it ignored. Its car caravan made little impression, and its most assertive line of political action was during the 1936 presidential election, when it pulled out all the stops in a hopeless bid to prevent Roosevelt's reelection.

Homing in on the Townsend Plan's strategy of endorsing congressional representatives provides a more focused appraisal of the collective action argument. These endorsements and the electoral aid they were to bring from committed Townsendites were made in return for vows or evidence of support for

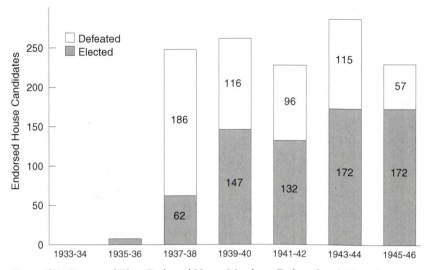

Figure C.3: Townsend Plan–Endorsed House Members, Defeated and Elected, 1933–46. During the 1934 elections for the 1935–36 House, the Townsend Plan made no official endorsements. *Source: Townsend Weekly*, Abraham Holtzman, *The Townsend Movement*, p. 127.

Townsend Plan legislation. This was perhaps the most consistent and as-sertive political action employed by the Townsend Plan, and the main way that the plan was represented in political processes was by way of endorsed representatives. Figure C.3, which tracks the Townsend endorsees elected to the House, establishes some connection between collective action and influ-ence. The failed electoral efforts of 1936 were repaid with little influence in 1937, and Congress upped old-age benefits in the Social Security Act amend-ments of 1939, right after elections that first sent many Townsend endorsees to Congress. The productivity of these efforts was, however, at best uneven. Before 1938 very few were endorsed, and only a small percentage elected. Yet the Townsend Plan influenced the Roosevelt administration in 1934. More important, the strategy returned a fairly consistent number of Townsend en-dorsees to the House over a decade's worth of elections starting in 1938, but the influence of the Townsend Plan varied greatly during this time. In the middle 1940s, notably, the Townsend Plan gained its greatest congressional representation, but old-age issues were off the political agenda.

Another line of argument concerning the impact of movements addresses how challengers make their claims. The literature on framing and the conse-quences of social movements suggests that a challenger's influence is related to the plausibility and resonance of its strategies of claims making. More plausible diagnoses of problems and proposed solutions are expected to be more effective in making a political impact, and less credible discursive moves should result in a loss of influence. As we have seen, the political discourse of the Townsend Plan resonated well at least with the medical metaphors of the framing literature. Given Dr. Townsend's background, he was said to have a "diagnosis" for the Depression and poverty in old age—that technology was reducing necessary labor time and producing unjust unemployment and poverty—as well as a "prescription" to ensure Americans would enjoy the abundance made possible by technology. The mandatory and rapid spending of generous old-age pensions would increase purchasing power, reduce the labor force, and end unemployment, while granting older Americans their just rewards for lives of productive citizenship. Creating artificial scarcity—one line pursued by the Roosevelt administration—was doomed, and immoral besides, given all the poverty. In alignment with this point of view, once the Townsend prescription seemed inappropriate, during the war, as military spending ended the Depression, the organization lost influence.

All the same, the experience of the Townsend Plan and the old-age pension movement suggests that only minimally resonant framing may be necessary for a movement to have an impact. The diagnoses and prescriptions of the Townsend Plan did not change much, but the Townsend Plan's pattern of influence varied during the Depression years, as did its coverage in the newspapers. Whether its claims resulted in a serious hearing seemed to depend on other factors, and the claims were only partially resonant among the general public and political leaders. The public tended to agree that old-age benefits should be closer to what the Townsend Plan was demanding. But political officials and other elites tended to denounce the proposal as being too expensive, misleading, and unlikely to work as claimed. Indeed, the Townsend Plan was often most influential when its arguments were under the greatest public attack. If Roosevelt was denouncing pension proposals as "untried panaceas" and "shortcuts to utopia," it was a sure sign that his policy proposals were tacking in their direction. What is more, never did the Townsend prescription for economic recovery through the mandatory spending of old-age pensions win acceptance from policy makers or the general public—including after "spenders" began to dominate within the administration in the late 1930s. When opinion polls registered support for the Townsend Plan, it was mainly because it was pointing in "the right direction" on old-age pensions.

Finally, there are political contextual or opportunity explanations for the influence of social movements. According to this line of argument, the productivity of challengers' collective action will be greater in more favorable political contexts. One way to appraise these ideas is to examine closely the fates of northern Democrats and left-wing party representatives in Congress, in relation to those of Republicans and southern Democrats, as northern Democrats and representatives farther to the left have been key backers of social policy and thus natural allies of social spending movements. This con-

Figure C.4: Size of Pro–Social Spender Margins in Congress, by Percentages, 1931–44. "Pro-spender" means likely supporters of generous, nationally controlled social programs. The margin is the difference between the pro-spenders and others in terms of the percentage of the house of Congress. See text. *Source: Congressional Quarterly.*

gressional "pro-spending" group should be all the more influential because throughout most of the Townsend Plan's challenge the president was Roosevelt, a northern Democrat in favor of social policy.[4]Figure C.4 shows that highly unfavorable political contexts meant no influence for the Townsend Plan. It had no impact in 1943 and 1944, when the ranks of the northern Democrats were decimated, the president focused on war, and a conservative coalition ruled Congress. Yet fluctuations in broadly favorable contexts did not correspond to the impact of the Townsend Plan. The plan had influence in 1934 during the proposal stage of the security bill, but not in 1935 or 1936 when the Congress was augmented with many new northern Democratic members after the midterm triumph in November 1934. The Townsend Plan had little influence in Congress when the political alignment was even better suited to social spending gains, in 1937 and 1938, but had great influence in 1939, after a midterm election in which pro-spenders took a drubbing.[5]

The lack of connection between the influence of the Townsend Plan and the political context was not a matter of underestimating the possibilities or seriously misreading them. Every January the *Townsend Weekly* would summarize the previous year, pronounce it as being the best ever for the Townsend Plan, and predict that the coming year would be better still. This occurred even in 1943, after support for Townsend clubs had dropped off sharply as the nation began its second year of war and as an anti–New Deal Congress was being seated. Still, the leadership seemed to understand that the fate of the old-age issue was connected to New Deal supporters in Congress. In consecutive issues the *Weekly* banner declared "New Townsend Plan Bill, Streamlined for War, Goes to Pension-Minded Congress," but then later noted on the inside pages that the "House Line-Up Threatens New Deal," and that Roosevelt's plans for improvements in old-age programs might be shelved. The Townsend Plan also routinely railed against "reactionary Republicans" and "poll-tax Democrats."[6]

In short, the evidence provides only some support for standard explanations. Some basic level of organized and highly mobilized support seemed to be necessary for the Townsend Plan to have an influence, as the resource mobilization view suggests. But there was no direct historical connection between the plan's mobilization and its influence. Moreover, sometimes the Townsend Plan's collective action strategies worked, and sometimes they did not. The organization's chief assertive strategy, contesting congressional elections, was productive only at times. What is more, the plan's diagnosis and prescription rarely changed over time, but its influence varied greatly. Finally, the Townsend Plan had no impact in unfavorable political contexts, as expected, but sometimes had an influence in circumstances that were only marginally favorable to social policy generally, and little influence at times when circumstances were greatly favorable. So what accounts for the varied influence of the Townsend Plan?

Explaining the Consequences of the Townsend Plan

My answer builds on these other points of view. For well-organized and well-mobilized challengers with at least marginally plausible claims, different sorts of strategies of collective action work best in different political contexts. To have an impact, challengers need to match strategies to meet changing political contexts. Here I summarize some of my expectations for the influence of the Townsend Plan and juxtapose them with some key results of its campaigns and episodes of old-age policy making. These claims and results appear in table C.1, which indicates that in some instances the Townsend Plan matched strategies to contexts, and in others it did not. The table also shows that when the Townsend Plan's strategies matched political contexts it was influential, and when it failed to do so it was not.

Two important, medium-run aspects of the political context concern the political regime and state bureaucracies related to the challenger's issue. If the political regime is supportive and the domestic bureaucrats are professionalized and supportive, limited protest based mainly on the evidence of mobilization is likely to be sufficient to provide increased collective benefits. By contrast,

TABLE C.1.
Collective Action Strategies Expected to Produce Collective Benefits, Given Specified Political Conditions, and Townsend Plan Campaigns, 1934–46

	State Bureaucrats	
Elected Officials	Strong and Aligned with Challenger's Interests	Weak and/or Opposed to Challenger's Interests
Aligned with challenger's constituency	Sheer mobilization, limited protest *(national level, 1934, 1938)* **(national level, 1935)** *(some states, late 1930s)*	Sanction or urge creation of state bureaus *(anti-lien campaign, 1939)*
Opposed or neutral to challenger's constituency	Sanction or displace elected officials *(national level, 1939)* *(states w/initiative drives, 1940s)* **(states w/out initiatives, 1940s)**	Highly assertive strategies **(California before 1939)**

Note: Campaigns in italics are ones in which the Townsend Plan matched strategy and context. Campaigns in bold are ones in which the Townsend Plan failed to match strategy and context, according to the model. In each instance, matching strategy and context led to gains by the Townsend Plan, and in each instance failing to match strategy and context resulted in no gains for the Townsend Plan.

achieving collective benefits through public policy is likely to be more difficult if neither a supportive regime nor administrative authority exists. When the regime is largely unfavorable to the challenger's claims and constituency, a challenger engaged only in limited protest would seem unlikely to influence the content of legislation or its passage. More assertive or bolder collective action would be needed—with electoral sanctions ranging from statements of endorsement in electoral contests to bids to recall legislators or attempting to eliminate them through a new party. If the state bureaucracy is unfavorably disposed to the challenger's constituency, it requires targeting. Assertive strategies might also produce results in relatively favorable political environments. Indeed, for challengers to make radical gains, they need to be highly mobilized, engage in coordinated and assertive strategies, provide plausible claims, and be in highly favorable contexts not of their own making. But in many instances, assertive strategies in favorable conditions might backfire and risk alienating potential allies within the polity and wasting energy and resources.

The policy situation is also an important part of the political context facing challengers. For reasons that have little to do with challengers, an issue related to their constituencies may find itself on or off the political agenda. Mobilized challengers have far greater chances to exert influence if their issue is already on the legislative agenda. It is easier to keep an issue from leaving the agenda than to place one on it. Challengers can attempt to advance the benefits in the legislation at hand or induce legislators to vote for the legislation, sometimes by gaining support for more radical legislation. An anti–social policy political alignment will generally ensure that augmentations in social policy do not get on the political agenda, but a favorable political alignment does not ensure that a challenger's issue will receive legislative attention. Similarly, a mobilized challenger can more easily influence the implementation of legislation that has recently been enacted. Over time, making a fundamental change in the nature of a policy becomes increasingly difficult as it becomes institutionalized.

As political circumstances become more difficult, represented by movement from the upper left-hand corner to the bottom right-hand corner of table C.1, more assertive or bolder collective action is required to produce collective benefits. By more assertive I mean the use of increasingly strong sanctions that influence things political actors value—often their positions, but also their beliefs—or that take over their functions or prerogatives.[7] These sanctions work largely by mobilizing large numbers of people behind a line of action. I avoid the usual equation between assertive and noninstitutional action, as institutional action is often more assertive than standard protests, which they provide stronger sanctions. The following examples give a sense of degrees of assertiveness in political institutional action by challengers. Engaging in educational campaigns and promoting the acceptance of a specific proposal or aid for a group is minimally assertive. Making public statements of endorsement for individual legislators or proposals goes further, and more assertive than that is engaging in protest campaigns targeting programs or administrators. Letter-writing campaigns to incumbents can be fairly assertive, depending on what the letters demand. Engaging in public campaigns to replace administrators subject to election or to prevent the appointments of others is more assertive still. Contesting the electoral prospects of individual legislators is similarly assertive. Bolder still are campaigns in polities with direct democratic devices, where a challenger can put its issue on the agenda, specify the proposal, and bid to have it voted into law. The passage of challenger-designed policies will also tend to promote its growth.

Challengers are also likely to benefit by targeting their actions to fit administrative or legislative contexts. If the relevant state bureaucratic actors are present and either supportive or neutral, and the political regime is not supportive of the challenger's group, collective action will be most productive if it focuses on elected officials. Such action might induce those who would otherwise be indifferent or hostile to legislation to support it or at least not to challenge it. If the political regime is supportive or neutral, and domestic bureaucrats are either absent or hostile to the challenger's constituency, domestic bureaucratic capabilities must be created or existing bureaucratic actors must be sanctioned. When both the political regime and the relevant state bureaucracy are unfavorably disposed to the challenger's constituency, only the most assertive strategies will be likely to win collective benefits. The most direct way to overcome these circumstances is for challengers to take political power through democratic processes, as through initiatives or creating new parties. Less assertive electoral strategies would work better than limited protest, which in turn would be better than minor educational or informational campaigns. In some circumstances, however, no collective action has hopes of being productive. Notably, the regime may be so unfavorable to the constituency or issue represented by the challenger that little can be done in the short run. In such instances it is best to focus on organizational efforts. For radical results, such as the generous and universal senior citizens' pensions demanded by the Townsend Plan, it will likely take highly favorable circumstances, high mobilization, and extensive and assertive action.

Matching strategies to contexts can happen either by design or inadvertently. Characteristics of movement organization can influence the probabilities of organizations making matches of strategy and situation. Organizational centralization has been claimed to allow the quickest reactions, but I argue the more important characteristics have to do with the capacities of the organization and the flexibility required to see that they are used. Those making decisions in the name of movements need to have specific claims-making, organizational, and political capacities, and a leadership structure that is flexible enough to allow these abilities to be deployed as needed. Leaders with particular skills need to be able to use them when the situation calls for them.

Townsend Plan Campaigns and Old-Age Policy

The Townsend Plan's history is helpful in appraising these claims because of the great number and variety of its campaigns and its fluctuating pattern of influence. Its actions ranged from merely trying to educate the public about the merits of the pension plan to attempting to unseat the president, and they took place under greatly varied circumstances. The Townsend Plan also contested old-age politics across many states of the union, whose polities varied quite dramatically.

Favorable Context, Strategy of Mobilization: Influencing the Administration, 1934

An example of applying an appropriate strategy to political circumstances came in 1934. Old-age and other social programs, notably unemployment insurance, were already on the political agenda as the Townsend Plan was just getting started, and in June Roosevelt called for the creation of the Committee on Economic Security to write a comprehensive bill for social policy. Although no one in the administration was admitting it, old-age policy apparently moved higher on the administration's list of priorities because of the Townsend Plan. Congressional legislation anticipated a program on the order of Old-Age Assistance, but with a lower matching formula and a smaller appropriation. An old-age annuity program was included. Aid to Dependent Children, also proposed by the CES, was funded at a lower matching rate than Old-Age Assistance, and health insurance, which was studied by the CES, was placed completely on the back burner.[8] All this happened, however, without much assertive action or even any self-conscious collective action by the Townsend Plan. For the most part, the Townsend Plan attempted to organize clubs in the West. The episode showed the value of organizing and mobilizing while an issue was on the agenda and the administration was generating new policy proposals.

Favorable Context, Inappropriate Strategy: Contesting Congress, 1935

By January 1935, the administration had written its economic security bill. Also, the political situation had changed for the better. The midterm congressional elections, which are always expected to lead to significant losses for the presidential party, instead brought great gains for the Democrats—all from the democratized North—in both houses of Congress, as well as for radical third parties. The administration went forward with its economic security bill as well as a work program that would amount to about one-tenth of the national income and about half of the budget.[9] The Townsend Plan adopted an explicit strategy, taking a much more assertive line. It presented a bill in Congress and launched an aggressive letter-writing campaign to members of the House Ways and Means Committee and other influential congressmen. Townsend Plan witnesses dismissed the administration's proposals as suitable for "paupers." The McGroarty bill received harsh criticism in return, and the Townsend Plan was forced to replace it. While the Townsend Plan was rewriting its bill, the House Ways and Means Committee was reducing the benefits in the administration's. Later, the Townsend Plan declined to lend its support to the best-supported House floor amendment, proposed by Isabella Greenway of Arizona, which upped the federal matching ratio for OAA and would have provided larger benefits to many more recipients. The Townsend Plan's actions were too assertive for its geographically localized mobilization.

Old-Age Off the National Political Agenda, on the Agenda of States, 1936–37

As 1936 began, the Townsend Plan had become a national phenomenon. It started to organize the entire country, with more than 7,000 Townsend clubs and a membership of 2 million.[10] Nonetheless, the Townsend Plan did not have much influence in Congress, where the organization targeted its pressure, but had at least indirect effects on state governments, which were demanding national certification for their new Old-Age Assistance programs far more rapidly than for similarly constructed Aid to the Blind and Aid to Dependent Children programs. In many states, notably those with extensive old-age pension support, the aged received something resembling pensions—relatively unfettered grants.[11] The difference between the impressive impact of the Townsend Plan at the state level, where it was not contesting the issue, and its lack of influence at the national level mainly had to do with differences in the place of old-age policy on political agendas. At the national level, the Townsend Plan did not have nearly enough support in Congress to force a vote through the discharge-petition process, unlike veterans' organizations, such as the American Legion, which successfully concluded a long campaign for their bonus bill. And the administration was sitting tight with its new security legislation. In the states, national incentives and the end of national emergency relief placed the old-age issue on the agenda.

Varied Contexts, Similar Strategies:
OAA in the States, 1936–1938

In its first years the Townsend Plan engaged in no plan of action to improve state Old-Age Assistance programs, but Townsend clubs were differentially mobilized across the states, which faced vastly different political circumstances. If one examines all states that were similar in having a prominent presence of Townsend clubs and being from a democratized polity not dominated by patronage parties, the Townsend Plan had a differential impact according to whether a favorable political regime was in power. States with Democratic or third-party regimes in power saw their benefit levels jump, slightly surpassing states that had gotten off to bigger head starts.[12] Still, the evidence suggests that the Townsend Plan lost opportunities to influence policy in these states. In California, one of the best mobilized states, the organization plan paid little attention to OAA politics and instead pressed the legislature to pass measures "memorializing" the national government to adopt the pension-recovery program. The Townsend Plan's "think-nationally, act-nationally" strategy combined with the sheer mobilization of clubs was not enough to boost California old-age policy, with its unfavorable regime: Republicans controlling the governor's mansion and the statehouse, and the California Department of Social Welfare sharing responsibility for old-age policy with the more restrictive county boards of supervisors.[13] In Colorado, by comparison, a pension organization begun by leaders that had broken with the Townsend Plan pressed for a state initiative to create generous old-age pensions where the political regime was similarly unfavorable. The National Annuity League succeeded not only in its drive to place its initiative on the ballot, putting immediate pressure on state officials to increase pensions; the initiative was approved in the general election. As a result, Colorado's version of Old-Age Assistance shot to the top of the nation's programs in terms of both benefits and coverage.

Old-Age Returns to the Political Agenda: The Impact of Mobilization, 1938

After the Townsend Plan's setbacks in 1936 and 1937, from the congressional investigation to Dr. Townsend's purging of key leadership, the organization made a comeback sparked by a reemphasis on organizing, a sharp economic decline in 1937–38, and a consensus among the administration and both parties in Congress that old-age policy needed to be revisited. Pension movements were also becoming big at the state level, as several groups were devoted to improving their OAA programs, notably Ham and Eggs, which had eclipsed the Townsend Plan in California.[14] In 1938, the Roosevelt administration and Congress placed old-age policy on the political agenda. The administration and liberal Democrats were concerned that the old-age payroll tax was building up reserves at the expense of the economy, whereas Republicans and other conservatives feared that the high productivity of the payroll tax would bring higher benefits. The Social Security Board also sought changes and with the aid of a Senate Advisory Council suggested increasing the starting date for social insurance benefits, providing huge windfalls for many workers who had paid almost nothing into the "system," and adding survivors' insurance and dependents' benefits. These proposals were supported by the administration despite the fact that health insurance was also being planned by a cabinet-level group. As in 1934, the Townsend Plan—and other old-age pension challengers—helped to move the old-age issue to a higher priority in the administration's thinking and spur the proposed benefits, largely by remobilizing in a period in which a pro-spending administration was revisiting the old-age issue.

Congress Ups the Ante: Assertive Strategy, Neutral Context, 1939

The new Congress that convened in 1939 was missing more than 90 northern Democrats in the House. Third-party candidates had all but been eliminated, and northern Democrats also had lost support in the Senate. The political configuration in Congress was only moderately favorable to social spending reform. But the Townsend Plan had for the first time focused its attention on congressional elections and had endorsed 147 winning House members. The influence of the Townsend Plan and the pension movement was evident in congressional amendments. Bucking the administration's proposals, Congress increased the maximum federal matching payments for OAA from $15 per person to $20. In the wake of a vote on a Townsend bill that produced more than 100 yeas, Congress was anxious to give something to the organization's aged constituency. The episode of influence contrasted greatly with that of 1935, when the Townsend Plan was unable to prevent decreases in proposed benefits for the aged in the Social Security Act.[15]

Unfavorable Administration, Assertive Action: California in 1939

Near the end of the 1930s, the Townsend Plan began to contest specific aspects of the California OAA law, especially the unfavorable administration of it, and in an increasingly assertive manner. In 1939, Townsendites marched on conservative county boards in Los Angeles and San Francisco, protesting their enforcement of liens on old-age beneficiaries' estates. According to these rulings, old-age beneficiaries could not bequeath their possessions, preventing many from applying for benefits. Townsendites asserted that California should provide pensions as a right. The bid for change helped to place the issue on the political agenda. At the start of the 1940 legislative session, Governor Culbert Olson asked for the repeal of the lien provision, despite the fact that he had previously stated that he wanted to avoid pension issues. Two repeal propositions passed by more than half a million votes with the support of the Townsend Plan.[16]

Influence over Agenda, Proposals, and, Almost, Legislation, 1940–41

By 1940, the administration had again seemingly completed its agenda on old age. Yet the Townsend Plan and the pension movement forced its return. The Townsend Plan was reaping organizing successes in the East and Midwest with its highest numbers of clubs and membership since 1936. State-level pension movements remained active in the West. The Townsend Plan's focused congressional endorsement campaign punished those who voted against its pension legislation and supported backers. In the presidential campaign, President Roosevelt and the Democratic platform called for a minimum old-age pension for all. The electorate returned Roosevelt to office and brought with him Democratic majorities large enough to improve social policy. Old-age policy was the main domestic issue in an agenda dominated by defense preparations. In a special committee led by California's Senator Sheridan Downey, a longtime proponent of the Townsend Plan, a minimum pension was agreed upon. Against its inclinations, the Social Security Board drew up plans for a two-tiered program that would add a universal old-age pension of $30 to the OASI program. Universal senior citizens' pensions had considerable support in Congress, and the Senate Finance Committee started hearings. But then the United States was attacked, and social policy was whisked from the political agenda. The pension movement had everything going for it—it was well organized and mobilized, facing a favorable political context, making plausible claims, and having engaged in successful assertive action that kept its issue on the agenda. But it ran out of time.[17]

A Loss of Influence, War, and a Conservative Coalition, 1942–45

The war forced the pension issue off the political agenda and presented the Townsend Plan with discursive and political problems. The war preparations and then mobilization for war had ended the Depression, minimizing the need for a recovery program. What was worse, demanding benefits for the aged was incongruent with the dominant political theme of national sacrifice. The Townsend Plan tried to revise its program, earmarking its tax for defense for the duration, but no one was paying attention. Then the elections of 1942 decimated the potential political alignment for social policy reform. A coalition of Republicans and southern Democrats delayed already scheduled increases in the old-age insurance payroll tax, despite the fact that the Townsend Plan had its best year ever in terms of endorsing members of the House. A moderate level of Townsend Plan strength in mobilization and success in its congressional endorsements were not enough to effect advances in old-age spending policy—once the congressional alignment turned conservative and the president was preoccupied by foreign affairs. Retrenchment occurred instead.[18]

Sixty-at-Sixty and Unfavorable Political Contexts in the States

The Townsend Plan turned its attention to the states, which were not fiscally involved in the war effort and were responsible for half of Old-Age Assistance, and embarked on drives for initiatives demanding $60 per month for all citizens sixty years old and older. By 1944 the Townsend Plan had placed Sixty-at-Sixty initiatives before the voters in Washington, Oregon, and California. As in the nation, however, there was a shift to the Republicans, and the initiatives lost in each state. But where initiatives were fought, old-age programs were advanced further than in comparable states. Assertive action in somewhat unfavorable political contexts proved effective. But these campaigns were the last hurrah for the Townsend Plan. Townsendites began to die off, and their ranks were not being replenished. The claims of the Townsend Plan, based on the program's ability to ensure prosperity, lost credibility as a postwar depression never surfaced.

The Rise of Social Security, 1949–1950, and
the Secondary Effect of the Movement

Soon the national political context became moderately favorable again for social policy, with the end of the war and the election of Harry S Truman and a Democratic Congress in 1948. Once again the Social Security Administration sought improvements in Old-Age and Survivors Insurance, its flagship social insurance program. A new round of debate culminated in the Social Security Amendments of 1950, which greatly improved OASI and gave us something like Social Security as we know it today. The Townsend Plan and the national old-age pension movement, having declined in numbers and having no plausible prescription for prosperity, had little influence on the process. It had narrowly missed its chance to change the nature of U.S. old-age policy, which was becoming further institutionalized, as more and more Americans received both OAA and OASI benefits. Still, the mobilizations of the previous fifteen years had a cumulative impact and altered the parameters of the debate. Conservative business groups feared the expansion of OAA in the more generous states and thus backed moderate increases in OASI benefits, while rejecting other social insurance initiatives. So did southern representatives who wanted to get a greater share of federal monies. In each state, cash-strapped departments of welfare hoped that the national government would pick up a greater share of the old-age tab.

Some Lessons of the Townsend Plan

One thing the Townsend Plan and U.S. old-age pension challengers demonstrated was that challengers can have impressive impacts even when their goals are not achieved. The Townsend Plan never passed its legislation, but it helped to alter the course of U.S. social policy. And challengers can have influence even when their leaders fail them, as happened often with the Townsend Plan. Another lesson is that challengers' influence on public policy is politically mediated in specific ways. Under certain political institutional conditions, notably restrictions on democratic practices and the entrenchment of patronage-oriented political parties, both the presence and the impact of state-oriented challengers are likely to be greatly dampened. Even when polities are structurally and systemically favorable, challengers need to match appropriate collective action strategies to situations. In addition, the place of an issue relative to the political agenda constitutes an important part of the political context. If the issue is on the political agenda, it greatly increases the probability of influence, but these opportunities are usually short-lived and shifting.

Another message from these results is that it is worth thinking through the complexity of challenger strategies as well as those of political contexts.

Challenger strategies that are often lumped together as "assimilative" or "institutional" usually include most of the lines of action available to challengers in democratic polities. Yet these actions can vary dramatically in terms of who they target, the sanctions they provide, and their productivity under different political circumstances. Making greater distinctions among these strategies according to assertiveness and direction matters, because collective action varies in its effectiveness according to the contexts in which it is undertaken.

Scholars, and possibly movement activists, too, should pay attention to aspects of challengers' mode of organization that promote strategic flexibility. Centralization in leadership may make it easier for leaders to alter strategy quickly, but the history of the Townsend Plan suggests that flexibility is far from inevitable in centralized organizations. Movements need many sorts of capabilities, including ones that apply to claims making, organizational matters, and legislative action, and there must be ways for those with expertise to influence strategic decision making. The Townsend Plan was hampered by the fact that the person calling the shots after its first two years had few skills. Possibly for this reason the Townsend Plan's average of matching strategies to situations was a low one, relying largely on changing contexts and coincidence rather than altering action to meet changing situations.

As scholars of social policy have long understood, social movements are usually not the only influences on policy making, even when they are particularly active. The political system matters quite a bit, as do left-center political coalitions, the actions of domestic bureaucrats, previous policies, and changes in public opinion. Some of the same reasons that made it difficult for the Townsend Plan to advance U.S. social policy, especially its poorly democratized political system, made it difficult for left-center coalitions to take power and for domestic bureaucrats to advance social policy while other countries were making progress. A complete analysis of the development of policies requires taking other actors and aspects of the political process far more seriously than social movement scholars tend to do. Social movement leaders cannot be blamed for exaggerating the influence of their actions, as Townsend surely did. It is central to their mission. But scholars need to sort out the processes by which different political actors maneuver in different political contexts to produce changes in state policy.

There are also implications for accepted theoretical accounts of the development of U.S. social policy. The old-age slant of U.S. social policy is often attributed to the power and savvy of the Social Security Administration, which is held to have been able to work around the barriers to social policy set up by the U.S. polity. But, as we have seen, in its salad days this body was quite weak and frequently outmaneuvered; at key points it was the pension movement that induced the administration and Congress to attend to old-age policy, with a cumulative effect. What is more, discussions of welfare, based on Aid to Dependent Children, suggest that all means-tested programs were similar and less valuable than social insurance programs, because welfare programs were designed for women. Although that is partly true, Old Age Assistance was far more generous than ADC, as well as the old-age insurance program, and this was due to the extensive mass pressure on OAA, a mobilization that involved women and men in equal measures. That sort of pressure was missing for ADC. Also, the U.S. welfare state is often claimed to have had its origins in the "big bang" that was the Social Security Act, which in turn is sometimes attributed to short-term contingencies, such as the rise to power of northern Democrats and short-lived mobilizations like Huey Long's Share Our Wealth or the first years of the Townsend Plan.[19] However, U.S. social policy was formed over more than a decade, and its shape was the result of both a sustained coalition of pro-spending forces in the White House and Congress and a persistent mobilization around old age. Had there not been both, U.S. social policy would have been even less extensive and certainly less focused on old age than it is today.

The Legacy of the Townsend Plan

The Townsend Plan had some notable shortcomings that are central to its legacy. The Townsend clubs did little in the way of creating a sophisticated, effective, or durable collective identity for the aged. The clubs' focus did not stray far from the pension proposal and its founder. Townsend clubs were at least as much fan clubs as challenger membership organizations. They also attached the program to standard rituals of pietistic Protestantism and American patriotism, a cultural repertoire that may have discouraged participation among nonnative white Americans. Although the Townsend Plan energized the aged who participated in its club activities, the central organization did not allow the clubs much leeway in independent political activity. Townsend clubs gave those aged people outside the clubs few materials with which to help to reshape their own political identities.

Worse than that, the Townsend Plan did little directly to aid the permanent political organization of the aged. The plan provided an unsound vehicle to organize the aged for the long haul. When the pension idea lost favor, so did the organization and its clubs. And the Townsend Plan could have done far more than it did to develop new leaders among the aged. To put its setback in perspective, Theda Skocpol has shown that of the only fifty-seven voluntary organizations that ever claimed as members at least 1 percent of the U.S. population, forty-three are still in existence. Despite its rapid growth, all-American appeal, and the fact that it targeted a demographic group constantly being replenished, the Townsend Plan went the way of the Farmers Alliance, the Industrial Workers of the World, and the second Ku Klux Klan.[20]

Most Americans born in 1934 are now receiving Social Security, but in that same lifetime the Townsend Plan went from national force to vague memory. If the Townsend Plan brings anything at all to mind, it is a leadership that was either living in a fantasy world or taking advantage of an elderly generation whose poverty was exceeded only by its gullibility. Nowadays when one reads about the Townsend Plan in the newspaper, it is usually in a letter to the editor whose author is hoping to demonstrate erudition in belittling some current proposal with a historical laughingstock. It is odd that an organization that spent so much time selling itself and its program and so innovatively should suffer such poor historical PR.

The fact that it is so little remembered and so negatively is not all the Townsend Plan's fault. As with most social movement organizations, the Townsend Plan did not leave extensive records. Its wispy historical traces are dwarfed by extensive archives of the Social Security Administration. With its many erudite former officials and enterprising scholars writing memoir after analysis, it has taken control over the historiography of American old age, often following Witte in portraying the Townsend Plan as an obstacle to the sort of rational policy exemplified by Social Security. Few of the Townsend Plan's leaders had the writer's impulse, and in any case all of them are dead, unable to forge an alternative historiography as younger activists of the 1960s have done. Also, Depression-era phenomena are often too bleak to think much about. Americans much prefer to relive the triumph of World War II. Even for those not put off by the 1930s, Townsend was not as colorful or exciting as his contemporaries Huey Long or Father Coughlin. The aged doctor's brand of charisma relied more on publicity than aura. Frank Capra could not cast the main character in Meet John Doe as an older man and expect to pack theaters. Townsend's longevity may also have hurt the cause of remembrance. It would have helped to have gone out in a hail of gunfire like Long or Dillinger. And the Townsend Plan has certainly been less than fortunate in its chroniclers. There have been no documentaries by Ken Burns, no volumes by Alan Brinkley, Taylor Branch, or Michael Kazin.

The mixed ideological message of the Townsend Plan leaders no doubt also limits its current appeal. Neither conservatives nor radicals recognize in the Townsendites their forebears. This is another unfortunate legacy and one that is more our own doing. In these polarized political times, patriotism and religion seem inextricably linked to militarism and social policies favoring the rich and harming the poor. But the Townsend Plan provided a model of how to link these red cultural themes with a blue program to fight injustice and poverty that is worth considering today.

There is no reason to end by accentuating the negative and focusing on what might have been. The Townsend Plan and the old-age pension movement influenced the American welfare state in its formative years and permanently tilted it toward old age. The Townsend Plan also helped to make the aged more formidable as a force on the American political scene and induced politicians for the first time to see the aged as a special category of citizens. Politicians of both parties feared the Townsendites and began to think of the aged as a group whose demands and wants were deserving of respect and attention. The Townsend Plan also demonstrated the value of mobilizing the aged and was soon copied by all manner of organizations.

Through their promotion of old-age policy, the Townsendites indirectly increased the political importance of the elderly for the long haul. The Townsend Plan helped to forge a ready-made set of issues around which older Americans could be mobilized in the future. By speeding up a process of state building in which the elderly were designated as extradeserving of governmental attention and receiving benefits through Old-Age Assistance and Social Security, the Townsend Plan put the state in charge of mobilizing senior citizens. The old-age organizations that followed, most famously the AARP, were based on recipients of Social Security. The Townsend Plan advanced forces that undermined it, but opened the way for others to carry on the cause.

ACKNOWLEDGMENTS _____

I HAVE BEEN WORKING on the issues in this book for almost as long as the Townsend Plan was a serious challenger and have incurred about as many debts. Unfortunately, I cannot discharge them by sales of paraphernalia or vitamin pills, so I hope this will do.

I am in the debt of the helpful staffs of many research libraries and institutions, including the National Archives; the Franklin D. Roosevelt Library; special collections units at the University of California, Los Angeles (Charles E. Young), the University of California, Berkeley (Bancroft), the University of Oregon, and Louisiana State University (Hill); the Oregon, Wisconsin, and Arizona Historical Societies; and last, and probably least, the Federal Bureau of Investigation.

I thank Chuck Myers of Princeton University Press and Lewis Bateman of Cambridge University Press for stimulating discussions of where to take the book. Chuck gets credit for the title. I thank Mark Bellis and Jennifer Nippins for getting the manuscript through production and Susan Ecklund for her fine copyediting. I thank, too, the editors of the series, Ira Katznelson, Martin Shefter, and Theda Skocpol.

I have presented versions of this work before several groups of colleagues, including at the Russell Sage Foundation; the sociology departments at the University of Arizona, Harvard University, Rutgers University, the University of California, San Diego, and the University of California, Irvine; the political science department of Yale University; the Workshop on 20th Century American Politics and Society at Columbia University; and the Politics, Power, and Protest Workshop at New York University. I thank all participants for making me think about these issues on my feet and out loud.

I also thank Eric Wanner, my fellow visiting scholars, Madge Spitaleri, and the staff at the Russell Sage Foundation in 2000–2001 for helping to jumpstart this project and making me believe that there was a book here instead of just a few more articles.

I am grateful to many colleagues for their reading of parts of the manuscript and comments on it, including Vanessa Barker, Edward D. Berkowitz, Neal Caren, Jeff Goodwin, Jack A. Goldstone, Brian Gratton, James M. Jasper, David S. Meyer, Sheera Joy Olasky, Francesca Polletta, Mildred A. Schwartz, Michael P. Young, and anonymous readers from Cambridge University Press and Princeton University Press. I would especially like to thank Jim and Jeff for many stimulating discussions over the years.

I express my deep appreciation to the friends and colleagues who worked with me through the years on articles about the Townsend Plan and the impact of movements: Bruce G. Carruthers, Yvonne Zylan, Mary Bernstein, Kathleen Dunleavy, Jane D. Poulsen, Michael P. Young, Drew Halfmann, and the members of Manhattan 269, the last Townsend club, Neal Caren and Sheera Joy Olasky. Who would have thought that New York City would be the final stronghold of the Townsend Plan? Now that we have rolled up our "God Bless America—with the Townsend Plan" banner and moved on, the only organized attacks on Social Security will be from the Right.

I want to thank as well my friends, especially Kim Blanton, and family— my brothers, Chuck and Francis, and my sister Kerry Garesché and their families, my sister Marybeth, and my parents, Charles and Mary Amenta—for their support over the years. I would also like to thank my one-and-a-half-year-old children, Gregory and Luisa, who will probably be turning the corner toward three by the time this is published. But I cannot because they are the reason this book did not appear two years ago as initially planned. They arrived instead, and I am grateful. As for Francesca, this is where the author usually thanks his lovely wife for all her typing, copyediting, and taking charge of the household. But that didn't happen, and I'm glad for that, too. She did more than her share of expert reading and listening and was always there when I needed her.

NOTES

Introduction: The Townsend Plan's Image Problem

1. Francis E. Townsend, with Jesse George, *New Horizons: An Autobiography* (Chicago: J. L. Stewart, 1943), p. 235.

2. Edwin E. Witte, *The Development of the Social Security Act: A Memorandum on the History of the Committee on Economic Security and Drafting and Legislative History of the Social Security Act* (1937; Madison: University of Wisconsin Press, 1962), pp. 95–96.

3. The locution "Townsend movement" has caught on among scholars, but I refer to the organization and phenomenon as the "Townsend Plan" for key historical and analytical reasons. Most of all, in its day the organization and its clubs were mainly referred to as the "Townsend Plan," which is how the *New York Times* index and other official sources have it. In secondary references, newspapers and magazines were as likely to use "Townsend organization," "Townsend clubs," "Townsendites," and "Townsend clubbers" as the more grandiose "Townsend movement." Searching the *New York Times* through ProQuest, while omitting "Townsend movement" from a list of terms including all the organization's official names, "Townsend clubs," and "Townsendites," will miss only 33 articles, whereas leaving out "Townsend Plan" will miss 555. (And searching for "Townsend movement" will yield no memorabilia on eBay.) Taking a name that served for both organization and program was a standard formulation for challengers of the day, as in Huey Long's Share Our Wealth and Upton Sinclair's End Poverty in California. The Townsend Plan's original name, Old Age Revolving Pensions, was thought to be less catchy and was abandoned. Also, Townsend eventually changed the name of the organization to the Townsend National Recovery Plan and then just the Townsend Plan. It was never called the "Townsend Movement." From the perspective of social movement scholarship, moreover, the organization and the Townsend clubs were not a "movement" so much as a movement organization in the wider old-age pension movement, which, by 1938, was no longer dominated by the Townsend Plan.

4. Paul Douglas, *Social Security in the United States: An Analysis and Appraisal of the Federal Social Security Act* (New York: McGraw-Hill, 1936), p. 73; Abraham Holtzman, *The Townsend Movement: A Political Study* (New York: Bookman, 1963), pp. 207–10; Frances Fox Piven and Richard A. Cloward, *Regulating the Poor: The Functions of Public Welfare*, 2nd ed. (New York: Vintage Books, 1993), chap. 3; Arthur M. Schlesinger Jr., *The Politics of Upheaval* (Boston: Houghton Mifflin, 1960), p. 43.

5. Witte, *The Development of the Social Security Act*, pp. 83–84; Frances Perkins, *The Roosevelt I Knew* (New York: Harper and Row, 1946), chap. 23.

6. The initial math was simple: 10 million aged pensioners at $200 per month would cost $24 billion per year, which was approximately half the nation's income in 1934. Edward D. Berkowitz, *America's Welfare State: From Roosevelt to Reagan* (Baltimore: Johns Hopkins University Press, 1991); Ann Shola Orloff, *The Politics of Pensions: A Comparative Analysis of Britain, Canada, and the United States, 1880–1940* (Madison: University of Wisconsin Press, 1993), chap. 9. See also W. Andrew Achen-

baum, "The Formative Years of Social Security: A Test Case of the Piven and Cloward Thesis," in *Social Welfare or Social Control: Some Historical Reflections on Regulating the Poor*, ed. Walter I. Trattner (Knoxville: University of Tennessee Press, 1983), pp. 67–89; Daniel J. B. Mitchell, *Pensions Politics and the Elderly: Historical Social Movements and Their Lessons for Our Aging Society* (Armonk, N.Y.: M. E. Sharpe, 2000).

7. For some examples, see William Kornhauser, *The Politics of Mass Society* (New York: Free Press, 1959); Neil Smelser, *Theory of Collective Behavior* (New York: Free Press, 1962).

8. *An Army of the Aged* (Caldwell, Idaho: Caxton Printers, 1936), pp. 14, 32–33; *The Psychology of Social Movements* (New York: Wiley, 1941), p. 169. See also Sheldon L. Messinger, "Organizational Transformation: A Case Study of a Declining Movement," *American Sociological Review* 20 (1955): 3–10. Other organizations in the old-age pension movement were treated similarly. See, for instance, Frank A. Pinner, Paul Jacobs, and Philip Selznick, *Old Age and Political Behavior: A Case Study* (Berkeley: University of California Press, 1959).

9. See Doug McAdam, John D. McCarthy, and Mayer N. Zald, "Introduction: Opportunities, Mobilizing Structures, and Framing Processes—Toward a Synthetic, Comparative Perspective on Social Movements," in *Comparative Perspectives on Social Movements: Political Opportunities, Mobilizing Structures, and Cultural Framings*, ed. Doug McAdam, John D. McCarthy, and Mayer N. Zald (New York: Cambridge University Press, 1996), pp. 1–22; Sidney Tarrow, *Power in Movement* (New York: Cambridge University Press, 1994).

10. For a review, see Edwin Amenta and Neal Caren, "The Legislative, Organizational, and Beneficiary Consequences of State-Oriented Challengers," *The Blackwell Companion to Social Movements*, ed. David A. Snow, Sarah A. Soule, and Hanspeter Kriesi (Oxford: Blackwell, 2004), chap. 20.

11. William Gamson also sees acceptance as an important dimension of success. William A. *The Strategy of Social Protest*, 2nd ed. (Belmont, Calif.: Wadsworth, 1990), pp. 34–37.

12. On resource mobilization, see John D. McCarthy and Mayer N. Zald, "The Enduring Vitality of the Resource Mobilization Theory of Social Movements," in *Handbook of Sociological Theory*, ed. Jonathon H. Turner (New York: Kluwer Academic/ Plenum, 2001), pp. 533–65.

13. On claims making and framing, see Charles Tilly, "From Interactions to Outcomes in Social Movements," in *How Social Movements Matter: Past Research, Present Problems, Future Developments*, Marco Giugni, Doug McAdam, and Charles Tilly (Minneapolis: University of Minnesota Press, 1999), pp. 253–70; Daniel M. Cress and David A. Snow, "The Outcomes of Homeless Mobilization: The Influence of Organization, Disruption, Political Mediation, and Framing," *American Journal of Sociology* 105 (2000): 1063–1104. On political opportunity, see Herbert P. Kitschelt, "Political Opportunity Structures and Political Protest: Anti-nuclear Movements in Four Democracies," *British Journal of Political Science* 16 (1986): 57–85. See chapter 1 for further discussion.

14. Witte also used that ploy. The epigraph at the beginning of the chapter, suggesting that the "Townsend movement" did more harm than good, is taken from a discussion of why the economic security bill stalled in Congress. Witte was also the author

of an anti–Townsend Plan press release. "Old Age Pension Organizations," September 6, 1934, National Archives, Record Group 47, box 22, Witte—personal file.

15. Technically speaking, choosing to study a challenger of suspected significance is selecting on the dependent variable—which can result in misleading conclusions. Gamson, *Strategy of Social Protest*, appendices b and c.

Chapter One: Success or Consequences, and U.S. Social Movements

1. William A. Gamson, *The Strategy of Social Protest*, 2nd ed. (Belmont, Calif.: Wadsworth, 1990). Initially published in 1975, Gamson's work sparked a great deal of debate, notably Jack A. Goldstone, "The Weakness of Organization: A New Look at Gamson's *The Strategy of Social Protest*," *American Journal of Sociology* 85 (1980): 1017–42. For a review, see Edwin Amenta and Neal Caren, "The Legislative, Organizational, and Beneficiary Consequences of State-Oriented Challengers," in *The Blackwell Companion to Social Movements*, ed. David A. Snow, Sarah A. Soule, and Hanspeter Kriesi (Oxford: Blackwell, 2004), chap. 20.

2. Gamson, *Strategy of Social Protest*, p. 29. See also Lee Ann Banaszak, *Why Movements Succeed or Fail: Opportunity, Culture, and the Struggle for Woman Suffrage* (Princeton, N.J.: Princeton University Press, 1996). For an early critique, see Joseph Gusfield, "Social Movements and Social Change: Perspectives of Linearity and Fluidity," in *Research in Social Movements, Conflict, and Change*, ed. Louis Kriesberg (Greenwich, Conn.: JAI Press, 1980), pp. 317–39.

3. Russell Hardin, *Collective Action* (Baltimore: Johns Hopkins University Press, 1982). The collective benefits standard is valuable even outside the context of standard rational-choice imagery and explanations. Scholars working in this tradition typically address contributions to collective action or mobilization. Once individuals contribute effort to collective action, say, money to a public television network, it is assumed that a definite amount of collective good, say, public television programming, will result. See Dennis Chong, *Collective Action and the Civil Rights Movement* (Chicago: University of Chicago Press, 1993). The path from resource mobilization to collective action to impacts on states, however, is not straightforward. Resources devoted to the Townsend Plan would not necessarily result in a set amount of a collective benefit—such as an increase in the old-age benefit payment.

4. Sidney Tarrow, *Power in Movement: Social Movements, Collective Action, and Politics* (New York: Cambridge University Press, 1994); Jane Mansbridge, *Why We Lost the ERA* (Chicago: University of Chicago Press, 1986); Sarah A. Soule and Susan Olzak, "When Do Social Movements Matter? The Politics of Contingency and the Equal Rights Amendment, 1972–1982," *American Sociological Review* 69 (2004): 473–97; David S. Meyer, *A Winter of Discontent: The Nuclear Freeze and American Politics* (New York: Praeger, 1990).

5. David Snyder and William J. Kelly, "Strategies for Investigating Violence and Social Change," in *The Dynamics of Social Movements*, ed. Mayer N. Zald and John D. McCarthy (Cambridge, MA: Winthrop Press, 1979).

6. The use of access or acceptance as a criterion for success also has problems. As Gamson notes, acceptance does not necessarily lead to new advantages—a situation

he refers to as co-option. Francis Fox Piven and Richard A. Cloward, *Poor People's Movements: Why They Succeed, How They Fail* (New York: Random House, 1977). Also, almost all challengers can gain some access to some state officials in democratic states, as through public forums, hearings, and interviews.

7. Steven Lukes, *Power: A Radical View* (London: Macmillan, 1974); Charles Tilly, *From Mobilization to Revolution* (Reading, Mass.: Addison-Wesley, 1978).

8. Of the fifty-three groups studied by Gamson, a sample representing the population of American challengers through 1945, thirty-three were mainly state oriented. Important examples of state-oriented social movements since then include the civil rights and environmental movements. Robert Dahl, *Polyarchy: Participation and Opposition* (New Haven, Conn.: London: Yale University Press, 1971).

9. On framing and consequences for social movements, see Daniel M. Cress and David A. Snow, "The Outcomes of Homeless Mobilization: The Influence of Organization, Disruption, Political Mediation, and Framing," *American Journal of Sociology* 105 (2000): 1063–1104. For noninstitutional action, see Doug McAdam, "Conceptual Origins, Current Problems, Future Directions," in *Comparative Perspectives on Social Movements: Political Opportunities, Mobilizing Structures, and Cultural Framings*, ed. Doug McAdam, John D. McCarthy, and Mayer N. Zald (New York: Cambridge University Press, 1996), chap. 1. For disruptive action, see Herbert P. Kitschelt, "Political Opportunity Structures and Political Protest: Anti-nuclear Movements in Four Democracies," *British Journal of Political Science* 16 (1986): 57–85. For unconventional action, see Russell Dalton, *Citizen Politics in Western Democracies: Public Opinion and Political Parties in the United States, Great Britain, West Germany, and France* (Chatham, N.J.: Chatham House, 1988); Elisabeth S. Clemens, *The People's Lobby: Organizational Innovation and the Rise of Interest Group Politics in the United States, 1890–1925* (Chicago: University of Chicago Press, 1997). On transgressive action, see Doug McAdam, Sidney Tarrow, and Charles Tilly, *Dynamics of Contention* (New York: Cambridge University Press, 2001).

10. Charles Tilly sees the effectiveness of challengers in their interactions with the state as being based on their worthiness, unity, numbers, and commitment. "From Interactions to Outcomes in Social Movements," in *How Social Movements Matter: Past Research, Present Problems, Future Developments*, ed. Marco Giugni, Doug McAdam, and Charles Tilly (Minneapolis: University of Minnesota Press, 1999), pp. 253–70.

11. See also Kitschelt, "Political Opportunity Structures and Political Protest"; J. Craig Jenkins, "Resource Mobilization Theory and the Study of Social Movements," *Annual Review of Sociology* 9 (1983): 527–53; Michael Lipsky, "Protest as Political Resource," *American Political Science Review* 62 (1968): 1144–58.

12. For reviews of the literatures on the development of social policy, see Edwin Amenta, "What We Know about Social Policy: Comparative and Historical Research in Comparative and Historical Perspective," in *Comparative and Historical Analysis*, ed. Dietrich Rueschemeyer and James Mahoney (New York: Cambridge University Press, 2003), chap. 3; Paul Pierson, "Three Worlds of Welfare State Research," *Comparative Political Studies* 33 (2000): 822–44; Edwin Amenta, Chris Bonastia, and Neal Caren, "U.S. Social Policy in Comparative and Historical Perspective: Concepts, Images, Arguments, and Research Strategies," *Annual Review of Sociology* 27 (2001): 213–34; Jeff Manza, "Political Sociological Models of the U.S. New Deal," *Annual Review of Sociology* 26 (2000): 297–322.

13. Charles Tilly, *Coercion, Capital, and European States, AD 992–1992* (Cambridge, Mass.: Blackwell, 1992); Hanspeter Kriesi, "The Political Opportunity Structure of New Social Movements: Its Impact on Their Mobilization," in *States and Social Movements*, ed. J. Craig Jenkins and Bert Klandermans (Minneapolis: University of Minnesota Press, 1995), chap. 7.

14. Evelyne Huber and John D. Stephens, *Development and Crises of the Welfare State: Parties and Policies in Global Markets* (Chicago: University of Chicago Press, 2001), pp. 4–5; Tilly, *From Mobilization to Revolution*; Edwin Amenta and Michael P. Young, "Democratic States and Social Movements: Theoretical Arguments and Hypotheses," *Social Problems* 57 (1999): 153–68.

15. V. O. Key, *Southern Politics in State and Nation* (New York: Knopf, 1949), chap. 14; McAdam, "Conceptual Origins, Current Problems, Future Directions"; Amenta and Young, "Democratic States and Social Movements."

16. On U.S. voter turnout, see Ruy A. Teixeira, *The Disappearing American Voter* (Washington, D.C.: Brookings, 1992), chap. 1; Frances Fox Piven and Richard A. Cloward, *Why Americans Don't Vote* (New York: Pantheon, 1989); J. Morgan Kousser, *The Shaping of Southern Politics: Suffrage Restriction and the Establishment of the One-Party South, 1880–1910* (New Haven, Conn.: Yale University Press, 1974); Walter Dean Burnham, *Critical Elections and the Mainsprings of American Politics* (New York: Norton, 1970), chap. 4. For the populists, see Lawrence Goodwyn, *The Populist Moment: A Short History of the Agrarian Revolt in America* (Oxford: Oxford University Press, 1978), pp. 56–58.

17. Theda Skocpol, *Protecting Soldiers and Mothers: The Political Origins of Social Policy in the United States* (Cambridge, Mass.: Harvard University Press, 1992), pp. 1–62.

18. Seymour M. Lipset and Stein Rokkan, "Cleavage Structures, Party Systems, and Voter Alignments," in *Party Systems and Voter Alignments*, ed. Seymour M. Lipset and Stein Rokkan (New York: Free Press, 1967), pp. 1–66; Seymour Martin Lipset and Gary Marks, *It Didn't Happen Here: Why Socialism Failed in the United States* (New York: Norton, 2000), chap. 2; Mildred A. Schwartz, "Continuity Strategies among Political Challengers: The Case of Social Credit," *American Review of Canadian Studies* 30 (2000): 455–77; Gamson, *Strategy of Social Protest*, pp. 277–85; Herbert Kitschelt, *The Logics of Party Formation* (Ithaca, N.Y.: Cornell University Press, 1989).

19. Clemens, *The People's Lobby*.

20. Kriesi, "The Political Opportunity Structure of New Social Movements"; Clarence Y. H. Lo, *Small Property versus Big Government: The Social Origins of the Property Tax Revolt* (Berkeley: University of California Press, 1990); Elizabeth Gerber, *The Populist Paradox: Interest Group Influence and the Promise of Direct Democracy* (Princeton, N.J.: Princeton University Press, 2001).

21. Mayhew refers to these as "traditional party organizations" and defines them as substantially autonomous, long-lasting, hierarchical, seeking to nominate candidates for a wide range of public offices, and relying substantially on material incentives. *Placing Parties in American Politics* (Princeton, N.J.: Princeton University Press, 1986), pp. 19–20, chap. 10. See also Ira Katznelson, *City Trenches: Urban Politics and the Patterning of Class in the United States* (New York: Pantheon, 1981). As Seymour Martin Lipset and Gary Marks note, the early establishment of these parties on a national basis made the United States stand out in comparison to early (male) democratizing

countries like Switzerland and Australia, neither of which expanded the electorate in the context of an existing party system. *It Didn't Happen Here*, chap. 2.

22. Martin Shefter, *Political Parties and the State: The American Historical Experience* (Princeton, N.J.: Princeton University Press, 1993), chaps. 3, 5; Amenta, *Bold Relief.*

23. State domestic bureaucracies are in the middle range, structurally speaking, and often influence only specific groups and issues. Skocpol, *Protecting Soldiers and Mothers*; Amenta, *Bold Relief*; Kitschelt, "Political Opportunity Structures and Political Protest."

24. Skocpol, *Protecting Soldiers and Mothers*. See also Paul Pierson, *Dismantling the Welfare State? Reagan, Thatcher, and the Politics of Retrenchment* (Cambridge: Cambridge University Press, 1994), chap. 1.

25. Piven and Cloward, *Poor People's Movements*; Bruce Western, "Postwar Unionization in Eighteen Advanced Capitalist Countries," *American Sociological Review* 58 (1993): 266–82.

26. Theda Skocpol, *Diminished Democracy: From Membership to Management in American Civic Life* (Norman: University of Oklahoma Press, 2003); John D. McCarthy and Mayer N. Zald, "The Enduring Vitality of the Resource Mobilization Theory of Social Movements," in *Handbook of Sociological Theory*, ed. Jonathon H. Turner (New York: Kluwer Academic/Plenum, 2001), pp. 533–65. On claims making, see Cress and Snow, "The Outcomes of Homeless Mobilization"; Myra Marx Ferree, William Anthony Gamson, Jurgen Gerhards, and Dieter Rucht, *Shaping Abortion Discourse: Democracy and the Public Sphere in Germany and the United States* (Cambridge: Cambridge University Press, 2002). On the impact of political contexts, see David S. Meyer and Debra C. Minkoff, "Conceptualizing Political Opportunity," *Social Forces* 82 (2004): 1457–92; Kitschelt, "Political Opportunity Structures and Political Protest." See also J. Craig Jenkins and Charles Perrow, "The Insurgency of the Powerless: Farm Worker Movements, 1946–1972," *American Sociological Review* 42 (1977): 249–68.

27. The argument focuses on specific political contexts, taking to heart criticisms that political opportunity concepts are often conceptualized at too broad a level. Jeff Goodwin and James M. Jasper, "Caught in a Winding, Snarling Vine: The Structural Bias of Political Process Theory," *Sociological Forum* 14 (1999): 27–54. The political mediation argument also differs from political opportunity arguments in that the latter tend to address the mobilization of challengers more than their political consequences. See Doug McAdam, *Political Process and the Development of Black Insurgency, 1930–1970*, 2nd ed. (Chicago: University of Chicago Press, 1999), introduction; Mayer N. Zald, "Ideologically Structured Action: An Enlarged Agenda for Social Movement Research," *Mobilization* 5 (2000): 31–36.

28. Edwin Amenta and Jane D. Poulsen, "Social Politics in Context: The Institutional Politics Theory and State-Level U.S. Social Spending Policies at the End of the New Deal," *Social Forces* 75 (1996): 33–60; Alexander Hicks, *Social Democracy and Welfare Capitalism: A Century of Income Security Politics* (Ithaca, N.Y.: Cornell University Press, 1999); Bert Klandermans and Dirk Oegema, "Campaigning for a Nuclear Freeze: Grass-roots Strategies and Local Governments in the Netherlands," *Research in Political Sociology* 3 (1987): 305–37.

29. Ann Shola Orloff, *The Politics of Pensions: A Comparative Analysis of Britain, Canada, and the United States, 1880–1940* (Madison: University of Wisconsin Press, 1993). On the difficulty of influencing military policy, see Marco Giugni, *Social Protest*

and Policy Change: Ecology, Antinuclear, and Peace Movements in Comparative Historical Perspective (Lanham, Md.: Rowman and Littlefield, 2004).

30. Challengers are often defined by action that they take, but I am defining challengers according to their outsider status in politics, the politically disadvantaged status of their constituency, and the bid to mobilize or invoke large numbers of people in campaigns to influence states.

31. Jeff Goodwin, *No Other Way Out: States and Revolutionary Movements, 1945–1991* (New York: Cambridge University Press, 2001). In their famous treatment, Piven and Cloward argue that mass defiance is likely to win concessions only under very unusual political conditions for poor people. *Poor Peoples' Movements*, chap. 1. See also Richard C. Fording, "The Conditional Effect of Violence as a Political Tactic: Mass Insurgency, Welfare Generosity, and Electoral Context in the American States," *American Journal of Political Science* 41 (1997): 1–29.

32. John Kingdon, *Agendas, Alternatives, and Public Policies* (Boston: Little, Brown, 1984); Paul Burstein, "Explaining State Action and the Expansion of Civil Rights: The Civil Rights Act of 1964," *Research in Political Sociology* 6 (1993): 117–37.

33. A key insight from historical institutionalism is that political decisions alter politics and the possibilities of group and coalition formation at a later point in time. Peter A. Hall and Rosemary C. R. Taylor, "Political Science and the Three New Institutionalisms," *Political Studies* 44 (1996): 936–57; Kathleen Thelen, "Historical Institutionalism in Comparative Politics," *Annual Review of Political Science* 2 (1999): 369–404. On policy monopolies, see Frank R. Baumgartner and Bryan Jones, *Agendas and Instability in American Politics* (Chicago: University of Chicago Press, 1993).

34. On the value of movement infrastructures, see Kenneth T. Andrews, *Freedom Is a Constant Struggle: The Mississippi Civil Rights Movement and Its Legacy* (Chicago: University of Chicago Press, 2004). On strategic capacities, see Marshall Louis Ganz, "Resources and Resourcefulness: Strategic Capacity in the Unionization of California Agriculture, 1959–1966," *American Journal of Sociology* 105 (2000): 1003–62.

35. James M. Jasper, *The Art of Moral Protest: Culture, Biography and Creativity in Social Movements* (Chicago: University of Chicago Press, 1997), chap. 10; Steve Valocchi, "The Unemployed Workers' Movement: A Reexamination of the Piven and Cloward Thesis," *Social Problems* 37 (1990): 191–205; Samuel Cohn, *When Strikes Make Sense—and Why: Lessons from Third Republic French Coal Miners* (New York: Plenum, 1993), p. 5.

36. Francesca Polletta, *Freedom Is an Endless Meeting: Democracy in American Social Movements* (Chicago: University of Chicago Press, 2002), chap. 1.

37. McCarthy and Zald, "Enduring Vitality of the Resource Mobilization Theory of Social Movements," pp. 533–65. Skocpol, *Protecting Soldiers and Mothers*, introduction.

38. Tilly, "From Interactions to Outcomes in Social Movements"; Amenta and Young, "Making an Impact"; Jennifer Earl, "Methods, Movements, and Outcomes: Methodological Difficulties in the Study of Extra-Movement Outcomes," *Research in Social Movements, Conflicts, and Change* 22 (2000): 3–25.

39. On cases, see Charles C. Ragin and Howard Becker, *What Is a Case? Exploring the Foundations of Social Inquiry* (New York: Cambridge University Press, 1992). On maximizing variation in independent variables, see Gary King, Robert O. Keohane,

and Sidney Verba, *Designing Social Inquiry: Scientific Inference in Qualitative Research* (Princeton, N.J.: Princeton University Press, 1994).

40. In some analyses across states and regarding votes, I rely on a group of coauthored studies employing multiple regression and qualitative comparative analyses, though for details I refer readers to specific articles.

41. McAdam, Tarrow, and Tilly, *Dynamics of Contention*; Hall and Taylor, "Political Science and the Three New Institutionalisms"; Thelen, "Historical Institutionalism in Comparative Politics."

Chapter Two: How the West Was Won Over

1. For the series of letters written by Townsend, see J. D. Gaydowski, "Eight Letters to the Editor: The Genesis of the Townsend National Recovery Plan," *Southern California Quarterly* 52 (1970): 365–82.

2. U.S. Congress, House of Representatives, *Hearings before the Select Committee Investigating Old-Age Pension Plans and Organizations*, 74th Cong., 2nd sess., vol. 1 (Washington, D.C.: U.S. Government Printing Office, 1936), pp. 121–23.

3. Francis E. Townsend, *New Horizons (An Autobiography)*, ed. Jesse George Murray (Chicago: J. L. Stewart 1943), pp. 1–110; Richard L Neuberger and Kelley Loe, *An Army of the Aged: A History and Analysis of the Townsend Old Age Pension Plan* (Caldwell, Idaho: Caxton Printers, 1936), chap. 2; Raymond Gram Swing, "Dr. Townsend Solves It All," *Nation*, March 6, 1935, pp. 268–70.

4. Townsend, *New Horizons*, pp. 105–36; Luther Whiteman and Samuel L. Lewis, *Glory Roads: The Psychological State of California* (New York: Crowell, 1936), pp. 64–65.

5. The story does not appear in Townsend's 1943 autobiography, and none of the major works on the Townsend Plan give it any credence. The story appears in Richard Milne, *That Man Townsend* (Los Angeles: Prosperity Publishing Comparny, 1935), p. 2, which was commissioned as a promotional giveaway to subscribers of the *Townsend Weekly*. Townsend liked at the time to recount the apocryphal story to others; see *Old-Age Pension Plans and Organizations*, pp. 753–54.

6. See, for instance, David A. Snow, R. Burke Rochford Jr., Steven K. Worden, and Robert D. Benford, "Frame Alignment Processes, Micromobilization, and Movement Participation," *American Sociological Review* 51 (1986): 464–81. See also Myra Marx Ferree, William Anthony Gamson, Jurgen Gerhards, and Dieter Rucht, *Shaping Abortion Discourse* (New York: Cambridge University Press, 2002). For a review, see David A. Snow, "Framing Processes, Ideology, and Discursive Fields," in *The Blackwell Companion to Social Movements*, ed. David A. Snow, Sarah A. Soule, and Hanspeter Kreisi (Malden, Mass.: Blackwell, 2004), chap. 17.

7. Gaydowski, "Eight Letters to the Editor." For descriptions of the proposal as it was developed in its first year, see the following pamphlets: [Francis E. Townsend and Robert Earl Clements, eds.], *Old Age Revolving Pensions: A Proposed National Plan* (Long Beach, Calif.: Old Age Revolving Pensions, 1934); [Francis E. Townsend and Robert Earl Clements, eds.], *Old Age Revolving Pensions: A National Plan Proposed by Dr. F. E. Townsend* (Long Beach, Calif.: Old Age Revolving Pensions, 1934); [Francis E. Townsend and Robert E. Clements, eds.], *The Townsend Plan* (Los Angeles: Old

Age Revolving Pensions, 1935). Of the 29 million families in the United States, 87 percent had incomes of less than $2,500 in 1935–36. The median family income was somewhere between $1,000 and $1,500 per year, far less than the $1,700 that Townsend called for, which was soon upgraded to $2,400. National Resources Committee, *Consumer Incomes in the United States: Their Distribution in 1935–1936* (Washington, D.C.: U.S. Government Printing Office, 1938). On dependency in old age, see Brian Gratton, "The Politics of Dependency Estimates: Social Security Board Statistics, 1935–1939," *Journal of Gerontology: Social Sciences* 52B (1997): S117–S124.

8. In his initial letter Townsend estimated that there were somewhere between 15 and 20 million Americans aged sixty and older, though there were only about 11 million in 1934. In the first official pamphlet, it was suggested that more than three-fourths of those over sixty were earning some money in order to subsist. Gaydowski, "Eight Letters to the Editor"; *Old Age Revolving Pensions: A Proposed National Plan*, p. 3.

9. *Old Age Revolving Pensions: A Proposed National Plan*, pp. 3, 11. Townsend came to believe that about 10 million would take the pension, whereas Clements saw the figure as approximately 8 million, approximately half of whom would give up employment.

10. For Pope's plan, see U. S. House of Representatives, *Hearings before the Committee on Labor on H.R. 1623*, 73rd Cong., 2nd sess. (Washington, D.C.: U.S. Government Printing Office, 1934); Abraham Holtzman, *The Townsend Movement: A Political Study* (New York: Bookman, 1963), pp. 25–26. On the twenty groups in San Francisco, see Whiteman and Lewis, *Glory Roads*, p. 4. On other Depression-fighting ideas, see Arthur M. Schlesinger Jr., *The Age of Roosevelt: The Politics of Upheaval* (Boston: Houghton Mifflin, 1960), chap. 3. McCord's 1931 lecture "Mercy Death for Surplus Labor" is printed in full in *Old-Age Pension Plans and Organizations*, pp. 758–64; Townsend and Murray, *New Horizons*.

11. *Old-Age Pension Plans and Organizations*, pp. 2–19. If real estate investors could not keep up payments, the land would revert to the lender, who was often also Clements.

12. *Old-Age Pension Plans and Organizations*, pp. 2–19.

13. Milne, *That Man Townsend*, pp. 25–26.

14. For the articles of incorporation, see Division of Special Collections, University of Oregon Library System (SCUO), "Townsend National Recovery Plan," box 115, folder 1. Some early records of Old Age Revolving Pensions (OARP), Ltd., the Prosperity Publishing Company, and the Townsend National Recovery Plan (TNRP), Inc., were gathered in November 1937 by Gilmour Young and J. W. Brinton, members of the TNRP board of directors, to determine the income tax liability of Dr. Townsend for those years. These wound up in the special collections division of the University of Oregon. See John C. Cuneo, "The Townsend Plan in Retrospect," Oral History Program, University of California, Los Angeles, Charles E. Young Research Library of Special Collections, University of California, Los Angeles (SCU-CLA), pp. 83–90. See also U.S. Senate Committee on Finance, *Hearings on S. 1130 [the Economic Security Act]* (Washington, D.C.: U.S. Government Printing Office, 1935), pp. 1045–46. The three members of OARP, Ltd., had control over the corporation and the right to appoint a board of directors, which were the same three people, though only the two founders participated. The floor painting story is from Milne, *That Man Townsend*, pp. 28–29, and is likely apocryphal. See also Townsend and Mur-

ray, *New Horizons*, pp. 144–45. On Clements's claims that he studied the economics of the pension-recovery program, see *Old-Age Pension Plans and Organizations*, pp. 13–15; Neuberger and Loe, *An Army of the Aged*, pp. 55–58; Holtzman, *The Townsend Movement*, pp. 66–67.

15. Almost all journalistic accounts of the day and the surviving documents from the early years point to Clements as the driving force behind the rise of the Townsend Plan. See, for instance, Neuberger and Loe, *An Army of the Aged*, pp. 64–65. In a *Time* magazine story that was the basis of the March of Time documentary short "Townsend Plan!" Townsend was referred to as "the Front," and Clements as "the Big Fellow," clearly indicating that Clements was running the show. "For Mothers and Fathers." *Time*, November 4, 1935, pp. 17–21. When the organization made its greatest gains and won the attention of the country, Townsend was not running it. His testimony before Congress in February 1935 exhibited a comprehensive ignorance of the organization. He was unable, for instance, to give even a ballpark estimate of the number of organizers in the field. U.S. House of Representatives, Committee on Ways and Means, *Hearings on H. R. 4120 [the Economic Security Act]* (Washington, D.C.: U.S. Government Printing Office, 1935), pp. 708–9. For Clements's admission that he had "control and charge" of "practically all administrative work," and for the organizer Clinton Wunder's concurring view, see *Old-Age Pension Plans and Organizations*, pp. 329, 361 (see p. 3 for Clements's voice not carrying). Similar impressions of Clements and his wife Thelma's control over the organization come from O. Otto Moore, who organized Townsend clubs in Denver and represented the Townsend Plan in Washington in 1935. *Mile High Harbor* (Denver, Colo.: Associated Publishers, 1947), pp. 26, 75. He refers to Clements as the "brains" of the organization, and to Clements and Thelma as the "dictators" of its policy. Moore referred to Townsend as the "head man only before the public and the press." On Thelma Clements's role, see Whiteman and Lewis, *Glory Roads*, pp. 75, 100. See also The Unofficial Observer [John Franklin Carter], *American Messiahs* (New York: Simon and Schuster, 1935), pp. 82–83. Clements described the Townsend Plan's division of labor as himself running the organization and Townsend speaking out for it. As Townsend put it, "I was to take care of the philosophical presentation of the plan; and all the money raising, financing, was to be left to the other side, to Mr. Clements." *Old-Age Pension Plans and Organizations*, pp. 627, 640, 671, 679–81, quotation on p. 719. Even that quote overstates Townsend's role. Because of all this evidence and the fact that the Townsend Plan was not going anywhere until Clements got hold of it and foundered afterward, it is difficult to take at face value the statements by Abraham Holtzman, the author of the most comprehensive study of the Townsend Plan, that it "revolved principally around one individual, Dr. Francis E. Townsend," that Clements "was never more than a 'co-founder,'" and that the Townsend Plan was "the personal creation and possession of Dr. Francis E. Townsend." Holtzman, *The Townsend Movement*, p. 58.

16. Because of Townsend's full-time efforts on behalf of the Townsend Plan, he was allowed to draw on the organization's funds "such sums as were necessary for him to adequately provide for his necessary personal and family expenses." Minutes of OARP, Ltd., Board of Directors, February 20, 1934, SCOU, TNRP, Inc., box 1, folder 1. According to Clements's later testimony, Thomas Collier was the first paid Townsend Plan representative, and there were a number of volunteers, including Joe Charlesbois and Baxter Rankine, who later became an officer in the organization. According to

Pierre Tomlinson, when he joined the organization in May there were only five approved promoters, including Collier and Chester MacDonald, the editor of the *Modern Crusader*. Clements claimed that he did not give his full attention to the organization until March. *Old-Age Pension Plans and Organizations*, pp. 20–21, 25, 482. See also Neuberger and Loe, *An Army of the Aged*, pp. 64–65.

17. Clements's 1936 testimony of the founders' taking salaries in March is somewhat at odds with the OARP, Ltd., reconstructed minutes, the originals through 1934 having been lost, which indicate that Townsend and Clements did not vote themselves salaries until June 1934, to start in July. Possibly they made official in June what they had already put into practice in March. According to the reconstructed minutes, they voted themselves expense money in July. See Minutes of OARP, Ltd., Board of Directors, June 12, 1934, July 20, 1934, March 19, 1935, SCUO, TNRP, Inc., box 1, folder 1; *Old-Age Pension Plans and Organizations*, pp. 340–41, 351–52.

18. John D. McCarthy and Mayer N. Zald, "Resource Mobilization and Social Movements: A Partial Theory," American Journal of Sociology 82 (1977): 1212–41; John D. McCarthy, "Mobilizing Structures: Constraints and Opportunities in Adopting, Adapting, and Inventing," In ed. Doug McAdam, John D. McCarthy, and Mayer N. Zald, *Comparative Perspectives on Social Movements*, (New York: Cambridge University Press, 1996), pp. 141–51; John D. McCarthy and Mayer N. Zald, "The Enduring Vitality of the Resource Mobilization Theory of Social Movements," in *The Handbook of Sociological Theory*, ed. Jonathan H. Turner (New York: Kluwer, 2002), pp. 533–65.

19. In their six months with the Townsend Plan, Tomlinson and Smith constructed a network of approximately 300 representatives and organizers. *Old-Age Pension Plans and Organizations*, pp. 473–84.

20. Clements's column ran in every issue and constituted all but two pages of the second issue of the *Modern Crusader*, June 13, 1934, pp. 2–15, whereas Townsend's column, "The Doctor's Own Page," ran more sporadically. Whiteman and Lewis, *Glory Roads*, p. 66.

21. *Old Age Revolving Pensions: A Proposed National Plan*, p. 6. The idea that greater productivity would lead to fewer jobs—more or less opposite to the conventional wisdom today—was also a staple among U.S. social scientists of the day. President's Committee on Social Trends, *Recent Social Trends in the United States* (New York: McGraw-Hill, 1933).

22. S. M. Dick, "O.A.R.P. Qualifies as Economic Relief Factor," *Modern Crusader*, July 17, 1934, p. 1.

23. R. E. Clements, "Your Questions Answered," *Modern Crusader*, June 13, 1934, p. 14. The life expectancy at the time for American men reaching age sixty was about another eleven years, for women another fifteen.

24. I am working with a definition of ideology that provides "a systematic set of assumptions, theories, and values that offer an interpretation of, and program for man in all aspects of his life or for society as a whole." Wilson, *Political Organizations*, p. 46. On populism as a style of political rhetoric, see Michael Kazin, *The Populist Persuasion: An American History* (New York: Basic Books, 1995). For a discussion of ideological currents in the rhetoric of the Townsend Plan, see Steven B. Burg, "The Gray Crusade: The Townsend Movement, Old Age Politics, and the Development of Social Security" (Ph.D. diss., thesis, University of Wisconsin, 1999), chap. 3. Townsend's pension-recovery proposal was referred to as "God's plan" in a popular Townsend club song that

provided substitute lyrics for "The Battle Hymn of the Republic." Frank Dyer, ed., *Townsend Convention Songbook* (Cleveland, Ohio: OARP, 1936), p. 2.

25. For an analysis and critique of the brand of populism offered by Long and Coughlin, see Alan Brinkley, *Voices of Protest* (New York: Vintage, 1984), chap. 7. Brinkley (p. 143) persuasively argues that Long and Coughlin evoked a distinctive ideology, though often muddled in presentation, that included "an affirmation of threatened values and institutions, a vision of a properly structured society in which those values and institutions could thrive, . . . an explanation of obstacles to this vision, a set of villains and scapegoats upon whom it was possible to blame contemporary problems . . . [and] a prescription for reform, resting upon a carefully restricted expansion of the role of government."

26. The discussion of the role of government and the critique of New Deal efforts appear in Townsend's first letters. Gaydowski, "Eight Letters to the Editor." This critique was toned down in Townsend Plan publications in 1934. The first pamphlet went so far as to reprint a speech of Roosevelt's from March 5, 1934, calling for increased purchasing power through the NRA. *Old Age Revolving Pensions: A Proposed National Plan*, pp. 2, 5, 13, 18. Townsend and Clements also professed faith in the government to perform the fiscal fine-tuning. *Old Age Revolving Pensions: A National Proposed by Dr. F. E. Townsend*, pp. 8, 12.

27. *Old-Age Pension Plans and Organizations*, pp. 475 (quotation), 660–61.

28. Sanders did not start franchising his chicken business until 1952, at age sixty-five. See www.kfc.com/about/colonel.htm. Dr. Townsend's was also a brand of sarsaparilla that was popular in the late nineteenth century.

29. Holtzman, *The Townsend Movement*, p. 40.

30. Cantril, *The Psychology of Social Movements*, p. 171.

31. The first version of the pension pamphlet was only eighteen pages, and the second version, which most club members received in 1934 and was also called *Old Age Revolving Pensions*, was twenty pages. The 1935 version, called *The Townsend Plan*, ran to thirty-two pages. The first year's booklets cost about 1.6 cents each to print, whereas the latter cost about 2.2 cents. *Old-Age Pension Plans and Organizations*, p. 134.

32. On the glamour of $200, see Milne, *That Man Townsend*, pp. 28–29; Russell Owen, "Townsend Talks of His Plan and Hopes," *New York Times Magazine*, December 29, 1935, p. 3. For a similar argument about the political motivation of these changes in plan, see Holtzman, *The Townsend Movement*, pp. 37–40.

33. Susan B. Hansen, *The Politics of Taxation: Revenue without Representation* (New York: Praeger, 1983), chap. 5; Holtzman, *The Townsend Movement*, pp. 38–40.

34. The change in the taxation scheme came sometime during the summer. As late as September, Townsend was still promoting the idea that a sales tax of 10 percent would be needed to fund the pensions. See, for instance, Townsend's "The Doctor's Own Page" column of September 15, 1934, *Modern Crusader*, p. 2; Robert Ordway Foote, "Pensions for All at 60, Idea from the West," *New York Times*, September 16, 1934, sec. IX, p. 6. The transactions tax of 2 percent was based on the 1929 level of total transactions, which was estimated at $1.2 trillion.

35. The political right perhaps had the most to fear from the pension program, because of the great taxation it implied. The politically engaged left would not like a regressive consumption tax, no matter what it was called. Edwin Amenta, *Bold Relief:*

Institutional Politics and the Origins of Modern American Social Policy (Princeton, N.J.: Princeton University Press, 1998), chap. 3.

36. For an extensive discussion of the items sold, see *Old-Age Pension Plans and Organizations*, pp. 78, 131–39. The first financial statement appears in *Modern Crusader*, August 7, 1934, p. 16. This statement indicates that OARP, Ltd., brought in $6,850, although its accounting practices, which counted pamphlets sent to organizers on speculation as "receipts," suggest that the amount might have been less than half this figure. Clements later stated that the corporation took in less than $7,000 in its first five months. "For Mothers and Fathers," *Time*, November 4, 1935, p. 20. Among the authorized booklets for sale by the end of the summer was a kind of catechism of the pension-recovery program, taken from Clements's "Your Questions Answered" column in the *Modern Crusader*. *Modern Crusader*, August 27, p. 13.

37. For the experience of O. Otto Moore, who became a speaker and representative for the Townsend Plan in Denver, see *Mile High Harbor*, pp. 18–20.

38. Something like the idea for Townsend clubs appeared in the first pamphlet, which called for groups to organize to better coordinate the amassing of signatures on petitions. *Old Age Revolving Pensions: A Proposed National Plan*, p. 16. By the second edition of the pamphlet, there was an explicit call to organize Townsend clubs. *Old Age Revolving Pensions: A National Plan Proposed by Dr. F. E. Townsend*, p. 16. Clements later stated that the reason for the creation of Townsend clubs was to "keep the enthusiasm" of Townsend sympathizers "at a high pitch." *Old-Age Pension Plans and Organizations*, pp. 26–27, 42–43. At first there was no limit to the size of clubs. Soon it was decided that clubs could be formed once local organizers had accumulated 100 members, 50 in less populated places. According to Clements's "Your Questions Answered" column, the organization had 274 "branch offices" in twenty states in the middle of 1934. *Modern Crusader*, June 13, 1934, p. 14. Some thirty states had these offices by the end of September 1934, though very likely these often included the addresses of club secretaries, as there were approximately 400 offices listed. *Modern Crusader*, September 15, 1934, p. 12; *Modern Crusader*, September 29, 1934, pp. 14–15.

39. Senate Committee on Finance, *Hearings on S. 1132*, p. 1048; Whiteman and Lewis, *Glory Roads*, pp. 74–75.

40. Most likely the subcontractors were paid separate commissions. *Old-Age Pension Plans and Organizations*, pp. 495–96.

41. Some of these forms from 1939 and afterward for California survive in papers of the state organizer John C. Cuneo. "Townsend National Recovery Plan, Inc." [compiled by James A. Mink, 1959], Charles E. Young Research Library, SCUCLA, collection 219, box 112.

42. "Henry Stone's" career as a Townsendite, to take one documented example, began by his talking over the pension plan with the owner of a local feed store, who had read about the program in the newspaper. One day a Townsend Plan organizer, working the territory, drove up and encouraged the store owner to convene a meeting. He induced Stone and several others to attend. At the meeting they started a club, with Stone signing up his wife, a boarder, and two others at 25 cents each. Stone's wife never participated much, though the boarder did. A "Mr. Barber," the first president of his club, convened the first meeting by hiring a Townsend speaker and renting a hall with his own money. Hadley Cantril, *The Psychology of Social Movements* (New York:

Wiley, 1941), pp. 194–98. The form was known as form 61. If the club were organized by the secretary without the aid of an organizer, the secretary of a 100-member club could keep $7.50 for his or her efforts and remit the remaining $17.50 to national headquarters. See also The Unofficial Observer, *American Messiahs*, p. 81.

43. On the Nonpartisan League, see Robert L. Morlan, *Political Prairie Fire: The Nonpartisan League, 1915–1922* (Minneapolis: University of Minnesota Press, 1955), chap. 2. At the rate of commission—$4 for each $16 two-year membership—it seems unlikely that Nonpartisan League organizers did much better than earn their expenses. As for OARP, Ltd., of the slightly more than $28,000 in disbursements (with slightly less than $30,000 in receipts) as of October 31, approximately $11,000 went to "organizers and organization expense," with salaries constituting another approximately $2,500. House Committee on Ways and Means, *Hearings on H.R. 4120*, pp. 721–22. Of the approximately $60,000 brought in by the end of 1934, about $20,000 went to organizers and organizing expenses, about $7,000 to commissions, and about $6,000 to salaries. The next largest expenses, of about $4,000 each, were for books, postage, and radio. According to Clements's later testimony, "receipts" for books and petitions were items out on consignment (or accounts receivable). Thus the approximately $25,000 in receipts for books in 1934 meant that there were about 100,000 books (costing about $1,600) in the hands of organizers with the prospect, as yet unfulfilled, of generating sales of 25 cents each. Senate Committee on Finances, *Hearings on S. 1130*, pp. 1070; *Old-Age Pension Plans and Organizations*, pp. 67, 134.

44. In their first two months, clubs yielded receipts of about $8,200, with the clubs' extension service (the Townsend Plan's radio operation) bringing in about the same amount. The clubs brought in $11,300 more in the last two months of the year, with the extension service bringing in about $8,200, for a total of approximately $36,000. House Committee on Ways and Means, *Hearings on H.R. 4120*, pp. 721–22; Senate Committee on Finances, *Hearings on S. 1130*, pp. 1048–49, 1066–69; *Old-Age Pension Plans and Organizations*, p. 76.

45. A field report from the *Townsend Weekly* suggested the format of meetings; see "California," May 27, 1935, p. 6; *Old-Age Pension Plans and Organizations*, p. 114. A club manual from circa 1939 indicates that they did not change much over time. "Townsend National Recovery Plan, Inc.," SCUCLA, collection 219, box 111.

46. Neuberger and Loe, *An Army of the Aged*, chap. 1. For detailed records of the meetings of Modesto (California) number 2, see "Townsend National Recovery Plan, Inc.," SCUCLA, collection 219, boxes 138, 139. For an extensive treatment of Townsend club meetings, see Burg, "The Gray Crusade," chap. 4.

47. James Q. Wilson, *Political Organizations*, 2nd ed. (Princeton, N.J.: Princeton University Press, 1995), chap. 3. On the benefits to one's reputation through participation in movement activity, see Dennis Chong, *Collective Action and the Civil Rights Movement* (Chicago: University of Chicago Press, 1992).

48. John D. McCarthy and Mayer Zald, "Resource Mobilization: A Partial Theory," *American Journal of Sociology* 82 (1977): 1212–41.

49. Elisabeth S. Clemens, *The Peoples' Lobby: Organizational Innovation and the Rise of Interest Group Politics in the United States, 1890–1925* (Chicago: University of Chicago Press, 1997), pp. 8–10. On new institutionalists in political sociology, see Peter A. Hall and Rosemary C. R. Taylor, "Political Science and the Three New Institutionalisms," *Political Studies* 44 (1996): 936–57.

50. Francesca Polletta, *Freedom Is an Endless Meeting: Democracy in American Social Movements* (Chicago: University of Chicago Press, 2002). On other membership organizations, see Theda Skocpol, "How Americans Became Civic," in *Civic Engagement in American Democracy*, ed. Theda Skocpol and Morris P. Fiorina (Washington, D.C., and New York: Brookings Institution and Russell Sage Foundation, 1999), chap. 2. On the distinction between officers and militants, see Wilson, *Political Organizations*, pp. 109–10. For the club setup and permit, see *Old-Age Pension Plans and Organizations*, pp. 127–30. For a member of a club whose charter was revoked, see *Old-Age Pension Plans and Organizations*, p.765. See also Holtzman, *The Townsend Movement*, pp. 68–70.

51. *Old-Age Pension Plans and Organizations*, pp. 349–50. For various unsuccessful bids to democratize the Townsend Plan, see Holtzman, *The Townsend Movement*, pp. 66–70.

52. MacDonald charged Townsend and Clements with stealing a 5,000-name subscription list, but nothing was ever proved, and without the list MacDonald's career in pension politics was finished. *Old-Age Pension Plans and Organizations*, pp. 161–63; Neuberger and Loe, *An Army of the Aged*, pp. 110–15; Holtzman, *The Townsend Movement*, pp. 71–72.

53. It was not made immediately clear that the "official" Townsend Plan newspaper was now being run for the profit of Townsend and Clements. The *Townsend Weekly* had its first run in January 1935, with a circulation of about 37,000, with perhaps a quarter of it paid. The paper had the word "Official" adjoining "Townsend Weekly" at its top. It was decided by the OARP, Ltd., board that the paper was to be under the control of the founders. Minutes of OARP, Ltd., Board of Directors, December 4, 1934, SCUO, TNRP, Inc., box 1, folder 1; Neuberger and Loe, *An Army of the Aged*, pp. 113–15; Holtzman, *The Townsend Movement*, p. 72.

54. The balance of the commissions to Tomlinson and Smith ran to $793.41. Tomlinson later claimed that he and Smith were shorted. *Old-Age Pension Plans and Organizations*, pp. 475–82. The meeting of the OARP, Ltd., Board (attended as always by Clements and Townsend only) in December gave Clements authorization to open state area and national offices where he deemed it desirable. See Minutes of OARP, Ltd., December 4, 1934, SCUO, TNRP, Inc., box 1, folder 1.

55. Later, state managers' club lists were supposed to include each club's location, its order of creation in its city or town, its officers, and the number of members, but these lists do not survive, and members themselves were never listed. Also, in 1934 there were as yet no state managers. *Old-Age Pension Plans and Organizations*, pp. 431, 872. In California, clubs were not required to report paying members until 1940. "Townsend National Recovery Plan, Inc." SCUCLA, collection 219, box 113.

56. "California Doctor Plans Old Age Utopia," *New York Times*, December 22, 1934, p. 15. The petitions at the end of the year asked members of Congress to introduce or support bills with the essentials of the old-age pension-recovery program. Senate Committee on Finances, *Hearings on S. 1130*, p. 1016–17. Townsend claimed 20 million petition signers in February 1935; House Committee on Ways and Means, *Hearings on H.R. 4120*, p. 752. However, these petitions were not presented to the bipartisan House Select Committee Investigating Old-Age Pensions Organizations until May 1936. Probably there were about 7 million, the vast bulk of which came in late 1935 and early 1936. On February 11, 1935, the *Townsend Weekly* admitted that Cali-

fornia had only approximately 1.5 million petition signers—which was probably an exaggeration, too. *Old-Age Pension Plans and Organizations*, pp. 341, 584.

57. Senate Committee on Finance, *Hearings on S. 1130*, pp. 1047–48.

58. One relatively contemporaneous account indicates that there were about 1,200 clubs at the end of 1934. Harry B. Presson, "Tells History of First Townsend Clubs," *National Weekly Townsend*, November 2, 1936, p. 10. Holtzman also estimates that there were somewhat more than 1,000 clubs at the end of 1934; *The Townsend Movement*, p. 67. Membership can be estimated by way of the official booklet, which cost 25 cents. Each booklet cost 1.6 cents to print, as Clements later testified, the corporation spent $4,108 on books, and there were about 257,000 booklets in existence by the end of 1934. Yet in the financial records the "receipts" for booklets included a charge for $24,808. This item, essentially an "accounts receivable" entry, suggests that about 100,000 of these booklets remained in the hands of organizers, waiting to be sold. Thus somewhat more than 158,000 books had been sold by the end of the year. Senate Committee on Finance, *Hearings on S. 1130*, p. 1069–70; *Old-Age Pension Plans and Organizations*, pp. 67, 134.

59. About 100 of the "state and divisional managers" of the 300 that Tomlinson and Smith claimed to have contracted out to by November 1934 were listed in Tomlinson's testimony, and the vast bulk of them were from California. Many of these were likely simply secretaries for a specific club. Other states mainly had one manager, as in the case of Iowa, Colorado, and Florida. It seems likely that Oregon and Washington at least had more than one subcontractor. *Old-Age Pension Plans and Organizations*, pp. 477–79.

60. Senate Committee on Finance, *Hearings on S. 1130*, p. 1069–70; *Old-Age Pension Plans and Organizations*, pp. 67, 134.

61. Minutes of OARP, Ltd., Board of Directors, November 15, 1934, December 4, 1934, SCUO, TNRP, Inc., box 1, folder 1; Holtzman, *The Townsend Movement*, p. 67.

Chapter Three: Behind the Townsend Plan's Rise and Initial Impact

1. Theda Skocpol, *Protecting Soldiers and Mothers: The Political Origins of Social Policy in the United States* (Cambridge, Mass.: Harvard University Press, 1992), chap. 2; W. H. Glasson, *Federal Military Pensions in the United States* (New York: Oxford University Press, 1918); Heywood Sanders, "Paying for the 'Bloody Shirt': The Politics of Civil War Pensions," in *Political Benefits*, ed. Barry Rundquist (Lexington, Mass.: Heath, 1980), pp. 137–60; U.S. Bureau of the Census, *Historical Statistics of the United States from Colonial Times to 1970* (Washington, D.C.: U.S. Government Printing Office, 1975), series F 1-5, Y 352–57, Y 998–1009, pp. 224, 1106, 1149.

2. Jackson K. Putnam, *Old-Age Politics in California: From Richardson to Reagan* (Stanford, Calif.: Stanford University Press, 1970), pp. 17–19; Jill Quadagno, *The Transformation of Old-Age Security: Class and Politics in the American Welfare State* (Chicago: University of Chicago Press, 1988), pp. 66–72; Gary M. Fink, *Labor's Search for Political Order: The Political Behavior of the Missouri Labor Movement, 1890–1940* (Columbia: University of Missouri Press, 1973); Skocpol, *Protecting Soldiers and Mothers*, chap. 4.

3. Royce D. Delmatier, Clarence F. McIntosh, and Earl G. Waters, *The Rumble of California Politics, 1848–1970* (New York: Wiley, 1970), chap. 7; Putnam, *Old-Age Politics in California*, chap. 2; U.S. Committee on Economic Security, *Social Security in America: The Factual Background of the Social Security Act as Summarized from Staff Reports to the Committee on Economic Security* (Washington, D.C.: U.S. Government Printing Office, 1937), p. 245; Ann Shola Orloff, *The Politics of Pensions* (Madison: University of Wisconsin Press, 1993), pp. 280–83.

4. Committee on Economic Security, *Social Security in America*, pp. 156–67.

5. Arthur M. Schlesinger Jr., *The Age of Roosevelt: The Crisis of the Old Order, 1919–1933* (Boston: Houghton Mifflin, 1957), pp. 390–95; Kenneth S. Davis, *FDR: The New York Years, 1928–1933* (New York: Random House, 1979), chaps. 3, 8; Jordan A. Schwarz, *The Interregnum of Despair: Hoover, Congress, and the Depression* (Urbana: University of Illinois Press, 1970), chap. 7; William R. Brock, *Welfare, Democracy, and the New Deal* (Cambridge: Cambridge University Press, 1988), chap. 4.

6. The margin in the Electoral College was 473 to 59. U.S. Bureau of the Census, *Historical Statistics of the United States from Colonial Times to 1970*, series Y 84–134, Y 135–86, pp. 1075, 1077.

7. Federal Works Agency, *Final Statistical Report of the FERA*, pp. 99–104; Josephine Chapin Brown, *Public Relief, 1929–1939* (New York: Holt, 1940), chaps. 8–12; Brock, *Welfare, Democracy and the New Deal*, pp. 162–73. Many states, including most of the former Confederacy, provided little funding for FERA aid and relied on the national government.

8. "Message to Congress Reviewing the Broad Objectives and Accomplishments of the Administration," in *The Public Papers and Addresses of Franklin D. Roosevelt* (PPAFDR), ed. Samuel I. Rosenman (New York: Random House, 1938), vol. 3, item 102 (June 8, 1934), pp. 287–93. The CES also included secretary of the treasury Henry Morgenthau, secretary of agriculture Henry Wallace, and attorney general Homer Cummings.

9. Milton Derber, "Growth and Expansion," in *Labor and the New Deal*, ed. Milton Derber and Edwin Young (Madison: University of Wisconsin Press, 1961), pp. 1–44; Bureau of the Census, *Historical Statistics*, series D 946–951, p. 178; Steve Fraser, "The 'Labor Question,'" in *The Rise and Fall of the New Deal Order, 1930–1980*, ed. Steve Fraser and Gary Gerstle (Princeton, N.J.: Princeton University Press, 1990), chap. 3; David Plotke, *Building a Democratic Political Order: Reshaping American Liberalism in the 1930s and 1940s* (New York: Cambridge University Press, 1996), chaps. 4 and 5.

10. T. Harry Williams, *Huey Long* (New York: Vintage, 1969); William Ivy Hair, *The Kingfish and His Realm: The Life and Times of Huey P. Long* (Baton Rouge: Louisiana State University Press, 1991).

11. Share Our Wealth would increase the minimum wage and limit hours for workers, purchase and store agricultural goods from farmers, and provide scholarships to students. World War I veterans' "bonuses," due in 1945, would be paid immediately. For an early version of the "Long Plan," see Huey Long Scrapbooks, Hill Memorial Library Special Collections (HMLSC), Louisiana State University, no. 18. A Share Our Wealth Society circular, dated February 19, 1934, includes six points: to limit poverty; to limit fortunes; old-age pensions ($30 per month, for those sixty and older); to limit the hours of work; to balance agricultural production with consumption; and to care

for the veterans of our wars. See also Brinkley, *Voices of Protest*, pp. 71–74; Donald R. McCoy, *Angry Voices: Left of Center Politics in the New Deal Era* (New York: Kennikat Press, 1967), pp. 122–23; Hair, *The Kingfish and His Realm*, chap. 15.

12. See Raymond G. Swing, *Forerunners of American Fascism* (New York: Julian Messner, 1935), chap. 3. On the Louisiana clubs, see Williams, *Huey Long*, p. 701; Brinkley, *Voices of Protest*, pp. 79–81. A number of useful articles appear in the Long Scrapbooks, HMLSC, especially no. 19; U.S. Department of Justice, FBI files on Huey P. Long, HMLSC, box 2, folder 58.

13. Upton Sinclair, *I, Governor of California, and How I Ended Poverty: A True Story of the Future* (Los Angeles: Upton Sinclair, 1933), pp. 21–24; Delmatier, McIntosh, and Waters, *Rumble of California Politics*, chap. 8; Putnam, *Old-Age Politics*, chap. 3; Arthur M. Schlesinger Jr., *The Age of Roosevelt: The Politics of Upheaval* (Boston: Houghton Mifflin, 1960), chap. 7; "Creel Sees Spread of Economic Cults," *New York Times*, October 2, 1934, p. 2.

14. Brinkley, *Voices of Protest*, chaps. 2–4, appendix III.

15. Daniels, *The Bonus March*; Dillingham, *Federal Aid to Veterans*; Davis R. B. Ross, *Preparing for Ulysses: Politics and Veterans during World War II* (New York: Columbia University Press, 1969), chap. 1; Bureau of the Census, *Historical Statistics*, series Y984–97, Y998–1009, pp. 1147, 1149.

16. Frances Fox Piven and Richard A. Cloward, *Poor People's Movements: Why They Succeed, How They Fail* (New York: Random House, 1977); Steve Valocchi, "The Unemployed Workers Movement of the 1930s: A Reexamination of the Piven and Cloward Thesis," *Social Problems* 37 (1990): 191–205. Farmers also mobilized through the Farmers' Holiday Association and other organizations. John L. Shover, *Cornbelt Rebellion: The Farmers' Holiday Association* (Urbana: University of Illinois Press, 1965).

17. These are simplifications of internally variegated positions. For a further discussion, see Doug McAdam, *Political Process and the Black Insurgency, 1930–1970*, 2nd ed. (Chicago: University of Chicago Press, 1999).

18. Lester V. Chandler, *America's Greatest Depression, 1929–1941* (New York: Harper and Row, 1970), p. 5.

19. On the impact of short-term political changes on social movements, see J. Craig Jenkins and Bert Klandermans, "The Politics of Social Protest," in *States and Social Movements*, ed. J. Craig Jenkins and Bert Klandermans (Minneapolis: University of Minnesota Press, 1995), chap. 1; Sidney Tarrow, "States and Opportunities: The Political Structuring of Social Movements," in *Comparative Perspectives on Social Movements: Opportunities, Mobilizing, Structures, and Cultural Framings*, ed. Doug McAdam, John D. McCarthy, and Mayer N. Zald (New York: Cambridge University Press, 1996), chap. 2.

20. See, for instance, Skocpol, *Protecting Soldiers and Mothers*, introduction.

21. Edwin Amenta and Michael P. Young, "Democratic States and Social Movements: Theoretical Arguments and Hypotheses," *Social Problems* 57 (1999): 153–68.

22. The American backwardness in old-age programs was pointed out to Townsendites. See "New Deal for Old People," *Modern Crusader*, September 29, 1934, p. 3.

23. Hanspeter Kriesi, "The Political Opportunity Structure of New Social Movements: Its Impact on Their Mobilization," in *States and Social Movements*, ed. J. Craig

Jenkins and Bert Klandermans (Minneapolis: University of Minnesota Press, 1995), chap. 7; Herbert P. Kitschelt, "Political Opportunity Structures and Political Protest: Anti-nuclear Movements in Four Democracies," *British Journal of Political Science* 16 (1986): 57–85.

24. On Social Credit, see Maurice Pinard, *The Rise of a Third Party: A Study in Crisis Politics* (Englewood Cliffs, N.J.: Prentice-Hall, 1971). On the Farmer-Labor Party, see Richard M. Valelly, *Radicalism in the States: The Minnesota Farmer-Labor Party and the American Political Economy* (Chicago: University of Chicago Press, 1989). On the Progressives, see John E. Miller, *Governor Philip F. La Follette, the Wisconsin Progressives, and the New Deal* (Columbia: University of Missouri Press, 1982).

25. Foote, "Pensions for All at 60, Idea from the West."

26. According to Tomlinson, Clements was in no hurry to have the Townsend bill passed and claimed that Clements wanted "the racket," as Tomlinson claimed Clements called the Townsend Plan, to go on for another two years. Tomlinson's account is questionable, though, given his bitterness about being forced out. *Hearings before the Select Committee Investigating Old-Age Pension Plans and Organizations*, p. 492. A Michigan state organizer, Jack Leisa, charged in 1936 that Townsend Plan leaders did not want a bill to be enacted right away and instead sought to gain a steady flow of members. Leisa was also fired, after only a month's service, and thus he, too, had reasons for negative testimony. See "Exhibit A [List of state area managers]," SCUO, TNRP, Inc., box 115, folder 4; *Old-Age Pension Plans and Organizations*, pp. 438–39.

27. For Clements's claim that Townsend wanted to start a new party, see *Old-Age Pension Plans and Organizations*, p. 329. For Townsend's view of the potential of the clubs, see his "The Doctor's Own Page" column, *Modern Crusader*, September 29, 1934, p. 2.

28. Townsend, for instance, wrote importunate form letters to incumbents: "To ascertain your stand on the Townsend Plan, we would greatly appreciate your answers, either 'yes' or 'no,' to the following questions: 1. Do you endorse the Townsend Plan in its entirety without qualifications of any sort? 2. Do you endorse the Townsend Plan with reservations? If so, what are they? 3. Are you against the Townsend Plan? If so, what are your objections? 4. In the event of your election to the United States Congress, would you champion the cause of the Townsend Plan and work for its enactment into law?" Congresswomen Isabella Greenway of Tucson, Arizona, got off the hook by responding politely and asking for literature about the pension proposal. See letter from F. E. Townsend to Isabella Greenway, October 25, 1934, and the November 15, 1934, response from Greenway to Townsend, Arizona Historical Society, Southern Arizona Division, Isabella Greenway papers, Collection MS 0311, box 37, folder 462.

29. Delmatier, McIntosh, and Waters, *Rumble of California Politics*, chap. 8; Putnam, *Old-Age Politics*, chaps. 3–4; Greg Mitchell, *The Campaign of the Century: Upton Sinclair's Race for Governor of California and the Birth of Media Politics* (New York: Random House, 1992). Sinclair stated that he would "put off the problem of pensions to see what the president does." Upton Sinclair, *Immediate EPIC* (Los Angeles: Upton Sinclair, 1934), p. 26; Upton Sinclair, *I, Candidate for Governor, and How I Got Licked* (Berkeley: University of California Press, 1994 [originally 1934, 1935]). Sinclair's EPIC lieutenant, Culbert Olsen, placed an ad in the *Modern Crusader* in favor of Sinclair and the Democratic Party. It implored Townsendites to "vote intelligently." His opponent Merriam trumpeted his status as a "churchman," while remaining silent

about the pension plan. Clements claimed that Dr. Townsend and the Townsend Plan were not supporting or opposing any candidate for governor. *Modern Crusader*, October 26, 1934, pp. 8, 9, 16. Sinclair lost with 879,537 votes to 1,138,620 for Merriam and 302,519 for Raymond Haight, a moderate candidate running on the Progressive ballot line. Arthur Krock attributed Sinclair's loss to Roosevelt's lukewarm support. "Tide Sweeps Nation, Democrats Clinch Two-Thirds Rule of the Senate," *New York Times*, November 7, 1934, p. 1. Tomlinson later claimed that Merriam had offered $12,000 for the Townsend Plan's endorsement, but that Townsend jumped the gun and the offer was withdrawn. *Old-Age Pension Plans and Organizations*, pp. 484–85.

30. Holtzman, *The Townsend Movement*, pp. 191–93.

31. For McGroarty's account of his connection with the Townsend Plan, see *Old-Age Pension Plans and Organizations*, pp. 774, 794; F. E. Townsend, "Your Pension Must Have Able Congressman," *Modern Crusader*, August 27, 1934, p. 13. On the demographics of California, see Daniel J. B. Mitchell, *Pensions, Politics, and the Elderly: Historic Social Movements and Their Lessons for Our Aging Society* (Armonk, N.Y.: M. E. Sharpe, 2000), pp. 20–22.

32. Schlesinger, *Politics of Upheaval*, pp. 142–46; Richard M. Valelly, *Radicalism in the States: The Minnesota Farmer-Labor Party and the American Political Economy* (Chicago: University of Chicago Press, 1989), pp. 168–69; James J. Lorence, *Gerald J. Boileau and the Progressive-Farmer Labor Alliance: Politics of the New Deal* (Columbia: University of Missouri Press), chap. 3.

33. Edwin Witte, *The Development of the Social Security Act: A Memorandum on the History of the Committee on Economic Security and Drafting and Legislative History of the Social Security Act* (Madison: University of Wisconsin Press, 1962); Frances Perkins, *The Roosevelt I Knew* (New York: Harper and Row, 1946), chap. 23; Arthur Altmeyer, *The Formative Years of Social Security* (Madison: University of Wisconsin Press, 1966), chaps. 1–2; J. Douglas Brown, *An American Philosophy of Social Security: Evolution and Issues* (Princeton, N.J.: Princeton University Press, 1972), chap. 1. Witte's contemporaneous account stresses the influence of the previous bills in Congress in determining the committee's agenda. Perkins's retrospective account is doubtfully reliable on the influence of the Townsend Plan, as she is mistaken on some of the basics in the chronology.

34. The FERA's support to the aged dwarfed the approximately 180,000 aided by state-level programs. "Estimates of Costs to the States in Providing Old-Age Assistance," *New York Times*, February 10, 1935, p. 26. The FERA's aid to female-headed households without breadwinners also eclipsed the mothers' pensions programs. In August 1934, approximately 719,000 children whose mothers were widowed, separated, or divorced received FERA aid, compared with 280,500 children aided by mothers' pensions. Committee on Economic Security, *Social Security in America*. For a discussion of Hopkins's views, see George McJimsey, *Harry Hopkins: Ally of the Poor and Defender of Democracy* (Cambridge, Mass.: Harvard University Press, 1987), chap. 6, especially pp. 95–97.

35. "Message to Congress Reviewing the Broad Objectives and Accomplishments of the Administration," in *PPAFDR*, vol. 3, item 102 (June 8, 1934), pp. 287–93. Roosevelt's quotation is from his "Annual Message to the Congress," *PPAFDR*, vol. 4, item 1 (January 4, 1935), pp. 19–20.

36. Witte, *The Development of the Social Security Act*, p. 25. Witte wrote the "Preliminary Outline of the Work of the Staff on the Committee on Economic Security" on August 10, as well as the "Preliminary Report of the Staff of the Committee on Economic Security," the staff's initial recommendations on September 26. National Archives, Reports of the Committee on Economic Security, Record Group 47, box 6, preliminary reports file 3. The Technical Board developed its own preliminary recommendations on October 1, with its final "preliminary" report dated October 9. See National Archives, RG 47, box 1, file 1. On the Advisory Council, see Sheryl R. Tynes, *Turning Points in Social Security: From "Cruel Hoax" to "Sacred Entitlement"* (Stanford, Calif.: Stanford University Press, 1996), pp. 45–46. Barbara Armstrong, professor of law at the University of California and the author of a comparative study that strongly supported social insurance, led the studies regarding old-age security. Hope Ridings Miller, "Hopes of Providing for the Needy Past 65 Based on FERA Program," *Washington Post*, December 18, 1934, p. 17. Murray Latimer of the Railroad Retirement Board and J. Douglas Brown of Princeton advised her. Latimer was the head of the Technical Board committee for this subject. See also J. Douglas Brown, *An American Philosophy of Social Security: Evolution and Issues* (Princeton, N.J.: Princeton University Press, 1972), chap. 1.

37. The staffer was Wilbur Cohen, who reported directly to Witte and was later known as "Mr. Social Security." The committee was somewhat at a disadvantage in its work because it had no publicity staff. "Old Age Pension Organizations," September 6, 1934, National Archives RG 47, box 22, Witte—personal file; "Social Problem Session Called Here Nov. 14–15," *Washington Post*, October 26, 1934, p. 4; Foote, "Pensions for All at 60, Idea from the West"; Witte, *The Development of the Social Security Act*, pp. 35–36; Edward D. Berkowitz, *Mr. Social Security: The Life of Wilbur J. Cohen* (Lawrence: University Press of Kansas, 1995), pp. 29–30; Burg, "The Gray Crusade," pp. 327–30.

38. Louis Stark, "Roosevelt Bars Plans Now for Broad Social Program; Seeks Job Insurance Only," *New York Times*, November 15, 1935, p. 1; Robert C. Albright, "Mustn't Become Dole, He Tells Economic Security Group," *Washington Post*, November 15, p. 1. Both articles indicate that Roosevelt was referring to the Townsend Plan.

39. See Burg, "The Gray Crusade," pp. 330–32.

40. Louis Stark, "Experts Push Plan for 'Real' Job Bill with Federal Aid," *New York Times*, November 16, 1935, p. 1. Witte claims that the president was misinterpreted in the *Times*; *The Development of the Social Security Act*, pp. 45–47. According to Arthur Altmeyer, an undersecretary of labor at the time and later the head of the Social Security Board, he had written the passage, not Witte, who was blamed for it. Altmeyer was trying to convey that the plan would be comprehensive and include unemployment compensation as the top priority, not just an old-age program. *The Formative Years of Social Security* (Madison: University of Wisconsin Press, 1966), pp. 13–14. If the president had wanted to delay old-age action because of his distaste for the Townsend Plan, it would mean that its influence was a wash—having helped to return old-age security to the national political agenda after helping to remove it.

41. U.S. Committee on Economic Security, *Report to the President* (Washington, D.C.: U.S. Government Printing Office, 1935), p. 9. As late as December 24, 1934, Roosevelt wanted to combine the legislation for the work program and other eco-

nomic security in one bill. Arthur W. Macmahon, John D. Millett, and Gladys Ogden, *The Administration of Federal Work Relief* (Chicago: Public Administration Service, 1941), pp. 26–27; Witte, *The Development of the Social Security Act*, p. 77; Altmeyer, *The Formative Years of Social Security*, pp. 12–13.

42. "Roosevelt to Make Jobs for 3,500,000 Now on Relief: Pushes His Social Program," *New York Times*, January 5, 1935, p. 1; "Budget Totals $8,520,413,609, $4,000,000,000 for New Jobs," *New York Times*, January 8, 1935, p. 1.

43. Those who did not qualify for regular benefits would receive lump-sum retirement benefits—or death benefits for their estates. The bill also included support for state and county medical services for pregnant women and mothers and their infants, as well as for public health services, and aid for disabled children. In addition, there were to be government-run voluntary annuities for those with relatively large incomes. The "Economic Security Act" is appended to the Committee on Economic Security, *Report to the President*; Robert C. Albright, "Congress Gets Social Program from Roosevelt to Provide Pensions and Job Insurance," *Washington Post*, January 18, 1935, p. 1.

44. In old-age insurance, as with Townsend's proposal, recipients would have to retire to receive the benefits. This provision was designed more to save money by providing disincentives to taking the payments than to boost employment.

45. Theda Skocpol and G. John Ikenberry, "The Political Formation of the American Welfare State in Historical and Comparative Perspective," *Comparative Social Research* 6 (1983): 87–148; Ann Shola Orloff, "The Political Origins of America's Belated Welfare State," in *The Politics of Social Policy in the United States*, ed. Margaret Weir, Ann Shola Orloff, and Theda Skocpol (Princeton, N.J.: Princeton University Press, 1988), pp. 37–80.

Chapter Four: The Townsend Plan versus Social Security

1. "The Forum," an unsigned feature on the *New York Times* op-ed page, ironically offered its more comprehensive "Ultimate Plan"; December 3, 1934, p. 16. See also "Townsend Here, Plans Old Age Pension Drive," *Washington Post*, December 12, 1934, p. 5; "California Doctor Plans Old Age Utopia," *New York Times*, December 22, 1934, p. 15; "Topics of the Times," *New York Times*, January 6, 1935, p. 16; "Townsend Plan Hit as a Vain Sacrifice," *New York Times*, January 6, 1935, sec. II, p. 1. *Time* magazine summarized sober criticisms by Mark Sullivan and Walter Lippman of the *New York Herald-Tribune*, as well as the more sarcastic ones of Westbrook Pegler of the Scripps-Howard newspaper chain. "Simple Plan," *Time*, January 14, 1935, p. 14. On Townsend's seeking a meeting with the president, see telegram from Frank Peterson to George Creel, October 12, 1934; letter from Townsend to Roosevelt, December 17, 1934; Marvin H. McIntyre to Townsend, December 18, 1934. McIntyre suggested that Townsend meet Frances Perkins instead. Franklin D. Roosevelt (FDR) Papers, Official File (OF) 1542, Townsend, Dr. Francis E., 1933–1935, FDR Library; Elliott Thurston, "Townsend Pension Bill to Make Debut before House Tomorrow," *Washington Post*, January 16, 1935, p. 1; "Townsend Pension Plan Goes to the House; Bill Calls for 2 Billions Outlay in Month," *New York Times*, January 17, 1935, p. 5; "Roosevelt Offers

His Security Plan for Jobless, the Aged and Widows; Program Splits Congress Party Lines," *New York Times*, January 18,1935, p. 1; Robert C. Albright, "Congress Gets Social Program," *Washington Post*, January 18, 1935, p. 1; "Social Services," *Time*, January 28, 1935, p. 22.

2. Raymond Clapper, "Between You and Me," *Washington Post*, January 17, 1935, p. 2. Clapper covered the Townsend Plan extensively in his column.

3. "Roosevelt to Make Jobs for 3,500,000 Now on Relief: Pushes His Social Program," *New York Times*, January 5, 1935, p. 1. Roosevelt's budget gave almost half to work projects. "Budget Totals $8,520,413,609, $4,000,000,000 for New Jobs," *New York Times*, January 8, 1935, p. 1. The administration routinely confused the term "pensions," which would imply benefits based on senior citizens' rights, with the benefits of Old-Age Assistance, which was presumably to go to the neediest only, presumably to make the OAA program seem more dignified. "Roosevelt to Ask 3 Social Measures," *New York Times*, January 8, 1935, p. 27.

4. The $2 billion to pay for the soldiers' bonus was considered a likely candidate to thwart the president's security plans. "Roosevelt Bars Bonus, but Veterans Defy Him," *Washington Post*, January 1, 1935, p. 1; "Congress Faces a Heavy Program," *New York Times*, January 2, 1935, p. 10. On the bonus, see Roger Daniels, *The Bonus March: An Episode of the Great Depression* (Westport, Conn.: Greenwood Press, 1971), especially chap. 9; Frederick Rudolph, "The American Liberty League, 1934–1940," *American Historical Review* 56 (1950): 19–33; George Wolfskill, *The Revolt of the Conservatives: A History of the American Liberty League, 1934–1944* (Boston: Houghton Mifflin, 1962).

5. *New York Times*, January 27, 1935, p. E9.

6. Arthur Krock, "Roosevelt, Long, or Townsend Our Social Security Choice," *New York Times*, January 18, 1935, p. 22. In the *Washington Post*, Robert C. Albright suggested that the Senate might decide to fund an old-age pension bill at the rate of $60 per month by way of sales taxes—most likely at the suggestion of Senator William Borah of Idaho. "Congress Gets Social Program from Roosevelt to Provide Pensions and Job Insurance," January 18, 1935, p. 1. See also "Townsend Plan Takes Spotlight," *Literary Digest*, February 2, 1935, pp. 7–8.

7. Democratic conservatives and Republicans criticized the costliness of the work relief program, and labor sympathizers in Congress argued that the administration's wage scale for relief work, below that of private industry, would lower private wages. "Work Relief Plan Criticized by Some," *New York Times*, January 8, 1935, p. 2. The House passed the bill on January 24, but it ran into trouble in the Senate. Republicans on the committee voted both for prevailing wages, which would increase the cost of the bill, and for cutting the appropriation in half, joining with liberals and conservative Democrats, depending on the issue. "Senate Body in Deadlock over Works," *Washington Post*, February 7, 1935, p. 1; Turner Catledge, "President's Aides Drive to Restore Relief Resolution," *New York Times*, February 11, 1935, p. 1. On the Lundeen bill, see "Roosevelt Limits Social Aid Grants," *New York Times*, January 12, 1935, p. 1; Witte, *The Development of the Social Security Act*, pp. 80, 85. On the liberal bloc, see "35 Members in House Drop Party Lines to Join in Drive for Liberal Legislation," *New York Times*, March 10, 1935, p. 1; James J. Lorence, *Gerald J. Boileau and the Progressive-Farmer Labor Alliance: Politics of the New Deal* (Columbia: University of Missouri Press,

1994). Long's futuristic *My First Days in the White House* claimed that there was no further hope from Roosevelt's policies. " 'Every Man a King' Drive by Long Is On," *New York Times*, January 10, 1935, p. 1.

8. "Townsend Pension Plan Goes to the House," *New York Times*. The bill, HR 3977, officially known as the Townsend Old-Age Revolving Pensions Act, appears in U.S. House of Representatives, Committee on Ways and Means, *Hearings on H.R. 4120 [the Economic Security Act]* 74th Cong., 1st sess. (Washington, D.C.: U.S. Government Printing Office, 1935), pp. 678–89.

9. According to O. Otto Moore, a Townsend Plan leader from Denver and a lobbyist, Dr. Townsend and Frank Peterson, the Townsend Plan publicist, wrote the bill with the help of a Washington lawyer and with the advice of a few congressmen. However, a letter from Townsend to Clements dated January 4, 1935, suggests that Townsend did not aid greatly in drafting the bill. In a letter to Clements, dated January 20, 1935, Peterson indicates that he assembled an advisory committee of about ten House members, including Congressmen McGroarty, Costello, Gearhart, and Ekwall. Peterson also states that administration leaders did not want to meet with the Townsend Plan representatives because it did not have as much support as it claimed and was printed in the newspapers. He saw the Townsend Plan's task as to achieve its reputed strength "before our strength is actually measured." U.S. Congress, House of Representatives, *Hearings before the Select Committee Investigating Old-Age Pension Plans and Organizations*, 74th Cong., 2nd sess., vol. 1 (Washington, D.C.: U.S. Government Printing Office, 1936), pp. 452–56, 873–85; O. Otto Moore, *Mile High Harbor* (Denver, Colo.: Associated Publishers, 1947), pp. 26–29.

10. Requests for letters to be sent to House members appeared in the *Townsend Weekly* from its first issue onward, listing all the members of Congress. "Below Are Listed the Men We Should Concentrate On," *Townsend Weekly*, January 21, 1935, p. 5. On Townsend's letters-as-orders statement, see his letter to Clements of January 4, 1935. See also "Bombardment of Congress Having Effect—Increase It Now, Urges Dr. Townsend," *Townsend Weekly*, February 11, 1935, p. 6. As Townsend wrote: "Make your letters pointed. Put the snap of command in them. After all you are talking to your servants." For an example of such a letter, sent to a friend of old-age benefits, see J. C. Adams to Isabella Greenway, February 11, 1935, Arizona Historical Society, Southern Arizona Division (AHSSAD), Isabella Greenway papers, collection MS 0311, box 35, folder 451. Adams wrote: "I do not know how you stand on the Townsend Pension plan, because you are a friend of the Roosevelts. But remember this, dear lady, *you belong to us. We* sent you to Congress, and *we* expect you to *help us*, regardless of the Roosevelts. We understand the Presidents [sic] willing to give us a dole of $15.00 a month. Bless his heart! It surely must hurt him to give such a munificent sum, and only ask for 4 billion + himself!" On sending an organizer to Texas, see Peterson's letter to Clements, January 20, 1935. *Old-Age Pension Plans and Organizations*, pp. 873–85. See also Luther Whiteman and Samuel L. Lewis, *Glory Roads: The Psychological State of California* (New York: Crowell, 1936), pp. 85–86; "Townsend Group Threatens Recall," *New York Times*, March 10, sec. IV, p. 6.

11. Witte's memo appears in Committee on Ways and Means, *Hearings on H.R. 4120*, pp. 894–96. For the testimony regarding the McGroarty bill, see Abraham Holtzman, *The Townsend Movement: A Political Study* (New York: Bookman, 1963), pp. 90–96.

12. On the testimony of Witte, Perkins, and Hopkins, respectively, see Committee on Ways and Means, *Hearings on H.R. 4120*, pp. 110–11, 200, 202, 215–17.

13. See the testimony of Herbert Benjamin of the National Council for Unemployment and Social Insurance, David Lasser of the Workers' Unemployed Union, and Benjamin Marsh of the Peoples' Lobby. Committee on Ways and Means, *Hearings on H.R. 4120*, pp. 596–97, 784, 478–79; Witte, *The Development of the Social Security Act*. The Lundeen bill, H.R. 2827, was expected to pay about $20 per week for each unemployed worker, when dependents ($3 additionally per week) were taken into account. The bill was estimated to cost about $10 billion per year, and it was being considered in the House by the Labor Committee. See the testimony by Mary Van Kleek, its author and a research director of the Russell Sage Foundation. Committee on Ways and Means, *Hearings on H.R. 4120*, pp. 931–38.

14. Epstein reported a survey of newspaper editors on the Townsend Plan, with most being in opposition. Epstein also attacked the administration's unemployment compensation and old-age annuity programs, which he saw as straying far from social insurance principles. Committee on Ways and Means, *Hearings on H.R. 4120*, pp. 558–61.

15. James Emery, representing the National Association of Manufacturers, attacked the payroll taxes in the administration's bill. Committee on Ways and Means, *Hearings on H.R. 4120*, pp. 1020–36.

16. Townsend's brief statement and avoidance of questioning by the Ways and Means Committee on Friday, February 1, were carefully planned. Moore appeared before the committee on February 8, accompanied by Hudson. "House Chiefs Plan Gag Rule to Guard Social Measure," *New York Times*, February 5, 1935, p. 1. For a discussion highly critical of the initial testimony, see Moore, *Mile High Harbor*, chap. 3.

17. In response to Congressman Samuel Hill's leading questions, Townsend admitted that someone gaining income from rents or interest would be eligible for the pension. On whether the pensioners could spend on luxuries, Townsend offered, "Let him buy whisky with it if he wants to kill himself off as quickly as he chooses." Townsend also argued that it would be fine if parents hired children, so long as the money was spent. Committee on Ways and Means, *Hearings on H.R. 4120*, pp. 685, 687, 718–19. The *Washington Post* indicated that the Townsend supporters had lost confidence about the passage of the bill; "Pension Plan Compromise, Aim in House," February 5, 1935, p. 4. The *New York Herald-Tribune* ran a headline trumpeting the wealthy who would receive pensions; "Dr. Townsend Would Pension Morgan, Ford," February 5, 1935, p. 5.

18. Townsend was cornered into admitting that there should be no tax on casual transactions or on interest payments to depositors, despite stipulations to the contrary in the McGroarty bill. Hudson and Moore disagreed among themselves on whether mortgage payments constituted a transaction and who would pay the tax. Townsend was also taken to task because his pension plan did not technically include a "revolving" fund, which in any case would be unconstitutional. Committee on Ways and Means, *Hearings on H.R. 4120*, pp. 689–90, 696–97, 1058–60.

19. On February 12, Robert Doane, the director of research of American Business Surveys in New York and whose study of the transactions tax was commissioned by the Townsend Plan, was the only Townsend witness who emerged unscathed. He suggested that the tax would bring in from $4 billion to $9 billion, but he did not sup-

port the McGroarty bill as written. As Doane put it: "[A transactions tax] might en-able us to reduce our current Government deficit, however the money might be ap-plied." Committee on Ways and Means, *Hearings on H.R. 4120*, pp. 1122, 1125. He was interpreted by some to mean that Congress could pay for the security bill through sales taxes rather than payroll taxes. "Federal Sales Tax Urged on Congress," *New York Times*, February 13, p. 33. The committee members also flushed out the disingenuous-ness of the Townsend Plan publicists' claims that the pension proposal would cost only two pennies on the dollar for each purchase.

20. Committee on Ways and Means, *Hearings on H.R. 4120*, pp. 738, 1051. Townsend suggestion of first granting pensions to those at age seventy-five was consid-ered quite damaging by Holtzman; *The Townsend Movement*, p. 95. See also Moore, *Mile High Harbor*, pp. 62–64.

21. "Dr. Witte Fallacy Corrected," *Townsend Weekly*, January 21, 1935, p. 1. In its standard overoptimistic manner, the *Weekly* predicted the triumph of the Townsend bill. "Predict Congress Stampede, Postal Inquiry of Organization Is Welcome," *Townsend Weekly*, February 4, 1935, p. 1. In the editorial "Taking the Rap," it was sug-gested that Roosevelt should be blamed for the unfriendly statements of Witte, Perkins, and Hopkins; *Townsend Weekly*, February 4, 1935, p. 12. The paper splashed Doane's testimony on its front page, claiming, contrary to fact, that the economist sup-ported the McGroarty bill; "R. R. Doane Enlists in Fight," *Townsend Weekly*, February 18, p. 1; "Dr. Townsend Addresses Ways and Means Committee," *Townsend Weekly*, February 18, p. 2; "No Compromise," *Townsend Weekly*, February 25, 1935, p. 1. Instead of owning up to his testimony, Townsend stated, "You should expect to see our remarks garbled in the opposition press." The investigation by the Post Office found that about 10 percent of the Townsend Plan revenues were being diverted by Clements and Townsend, an amount not inconsistent with a liberal interpretation of their traveling expenses. C. E. Webster, F. E. Smith, Post Office Dept. Los Angeles, CA, April 1, 1935, "Re: Alleged violation of Section 2350, Postal Laws and Regulations of 1932 by Old Age Revolving Pensions, Ltd," FDR Papers, OF 1542, Townsend, Dr. Francis E., 1933–1935, FDR Library.

22. On Townsend's admissions that the transactions tax is a sales tax, that farmers selling livestock would need to be taxed, that he opposes saving, and that the poor mainly pay sales taxes, see U.S. Senate Committee on Finance, *Hearings on S. 1130 [the Economic Security Act]* (Washington, D.C.: U.S. Government Printing Office, 1935), pp. 1018, 1027, 1030, 1035.

23. Townsend admitted that he was not on the strategy board of the Townsend Plan and that he did not know how much money had been raised for the congressional fund. (The strategy board included C. H. Randall, Frank Arbuckle, W. D. Wood, C. N. John-ston, George Snow, W. H. Mitchell, H. H. Fuller, E. F. Zimmerman, and Max Lowen-thal, all of southern California.) Senate Finance Committee, *Hearings on S. 1130*, pp. 1044, 1051. Clements's testimony, beginning on p. 1051, indicated that the organiza-tion had taken in approximately $50,000 and that the print run of the *Weekly* in-creased from 37,000 in the first week, to 50,000 in the second, to 75,000 in the third. Clements was able to claim that he and Townsend had made no money from the paper (p. 1054) or the Townsend Plan (p. 1061), though Townsend was unaware that he was receiving salary, rather than just expenses (p. 1062). "Townsend Queried on Pension

Plan," *New York Times*, February 17, 1935, p. 18; "Senators Balk Dr. Townsend, Bar His Plan," *Washington Post*, February 17, 1935, p. 3.

24. Some members argued against granting authority to a temporary agency, perhaps fearing that the agency would become permanent. Others were apparently upset by Hopkins's decision to pay a minimum wage of 55 cents per hour on federal work relief projects, and his withholding of funds to unforthcoming states under the FERA was legendary. "Votes to Separate FERA and Age Fund," *New York Times*, February 15, 1935, p. 2. The FERA's authority over Aid to Dependent Children was removed the next day. "Restricts Child Aid in Social Security," *New York Times*, February 16, 1935, p. 2.

25. "Votes to Separate FERA and Age Fund," *New York Times*, February 15, 1935, p. 2; Witte, *The Development of the Social Security Act*, pp. 144–45.

26. "Solons Battle Movement for Security Bill," *Arizona Daily Star*, March 18, 1935.

27. The payroll taxes were to increase in steps of .5 percent on employers and employees every three years, until reaching a maximum rate of 3 percent each in 1949. "Age Pension Cost Put at Big Figure," *New York Times*, January 20, 1935, p. 2. For Morgenthau's testimony regarding the tax rates, on February 5, see *Hearings on H.R. 4120*, p. 898. "Morgenthau Asks Changes in Social Bill," *Washington Post*, February 6, 1935 p. 1. According to Witte, the impetus behind the speedup in the taxation schedules was the president's desire that the programs be sustained by these taxes until 1980. Witte, *The Development of the Social Security Act*, pp. 146–52. The Ways and Means Committee had stopped considering the security bill in March and commissioned its legislative staff to rewrite it. Turner Catledge, "Roosevelt Starts 3d Year with Test," *New York Times*, March 4, 1935, p. 1. Some changes were also made in the benefit schedule, with somewhat larger benefits going to those with relatively low wages. See "Recast Social Bill Ready for House: 'Gag' Rule Sought," *New York Times*, April 3, 1935, p. 1.

28. Under the pressure of Harry Hopkins, the Committee on Economic Security had covered these groups in the administration's bill, despite the opposition of the staff of the CES. But because of potential difficulties in collecting these taxes, Secretary Morgenthau testified that these groups should be excluded. This disagreement was settled by Ways and Means in favor of Morgenthau. It has been argued that the exclusion of these groups was designed to harm African Americans, but Charles H. Houston, representing the NAACP, objected to the administration's *initial* bill regarding old-age annuities and unemployment compensation because many black Americans would be excluded, including sharecroppers and cash tenants, as well as most domestic servants. For Houston testimony on February 1 and Morgenthau's testimony four days later regarding exclusions, see House Committee on Ways and Means, *Hearings on H.R. 4120*, pp. 796–97, pp. 901–2. Demands from church groups for an exemption from the payroll taxes were also agreed to, but a bid by employers with retirement programs to exempt themselves from the tax was fought off. "House Leaders Ask Roosevelt's Pension Stand," *Washington Post*, February 12, 1935, p. 2; Witte, *Development of the Social Security Act*, pp. 152–54; "Recast Social Bill Ready for House: 'Gag' Rule Sought," *New York Times*, April 3, 1935, p. 1. On race and the Social Security Act, see Robert C. Lieberman, "Race and the Organization of Social Welfare Policy," in *Classifying by Race*, ed. Paul Peterson (Princeton, N.J.: Princeton University Press, 1995),

chap. 7; Gareth Davies and Martha Derthick, "Race and Social Welfare Policy: The Social Security Act of 1935," *Political Science Quarterly* 112 (1997): 217–35.

29. Charles Randall, "Statement by the National Strategy Committee of the Townsend Movement," *Townsend Weekly*, March 18, 1935, p. 1; Daniel, *The Bonus March*, pp. 219–31.

30. The supplementary taxes included a 10 percent increase in the federal income tax, a 2 percent inheritance tax, and a 2 percent tax on gifts exceeding $500. See Holtzman, *The Townsend Plan*, pp. 96–98. Moore, *Mile High Harbor*, pp. 65–67, claims that he, Hudson, and Daniel Carmichael wrote the bill, in consultation with Congressman Knutson of Minnesota and other sympathetic members of the House.

31. The former national head of the Fraternal Order of Eagles, George Nordlin, who served on the Advisory Council of the CES, attacked the Townsend Plan's approach as providing false hope. Nordlin, however, argued in favor of flat and generous pensions and against the CES's justifications for the annuity program, saying that an aged person should be qualified for a pension by service to society, not through payroll-tax payments, and that anyone reaching retirement age had already long been paying taxes. House Committee on Ways and Means, *Hearings on H.R. 4120*, pp. 475, 477.

32. Susan B. Hansen *The Politics of Taxation: Revenue without Representation* (New York: Praeger, 1983), chap. 5; Sven Steinmo, *Taxation and Democracy: Swedish, British, and American Approaches to Financing the Modern State* (New Haven, Conn.: Yale University Press, 1993).

33. The second McGroarty bill warranted only one-sentence coverage in the "Day in Washington" column in the *New York Times*, April 2, 1936, p. 16.

34. "Recast Social Bill Ready for House: 'Gag' Rule Sought," p. 1. After the opponents of the administration's bill lost 289 to 103 on a procedural vote on April 11, McGroarty conceded defeat. "House Deals Blow to Townsend Plan," *New York Times*, April 12, 1935, p. 1; Douglas Warrenfels, "Gag Cry Fails, House Leaders Fix Procedure on Social Bill," *Washington Post*, April 12, 1935, p. 1. Telegrams sent to the Committee on Economic Security to demand the passage of the second McGroarty bill, gathered and forwarded by Louis Howe, are in the FDR Papers, OF 1542, Townsend, Dr. Francis E., 1933–1935, FDR Library.

35. Monaghan's Townsend amendment called for universal federal pensions of $50 immediately and then of $200 after five years, as well as a transactions tax of 2 percent. Although there was no roll call vote, there was a division vote. The Lundeen bill went down 158 to 40 on a teller vote. "House Beats 25 Attacks on Social Security Bill; Rejects Townsend Plan," *New York Times*, April 19, 1935, p. 1; "House Routs Radical Bills for Security," *Washington Post*, April 19, p. 1. See also the discussion in Witte, *The Development of the Social Security Act*, pp. 97–99; "Friends of Townsend Plan in Congress Recorded for Favorable Standing Vote," *Townsend Weekly*, June 3, 1935, p. 1. For scholars claiming the significance of the low vote totals for the Townsend amendment, see, for instance, Frances Fox Piven and Richard A. Cloward, *Regulating the Poor: The Functions of Public Welfare*, updated edition (New York: Vintage, 1993), p. 101.

36. The compromise on work program wages was that workers would be paid the prevailing hourly wage rate, but a monthly security wage sum. The finance committee restored the voluntary annuity program to the bill, which was later dropped. Witte, *The Development of the Social Security Act*, pp. 99–104.

37. Felix Bruner, "New Congress Likely to Enact Social Security," *Washington Post*, December 26, 1934, p. 3. For Roosevelt's message, see "The President Vetoes the Bonus Bill," *PPAFDR*, vol. 4, item 62 (May 22, 1935), pp. 182–93.

38. "Federal Sales Tax Urged on Congress," *New York Times*, February 13, 1935, p. 33.

39. Witte, *The Development of the Social Security Act*, p. 103.

40. Administration witnesses were doubtless counting on the fact that some states would not adopt OAA programs right away, and many others would provide neither generous nor extensive benefits. As for the fiscal connection between the old-age programs, Witte's testimony made this explicit: "In the early years of this system . . . there will be enough money brought into the United States Treasury so that the contributions [sic] toward the pensions [OAA] can be borrowed from the annuity fund. . . . [A]t the beginning you do not have to worry where this $50 million or $125 million the next year is coming from." He also claimed that if "everybody that could qualify at the present time would be on a pension from the very beginning, and that the average pension would be as high as $25 . . . you would have a cost of $136 million." Frances Perkins testified along the same lines: "Old-age pensions [OAA] and old-age annuities have been thought of as having in mind the same general principle, that is, the prevention of poverty and need among aged persons. It has, therefore, been our conception that the wise way to proceed would be for the Government to borrow from the old-age annuity fund to pay for old-age pensions [assistance]." In short, there was certainly no "lockbox" intended for the initial old-age annuity taxes, which were intended to pay for both programs. When questioned by Congressman Allen T. Treadway, a Republican from Massachusetts who calculated the national cost of OAA at about $700 million per year rather than $150 million, Perkins referred to this estimated cost as being that over and above the revenues generated by payroll tax for the old-age annuity program. For Witte, see *Hearings on H.R. 4120*, pp. 109, 125; for Perkins, pp. 194–98, (quotation on 194); "Only Million Aged Listed for Pension," *New York Times*, February 10, 1935, p. 26.

41. This is the view notably of Abraham Holtzman, *The Townsend Movement*.

42. Witte makes the distinction very clearly in his testimony before a skeptical Ways and Means Committee. *Hearings on H.R. 4120*, p. 109.

43. The points were made by some supporters of radical alternatives, such as the Lundeen bill. Because of potential constitutional issues, the taxation could be earmarked only in a symbolic way, rather than legislatively.

44. Margaret Weir, Ann Shola Orloff, and Theda Skocpol, "Understanding American Social Politics," in *The Politics of Social Policy in the United States*, ed. Margaret Weir, Ann Shola Orloff, and Theda Skocpol (Princeton, N.J.: Princeton University Press, 1988), 3–27.

45. The sort of silver lining the leadership initially perceived and claimed was unhelpful, too. The *Townsend Weekly* honored the thirty-three House members who voted against the security bill, a group mainly consisting of conservative Republicans who had no interest in old-age programs, much less one as expensive as Townsend's. "Vote Reveals Townsend Plan Friends in House, Thirty-three Courageous Men Brave Administration Whip to Vote McGroarty Amendment," *Townsend Weekly*, April 29, 1935, p. 1; "Honor Roll Noted," *Townsend Weekly*, April 29, 1935, p. 3. Only weeks later did they make the correction, replacing this group with the "honor roll" of the

fifty-six who stood up for Monaghan's amendment. "How Congressmen Voted," *Townsend Weekly*, June 3, 1935, p. 1.

46. Alan Brinkley, *Voices of Protest: Huey Long, Father Coughlin and the Great Depression* (New York: Random House, 1982), pp. 6–7; "The Pied Pipers," *Time*, March 18, 1935, p. 14. Long appeared on *Time's* cover on April 1, 1935.

47. Emil Hurja Papers, FDR Library, "Materials Relating to the 'National Inquirer' Presidential Preference Polls," box 72. The states were Colorado, Illinois, New Jersey, and Ohio. By discounting a sample of relief recipients, Hurja underestimated the support of Roosevelt but apparently influenced the president, who saw the election as close and running along the lines of the poll. Edwin Amenta, Kathleen Dunleavy, and Mary Bernstein, "Stolen Thunder? Huey Long's Share Our Wealth, Political Mediation, and the Second New Deal," *American Sociological Review* 59 (1994): 678–702. Farley gathered his own intelligence about the election, sending letters inquiring about Roosevelt's chances to congressmen, heads of local Democratic committees, newspaper editors, and lawyers, and guessed the results of each state correctly. See James A. Farley, *Behind the Ballots: The Personal History of a Politician* (New York: Harcourt, Brace, 1938), pp. 321–28; Papers of the Democratic National Committee, FDR Library, boxes 1093–1103. Several other magazine articles discussing the potential impact of Long appear in the T. Harry Williams Papers, Hill Memorial Library Special Collections, Louisiana State University, Baton Rouge, Louisiana, box 6, folder 47.

48. "A Message to the Congress on Tax Revision," *PPAFDR*, vol. 4, item 38 (June 19, 1935), pp. 270–77. Most historical accounts agree that Long and Share Our Wealth did not place these New Deal programs on the political agenda. See James MacGregor Burns, *The Lion and the Fox* (New York: Harcourt, Brace and World, 1956), pp. 210–15, 220–26; William E. Leuchtenburg, *Franklin D. Roosevelt and the New Deal* (New York: Harper and Row, 1963), p. 100.

49. Brinkley, *Voices of Protest*, p. 82; Williams, *Huey Long*, pp. 836–37; Schlesinger, *The Politics of Upheaval*, chap. 18; Mark H. Leff, *The Limits of Symbolic Reform: The New Deal and Taxation, 1933–1939* (Cambridge: Cambridge University Press), chap. 3.

50. Jane Mansbridge, *Why We Lost the ERA* (Chicago: University of Chicago Press, 1986). See also Michael Lipsky, "Protest as Political Resource," *American Political Science Review* 62 (1968): 1144–58; Anya Bernstein, *The Moderation Dilemma: Legislative Coalitions and the Politics of Family and Medical Leave* (Pittsburgh: University of Pittsburgh Press, 2001).

51. See, for instance, "Townsend Triumphs," *Townsend Weekly*, March 25, 1935, p. 1; "Bill Retains Basic Features," *Townsend Weekly*, April 15, 1935, p. 1.

52. This was the view of Richard L. Neuberger, who covered the Townsend Plan for the *Nation* and the *New York Times*. See "The Townsend Plan Exposed," *Nation*, October 30, 1935, p. 505.

53. Peterson was one of the sources for the Neuberger's "The Townsend Plan Exposed." See also "A Judas Revealed," *Townsend Weekly*, June 3, 1935, p. 1. Moore, and Daniel Carmichael, another member of the lobbying group, broke with Clements apparently over what he felt were excessive demands for funds for the largely abandoned congressional campaign and inaugurated the National Annuity League. *Old-Age Pension Plans and Organizations*, pp. 701–4, 716–18.

Chapter Five: A National Challenger

1. R. E. Clements, "Plan Leaders Announce Goal for Double Membership and Victory Fund before July 4," *Townsend Weekly*, May 13, 1935, p. 1. As Clements put it, "The recent vote in Congress on the Administration's Economic Security bill proved that wherever in the United States the Townsend Clubs were strongly organized, our Representatives were ready to support the Townsend bill." "Tabulation Shows Plan Strength in Nation's Congress," *Townsend Weekly*, June 10, 1935, p. 1.

2. See Clements's testimony in U.S. Senate Committee on Finance, *Hearings on S. 1130 [the Economic Security Act]* (Washington, D.C.: U.S. Government Printing Office, 1935), p. 1054. Circulation reached only 150,000 in July, after having gone over 115,000 by April. In its first issues, the *Townsend Weekly* routinely listed its circulation in advertisements for it. *Hearings before the Select Committee Investigating Old-Age Pension Plans and Organizations*, pp. 166–71. To estimate the revenues for each quarter, I subtract revenues for "books, petitions, and literature" as well as "cash" carried over from the previous quarter. According to Clements's testimony in 1936, the "accounts receivable" line included money already received by OARP, Ltd., whereas petitions, books, and literature constituted material out on consignment—what most accountants would consider "accounts receivable." *Old-Age Pension Plans and Organizations*, pp. 67, 80–81. For the revenues for the last quarter, see *Hearings on S. 1130*, pp. 1048–49. For the last quarter of 1934, I extrapolated, using the totals and the revenues for each of the last two months, which are calculated separately for the organization. *Townsend Weekly*, May 27, 1935, p. 2; August 5, 1935, p. 2. Clements estimated that there were 3,500 Townsend clubs in late July, which is probably an overestimate by about 500. "Townsend's Aides Open Office Here," *New York Times*, July 28, 1935, sec. II, p. 3.

3. Clements, "Plan Leaders Announce Goal for Double Membership"; "Townsend Group Opens State Drive," *New York Times*, July 13, 1935, p. 11; "Townsend's Aides Open Office Here," sec. II, p. 3. On Wunder, see *Old-Age Pension Plans and Organizations*, p. 849.

4. Clements, "Plan Leaders Announce Goal for Double Membership." See also *Old-Age Pension Plans and Organizations*, pp. 39–56.

5. Clements, "Plan Leaders Announce Goal for Double Membership." On the value of gaining resources and support from the beneficiary group rather than from other sources, see Doug McAdam, *Political Process and the Development of Black Insurgency* (Chicago: University of Chicago Press, 1982); Aldon D. Morris, *The Origins of the Civil Rights Movement: Black Communities Organizing for Change* (New York: Free Press, 1984).

6. Clements, "Plan Leaders Announce Goal for Double Membership"; "National Legion Import Stressed by Headquarters," *Townsend Weekly*, July 15, 1935, p. 1.

7. Clements indicated later that at no time did he and Townsend discuss giving the clubs a greater role in the Townsend Plan. *Old-Age Pension Plans and Organizations*, pp. 349–50. For Walter Townsend's resignation, see "Special Meeting of Directors," minutes, June 28, 1935, SCUO, "Townsend National Recovery Plan," box 115, folder 1.

8. R. E. Clements, "Putting Them on Record," *Townsend Weekly*, April 29, 1935, p. 3. The questionnaire to be sent to members of Congress is printed on this page.

9. Ibid. Clements, "Plan Leaders Announce Goal for Double Membership." Franklin Roudybush called Senator Long's filibuster, which prevented funding for the Social Security Board, "a great tactical victory for the Townsend Plan. Townsend leaders will lead a terrific drive to substitute the Townsend Plan for the Administration program in January." *National Townsend Weekly*, September 9, 1935, p. 6.

10. Clements, "Putting Them on Record"; Clements, "Plan Leaders Announce Goal for Double Membership." For women's, farmer, and labor groups, see Elisabeth S. Clemens, *The People's Lobby* (Chicago: University of Chicago Press, 1997). For the Anti-Saloon League, see Peter H. Odegard, *Pressure Politics: The Story of the Anti-Saloon League* (New York: Octogon Books, 1966); Ann-Marie E. Szymanski, *Pathways to Prohibition: Radicals, Moderates, and Social Movement Outcomes* (Durham, N.C.: Duke University Press, 2003).

11. New bylaws for OARP, Ltd., the Townsend Plan organization, were adopted the same day. "Special Meeting of Directors," minutes, June 28, 1935; "By-Laws of Old Age Revolving Pensions, Ltd. Amended"; SCUO, "Townsend National Recovery Plan," box 115, folder 1; "Townsend Weekly Moves Editorial Offices to East," *Townsend Weekly*, July 22, 1935, p. 1.

12. Roudybush was probably a stringer writing under a pen name.

13. The newspaper's health was evident in its array of advertisements. There were many low-budget ads touting mail-order products to alleviate the physical ailments of old age—rheumatism, sinus trouble, eczema, foot pain, and the like—some of the products of questionable value, like "Turtoil," a supposed life-enhancing substance extracted from turtles, and the "Hollywood," a weight-reduction device. There were also recurrent ads for get-rich-quick schemes, such as raising "giant frogs," and come-ons asking readers "Can You Find the Quintuplets?" to generate mailing lists of the credulous. In the Southern California edition, however, the *Weekly* drew slick ads for brand-name Helm's Olympic Bread, Holly Cleanser, Gilmore Red Lion gasoline and Lion Head motor oil, and Le Roy Gordon Beauty Salons, among others, and page-long ads from the Safeway and A&P grocery chains. A multiple advertiser was Dr. S. M. Cowen, "credit dentist," from Los Angeles, who also held speaking contests for Townsendites.

14. See description of the Radio Extension Division in the first issue of the *Townsend Weekly*, January 21, 1935, p. 1.

15. For the feud with Peterson and the appointment of Gurley, see Neuberger, "The Townsend Plan Exposed." Also Richard L. Neuberger and Kelly Loe, "The Old People's Crusade," *Harper's Monthly*, March 1936, pp. 426–38. For Townsend's response to Peterson, see "A Judas Revealed," *Townsend Weekly*, June 3, p. 1. For the regional directors, see the listing in the *National Townsend Weekly*, September 16, 1935, p. 7. On regional offices, see *Old-Age Pension Plans and Organizations*, pp. 30–35.

16. "Exhibit 'A' [list of state area organizers for Midwest, East, and South regions of OARP, Ltd., compiled by Gilmour Young]," TNRP, Inc., SCUO, box 115, folder 4; "All Records Broken in Two Short Years for Townsend Plan," *National Townsend Weekly*, January 27, 1936, p. 1.

17. "Many Congressmen Put On Record by Questionnaire Declare in Favor of Plan," *Townsend Weekly*, July 22, 1935. Townsend Plan booklets now included a club membership card, detachable from the front cover. F. E. Townsend and R. E. Clements, eds., *The Townsend Plan* (Washington, D.C.: OARP, 1935).

18. "Nation Is Watching Historic Gathering of Townsend Clubs," *National Townsend Weekly*, September 23, p. 1; "Seven Thousand at O.A.R.P. Convention Endorse Townsend," *National Townsend Weekly*, p. 1; "For Mothers and Fathers," *Time*, November 4, 1935, pp. 17–20; "Pension Will Win, Dr. Townsend Says," *New York Times*, October 25, 1935, p. 2; "Townsend Plan Held a 'New Deck,'" *New York Times*, October 26, 1935, p. 5; "'36 'Friends' to Get Townsend Votes," *New York Times*, October 27, 1935, p. 9; Harry Thornton Moore, "Just Folks in Utopia," *New Republic*, November 13, 1935, pp. 9–10. The reporter Richard L. Neuberger, however, was trumpeting the claims of Frank Peterson, the dismissed publicity director, that the Townsend Plan was a racket and that Clements and Townsend did not want the McGroarty bill to pass, seeking instead to soak the aged club members through the Prosperity Publishing Company, which he claimed was generating for the founders $2,000 per month. "The Townsend Plan Exposed," *Nation*, October 30, 1935, pp. 505–7. President Roosevelt apparently read an account of the convention written by the daughter of Charles Merriam, a consultant to the administration and a University of Chicago professor. E. Merriam, "Impressions of the 1st Natl. Convention of Townsend Clubs," FDR Papers, Official File 1542, Townsend, Dr. Francis E., 1933–1935, FDR Library.

19. "Main, Townsend Plan Candidate, Is Victor in Michigan Republican Congress Primary," *New York Times*, November 20, 1935, p. 1; S. J. Duncan-Clark, "Townsend Chief Sees Sweep in '36," *New York Times*, November 24, 1935, p. E7; "Politicians Worry over Townsendism," *New York Times*, November 24, 1935, p. N10; Duncan Aikman, "Townsendites Plant Pension Dynamite under 1936 Polls," *Washington Post*, December 1, 1935, p. B5; "Townsendite Wins in House Election," *New York Times*, December 18, 1935, p. 1; "Michigan Result Is a Signal Victory for Townsend Forces," *National Townsend Weekly*, December 23, p. 1; "Townsend Group Queries Congress," *New York Times*, December 15, 1935, p. 1; Arthur Krock, "Townsend Plan Foes Warn of Effect and Offer 'Substitute,'" *New York Times*, December 17, 1935, p. 22; Gladys H. Kelsey, "Townsend Victory Denied," *New York Times*, December 22, 1935, sec. IV, p. 11. *New York Times* analysts saw a significant influence of the Townsend organization on the outcome. See also John Leland Mechem, "Did Townsend Win in Michigan?" *Review of Reviews*, March 1936, p. 45.

20. Some newspapers were printing exaggerated claims that 250 new clubs were being started weekly. "New Attitude Noted for Townsend Plan In Questionnaire," *National Townsend Weekly*, December 30, 1935, p. 1; *Old-Age Pension Plans and Organizations*, p. 83; Duncan-Clark, "Townsend Chief Sees Sweep in '36"; "39 in House Listed for Townsend Plan," *New York Times*, December 29, 1935, p. 14; "Townsend Bill as 'Rider,'" *New York Times*, January 12, 1936, p. 17.

21. Henry Hazlitt, "Townsend's Plan Explained and Analyzed," *New York Times*, December 22, 1935, sec. IV, p. 3; "Townsend Theory Collapsed in 1793," *New York Times*, December 22, 1935, sec. II, p. 2; Kelsey, "Townsend Victory Denied"; "The Townsend Plan," a lecture by Father Charles E. Coughlin, December 22, 1935, the Radio League of the Little Flower, Royal Oak Michigan. Coughlin was in favor of generous treatment of the aged and the stimulation of the economy, but he put a higher priority on decent wages for workers and the end of private control of banking. Russell Owen, "Townsend Talks of His Plan and Hopes," *New York Times Magazine*, December

29, 1935, p. 3. Altogether, Dr. Townsend or the Townsend Plan, or both, figured in sixty-seven *New York Times* articles in December 1935.

22. Bosley Crowther, "'Time' Marches Off," *New York Times*, July 15, 1951, p. X1; Raymond Fielding, *The March of Time, 1935–1951* (New York: Oxford University Press, 1978).

23. U.S.A.! [Townsend Plan], executive producer, Louis de Rochemont (released January 1936), *The March of Time*, Time, Inc. The speaker at the San Francisco meeting was likely Edward Margett, the state area organizer for northern California.

24. Starting in the fall of 1935, Gallup reported the results of AIPO polls each Sunday on the front page of the Weekly News Magazine of the *Washington Post*. "Americans Reveal Their Hopes and Fears in Nation-Wide Poll," *Washington Post*, December 15, 1935, sec. III, p. 1. The polls on old-age pensions were taken in December, but Gallup did not ask about the Townsend Plan or the pension-recovery proposal as such. Also, the median response to an open-ended question regarding the qualifying age was sixty years old, similar to Townsend's retirement age, rather than sixty-five, the administration's. "Nation 9 to 1 for Old Age Pensions; Against the Townsend Plan"; Dr. George Gallup, "Americans Vote 89% For Government Aids"; Gallup, "Townsend Plan Threat Affects Both Parties," *Washington Post*, January 12, 1936, sec. III, p. 1. For the Townsend Plan's response, see "Figures Set by Institute Found Unfair," *National Townsend Weekly*, January 27, 1936, p. 1.

25. Gallup, "Townsend Plan Threat Affects Both Parties," p. 1. The differences between the two March polls were due perhaps to the unreliability of newly emerging political polling techniques, but another possibility is that the Townsend Plan received a bump in support because the polling was done the day after a failed vote in the House seeking to reduce the appropriation for the investigation of the organization. The results appear in Hadley Cantril and Mildred Strunk, eds., *Public Opinion, 1935–1946* (Princeton, N.J.: Princeton University Press, 1951), p. 542. However, the raw data on the March polls do not survive.

26. Using Clements's estimate of 7,000 clubs and a survey of clubs later taken by Congressman John Tolan that indicated there were slightly more than 300 members per club. Holtzman reckons that 2.2 million were members of Townsend clubs. Holtzman, *The Townsend Movement*, p. 49. However, membership reported by club leaders is no doubt somewhat inflated. Also, through the first quarter of 1936, the Townsend Plan's total revenues to date were less than $1 million. If each member had to pay a quarter to join, the upper limit would be less than 4 million members. Because the organization raised revenues in ways other than the membership fee, which likely accounted for half or less of the revenues, the paying club membership was no doubt far lower than 4 million, closer to 2 million. My own estimate of the maximum number of clubs for this period is slightly less than 8,000, with approximately 250 members per club. "Townsend Roll Call of House Members Has Lone Deserter," *National Townsend Weekly*, February 3, 1936, p. 1. See also "House to Expedite Townsend Inquiry," *New York Times*, January 30, 1936, p. 7. For wildly inflated estimates of Townsend club support, see "House Chooses Group to Study Townsend Plan," *Washington Post*, February 23, 1936, p. 2; "77 Economists, League Score Townsend Plan," *Washington Post*, February 24, 1936, p. 2; Felix F. Bruner, "Clements Resigns Post in Rift with Townsend over Pension Policies," *Washington Post*, March 25, 1936, p. 1.

27. Charles Tilly and Jack A. Goldstone note that aspects of the political context that promote the success of challengers and threats to them are not opposite sides of the same conceptual coin. "Threat (and Opportunity): Popular Action and State Response in the Dynamics of Contentious Action," in *Silence and Voice in the Study of Contentious Politics*, ed. Ronald R. Aminzade, Jack A. Goldstone, Doug McAdam, Elizabeth J. Perry, William H. Sewell Jr., Sidney Tarrow, and Charles Tilly (New York: Cambridge University Press, 2001), chap. 7.

28. Reporters would home in on larger events such as the Townsend conventions, which overrepresented the more steadfast and well-off among the Townsendites, as conventioneers had to be elected and pay their way. The journalism after the Townsend Plan's peak examined a much more narrow membership base that likely differed systematically from the previously great ranks of Townsendites. For one account purporting to depict the typical Townsendite, see Russell Porter, "Looking for Utopia along the Townsend Trail," *New York Times*, February 5, 1939, sec. VII, pp. 4–5, 13. These later accounts can be augmented by partial lists of secretary-reported club members collected in California, although these, too, are incomplete. See "The Townsend National Recovery Plan, Inc." [papers of John C. Cuneo, compiled by James A. Mink, 1959], Charles E. Young Library, SCUCLA, collection 219, boxes 113–15.

29. The American Institute of Public Opinion poll of January 1939 also ran in the *Washington Post* and indicated that the support for the Townsend Plan was inversely related to income, a result that was also doubtless true for 1936 but was not explored or known at the time. Dr. George Gallup, "Poll Voters Favor $40-a-Month Payment," *Washington Post*, February 26, 1939, III, p. 2. For a further analysis of the 1939 poll results, see Cantril, *The Psychology of Social Movements*, pp. 192–93. For the results of several polls regarding old-age pensions, including some on the Townsend plan, see Cantril and Strunk, *Public Opinion, 1935–1946*, pp. 541–46.

30. A "poll" was published in the *Townsend Weekly* in 1953, supposedly describing the average Townsendite. See Holtzman, *The Townsend Movement*, p. 48.

31. The approximately 8 million men and women in the United States sixty-five years of age and older constituted about 6.3 percent of the population. Approximately 2 million were in the labor force. There were an additional approximately 10 million people in the United States of ages fifty-five through sixty-four years, or about 7.8 percent of the population. If Townsend clubs had 2 million members, they would have enrolled about one-ninth of the U.S. population fifty-five years old and older. Bureau of the Census, *Historical Statistics of the United States: Colonial Times to 1957* (Washington, D.C.: U.S. Government Printing Office, 1960), series A22, A32, A33, 8, A84, 10 D25, 71. For dependency among the aged and the unreliability of official reports, see Brian Gratton, "The Politics of Dependency Estimates: Social Security Board Statistics, 1935–1939," *Journal of Gerontology: Social Sciences* 52B (1997): pp. S117–S124.

32. Cuneo, "The Townsend Plan in Retrospect," pp. 30–31.

33. Of the approximately 8 million men and women in the United States sixty-five years of age and older, approximately 0.5 million were African American, and slightly less than 2 million were foreign born. Bureau of the Census, *Historical Statistics*, series A33, A84, pp. 8, 10; "Negro Club Has Large Membership," *Townsend National Weekly*, March 15, 1937, p. 16; "Poll Taxers Oppose Plan Campaigners," *Townsend National Weekly*, November 6, 1943, p. 11. The organizer for California, John C. Cuneo, also

claimed that African Americans were not well represented in clubs in his state. "The Townsend Plan in Retrospect," p. 30.

34. Relying on women for the housekeeping functions of Townsend clubs became more exaggerated later, after 1936. See chapter 7.

35. Harry B. Presson, "Tells History of First Townsend Clubs," *National Townsend Weekly*, November 2, 1936 p. 10; Holtzman, *The Townsend Movement*, pp. 50–51. Both Presson and Holtzman are counting club charters. Presson includes all that were ever granted through October 1936, without apparently subtracting those that had broken away, had disbanded earlier, or had failed to send in new charters for TNRP, Inc. His account, though incomplete and focusing on only the best-organized states, provides a good indication of the number of clubs in the spring of 1936, before the Townsend Plan was investigated in spring 1936. As we will see, in the summer and fall of 1936 many clubs dropped out of existence or decided against requesting charters from the new Townsend Plan organization, and few new ones started. As for the total number of clubs at this peak, Presson refers to the statement of Gilmour Young, who asserted at the July 1936 convention that 9,000 club charters were in existence. Yet when Presson lists all the highest states in terms of clubs and enumerates them, the total amounts to less than 6,700. Probably there were about 1,000 charters among all the less well represented states, bringing a total of slightly less than 8,000. Holtzman includes all the clubs ever in existence, from a 1950 letter from Harrison Hiles, an executive secretary of the Townsend Plan since 1937, the total number of clubs being approximately 12,300. At least 3,300 clubs and perhaps as many as 5,000 were initiated in the fifteen years after mid-1936. In the analyses below, to estimate the number of clubs per state, I start with Presson's figures and adjust them according to mentions by the state in the *Townsend Weekly* and information from the *Townsend Weekly* later in the 1930s on club drives, using Holtzman's numbers as the maximum.

36. Harry B. Presson, "Solid Base Is Starting Point—We've Got It!" *National Townsend Weekly*, November 9, 1936, p. 4. He considered 400 members to be a reasonable average to seek, although this figure probably well overstated the average club membership in 1936.

37. Presson, "Tells History of First Townsend Clubs."

38. Abraham Holtzman offered hypotheses for the differential regional dispersion of clubs that ran along old-school lines—that rural areas and the South in particular escaped the worst effects of the Depression, thus hindering recruitment for the Townsend Plan. *The Townsend Movement*, pp. 53–55.

39. Holtzman also conjectured that the major political parties discourage challenges, noting that party systems in the West were more open. Holtzman, *The Townsend Movement*, pp. 53–55; Townsend and Murray, *New Horizons*, p. 151. Neuberger and Loe referred to Townsendites as "Methodist picnic people." Townsend himself often emphasized that he was raised as a Methodist. A reporter at a Townsend convention referred to members as "WCTU types." David Harry Bennett, *Demagogues in the Depression* (New Brunswick, N.J.: Rutgers University Press, 1969), p. 175. The club news in the *Townsend Weekly* often indicated that Townsend clubs met in churches, which likely provided recruits as well and thus may have constituted a physical and social infrastructure for political involvement. On civic engagement generally, see Theda Skocpol and Morris P. Fiorina, eds., *Civic Engagement in American*

Democracy (Washington, D.C., and New York: Brookings Institution and Russell Sage Foundation, 1999).

40. These analyses were undertaken by the author (detailed results available on request).

41. Multiple regression finds that a measure of voting participation in the 1932 presidential election and David Mayhew's traditional party organization measure are strongly significant in predicting estimated Townsend clubs per congressional district in 1936, when other measures are included. For an analysis of Holtzman's measure of clubs and the definition of measures used here on the estimated number of clubs in 1936, see Edwin Amenta and Yvonne Zylan, "It Happened Here: Political Opportunity, the New Institutionalism, and the Townsend Movement," *American Sociological Review* 56 (1991): 250–65.

42. T.R.B., "Washington Week in Review"; "Calls Borah Opportunist," *New York Times*, January 30, 1936, p. 9. According to one state area manager, on a walk to the Lincoln Monument Townsend allegedly said, "It might be me sitting up there." *Old-Age Pension Plans and Organizations*, pp. 900–901.

43. "For Mothers and Fathers," *Time*, November 4, 1935, pp. 17–20. In most of its coverage, the *Washington Post* professed what it considered common knowledge: that Clements was the "brains" of the organization and Townsend the "front." See Felix F. Bruner, "Clements Resigns Post in Rift with Townsend over Pension Policies," March 25, 1936, p. 1.

44. "Townsend to Back 300 for Congress," *New York Times*, February 22, 1936, p. 2; "Clements Discusses Salaries," *New York Times*, February 23, 1936, p. 11. Clements claimed that he and Townsend took salaries of $100 per week from OARP, Ltd., and $50 per week from the *Weekly*. They had apparently raised their OARP salaries from $100 per week to $250 per week at the beginning of the year, but a retroactive raise may have been part of Clements's buyout deal. *Old-Age Pension Plans and Organizations*, p. 355.

45. "Quits Townsend Post," *New York Times*, January 21, 1936, p. 2. For Wunder's complaints against Clements and vice versa, see *Old-Age Pension Plans and Organizations*, pp. 360–61, 842–47, 859–60, 880–81. Clements had charged him with personally profiting, $500 per appearance, from a speaking tour in which he debated others regarding the Townsend pension-recovery plan, using the organization's contacts to publicize the debates. Other leaders had their own ideas about how best to promote the plan—notably Edward Margett, the state organizer for northern California, and Representative Monaghan, whose Townsendite amendment to the Social Security Act was the basis of the *Townsend Weekly* congressional honor roll. He read an extensive letter criticizing Clements the day that the House voted for the inquiry, possibly bridling against his inability to alter the McGroarty bill. "Townsend Inquiry Is Voted by House, Only 4 Objecting," *New York Times*, February 20, 1936, p. 1.

46. "Would Bar Dual Party System," *New York Times*, February 23, 1936, p. 11. Townsend claimed the existence of 7,000 clubs but also, implausibly, that they were growing at a rate of 1,000 per week and that he would like to use them to replace the two-party system. "GOP Reports Big Donations: $261,387 Total," *Washington Post*, March 14, 1936, p. 2. See also Townsend's September 1935 letter to Clements, in *Old-Age Pension Plans and Organizations*, pp. 596–97.

47. See Townsend's letters to Clements dated July 25, 1935, and September 4, 1935, in *Old-Age Pension Plans and Organizations*, pp. 596–97, 668. The Townsend Plan was exploring the creation of a third party but only as a safeguard "against connivance of the old parties" and probably to mollify Townsend. "A Statement," *National Townsend Weekly*, December 23, 1935, p. 1; "Townsend Rejects National Ticket," *New York Times*, February 21, 1936, p. 2. At a rally Townsend collected $1,700 to explore the possibility of creating a new political party. "Calls Borah Opportunist," *New York Times*, January 30, 1936, p. 9; Richard L. Neuberger, "Borah Loses Aid of Townsendites," *New York Times*, February 23, 1936, sec. IV, p. 11. For Clements's view of the differences in strategic vision between himself and Townsend, see *Old-Age Pension Plans and Organizations*, pp. 329, 354.

48. "Townsend Rejects National Ticket," *New York Times*, February 21, 1936, p. 2; "McGroarty Sees Misunderstanding," *New York Times*, February 21, 1936, p. 2; "Townsend Men Split over Coast Primary," *New York Times*, March 22, 1936, p. 39. McGroarty claimed no presidential ambitions, only a Democratic convention delegation pledged to secure a Townsend plank in the platform. For the *Townsend Weekly's* account, see "Founder Says Present Aim Is for Townsend Congress," March 2, 1936, p. 2.

49. For Townsend's suggestions for converting the transactions tax into something like a gross income tax, see Dr. Francis E. Townsend, "Adventure," *National Townsend Weekly*, December 23, 1935, p. 2. To counter "unfounded rumors" that the Townsend Plan had abandoned the tax, see R. E. Clements, "A Statement," *National Townsend Weekly*, February 20, 1936, p. 1. On McGroarty, see "No Retreat in McGroarty Bill: Transactions Tax Purpose Is Understood by Supporters States National Headquarters," *National Townsend Weekly*, March 2, 1936, p. 1; "McGroarty to Talk to Nation," *National Townsend Weekly*, March 16, 1936, p. 1; "McGroarty Opposes Bond Plan," *New York Times*, April 1, 1936, p.13. Townsend also opposed the incomes test for the bill. For more on his disagreements, see *Old-Age Pension Plans and Organizations*, pp. 689–93.

50. Alan Brinkley, *Voices of Protest: Huey Long, Father Coughlin, and the Great Depression* (New York: Vintage, 1982), chaps. 4–6; Michael Kazin, *The Populist Persuasion: An American History* (New York: Basic Books, 1995), chap. 5; Charles J. Tull, *Father Coughlin and the New Deal* (Syracuse, N.Y.: Syracuse University Press, 1965).

51. Brinkley, *Voices of Protest*, pp. 187–93.

Chapter Six: Dr. Townsend, Now at the Helm

1. Paul W. Ward, "How Strong Is the Townsend Plan?" *Nation*, January 8, 1936, pp. 37–38.

2. Charles McKinley and Robert W. Frase, *Launching Social Security: A Capture-and-Record Account, 1935–1937* (Madison: University of Wisconsin Press, 1970), pp. 23, 26, 149; Blanche D. Coll, *Safety Net: Welfare and Social Security, 1929–1979* (New Brunswick, N.J.: Rutgers University Press, 1995), pp. 81–84; U.S. Committee on Economic Security, *Social Security in America* (Washington, D.C.: U.S. Government Printing Office, 1937), pp. 164, 238.

3. Coll, *Safety Net*, pp. 84–88; Jerry R. Cates, *Insuring Inequality: Administrative Leadership in Social Security, 1935–54* (Ann Arbor: University of Michigan Press, 1983), pp. 112–14. Within the Social Security Board, the Bureau of Public Assistance argued that individual investigations were required under the law, while the general counsel, Thomas Eliot, argued that the term "need" appeared only in the preamble of the Social Security Act, and thus need-assessment was not required. The board itself, a three-person politically appointed group, stood firm against flat pension programs but not against programs that employed exemptions of income or property or both to produce something like flat pensions.

4. McKinley and Frase, *Launching Social Security*, pp. 145–46, 149.

5. Cates, *Insuring Inequality*; O. Otto Moore, *Mile High Harbor* (Denver, Colo.: Associated Publishers, 1947); Jackson K. Putnam, *Old Age Politics in California: From Richardson to Reagan* (Stanford, Calif.: Stanford University Press, 1971), pp. 65–69, 75–80.

6. If one examines all states that were similar in having a prominent presence of Townsend clubs and being from a democratized polity not dominated by patronage parties, the Townsend Plan had a differential impact according to whether a favorable political regime was in power. In some instances (Colorado, Idaho, Minnesota, Montana, and Wyoming), Democrats or left-wing parties controlled the government for most of the period after 1935, and in other cases (California and New Hampshire) they did not. For the two states without favorable regimes in power during the 1935–38 period, the average old-age benefit prior to the Townsend Plan was 47.1 percent of the state's per capita income. By 1939, this figure had increased only to 52.6 percent—or about a 5.5 percentage point increase. By contrast, the five states with Democratic or third-party regimes in power saw their benefit levels jump from 27.4 percent of per capita income to 53.3 percent—a much more substantial increase, slightly surpassing states that had a big head start.

7. Long's filibuster was over a different issue. The third board member was the Democrat Vincent Miles. Altmeyer was elevated to chairman in 1936, when Winant resigned. McKinley and Frase, *Launching Social Security*, pp. 17–19.

8. Roger Daniels, *The Bonus March: An Episode of the Great Depression* (Westport, Conn.: Greenwood, 1971), chaps. 3, 9. See also William P. Dillingham, *Federal Aid to Veterans, 1917–1941* (Gainesville: University of Florida Press, 1952). To pay for the veterans' bonuses in 1936, the administration sought and won a tax on undistributed business profits, as well as more fiscally substantial increases in corporate income taxes. These provided more revenue, $800 million per year, than the previous year's "soak-the-rich" taxes. Arthur M. Schlesinger Jr., *The Politics of Upheaval* (Boston: Houghton Mifflin, 1960), pp. 509–512; Mark H. Leff, *The Limits of Symbolic Reform: The New Deal and Taxation, 1933–1939* (Cambridge: Cambridge University Press, 1984), pp. 169–85.

9. Harry D. Gideonse, ed., *The Economic Meaning of the Townsend Plan* (Chicago: University of Chicago Press, 1936); National Industrial Conference Board, *The Townsend Scheme* (New York: National Industrial Conference Board, 1936); Nicholas Roosevelt, *The Townsend Plan: Taxing for Sixty* (New York: Doubleday, Doran and Company, 1936); Twentieth Century Fund Committee on Old Age Security, *The Townsend Crusade* (New York: Twentieth Century Fund, 1936). This group, which in-

cluded the former longtime head of the Children's Bureau and social policy advocate Edith Abbott, called for adequate old-age "pensions." National Association of Manufacturers (NAM), "A Fireside Chat on the Townsend Plan" (New York: NAM, 1936). Richard L. Neuberger, who was covering the Townsend Plan and clubs for various publications, coauthored a book that came out later in the year, *An Army of the Aged*, whose thesis was that the Townsend Plan was a racket. Richard L. Neuberger and Kelley Loe, *An Army of the Aged* (Caldwell, Idaho: Caxton Publishers, 1936). For books taking a favorable point of view, winning the Townsend seal of approval, see Morgan Dorman, *Age before Booty: An Explanation of the Townsend Plan* (New York: Putnam, 1936), and Sheridan Downey, *Why I Believe in the Townsend Plan* (Sacramento, Calif.: Sheridan Downey, 1936).

10. "House to Expedite Townsend Inquiry," *New York Times*, January 30, 1936, p. 7. Bell would have been unlikely, however, to unseat the current incumbent, Champ Clark, and perhaps was hoping that Truman would fail.

11. "Both Parties Back Townsend Inquiry," *New York Times*, February 13, 1936, p. 1; Robert C. Albright, "House Votes Investigation of Townsend Plan, 240–4," *Washington Post*, February 20, 1936, p. 1; "Townsend Inquiry Is Voted by House, Only 4 Objecting," *New York Times*, February 20, 1936, p. 1; T.R.B. [Richard L. Strout], "Washington Week in Review," *New Republic*, June 10, 1936, pp. 128–129. See also Holtzman, *The Townsend Movement*, chap. 7; Burg, *The Gray Crusade*, pp. 368–73.

12. "House Chooses Group to Study Townsend Plan," *Washington Post*, February 23, 1936, p. 2; "Committee Named on Pension Inquiry," *New York Times*, February 23, 1936, p. 11; "National Headquarters Invites Politicians to Fulfill Threat of Investigation by Congress," *National Townsend Weekly*, February 24, 1936, p. 1; "Townsend Bloc Charges 'Trick' In Inquiry Fund," *Washington Post*, March 14, 1936, p. 2; "Townsend Inquiry Gets $50,000 Fund," *New York Times*, March 14, 1936, p. 2; Staff Correspondent, "Enemies of Townsend Plan Unmasked by Demand for Unreasonable Probe Fund," *National Townsend Weekly*, March 30, 1936, p. 1; "Appropriation Vote Indicates Plan Strength," *National Townsend Weekly*, March 30, 1936, p. 5.

13. Clements clearly saw the potential trouble that might be caused by the investigation. "Secretary Assails Inquiry," *New York Times*, February 20, 1936, p. 2; "National Headquarters Invites Politicians to Fulfill Threat of Investigation by Congress," *National Townsend Weekly*, February 24, 1936, p. 1; "Outcome of Investigation May Prove Big Boomerang Think Many Congressmen," *National Townsend Weekly*, March 30, 1936, p. 1.

14. "Secretary Assails Inquiry," *New York Times*; "Townsend Is Cast for Major Role in the House Inquiry into His Plan," *New York Times*, February 21, 1936, p. 1.

15. "Townsend Is Cast for Major Role in the House Inquiry into His Plan," *New York Times*; Ward, "How Strong Is the Townsend Plan?" *Nation*.

16. See chap. 5, n. 47, above.

17. "Townsend Men Split over Coast Primary," *New York Times*, March 22, 1936, p. 39. Townsend wrote a supporting introduction to Downey's *Why I Believe in the Townsend Plan*.

18. Clements's view was that Walter Townsend had resigned as both director and member, and thus the new board had no standing. The amended bylaws of OARP, Ltd., adopted June 28, 1935, are unclear as to whether members or the board con-

trolled the corporation. There is nothing to indicate in the minutes of the Special Meeting of the Board of Directors that Walter Townsend resigned as a *member* of the corporation. Townsend added Reverend A. J. Wright of Cleveland and Gilmour Young of San Francisco, the latter an ally of Edward Margett, to the board, apparently before March 9, contrary to the report in the *Weekly*. "A Message from Our Leader," *National Townsend Weekly*, March 16, p. 16; "Townsend Inquiry Eagerly Awaited," *New York Times*, March 26, 1936, p. 2; "Clements Conduct Exposed by New Board of Directors," *National Townsend Weekly*, April 13, 1936, p. 7; *Old-Age Pension Plans and Organizations*, pp. 357–58.

19. "Dr. Townsend's Chief Aide Quits in Split on 'Fundamental' Policies," *New York Times*, March 25, 1936, p. 1; Felix F. Bruner, "Clements Resigns Post in Rift with Townsend over Pension Policies," *Washington Post*, March 25, 1936, p. 1; "Townsend Plan: Rift and Inquiry," *Literary Digest*, April 4, 1936. Clements's statement ran in full in the *Weekly*, which placed it on page 2. "Clements Announces His Resignation as National Secretary of O.A.R.P.," *National Townsend Weekly*, March 30, p. 2. The terms of the sale of Clements's stock to Townsend are outlined in a "Memorandum of Agreement," between the two, March 20, 1936. Townsend agreed to transfer nine of Clements ten shares (of twenty altogether) to OARP, Ltd. TNRP, Inc., University of Oregon Library, Division of Special Collections and University Archives (SCUO), box 115, folder 1.

20. "$1,800–$2,000 Fees in Month Reported for Townsend Aide," *New York Times*, March 27, 1936, p. 1; Edward T. Folliard, "Townsend Lieutenant Got $1,800 a Month, House Inquiry Is Told," *Washington Post*, March 27, 1936, p. 1; "$952,000 Received by Townsend Plan since Its Inception," *New York Times*, March 28, 1936, p. 1; "Pension Post Paid $12,585 to Clements, Inquiry Told," *Washington Post*, March 28, 1936, p. 1; Duncan Aikman, "Townsend Movement Facing Hard Trials," *New York Times*, March 29, 1936, sec. IV, p. 12; *Old-Age Pension Plans and Organizations*, pp. 56–58.

21. "Millions in It, Dr. Townsend Wrote of Plan," *New York Post*, April 1, 1936, p. 1; "Dr. Townsend Had Vision of Plan Paying 'Millions,'" *New York Times*, April 2, 1936, p. 1; "Townsendites Broke Voting Laws, House Group Is Told," *Washington Post*, April 2, 1936, p. 1; "Charges Townsend Failed to Turn in $1,700 Collections," *New York Times*, April 3, 1936, p. 1; "Gift Never Paid into Age Fund, House Is Told," *Washington Post*, April 3, 1936, p. 1; *Old-Age Pension Plans and Organizations*, pp. 178–93. Newspaper headlines irresponsibly homed in on a letter by Townsend considering a new fund-raising strategy that the doctor estimated might generate "millions" of dollars. The committee prompted Clements to explain the essentially undemocratic nature of the organization as well as the Townsend National Legion, which numbered 11,000. Clements twitted Townsend's third-party aspirations, revealing to the committee that he had withheld $1,700 in receipts from a mass meeting on February 20 in Los Angeles to explore the creation of a Townsend party. On the Townsend Legion, see *Old-Age Pension Plans and Organizations*, pp. 94–97, 137; T.R.B., "Washington Notes."

22. Gomer Smith was already vice president, and Gilmour Young was named secretary. The regional directors added to the board, aside from Wunder, were John B. Kiefer, the midwestern regional director; Frank Arbuckle, the new western regional director and an ally of Sheridan Downey; and Nathan J. Roberts, the southern regional

director. Townsend retained majority ownership of the *Weekly*, but only 10 percent of its profits would go to him, with the rest being assigned to OARP, Ltd. Townsend clubs were authorized to choose a national advisory committee, with one representative from each state. A second national convention of Townsend clubs was called for the summer. "M'Groarty Quits Townsend Camp," *New York Times*, March 31, 1936, p. 1; "Drastic Shake-Up in Townsend Group," *New York Times*, April 1, 1936, p. 1; Duncan Aikman, "Inquiry and Rifts Stagger the OARP," *New York Times*, April 5, 1936, sec. IV, p. 12; Laura Vitray, "Congressional Investigators Turn Spy Glasses on Dr. Townsend," *Washington Post*, April 5, 1936, sec. III, p. 3; "Townsend Plan's Change of Drivers," *Literary Digest*, April 11, 1936, p. 10.

23. "National Board of Directors' Meeting April 6th and 7th, 1936 [of OARP, Ltd.]," SCUO, box 115, folder 1; "Townsend Chiefs Act to Oust Coast Head," *New York Times*, April 7, 1936, p. 30; "Townsend Board Is Reorganizing," *New York Times*, April 8, 1936, p. 6; "Los Angeles Club Withdraws," *New York Times*, April 8, 1936, p. 6; "Townsend Plan's Change of Drivers"; "Townsend Finds Cause Spreading," *New York Times*, April 12, 1936, p. 6. The board of directors also appointed a new treasurer, Baxter Rankine, who had served as Clements's assistant almost from the beginning, and who now joined the board. For the *National Townsend Weekly*'s version of these events, see "Clements Conduct Exposed by New Board of Directors," April 13, 1936, p. 7; "Dr. Townsend Picks Seven Members Representing Every Section of Land; Turns Profits from Weekly to the Townsend Plan," April 13, 1936, p. 1; "National OARP Board Charts Future Course of Movement in Resolutions," April 27, 1936, p. 1; "Townsend Clubs Called to Choose Members for National Advisory Body," April 27, 1936, p. 1. On Clements's efforts to get Walter Townsend to sign a statement, see Arthur Carlyle O'Byrne, "The Political Significance of the Townsend Movement in California, 1934–1950" (M.A. thesis, University of Southern California, Los Angeles, 1953).

24. "Townsend's Aide Received $77,780," *New York Times*, April 24, 1936, p. 4; "Says Townsend Chief Hinted of Other Aims," *New York Times*, April 29, 1936, p. 4; "Says Dr. Townsend Had Need of Cash," *New York Times*, May 1, 1936, p. 16. Moore also provided some headline-worthy quotes: Clements supposedly said he did not "give a damn about the old people," and Townsend supposedly dismissed some supporters as "old fossils."

25. When it first called Townsend to the witness stand on May 5, the committee found itself short of expected evidence and was forced to take a two-week adjournment. "Townsend Inquiry Is Put Off 2 Weeks," *New York Times*, May 6, 1936, p. 3; "Twelve Thousand Pounds of Townsend Petitions on Way to Nation's Capital," *National Townsend Weekly*, May 11, 1936, p. 1; " 'Joan of Arc' Greeted by Tolan," *National Townsend Weekly*, May 25, 1936, p. 2; "Townsend Blames Roosevelt Regime for 'Hostile' Probe," *New York Times*, May 20, 1936, p. 1; "Townsend Admits a Plan to License Farms to Get Tax," *New York Times*, May 21, 1936, p. 1; "Townsend Bolts Inquiry over Fraud Charge," *New York Times*, May 22, 1936, p. 1. The third "member" of OARP, Ltd., was now Gilmour Young. Although Townsend was probably unaware of it, the *Weekly* had published an accounting of the expenditures from the 1935 congressional fund. "Financial Statement: Expenditures from Congressional Fund," *Townsend Weekly*, June 3, 1935, p. 2. On the Townsendgrams, see *Old-Age Pension Plans and Organizations*, pp. 716–37.

26. After the first week of testimony, Duncan Aikman wrote in the *New York Times* "Week in Review" that Washington experts were divided over whether the investigation would harm or aid the Townsend Plan, but after the second week his summary was that things had changed dramatically because of factionalism within the Townsend Plan. "Townsend Movement Facing Hard Trials"; "Inquiry and Rifts Stagger the OARP." Alfred J. Wright, an Ohio state organizer and minister who was recently elevated to the board of directors, was ousted by Townsend when he defied the doctor's order to ignore the committee's subpoena. "Townsendite Held as Ex-Bootlegger," *New York Times*, June 3, 1936, p. 4. On Wunder's profane letters and Margett's indictments, see *Old-Age Pension Plans and Organizations*, pp. 842–47, 916–22; T.R.B., "Washington Notes."

27. Dr. Francis E. Townsend, "Most Salaries Are to Be Paid by Weekly," *National Townsend Weekly*, May 4, 1936, p. 8; "Margett Will Direct Nation Wide Publicity," *National Townsend Weekly*, May 11, 1936, p. 1; On Wright, see *Old-Age Pension Plans and Organizations*, pp. 886–87.

28. For a statement of April 4 from a club secretary in Maine that no more quotas would be forthcoming, see *Old-Age Pension Plans and Organizations*, p. 866; Richard L. Neuberger, "Townsend Dimes Fall Off," *New York Times*, April 12, 1936, sec. IV, p. 11; "Townsend Clubs Voting on Support," *New York Times*, April 19, 1936, p. 28; "Caravan Ends Triumphal March on Washington as Crowds Roar Greetings," *National Townsend Weekly*, May 25, 1936, p. 1.

29. "Says Income Fell, Then Rose," *New York Times*, June 3, 1936, p. 4. According to figures from the *National Townsend Weekly* (July 27, 1936, p. 31), OARP, Ltd., brought in $604,000 in the nine-month period ending on June 30, 1936. In figures presented at the July convention, OARP brought in $983,131 from its inception through June 30, 1936, leaving only $31,000 for the second quarter in 1936. Quotas were not being met, as a million members generating a dime per month would have meant $300,000 per quarter. Townsend, "Most Salaries Are to Be Paid by Weekly," p. 8; "Headquarters of O.A.R.P. to Be in Chicago," *National Townsend Weekly* [eastern edition], May 25, 1936, p. 1; Neuberger, "Townsend Dimes Fall Off."

30. Duncan Aikman, "Townsend and Foes Both in Difficulties"; T.R.B., "Washington Notes"; "Townsend Cited," *Literary Digest*, June 6, 1936, p. 5.

31. Alan Brinkley, *Voices of Protest: Huey Long, Father Coughlin and the Great Depression* (New York: Random House, 1982), pp. 77–79; David H. Bennett, *Demagogues in the Depression: American Radicals and the Union Party, 1932–1936* (New Brunswick, N.J.: Rutgers University Press, 1969), chap. 3; Glen Jeansonne, *Gerald L. K. Smith: Minister of Hate* (New Haven, Conn.: Yale University Press, 1988).

32. Staff correspondent, "New Educational Field Opened," *National Townsend Weekly*, May 11, 1936, pp. 10–11. Some of the films remain available in SPUO.

33. "National Board of Directors' Meeting April 6th and 7th, 1936 [of OARP, Ltd.]"; "National Board Meeting, May 1st & 2nd, 1936 [OARP, Ltd.]," SPUO, box 115, folder 1; "Townsend Taboos Party Alliances on Convention Eve," *New York Times*, July 15, 1936, p. 1.

34. The Socialist Norman Thomas was the only candidate who accepted an invitation to speak, and he drew headlines when he compared Townsend's recovery plan to prescribing cough drops to fight tuberculosis. "Thomas Tells Convention of Townsend Plan Flaws; Delegates Donate $30,000," *New York Times*, July 19, 1936, p. 1.

35. "Founder Greets Assembly in Inspiring Talk"; "Detailed Proceedings of Convention," *National Townsend Weekly*, July 27, 1936, pp. 3, 7. As Townsend put it: "Why should we pussyfoot, why should we hedge, why should we not call a spade a spade. This administration, instead of profiting by the mistakes of the preceding one, has gone on blindly intensifying those same mistakes and adding to them an infinite variety of new ones." See also the accounts of the convention in Bennett, *Demagogues in the Depression*, pp. 7–16. Thomas L. Stokes, *Chip off My Shoulder* (Princeton, N.J.: Princeton University Press, 1940), pp. 412–18. On Coughlin's support of Lemke and his role at the Townsend convention, see Brinkley, *Voices of Protest*, pp. 254–62; "Townsend Yields on 'Rebel' Aide Who Spoke in President's Defense," *New York Times*, July 18, 1936, p. 1; Duncan Aikman, "Townsend Convention Is Swayed by Oratory," *New York Times*, July 19, 1936, sec. IV, p. 6; "Townsend Makes Public Reasons for Dismissals," *National Townsend Weekly*, September 7, 1936, p. 1. In addition, former board member Alfred J. Wright used the forum to file a suit, along with George Highley and some California Townsend club members, to require OARP, Ltd., to account for its expenditures or be placed in receivership. Townsend soon dumped from the board of directors Gomer Smith, as well as Clinton Wunder and Jack Kiefer, because of their pro-Roosevelt views. The founder also charged Wunder and Kiefer with exchanging obscene letters and public drunkenness. The regional director for the South, Nathan Roberts, resigned in protest, and the article would later be the subject of a libel suit by Kiefer. A California Democratic Party official saw the convention as reducing the ability of the Townsend Plan to swing votes away from Roosevelt. Letter from Henry A. Briggs to James A. Farley, July 27, 1936, Democratic National Committee Papers, Correspondence of James Farley, box 1092, California, FDR Library.

36. The move was due partly to the lawsuit and partly to insulate educational and club matters from fund-raising. The Townsend Plan secretary, Gilmour Young, was the third member. The board of directors included Townsend, Young, the treasurer Baxter Rankine, business manager Harrison Hiles, and Edward Trefz. The new Townsend Plan corporation was still to collect the membership fees, but the publishing company was to subsidize the work of the corporation. Minutes of the First Meeting of the Board of Directors of Townsend National Recovery Plan, Inc., September 26, 1936, p. 5. In October, Townsend's wife, Minnie, was added to the membership of the corporation, along with their granddaughter Heloise Shevling. Minutes of the Special Meeting of the Members of the Townsend National Recovery Plan, Inc., SCUO, box 115, folder 1.

37. All moneymaking functions were to be handed over to the Prosperity Publishing Company, whose stock was owned almost entirely by Townsend. Although he had agreed to donate almost half of the stock of the company to OARP, Ltd., in March, Townsend had the latter refuse the gift. "Special Meeting of the Board of Directors [sic] of the Townsend Plan, Ltd., September 4, 1936," minutes [actually a meeting of "members"]; "Minutes of the Special Meeting of the Board of Directors of the Townsend Plan, Ltd.," September 25, 1936; Letter from F. E. Townsend to Harrison Hiles, October 3, 1936, SCUO, box 115, folder 1; "New Financial Plan Proposed for Movement," "Official Bulletin #11," *National Townsend Weekly*, August 17, 1936, pp. 1, 20; John S. Tucker, "Membership Dues Plan Wins Hearty Approval of Enthusiastic Units," "National Bulletin #12," *National Townsend Weekly*, August 24, 1936, pp. 1, 20; "Minutes of the First Meeting of the Board of Directors of Townsend National Recovery Plan, Inc.," September 26, 1936, SCUO, box 115, folder 1.

38. "'Bury Old Parties,' Urges Townsend," *New York Times*, July 24, 1936, p. 7; J. W. Brinton, "Don't Throw Your Votes Away on Roosevelt or Landon—If You Want the Townsend Plan Put in Operation Next Year," *National Townsend Weekly*, September 14, 1936, pp. 10–11; P. M. McEvoy, "Townsend Millions Can Elect President," Dr. F. E. Townsend, "Dr. Townsend Tells Why He Is Supporting Wm. Lemke," "Presidential Opposition Delayed the Payment of Bonus for 15 Years," and J. W. Brinton, "Don't Throw Your Votes Away Nov. 3—Make Them Count," *National Townsend Weekly*, October 19, 1936, pp. 1, 2, 10–11. According to projections in the *Weekly*, Roosevelt, Landon, and Lemke would each win sixteen states. The Townsend threat in California was not, however, taken very seriously by Democrats. Byron N. Scott to James A. Farley, October 15, 1936, Democratic National Committee Papers, Correspondence of James Farley, box 1092, California, FDR Library.

39. Richard L. Neuberger, "Townsend Power Ebbs in the West," *New York Times*, August 23, 1936, sec. IV, p. 7.

40. The small amount of newsprint devoted to congressional choices was in stark contrast to the extensive attention to the presidential election. For how the congressional endorsement process was supposed to work, see "National Board of Directors' Meeting April 6th and 7th, 1936 [of OARP, Ltd.]"; "Townsendites Put Vote at 10,000,000," *New York Times*, October 18, 1936, sec. II, p. 12; Gilmour Young, "200 Endorsed Candidates on Ballot November 3," *National Townsend Weekly*, October 19, 1936, p. 1; "Townsend-Endorsed Candidates for Congress," *National Townsend Weekly*, November 2, 1936, p. 5.

41. In Michigan, for instance, the *Weekly* had listed six endorsed candidates before the election and claimed that five Townsend supporters were elected, but none of the five supposed supporters were among the six previously listed. P. M. McEvoy, "Townsendites Elect 109—Eight Senators—101 Congressmen," *National Townsend Weekly*, November 16, 1936 p. 1; "Elected Candidates," *Townsend National Weekly*, November 30, 1936, p. 5; "Townsend Bloc Melted," *New York Times*, November 8, 1936, p. 32.

42. Perhaps not as badly as Father Coughlin, who disbanded his National Union for Social Justice as a result of the defeat. Brinkley, *Voices of Protest*, p. 261; George P. West, "Townsend Strives to Offset Defeat," *New York Times*, November 15, 1936, sec. IV, p. 7.

43. "Letter from Dr. Francis E. Townsend to My California Friends," January 27, 1937, SPUO, box 115, folder 1.

Chapter Seven: The Rise of a Pension Movement

1. On Johnson, see U.S. House of Representatives, Committee on Ways and Means, *Hearings Relative to the Social Security Act Amendments of 1939*, 76th Cong., 1st sess. (Washington, D.C.: U.S. Government Printing Office, 1939), vol. 1, pp. 115–16, 119.

2. "Few Heed Townsend Call," *New York Times*, January 16, 1937, p. 12. The GWA also removed the means test from the McGroarty bill, defined transactions more crisply, provided restrictions on how the pensions might be spent, especially regarding gifts, penalties for violating the law, and would repeal the old-age spending provisions

of the Social Security Act. For the bill, see "The General Welfare Act of 1937" [analyzed by Arthur L. Johnson] (Chicago: TNRP, Inc., 1937); Arthur L. Johnson, "Analysis of the New Townsend Recovery Plan Bill—General Welfare Act of 1937," *Townsend National Weekly*, January 25, 1937, p. 8; "Townsend National Weekly Making Great Gains," *Townsend National Weekly*, January 25, 1937, p. 1; "Open Townsend Bill Drive," *Townsend National Weekly*, January 25, 1937, p. 1.

3. The loans were to pay 4 percent interest. Also inaugurated that year was the Townsend Foundation. "Townsend Changes Plans," *New York Times*, January 4, 1937, p. 11; Duncan Aikman, "Twilight of Townsend Plan as a Political Force Is Seen in Congress," *New York Times*, January 24, 1937, sec. IV, p. 6; Dr. Francis E. Townsend, "No High Salaries Paid at National Headquarters," *Townsend National Weekly*, January 25, p. 16; "Women's Auxiliaries Organizing Everywhere to Increase Activities," *Townsend National Weekly*, April 5, 1937, p. 7; J. W. Brinton, "I Was Just Thinking," *Townsend National Weekly*, April 12, p. 14; J. W. Brinton, "A Personal Word to Townsend Members," *Townsend National Weekly*, May 13, 1937, p. 16; "Dr. Townsend Asks for a $5,000,000 Loan for Campaign to Put Over His Pension Plan," *New York Times*, March 30, 1937, p. 1; "Nation-Wide Program Launched: Five Million Dollars Being Raised to Finance Recovery Plan," *Townsend National* Weekly, April 5, 1937, p. 1.

4. He was convicted on two counts—failing to answer a subpoena and refusing to answer questions. His fine was $100. "Townsend on Trial in Contempt Case," *New York Times*, February 24, 1937, p. 2; "Townsend Is Sentenced to 30 Days in Jail; His Pension Plan Cannot Be Halted, He Says," *New York Times*, March 13, 1937, p. 1; "Dr. Townsend Found Guilty," *Townsend National Weekly*, March 8, 1937, p. 1. *Life* ran a nine-photo spread on Curtis C. Fleming of Chelan, Washington, who spent all the money in twelve days. "A Townsendite Spends $200," February 8, 1937, pp. 52–53; "Chelan, Wash., Starts Townsend Plan Trial: Give Man 'Tagged' $200 to Spend in Month," *New York Times*, January 18, 1937, p. 1; Richard L. Neuberger, "Townsend Tests Revive Movement," *New York Times*, January 31, 1937, sec. IV, p. 10; "Townsend Plan Test Is Begun in New Jersey," *New York Times*, May 2, 1937, sec. II, p. 2.

5. Only 59 signatures were listed, however. A second line of action was a letter to Chairman Doughton, asking him to hold hearings on Townsend legislation. "Ways and Means Committee Splits 16 to 7 on Party Vote," *Townsend National Weekly*, April 26, 1937, p. 1; "Double Drive Under Way to Force Action on Townsend Plan Bill," May 3, 1937, p. 1; "Townsend Bill Petition to Discharge Committee Climbing toward Goal," *Townsend National Weekly*, May 10, 1937, p. 1.

6. Townsend was also likely frustrated by the bottling of the Townsend Plan's legislation in committee by the Democratic leadership, whose moves he traced to the president. F. E. Townsend, "My Attitude on the Supreme Court Issue," *Townsend National Weekly*, May 31, 1937, p. 16; J. W. Brinton, "I Was Just Thinking," *Townsend National Weekly*, June 6, 1937, p. 16; "Associates Rebel against Townsend," *New York Times*, June 5, 1937, p. 1; "Congress Backer Balking," *New York Times*, June 5, 1937, p. 4; "Twelve Leaders Quit Dr. Townsend," *New York Times*, June 6, 1937, p. 20; Committee on Ways and Means, *Hearings Relative to the Social Security Act Amendments of 1939*, vol. 1, pp. 93–95, 97, 109–10, 116–18.

7. Louther Horne, "Townsend Movement Shaken," *New York Times*, June 13, 1937, sec. IV, p. 6; J. W. Brinton, "I Was Just Thinking," *Townsend National Weekly*, June 6, 1937, p. 16; "Leader of Duped Mutineers Sought for Betrayal of Fiduciary

Trust," *Townsend National Weekly*, June 13, 1937, p. 1; Dr. Francis E. Townsend, "Message of Founder to Nation," *Townsend National Weekly*, June 13, 1937, p. 16; "Pension for Dr. Townsend Proposed by House Group," *New York Times*, June 21, 1937, p. 6; E. J. Speake, "Brinton Tactics Forced Others to Resign with Him, Plan Aide Charges," *Townsend National Weekly*, August 23, 1937, p. 1; "Facts Presented by Loyal National Headquarters Aides Wholly Refute Anonymous Attack on Plan Founder," *Townsend National Weekly*, August 23, 1937, p. 1. For the origins of the General Welfare Federation, see Committee on Ways and Means, *Hearings Relative to the Social Security Act Amendments of 1939*, vol. 1, pp. 117–18, 122–26.

8. The six principles, or "corollaries," to the Townsend National Recovery Plan proper, were to restore control over credit to the government; drastic immigration laws; buy American; homes not to be confiscated by unjust property evaluation and taxation; minimum wages equal to the retirement annuity; and no changes in government except through constitutional amendment. The call for a constitutional convention was based on Townsend's fear that a Supreme Court packed by Roosevelt would rule Townsend legislation unconstitutional. "State Petition Move Inaugurated to Make Townsend Plan Amendment to Constitution, Insuring Victory," *Townsend National Weekly*, July 5, 1937, p. 1; "Unpopularity of Social Security to Spur Drive," *Townsend National Weekly*, August 16, 1937, p. 1; "Petition Drive Spreads in All State Sectors," *Townsend National Weekly*, November 15, 1937, p. 1; "Townsend Plan Principles," *Townsend National Weekly*, July 5, 1937, p. 8.

9. "The Open Forum," *Townsend National Weekly*, June 28, 1937, p. 3. For another letter, see *Townsend National Weekly*, August 2, 1937, p. 7.

10. On leadership and contention, see Ron Aminzade, Jack A. Goldstone, and Elizabeth J. Perry, "Leadership Dynamics and Dynamics of Contention," in *Silence and Voice in the Study of Contentious Politics*, ed. Ronald R. Aminzade, Jack A. Goldstone, Doug McAdam, Elizabeth J. Perry, William H. Sewell Jr., Sidney Tarrow, and Charles Tilly (New York: Cambridge University Press, 2001), chap. 4.

11. Henry D. Fetter, *Taking on the Yankees: Winning and Losing and the Business of Baseball, 1903–2003* (New York: Norton, 2003), chap. 11.

12. E. J. Speake was now the head of the National Organization Department, responsible for clubs. "Otis J. Bouma Chosen to Head TNRP Washington Efforts to Win Consideration for Bill," *Townsend National Weekly*, November 22, 1937, p. 1; "Growing Clubs Tell How They Sign Members," *Townsend National Weekly*, November 29, 1937, p. 7.

13. The Los Angeles convention assented to the new Townsend Plan policy for clubs to remit $1 per month in revenues. "Official Club Bulletin No. 31," April 18, 1938, p. 5; "Townsend Avers Pledge of Clubs Is Forward Step," *Townsend National Weekly*, July 18, 1938, p. 1.

14. E. J. Speake claimed that 78,000 members joined during "Out to Win." By the end of the year, another 100 or so clubs were formed apparently. That year the TNRP, Inc., brought in $150,000 in membership fees, which means an upper limit of 600,000 members. However, Townsend clubbers would sign up many nonparticipants, and probably the total number of active members was a little more than half that. "Campaign Launched to Increase Voting Strength in All Districts to 20,000 for Plan Enactment," *Townsend National Weekly*, September 12, 1938, p. 1; "States Vying for New Members; Many More Clubs Are Formed as Organization Increases Strength,"

Townsend National Weekly, October 3, 1938, p. 1; "500 New Charters Issued: Out-to-Win Drive Spurs Members to Launch New Clubs," *Townsend National Weekly*, October 10, 1938, p. 1; "Charters Go to Many More New Townsend Clubs," *Townsend National Weekly*, November 14, 1938, p. 1; "Election Success Brings More New Clubs into Fold," *Townsend National Weekly*, November 28, 1938, p. 1; "78,000 Members Join Club Ranks in Biggest Drive," *Townsend National Weekly*, December 26, 1938, p. 5; "Every Town Drive to Succeed, Rehearsals Show," *Townsend National Weekly*, January 30, 1939, p. 10; "Statement of Income and Expenses," *Townsend National Weekly*, July 14, 1939, p. 24.

15. Townsend brazenly proposed that the president form a coalition government. Roosevelt demurred but politely asked Townsend to visit again. "Townsend Opposes Pleas to Pardon Him: Call Moves 'Useless,' 'Political Gestures,'" *New York Times*, April 16, 1938, p. 2; "Townsend Freed, Feels 'Vindicated,'" *New York Times*, April 19, 1938, p. 1; "Townsend's Thanks Given to Roosevelt," *New York Times*, April 22, 1938, p. 2; Otis J. Bouma, "Pardon Reaches Dr. Townsend at the Jail's Door," *Townsend National Weekly*, May 2, 1938, p. 1.

16. "Official Club Bulletin No. 11," *Townsend National Weekly*, November 29, 1937, p. 2; "The Congressional Boards," *Townsend National Weekly*, November 29, 1937, p. 4.

17. L. W. Jeffery, "Jeffery Reveals TNRP Political Strategy Moves," *Townsend National Weekly*, May 23, 1938, p. 1; House Ways and Means Committee, *Hearings Relative to the Social Security Act Amendments of 1939*, vol. 1, pp. 445–50; Frederick R. Barkley, "'Short Cuts to Utopia' Grow Apace," *New York Times*, August 21, 1938, sec. IV, p. 7; "Intrigue Stops Move to Secure Hearing on GWA," *Townsend National Weekly*, April 4, 1938, p. 1; "Ways, Means Body Chairman Opposed by Plan Advocate," *Townsend National Weekly*, September 5, 1938, p. 1.

18. "Press Surprised at New Strength Shown by Ballots," *Townsend National Weekly*, September 26, 1938, p. 1; "Founder Embarks for Hawaii to Make Detailed Investigation of Transactions Tax in Operation," *Townsend National Weekly*, October 10, 1938, p. 1; "How Big List of Candidacies Was Selected for Club Support Told by Jeffrey in Interview," *Townsend National Weekly*, October 31, 1938.

19. On unemployment, see U.S. Bureau of the Census, *Historical Statistics of the United States: Colonial Times to 1957* (Washington, D.C.: U. S. Government Printing Office, 1958). For gross domestic product figures, see the Bureau of Economic Analysis (http://www.bea.doc.gov/bea/dn1.htm).

20. Altmeyer suggests that two unnamed Treasury Department officials, probably Harry White and Leon Henderson, demanded that he support flat pensions on the Townsend model because these would be easier to manipulate. *The Formative Years*, pp. 108–10; "Eccles Urges More Buying," *Townsend National Weekly*, April 10, 1938, p. 13; Alan Brinkley, *The End of Reform: New Deal Liberalism in Recession and War* (New York: Vintage, 1996), chaps. 4, 5.

21. *Townsend National Weekly*, August 8, 1938, p. 11.

22. For the Social Security Board's trials in registering employees and administering the lump-sum benefits, see Charles McKinley and Robert W. Frase, *Launching Social Security: A Capture-and-Record Account, 1935–1937* (Madison: University of Wisconsin Press, 1970), pp. 329–73; Louis Stark, "Social Security 3 Years Old," *New York Times*, August 7, 1938, sec. IV, p. 6

23. Daniel J. B. Mitchell, *Pensions Politics and the Elderly: Historic Social Movements and Their Lessons for Our Aging Society* (Armonk, N.Y.: M. E. Sharpe, 2000), chaps. 2, 3; Jackson K. Putnam, *Old-Age Politics in California: From Richardson to Reagan* (Stanford, Calif.: Stanford University Press, 1970), chap. 6; Bill Edward Fitzgerald, "Pension Politics in California" (M.A. thesis, University of California, 1951), pp. 30–61; Frank A. Pinner, Paul Jacobs, and Philip Selznick, *Old Age and Political Behavior: A Case Study* (Berkeley: University of California Press, 1959), pp. 4–5; Royce D. Delmatier, Clarence F. McIntosh, and Earl G. Waters, *The Rumble of California Politics, 1848–1970* (New York: Wiley, 1970), chap. 6; Michael Paul Rogin and John L. Shover, *Political Change in California: Critical Elections and Social Movements, 1890–1966* (Westport, Conn.: Greenwood Press, 1970), chaps. 2, 3; Russell B. Porter, "'Ham and Eggs' Plan Buoys Coast Aged," *New York Times*, October 1, 1938, p. 19; Dillard Stokes, "Roosevelt and Browder Condemn It," *Washington Post*, September 18, 1938, p. B4.

24. Mitchell, *Pensions Politics*, chaps. 2, 3; Putnam, *Old-Age Politics in California*, chap. 6; Fitzgerald, "Pension Politics in California"; Robert E. Burke, *Olson's New Deal for California* (Berkeley: University of California Press, 1953); Barkley, "'Short Cuts to Utopia' Grow Apace," p. 7; Russell B. Porter, "'$30-a-Week' Plan Aims at All States," *New York Times*, October 2, 1938, p. 13.

25. The Allens estimated the number of potential pensioners as being between 500,000 and 800,000. The scrip money or "warrants," as they were named, would be issued by the state and circulated among the willing; state agencies were bound to accept them. The size of dollar bills, the warrants would be subject to a two-cent stamp tax each week to help pay for themselves and promote their circulation. *Ham and Eggs for Californians: Life Begins at Fifty, $30 a Week for Life, Questions and Answers* (Hollywood, Calif.: Petition Campaign Committee for Thirty Dollars a Week for Life California State Pension Plan, 1938); Mitchell, *Pensions Politics*, chaps. 2, 3; Putnam, *Old-Age Politics in California*, chap. 6; Barkley, "'Short Cuts to Utopia' Grow Apace"; Porter, "'$30-a-Week' Plan Aims at All States."

26. The Arkansas initiative was thrown off the ballots by the courts. In Missouri there was a proposal to lower the pension age from seventy to sixty-five. Barkley, "'Short Cuts to Utopia' Grow Apace"; A. R. Buckingham, "Tent Show and Beans Bid for Kansas Votes," *New York Times*, September 18, 1938, sec. IV, p. 6; Russell B. Porter, "Oregon Is Heading for Pensions Vote," *New York Times*, September 26, 1938, p. 9; Richard L. Strout, "Social Security Program Becomes Political Ogre," *Christian Science Monitor*, October 6, 1938, p. 1; Russell B. Porter, "Seek Pension Rise for North Dakota," *New York Times*, October 11, 1938, p. 10; Russell B. Porter, "Langer Fights Nye with $40 Pensions," *New York Times*, October 12, 1938, p. 14; Frederick R. Barkley, "Pension Drive Pressure Is Felt at Washington," *New York Times*, October 23, 1938, sec. IV, p. 6; "Age Pensions Major Issue," *Los Angeles Times*, November 9, 1938, p. 3.

27. The Colorado program guaranteed $45 per month in income per aged OAA recipient, meaning that the average OAA benefit was lower than that figure. Russell B. Porter, "Old-Age Pensions Burden Colorado," *New York Times*, October 6, 1938, p. 9.

28. John C. Cuneo, "The Townsend Plan in Retrospect," UCLA Oral History Program, 1970, p. 76. Business organizations in California had sponsored a proposition limiting picketing and other collective action by labor. Russell B. Porter, "Drive Hard to Bar $30 Pensions Plan," *New York Times*, October 4, 1938, p. 2; "Pension Campaign

Turns to Congress," *New York Times*, November 13, 1938, sec. IV, p. 10; Mitchell, *Pensions Politics*, chaps. 2, 3; Putnam, *Old-Age Politics in California*, chap. 6; Dr. Francis E. Townsend, "Founder Deplores State Effort for Larger Pensions," *Townsend National Weekly*, April 18, 1938, p. 1; Staff Writer, "State Pensions Scheme Built on Untrue Premise," *Townsend National Weekly*, August 15, 1938, p. 1.

29. Russell B. Porter, " '$30-a-Week' Plan Aims at All States," *New York Times*, October 2, 1938, p. 13; "Pension for the Aged Retained in Colorado," *New York Times*, November 9, 1938, p. 9; "Without Excuse," *Los Angeles Times*, November 12, 1938, p. 4.

30. "Victory Perches on Townsend Banner as Chosen Candidates Win on Wide Political Front," *Townsend National Weekly*, November 21, 1938, p. 1; Edwin Amenta, Bruce G. Carruthers, and Yvonne Zylan, "A Hero for the Aged? The Townsend Movement, the Political Mediation Model, and U.S. Old-Age Policy, 1934–1950," *American Journal of Sociology* 98 (1992): 308–39; Abraham Holtzman, *The Townsend Movement: A Political Study* (New York: Bookman, 1963), chap. 6.

31. "Industrialists Fighting Roosevelt by Tax Warning on Pay Envelopes," *New York Times*, October 24, 1936, p. 1; "Stress Tax on Pay in Final Vote Drive," *New York Times*, October 25, 1936, p. 2; Edward D. Berkowitz, "The First Advisory Council and the 1939 Amendments," in *Social Security after Fifty: Successes and Failures*, ed. Edward D. Berkowitz (Westport, Conn.: Greenwood Press, 1987), chap. 3.

32. Abraham Epstein, "Letter to Editor," *New York Times*, June 28, 1938, p. 18; "Congress Is Urged to Alter Labor Act," *New York Times*, December 16, 1938, p. 1; "Pay-as-You-Go Plan Urged on Security," *New York Times*, March 26, 1939, p. 5; Arthur Altmeyer, *The Formative Years of Social Security* (Madison: University of Wisconsin Press, 1966), pp. 88–90; Mark H. Leff, "Speculating in Social Security Futures," in *Social Security: The First Half-Century*, ed. Gerald D. Nash, Joel H. Pugach, and Richard F. Tomasson (Albuquerque: University of New Mexico Press, 1987), pp. 243–78; Berkowitz, "The First Advisory Council and the 1939 Amendments."

33. A Twentieth Century Fund study based on research by the Committee on Social Security of the Social Science Research Council agreed with the Social Security Board. "Sounder Law Asked on Social Security by National Group," *New York Times*, January 4, 1937, p. 1; Security Act Held Far Too Limited," *New York Times*, July 11, 1937, sec. II, p. 1. For Epstein's views, see "How Shall the Social Security Act Be Amended?" House Ways and Means Committee, *Hearings Relative to the Social Security Act Amendments of 1939*, vol. 2, pp. 1055–65.

34. "House Republicans Ask Security Shifts," *New York Times*, February 2, 1937, p. 7; "Hoover Asks Help for Middle Class as Forgotten Men," *New York Times*, October 27, 1937, p. 1. Among the *Times* editorials were "Financial Hocus-Pocus," November 6, 1937, p. 16; "The Pious Fraud," August 9, 1938, p. 18; "The Reserve Fund," September 5, 1938, p. 14.

35. Altmeyer, *The Formative Years of Social Security*, chap. 3. His September memorandum appears on pp. 295–97. For a definitive account, see Berkowitz, "The First Advisory Council and the 1939 Amendments." See also Martha Derthick, *Policymaking for Social Security* (Washington, D.C.: Brookings Institution, 1979), pp. 90–92; Sheryl N. Tynes, *Turning Points in Social Security: From "Cruel Hoax" to "Sacred Entitlement"* (Stanford, Calif.: Stanford University Press, 1996), pp. 82–83; Edward D. Berkowitz, *Mr. Social Security: The Life of Wilbur J. Cohen* (Lawrence: University Press of Kansas,

1995), pp. 47–48; Luther A. Huston, "Social Security Law Is Studied for Changes," *New York Times*, January 10, 1937, sec. IV, p. 7; Henry H. Dorris, "Security Program Past Trial Stage," *New York Times*, September 4, 1938, sec. IV, p. 10.

36. The interdepartmental committee called for increases in federal public health expenditures, expansion of maternal and child health services, grants to build and expand hospitals, aid to state medical programs for the needy, grants-in-aid to establish temporary disability insurance at the state level, and a general program of publicly supported medical care. Altmeyer, *The Formative Years of Social Security*, pp. 93–96, 295–97; Paul Starr, *The Social Transformation of American Medicine: The Rise of a Sovereign Profession and the Making of a Vast Industry* (New York: Basic Books, 1982), pp. 275–280.

37. The council proposed to end the lump-sum death benefits and to reduce benefits for those at the upper end of the economic spectrum. *The Final Report of the Advisory Council on Social Security* is reprinted in Way and Means Committee, *Hearings Relative to the Social Security Act Amendments of 1939*, vol. 1, pp. 18–43. Altmeyer, *The Formative Years*, pp. 90–92; Berkowitz, "The First Advisory Council and the 1939 Amendments"; Robert Ball, "The 1939 Amendments to the Social Security Act and What Followed," in Project on the Federal Social Role, *The Report of the Committee on Economic Security of 1935: And Other Basic Documents Relating to the Development of the Social Security Act* (Washington, D.C.: National Conference on Social Welfare, 1985), chap. 6.

38. The council called for covering almost 15 million additional persons, including nonprofit organizations and their workers proposed for immediate coverage. Louis Stark, "Security Program Proposed to Cover Added 14,800,000," *New York Times*, December 19, 1938, p. 1; "Negroes File Plea on Social Security," *New York Times*, January 15, 1937, p. 7.

39. The council suggested the creation of a specific fund with trustees appointed to oversee it. One business representative wrote a dissent, claiming that payroll tax rates should not be increased. *The Final Report of the Advisory Council on Social Security*, pp. 18–43; "Report to Urge U.S. Share Old-Age Tax," *New York Times*, November 21, 1938, p. 1; Stark, "Security Program Proposed to Cover Added 14,800,000."

40. The council called for the benefit program to be broadened to include benefits for dependent "wives," "widows," and children of covered workers. See *The Final Report of the Advisory Council on Social Security*; Julia S. O'Connor, Ann Shola Orloff, and Sheila Shaver, *States, Markets, Families: Gender, Liberalism and Social Policy in Australia, Canada, Great Britain and the United States* (Cambridge: Cambridge University Press, 1999), chap. 1; Diana Sainsbury, "Women's and Men's Social Rights: Gendering Dimensions of Welfare States," in *Gendering Welfare States*, ed. Diane Sainsbury (London: Sage, 1994), chap. 10.

41. The board also suggested elevating Aid to Dependent Children to a one-to-one matching basis—the same as OAA. The board's Bureau of Research and Statistics had overestimated the need of the aged in 1937 in order to make a case for the constitutionality of the old-age annuity titles. According to the board's findings in 1939, however, dependent children were in significantly greater need than the aged. Brian Gratton, "The Politics of Dependency Estimates: Social Security Board Statistics, 1935–1939," *Journal of Gerontology: Social Sciences* 52B (1997): S117–S124; Blanche D. Coll, *Safety Net: Welfare and Social Security, 1929–1979* (New Brunswick, N.J.: Rutgers University Press, 1995), pp. 91–94.

42. The recommendations of the Social Security Board, *Proposed Changes in the Social Security Act*, appear in House Ways and Means Committee, *Hearings Relative to the Social Security Act Amendments of 1939*, vol. 1, pp. 3–17; Louis Stark, "Changes Expected Soon in Social Security Act," *New York Times*, December 4, 1938, sec. IV, p. 7. In this article, the board floated the idea that a health insurance proposal might also be added. Louis Stark, "Projects Wider Aid," *New York Times*, January 17, 1939, p. 1. The BPA was convinced that family budgeting by way of detailed assessment of need was the best way to ensure fairness and adequacy in granting aid. Huston, "Social Security Law Is Studied for Changes," p. 7; Altmeyer, *The Formative Years*, chap. 2; McKinley and Frase, *Launching Social Security*, pp. 169–74; Martha Derthick, *Policymaking for Social Security* (Washington, D.C.: Brookings Institution, 1979), pp. 90–92; Nancy K. Cauthen and Edwin Amenta, "Not for Widows Only: Institutional Politics and the Formative Years of Aid to Dependent Children," *American Sociological Review* 60 (1996): 427–48.

43. House Ways and Means Committee, *Hearings Relative to the Social Security Act Amendments of 1939*, vol. 1, pp. 1–2.

44. Arthur Krock, "Taxpayers Revolt," *New York Times*, November 10, 1938, p. 1; Arthur Krock, "New Congress in Revisionist Mood," *New York Times*, January 1, 1939, p. 53.

45. Edwin Witte first suggested speeding up the payments in early 1936, in order to "check the support given to impossible old-age pension schemes." Quoted in Tynes, *Turning Points in Social Security*, p. 79. The allowances for wives would be added to the checks of retired male wage earners.

46. Frank R. Baumgartner and Bryan Jones, *Agendas and Instability in American Politics* (Chicago: University of Chicago Press, 1993).

Chapter Eight: The Townsend Plan versus Social Security, Part 2

1. Russell Porter, "Looking for Utopia along the Townsend Trail," *New York Times*, February 5, 1939, sec. VII, pp. 4–5, 13.

2. "See Quiet Session in the Domestic Field," *New York Times*, January 4, 1939, p. 1; Turner Catledge, "Aims of President," *New York Times*, January 5, 1939, p. 1; Turner Catledge, "WPA Cost Amazes," *New York Times*, January 6, 1939, p. 1; Felix Belair Jr., "Debt Is Near Limit," *New York Times*, January 6, 1939, p. 1; Louis Stark, "Roosevelt Asks Extension of the Social Security Act to More Aged and Children," *New York Times*, January 17, 1939, p. 1.

3. However, Silva testified that HR 2's taxation provisions should be converted into a simpler gross income tax like Hawaii's. Dr. Townsend also boasted that he eventually anticipated pensions of $300 per month, undermining the Townsend Plan leadership's desire to make its legislation seem moderate. U.S. House of Representatives, Committee on Ways and Means, *Hearings Relative to the Social Security Act Amendments of 1939*, 76th Cong., 1st sess., vol. 1 (U.S. Government Printing Office, 1940), pp. 507–22, 544–68, 597, 615–17, 623, vol. 2, pp. 1341–43.

4. House Ways and Means Committee, *Hearings Relative to the Social Security Act Amendments of 1939*, vol. 1, pp. 195 (Johnson), 785–885 (some economists), vol. 2, pp. 887–942, 950–77, 980–1003 (more economists), 1005–65 (Epstein); "Committee

of House Told Townsendites Defraud Aged," *Los Angeles Times*, February 4, 1939, p. 5; "Economists Decry Age Pension Plans," *New York Times*, February 24, 1939, p. 9.

5. HR 2 appears in House Ways and Means Committee, *Hearings Relative to the Social Security Act Amendments of 1939*, vol. 1, pp. 282–88. For Townsend's statement, see p. 660. Hugh Russell Fraser, "Joe Hendricks, Florida Friend, Introduces Act," *Townsend National Weekly*, January 16, 1939, p. 1; Roy J. Webb, "Committee Fair during Hearing, Webb Declares," *Townsend National Weekly*, March 13, 1939, p. 1. For details, see Abraham Holtzman, *The Townsend Movement: A Political Study* (New York: Bookman, 1963), pp. 107–15.

6. House Ways and Means Committee, *Hearings Relative to the Social Security Act Amendments of 1939*, vol. 1, pp. 71–79 (HR 11), 114–214 (Johnson), vol. 3, pp. 1999–2003 (Voorhis). For more on the General Welfare Federation, see Luther A. Huston, "Federal Pension Drive Is Unshaken by Rebuffs," *New York Times*, November 5, 1939, p. 75.

7. Lasser opposed the transactions and gross income taxes, which he considered regressive, and his desire for alliance with the Townsend Plan went unrequited. House Ways and Means Committee, *Hearings Relative to the Social Security Act Amendments of 1939*, vol. 1, pp. 766–69 (Patman), vol. 2, pp. 1184–1211 (Lasser), vol. 3, pp. 1999–2003 (Voorhis); "Fusion of Jobless and Aged Planned," *New York Times*, February 12, 1939, p. 1; "Scores Security Tax Act," *New York Times*, February 13, 1939, p. 13; "Workers Alliance Offers Tax Plan," *New York Times*, February 13, 1939, p. 10; "Woodrum Decries Cost of Administering WPA," *Townsend National Weekly*, April 17, 1939, p. 5.

8. On the potential influence of public opinion on social policy, see Paul Burstein and April Linton, "The Impact of Political Parties, Interest Groups, and Social Movement Organizations on Public Policy: Some Recent Evidence and Theoretical Concerns," *Social Forces* 81 (2002): 381–408; Jeff Manza and Fay Lomax Cook, "A Democratic Polity? Three Views of Policy Responsiveness to Public Opinion in the United States," *American Politics Research* 30 (2002): 630–67; Dr. George Gallup, "Political Strength of Pension Movements Growing, Survey Shows," *Washington Post*, February 26, 1939, pp. B2–3; "Old-Age Pensions Favored in Survey," *New York Times*, February 26, 1939, p. 7.

9. Polling data unavailable to the public indicated that the support for the generous and universal pension plan in 1939 was twice as high as Gallup was suggesting, but still had decreased since its heyday in 1936. Gallup apparently devised the one-fifth result by counting those with an opinion in favor of the Townsend Plan (about 40 percent) who were also able to "identify" that the pension proposal aspired to provide $200 per month (about half of them). In the 1936 poll, Gallup had declared that those who favored the Townsend Plan were the 4 percent who offered $200 per month in response to an open-ended question about their preferred pension amount. Gallup did not, however, present the result that approximately 40 percent of the public with an opinion on the Townsend Plan was in favor of it and that 95 percent of the sample had heard of it. High as it was, this support in 1939 was somewhat lower than that recorded in two unreleased AIPO polls taken in March 1936 (see chapter 5). Gallup construed the Townsend Plan–sponsored benefits to mean strictly the $200 maximum, despite the fact that all sponsored Townsend legislation since April 1935 was projected to provide much less. Gallup, "Political Strength of Pension Movements Grow-

ing, Survey Shows." The data for the poll survive. In a logistical regression analysis of
the support for the Townsend Plan, the strongest predictors were income measures;
the lower the income, the greater the support. Indicators of receiving "relief" and being "poor" were strongly positively associated with support for the Townsend Plan,
while owning a phone was negatively associated with support, as was being wealthy. In
addition, age or being a union member, a woman, or a supporter of Roosevelt were all
positively and significantly related to support for the Townsend Plan, when controlling for income and the others. (Detailed results available from author.) Gallup reported that the approval of the Townsend Plan was greatest among those who favored
the New Deal, with the support for both running inversely to income. The *Townsend
Weekly* hailed the results: "Gallup Survey Shows People Want Pensions," *Townsend
National Weekly*, March 13, 1939, p. 1. In a previous and well-publicized poll, Gallup
had shown that people of lower incomes were strongly in favor of the New Deal.
Dr. George Gallup, "Marginal Earners Seen for New Deal," *New York Times*, August
24, 1938, p. 10.

10. The drive was led by Paul Chase and Harrison N. Hiles of the national headquarters and the twenty-nine national representatives. The *Weekly* did not consis-
tently list the results all in the manner of the Out to Win drive. Near the end of Every
Town, Chase claimed that more than 1,300 clubs had been organized. Given the other
information in the *Weekly* and its revenue statements, this seems close to correct. According to the *Weekly*, Hiles, a personal assistant to Dr. Townsend, organized more
than 400 clubs. At the official end of the Every Town drive in June, the participating
membership in Townsend clubs likely had gone over the half-million mark. Ascertaining the number of participating new Townsendites is difficult, however, signaled by the
case of a man in Bellingham, Washington, who bought memberships for sixty-three
members of his family. "17320 Villages in U.S. Charted for Organizers," *Townsend National Weekly*, January 16, 1939, p. 1; E. J. Speake, "Launch New Legion Drive: Seek
100,000 Members from Business and Professional Field," *Townsend National Weekly*,
January 16, 1939, p. 4; "Official Club Bulletin No. 75," *Townsend National Weekly*, Feb-
ruary 20, 1939, p. 5; "Solons Face New Demand for Measure," *Townsend National
Weekly*, March 20, 1939, p. 1; "March Record Hits New High in Club Drive,"
Townsend National Weekly, March 27, 1939, p. 1; "Drive Gains 400 Percent in 7
States," *Townsend National Weekly*, April 24, 1939, p. 1; Paul Chase, "1000th New
Club Is Formed: Latest Charter Given Group in Southern State," *Townsend National
Weekly*, May 5, 1939, p. 1; "New Club Drive Hit Stride as Deadline Appears,"
Townsend National Weekly, May 19, p. 1; "Letters Bring In 20,000 New Members, 466
Clubs from 44 States and Alaska," *Townsend National Weekly*, May 19, p. 4; Dr. Hal C.
Long, "Family Drive Spurs Growth in Washington," *Townsend National Weekly*, April
24, 1939, p. 1. The circulation of the *Weekly*, which again ran twelve pages, was
600,000 and rising.

11. "Job Aid Revision Bars New Groups," *New York Times*, March 11, 1939, p. 19.

12. Witte stated that a reserve of only $32 billion was expected by 1980 initially,
and most of this was to be "interest." He also noted that the original estimate of covered workers by 1980 was wildly underestimated. Fuller, the NAM representative,
tried to avoid expressing a preference on HR 2, as his organization did not address
it, but noted his personal opposition. Partially to appease business interests, an
administration-approved bill created a $3,000 ceiling on covered payrolls for unem-

ployment compensation, similar to the ceiling already in effect for the national, Title VII payroll taxes. House Ways and Means Committee, *Hearings Relative to the Social Security Act Amendments of 1939*, vol. 2, pp. 1213–93 (Brown), 1753–1812 (Witte), vol. 3, pp. 2069–87 (Fuller); "Forecasts Big Rise in Security Costs," *New York Times*, March 18, 1939, p. 18.

13. Morgenthau presented four alternatives, the most forgiving being "No increase in tax through 1942; thereafter tax schedule of present law." *Hearings Relative to the Social Security Act Amendments of 1939*, vol. 3, pp. 2111–20; "Morgenthau Acts," *New York Times*, March 25, 1939, p. 1. The editorial page of the *Times* hailed Morgenthau's decision. "End of the Huge Reserve Fund," *New York Times*, March 25, 1939, p. 14; Turner Catledge, "Administration Yields on Social Security Tax," *New York Times*, March 26, 1939, sec. IV, p. 6. The Chamber of Commerce responded that the payroll taxes be frozen permanently at 2 percent and that old-age benefits be provided on a pay-as-you-go basis according to the revenues generated. "Pay-as-You-Go Plan Urged on Security," *New York Times*, March 26, 1939, p. 5.

14. House Ways and Means Committee, *Hearings Relative to the Social Security Act Amendments of 1939*, vol. 2 (testimony of Altmeyer); "Asks Pension Plan for Security Pay," *New York Times*, March 30, 1939, p. 11; "The New Pension Scale," *New York Times*, April 1, 1939, p. 18; Mark H. Leff, "Speculating in Social Security Futures," in *Social Security: The First Half-Century*, ed. Gerald D. Nash, Joel H. Pugach, and Richard F. Tomasson (Albuquerque: University of New Mexico Press, 1987), pp. 243–78.

15. The Democrats' plot was brewing at least since Townsend Plan officials' testimony at the hearings. "House Leaders Favor Townsend Plan Vote to Mark Backers and Crush Movement," *New York Times*, February 26, 1939, p. 7; "Seek Vote to Kill Townsend Bill," *New York Times*, March 17, 1939, p. 13.

16. "Townsend Plan Vote Forecast in House," *New York Times*, May 20, 1939, p. 7; "Wise Democrats Show Necessity for Floor Vote," *Townsend National Weekly*, April 10, 1939, p. 1.

17. Doughton claimed to have received 25,000 letters urging that the bill be sent to the floor. He also argued against it, providing a disingenuous table showing how much each state would have to pay in taxes to support pensions of $200-per month. Other committee members from both sides of the aisle also spoke out against the bill. "Townsend Bill Put Up to Whole House," *New York Times*, May 25, 1939, p. 13; Arthur Krock, "Some Republican Chickens Coming Home to Roost," *New York Times*, May 25, 1939, p. 24; "A 'Townsend' Plan Stirs House Clash," *New York Times*, May 26, 1939, p. 7; "Townsend Plan Bill Is Hastened in House," *New York Times*, May 27, 1939, p. 3; "Charges Fly Fast on Townsend Plan," *New York Times*, June 1, 1939, p. 2; "House Rings with Anxiety of Members to Tell Why They Will or Will Not Back Scheme"; "Huge Burden Pointed Out," *New York Times*, June 1, 1939, p. 2; " 'We Have Just Begun to Fight,' Founder Says after House Vote," *Townsend National Weekly*, June 16, p. 1. See also Holtzman, *The Townsend Movement*, pp. 115–20.

18. The vote total includes four votes paired for and against it. In favor were 56 Republicans, 42 Democrats, 2 Progressives, and 1 Farmer-Labor representative. In opposition were 108 Republicans, 197 Democrats, and the one representative of the American Labor Party. "Townsend Pension Rejected, 302–97," *New York Times*, June 2, pp. 1, 10; "The Townsend Plan Vote," *New York Times*, June 2, 1939, p. 22; Arthur Krock,

"Party Attitudes toward Spending Not Diverse," *New York Times*, June 2, 1939, p. 23; Robert C. Albright, "Townsend Plan Loses as 34 Desert It," *Washington Post*, June 2, 1939, p. 1; Warren B. Francis, "Townsend Rout Made Complete," *Los Angeles Times*, June 4, 1939, p. 5; "Townsend Plan's Strength Indicated by Analysis of Roll Call Vote in Congress," *Townsend National Weekly*, September 15, 1939, p. 3.

19. The increased matching amount of $20 would again put OAA ahead of the similarly constructed Aid to Dependent Children program, whose matching amount was not increased despite the fact that need was similar and coverage was much lower for dependent children than for the dependent aged. The committee did not take up the Social Security Board's suggestion to place hiring for the assistance programs on a merit basis. *The Formative Years*, pp. 102–5; "House Group Asks Age Tax 'Freezing,'" *New York Times*, April 29, 1939, p. 4; Henry N. Dorris, "Cut in Payroll Tax for Job Insurance Is Put Up to House," *New York Times*, May 4, 1939, p. 1; Frederick R. Barkley, "Townsend Defeat Aids New Security Program," *New York Times*, June 4, 1939, sec. IV, p. 7; "Security Changes Speed in House," *New York Times*, June 7, 1939, p. 2; Cates, *Insuring Inequality*, chap. 5; Coll, *Safety Net*, pp. 91–102, 110–11. Even Roosevelt backed away from variable grants once the debate focused on their exempting some states of making fair contributions. U.S. Congress, Senate Finance Committee, *Hearings before the Committee on Finance on HR 6635*, 76th Cong., 1st sess. (Washington, D.C.: U.S. Government Printing Office, 1939), pp. 86–88; Altmeyer, *The Formative Years*, p. 105.

20. An amendment by Senator Edwin Johnson, a Colorado Democrat, however, required that each state spend at least $10 per recipient to qualify for any federal funds. This would nullify the potential gains of the least generous states, and, backed by northern Democratic liberals and Republicans, Johnson's amendment passed 37 to 31. The conferees dropped his amendment, too, but added to the cost of the bill by agreeing to pay regular "insurance" benefits, pensions essentially, to those who turned sixty-five in 1939, a pet issue of Senator Robert La Follette. "Abandons Pension Move," *New York Times*, July 8, 1939, p. 2; "Senators Support Higher Pensions," *New York Times*, July 11, 1939, p. 5; "Federal Increase in Pensions Share Voted by Senate," *New York Times*, July 13, 1939, p. 1; Charles W. Hurd, "Pension Increase with String on It Voted by Senate," *New York Times*, July 14, 1939, p. 1; "House Leaders Aim at Quick Ending," *New York Times*, August 2, 1939, p. 1; Turner Catledge, "Congress Quits Sine Die at 6:35 P.M.; $119,000,000 More Voted for Crop Loans; Social Security Tax Cut $905,000,000," *New York Times*, August 6, 1939, p. 1.

21. The Townsend Plan had caught wind of the move to increase the matching formula far before it happened, also suggesting that this move came in response to it and other pension mobilizations. "Doughton Hurries to Forestall All Plan's Proposals," *Townsend National Weekly*, October 25, 1938, p. 1; Senate Finance Committee, *Hearings on HR 6635*, p. 188. Luther A. Huston reported that the Social Security Act Amendments "represent Congress's answer to movements in support of vastly liberalized old-age pensions and its passage is considered politically important by both parties." See "Congress Wind-Up on or Near July 15 Again Is Predicted," *New York Times*, July 3, 1939, p. 1; Albright, "Townsend Plan Loses as 34 Desert It."

22. Catledge, "Congress Quits Sine Die at 6:35 P.M.," *New York Times*.

23. Witte thought the version proposed by the General Welfare Federation, which he disparaged as a "baby" Townsend plan, was the likeliest candidate for adoption. "Dr. Witte Further Explains the Pending Bill," *New York Times*, July 2, 1939, sec. IV, p. 9.

24. "You Can't Teach an Old Dog," *Townsend National Weekly*, June 23, 1939, p. 6; "Townsend Plan's Strength Indicated by Analysis of Roll Call Vote in Congress," *Townsend National Weekly*, September 15, 1939, p. 3. A multiple regression analysis of the vote indicates that being endorsed and Townsend club activity were both significant predictors of voting for HR 6466, after controlling for many other possible influences on the vote. Club activity and having a state-level pension initiative influenced voting for Lee's pension amendment. Edwin Amenta, Neal Caren, and Sheera Joy Olasky, "Age for Leisure? Political Mediation and the Impact of the Pension Movement on U.S. Old-Age Policy," *American Sociological Review* 70 (2005): 516–38.

25. The Townsend Plan continued to refer to the new effort as "Every Town a Townsend Town," even though that drive had been scheduled to end in June. The Townsend Trailblazers League was led by F. Manley Goldberry, and Townsendites could "join" by contributing a dollar or more to the effort. In Massachusetts, the Trailblazers took aim at Allen Treadway, the ranking Republican of the Ways and Means Committee. "Flying Squads Build Clubs to Beat Plan Foes," *Townsend National Weekly*, June 30, 1939, p. 1; "Another Answer to Capitol Hill," *Townsend National Weekly*, June 30, 1939, p. 6; "Form New Clubs as Answer When Vote Is Adverse," *Townsend National Weekly*, July 14, 1939, p. 9; "Trailblazers Move against Treadway; Squad Launches Massachusetts Drive," *Townsend National Weekly*, July 21, 1939, p. 1; "Dr. Townsend Says . . . ," *Townsend National Weekly*, August 11, 1939, p. 7.

26. "Social Security Plans Revised in Attempt to Head Off Townsend," *Townsend National Weekly*, July 7, 1939, p. 3; "25 Percent Gain in New Clubs Scored Last Month," *Townsend National Weekly*, October 20, 1939, p. 1; B. G. Rankine, "Organization Scores Great Progress since Convention," *Townsend National Weekly*, November 17, 1939, p. 11; B. G. Rankine, "Volunteer Trailblazers Bring in Many New Clubs," *Townsend National Weekly*, January 6, 1940, p. 5.

27. "Dr. Townsend Gives Details of Legislation," *Townsend National Weekly*, February 17, 1940, p. 1. The March 16 issue of the *Weekly* printed the bill in its entirety.

28. "Movement above Parties, Declare Representatives Making Recommendation," *Townsend National Weekly*, January 10, 1940, p. 1; "Will See That Plan's Backers Go to Congress," *Townsend National Weekly*, January 17, 1940, p. 1. At the 1939 convention it was agreed that the 1940 convention would take place before those of the major parties to prevent the organization from being embroiled in presidential politics. Holtzman, *The Townsend Movement*, pp. 126–35.

29. Dr. F. E. Townsend, "Urges Voters to Think," *Townsend National Weekly*, October 12, 1940, p. 1; L. J. Jeffery, "Jeffery Tells Strategy," *Townsend National Weekly*, October 26, 1940, p. 1. The Townsend Plan ultimately failed to endorse two of the "immortals," while endorsing four of the "betrayers," but these minor mix-ups compared favorably to the massive failure in 1936 to endorse members of the "honor roll," who had voted for a Townsend amendment. Cf. Holtzman, *The Townsend Movement*, pp. 132–33, 138.

30. However, Olson vetoed measures that voted more funds for counties to defray old-age expenditures and granted benefits to inmates of private charitable institutions, because the legislature had failed to pass his proposed tax increase. Putnam, *Old-Age Politics in California*, chap. 7; Burke, *Olson's New Deal for California*, p. 75.

31. A clause in the proposal prohibited restrictions on commerce, making some labor groups fear that it would outlaw picketing. Robert O. Foote, "New Pension Fight

Stirs California," *New York Times*, June 4, 1939, p. E7; "Ham-Egg Campaign the Wierdest [*sic*] Ever," *New York Times*, August 13, 1939, p. E10; "Victory Is Possible for Ham and Eggs," *New York Times*, October 29, 1939, p. 43; Byron Darnton, "Ham-Egg Throng Gets Final Order," *New York Times*, November 6, 1939, p. 14; Putnam, *Old-Age Politics in California*, chap. 6; Burke, *Olson's New Deal for California*, pp. 107–12; Mitchell, *Pensions Politics and the Elderly*, pp. 43–47.

32. OAA programs had to be administered similarly across counties in order to retain their certification. Putnam, *Old-Age Politics in California*, pp. 69–70; Arthur Carlyle O'Byrne, "The Political Significance of the Townsend Movement in California, 1934–1950" (M.A. thesis, University of Southern California, Los Angeles, 1953), pp. 40, 42–43; John C. Cuneo, "The Townsend Plan in Retrospect," UCLA Oral History Program, 1970, p. 66; "Abolish Relief Liens," *Townsend National Weekly*, November 23, 1940, p. 3; "California Clubs Get New Law," *Townsend National Weekly*, November 30, 1940, p. 3.

33. Putnam, *Old-Age Politics in California*, pp. 119, 123–24; *Townsend National Weekly*.

34. Detailed results are available from the author. In a multiple regression analysis across all states from 1936 through 1950, having any pension initiative on a ballot at any time was worth about $1.37 in 1950 dollars, when all other influences on OAA benefits are controlled for. Amenta, Caren, and Olasky, "Age for Leisure?"

Chapter Nine: The Elusive Double Victory

1. The Democratic party platform called for "a minimum pension for all who have reached the age of retirement and are not gainfully employed." Donald Bruce Johnson and Kirk H. Porter, *National Party Platforms, 1840–1972* (Urbana: University of Illinois Press, 1973), p. 387; Congressional Quarterly, *Guide To U.S. Elections* (Washington, D.C.: Congressional Quarterly, 1985), p. 34; "Pension Bill Due in 1941," *Townsend National Weekly*, November 23, 1940, p. 1; "Plan Wins Sweeping Victory; Elects 135 to Congress," *Townsend National Weekly*, November 23, 1940, p. 1.

2. Larger benefits, as well as insurance coverage for dependents and survivors, would go to workers in covered employment. Arthur Altmeyer, *The Formative Years of Social Security* (Madison: University of Wisconsin Press, 1968), pp. 122–26; Richard L. Strout, "Fair Federal Aid for Aged Being Mapped in All States," *Christian Science Monitor*, March 15, 1941, p. 6; Jerry R. Cates, *Insuring Inequality* (Ann Arbor: University of Michigan Press, 1983), pp. 70–72.

3. Richard L. Strout, "Intimate Message from Washington," *Christian Science Monitor*, January 7, 1941, p. 1; Strout, "Fair Federal Aid for Aged Being Mapped in All States"; "Foresees Bread Riots and Disaster When Defense Boom Ceases," *Townsend National Weekly*, August 9, 1941, p. 1; "Founder Testifies before Committee," *Townsend National Weekly*, August 9, 1941, p. 2.

4. The Townsend Plan bill, HR 1036, was introduced and included a 2 percent gross income tax on individuals and businesses in excess of $3,000 annually. The revenue was to be divided among those sixty years and older who agreed to refrain from employment. Pensions were to be spent within thirty days of their receipt. Some 109 House members signed the discharge petition by June 17. The letters to Doughton

were claimed to number approximately 100,000. "Seeks to Double Rolls," *Townsend National Weekly*, December 7, 1940, p. 1; "So Business Is Booming," *Townsend National Weekly*, December 7, 1940, p. 8; "Need 5000 Clubs," *Townsend National Weekly*, December 28, 1940; Sherman J. Bainbridge, "Editor Reports Progress," *Townsend National Weekly*, February 22, 1941, p. 1; L. W. Jeffery, "Here's How Plan Will Be Handled," *Townsend National Weekly*, February 22, 1941, p. 3; "Steering Group Elects," *Townsend National Weekly*, March 8, 1941, p. 1; "Plan Cost 'Trifle,' Says Sen. Wheeler, Cites War Spending," *Townsend National Weekly*, April 5, 1941, p. 1; Sherman J. Bainbridge, "Downey Clinches Hearing," *Townsend National Weekly*, May 3, 1941, p. 1; "March on Buffalo All Set," *Townsend National Weekly*, June 7, 1941, p. 1; L. W. Jeffery, "Cheer Action on Bill," *Townsend National Weekly*, June 7, 1941, p. 3; "Petition Due on Floor," *Townsend National Weekly*, June 14, p. 1; "Hit Solons from All over U.S.," *Townsend National Weekly*, November 29, 1941, p. 1; "Townsend Letters Swamp Committee Chairman," *Townsend National Weekly*, November 8, 1941, p. 1.

5. "30 States Vote on a Variety of Proposals," *Washington Post*, November 6, 1940, p. 5.

6. The specific reform being proposed was greatly to increase coverage for the OASI program and add the universal old-age floor to it. It was being sold as a way to curb inflation. Richard L. Strout, "President Ties Price Curb to Social Reform," *Christian Science Monitor*, October 1, 1941, p. 1; Blanche D. Coll, *Safety Net: Welfare and Social Security, 1929–1979* (New Brunswick, N.J.: Rutgers University Press, 1995), pp. 125–26; Cates, *Insuring Inequality*, chap. 3; "Founder Surprised at Pension Delay," *Townsend National Weekly*, September 6, 1941, p. 1; Dr. F. E. Townsend, "Flash!" *Townsend National Weekly*, September 6, 1941, p. 1; "The Downey Report," *Townsend National Weekly*, September 13, 1941, p. 4.

7. John Morton Blum, ed., *From the Morgenthau Diaries: Years of Urgency, 1938–1941* (Boston: Houghton Mifflin, 1964), pp. 304–18.

8. John Morton Blum, ed., *From the Morgenthau Diaries: The War Years, 1941–1945* (Boston: Houghton Mifflin, 1967), chap. 2; Sidney Ratner, *Taxation and Democracy in America* (New York: Norton, 1943), pp. 501–8; John F. Witte, *The Politics and Development of the Federal Income Tax* (Madison: University of Wisconsin Press, 1985), pp. 111–15; Eliot Brownlee, *Federal Taxation in America: A Short History* (New York: Cambridge University Press, 1996), pp. 91–94. Secretary of the Treasury Henry Morgenthau proposed a radical spending tax, and conservative opponents wanted to pass a sales tax, but Congress eventually decided to make highly progressive income taxes the centerpiece of its efforts.

9. Edwin Amenta, *Bold Relief: Institutional Politics and the Origins of Modern American Social Policy* (Princeton, N.J.: Princeton University Press, 1998), pp. 193–96.

10. Townsend's ill-advised editorial accused Roosevelt's war bond drive of producing a "Hitler government without a Hitler." Soon Townsend club halls were being converted to defense purposes, and Townsend clubs sold war bonds, but the revenues of the TNRP, Inc. dropped by 15 percent from January 1941 to January 1942. Dr. F. E. Townsend, "As Townsendites See It," *Townsend National Weekly*, January 24, 1942, p. 1; Sherman J. Bainbridge, "Delay Issue Urging Plan as Aid in War," *Townsend National Weekly*, January 31, 1942, p. 1; "'Black-out' Club Hall for Defense," *Townsend National Weekly*, January 31, 1942, p. 6; "Steering Group Opens New Drive for Petition Signers," *Townsend National Weekly*, February 7, 1942, p. 3;

"Delinquent Campaign Begins," *Townsend National Weekly*, February 7, 1942, p. 11; "An Earnest Plea," *Townsend National Weekly*, February 14, 1942, p. 4.

11. "52 Solons Needed for Plan Hearing This Session," *Townsend National Weekly*, February 14, 1942, p. 3; "Our Double Victory Campaign," *Townsend National Weekly*, July 31, 1942, p. 10; "Clubs Re-double Efforts as Townsend Plan Drive Is Called 'Un-Patriotic,'" *Townsend National Weekly*, August 1, 1942, p. 1.

12. Congressional Quarterly, *Guide to U.S. Congress* (Washington, D.C.: Congressional Quarterly, 1985), p. 896; "Townsendites List Friends to Be Aided at Polls Nov. 3," *Townsend National Weekly*, October 17, 1942, p. 2; "Plan Aid Puts Pension Friends in Majority of 78th Congress," *Townsend National Weekly*, November 21, 1942, p. 1; "Townsend Plan Forces Stronger Than Ever in '43," *Townsend National Weekly*, December 5, 1942, p. 2; Amenta, *Bold Relief*, chap. 6.

13. "Plan Executive L. W. Jeffery Resigns on Advice of Physician," *Townsend National Weekly*, August 2, 1941, p. 2; "'If People Ever Get to Vote, They'll Get Their Pensions,' Congress Told," *Townsend National Weekly*, April 5, 1942, p. 1. On Bainbridge's early career, see Daniel J. B. Mitchell, *Pensions Politics and the Elderly: Historic Social Movements and Their Lessons for Our Aging Society* (Armonk, N.Y.: M. E. Sharpe, 2000), pp. 27, 42–43.

14. "Measures Differ in Effect on People," *Townsend National Weekly*, September 5, 1942, p. 1; "Post-war Collapse Is Feared," *Townsend National Weekly*, February 14, 1942, p. 1; "Townsend Nat'l. Weekly Commended for Coverage of Nazi-Patent Deals," *Townsend National Weekly*, June 6, 1942, p. 3; "Charge Plants Turn Away Negroes Seeking War Jobs," *Townsend National Weekly*, November 28, 1942, p. 3; "Upper Salaried Brackets Spare Selves at Cost to War Effort," *Townsend National Weekly*, December 5, 1942, p. 1; Dr. Francis E. Townsend, "Townsend Plan Widens Base, Says Founder," *Townsend National Weekly*, March 6, 1943, p. 1; Russell Saville, "Progress in Washington," *Townsend National Weekly*, May 29, 1943, p. 1; "Townsend Ads Compel FDR Action on Higher Pensions," *Townsend National Weekly*, June 12, 1943, p. 1.

15. Alan Brinkley, *The End of Reform: New Deal Liberalism in Recession and War* (New York: Knopf, 1995), pp. 254–57; Ira Katznelson and Bruce Pietrykowski, "Rebuilding the American State: Evidence from the 1940s," *Studies in American Political Development* 5 (1991): 301–99; Marion Clawson, *New Deal Planning: The National Resources Planning Board* (Baltimore: Johns Hopkins University Press, 1981), chaps. 15–19; "WPA Exit Hits Aged Needy; Ends Tiny Help," *Townsend National Weekly*, January 2, 1943, p. 5; "Woman Writes Security Report; Omits the Aged," *Townsend National Weekly*, April 10, 1943, p. 3; "Don't Be Afraid of Brains," *Townsend National Weekly*, April 10, 1943, p. 8; "A Message to Liberals," *Townsend National Weekly*, December 4, 1943, p. 1.

16. District council chairs agreed for a Sixty-at-Sixty measure for California. The petition for a constitutional amendment was to include a 3-percent gross income tax, the prorating of it to all over age sixty and the totally disabled, but no less than $60 per month, and the repeal of the sales tax. The reasons eventually provided for the switch were that state action would give Congress a "shot in the arm" leading it to act, that the Townsend Plan had always stood for immediate gains for the aged, that state programs will show that the Townsend approach is workable and aids business, and that pressure from the rest of nation will result when it sees Townsendism working

elsewhere. "Chairmen of 23 Councils Vote 'Aye' on Big Program," *Townsend National Weekly*, July 31, p. 1; Dr. Francis E. Townsend, "Yes I Have Changed My Mind," *Townsend National Weekly*, August 7, 1943, p. 1; "Launch State Programs Right Now," *Townsend National Weekly*, August 7, 1943, p. 6.

17. "Assemblies Already Have Given Okay," *Townsend National Weekly*, August 7, 1943, p. 1.

18. "Chairmen of 23 Councils Vote 'Aye' on Big Program," p. 1. On developments in state-level OAA programs in 1943, see Dorothea Kahn, "Pensions Tend Higher throughout Nation," *Christian Science Monitor*, July 23, 1943, p. 12; "California Paying $90,000,000 to Aged," *New York Times*, October 31, 1943, p. 37.

19. Self-reported Townsend club membership in California dipped only from 39,500 in 1942 to 35,000 in 1943. California revenues more than doubled over those of the previous year, advancing from $242,000 to $510,000. Edwin Amenta, Drew T. Half-mann, and Michael P. Young, "The Strategies and Contexts of Social Protest: Political Mediation and the Impact of the Townsend Movement in California," *Mobilization* 1 (1999): 1–24. The state organizer John C. Cuneo recalled the early 1940s as being the heyday of the Townsend Plan in California. "The Townsend Plan in Retrospect," Oral History Program, SCUCLA, 1970, p. 27. See also Abraham Holtzman, *The Townsend Movement: A Political Study* (New York: Bookman, 1963), pp. 193–98.

20. Edwin Amenta, "Political Contexts, Challenger Strategies, and Mobilization: Explaining the Impact of the Townsend Plan," in *Routing the Opposition*, ed. David S. Meyer, Valerie Jenness, and Helen Ingram (Minneapolis: University of Minnesota Press, 2005); Amenta, Halfmann, and Young, "The Strategies and Contexts of Social Protest."

21. Richard L. Strout, "U.S. Warned That Crash Lies Ahead," *Christian Science Monitor*, July 22, 1946, p. 3. Military expenditures declined to $18 billion in 1950 but remained much higher than the $1 billion of 1938 and skyrocketed again with the Korean War. U.S. Bureau of the Census, *Historical Statistics of the United States: Colonial Times to 1957* (Washington, D.C.: U.S. Government Printing Office, 1960), series F4, Y414, pp. 139, 723.

22. It is ironic that veterans were viewed as the lesser of fiscal evils, given the historical experience of the bidding up of Civil War veterans' benefits in the nineteenth century. Amenta, *Bold Relief*, p. 202.

23. Jesse George Murray, "First of 12 Grass-Root Regional Councils Is Finally Elected," *Townsend National Weekly*, December 18, 1943, p. 11; "14 Units in State to Desert Townsend," *New York Times*, September 29, 1946, p. 2. For a detailed discussion of this fight, see Holtzman, *The Townsend Movement*, pp. 74–76. For all its expertise, the new organization lacked the brand-name recognition of Dr. Townsend. A ProQuest search turned up only one article concerning the American Pension Committee in the *New York Times*.

24. Holtzman, *The Townsend Movement*, pp. 151–52; Hartmann, *The 80th Congress*, pp. 74–79, 95–96, 132–37; Witte, *The Federal Income Tax*, pp. 131–44; W. Elliot Brownlee, *Federal Taxation in America: A Short History* (New York: Cambridge University Press, 1996), chap. 3.

25. Holtzman, *The Townsend Movement*, pp. 78–83; "Then and Now: Dr. Francis E. Townsend Gave Wide-Eyed Hope to Millions, Is Still a Crusader," *New York Times*

Magazine, May 30, 1948, p. 27; "Townsendites Want 'Action,'" *New York Times*, June 6, 1948, p. E7.

26. Jackson K. Putnam, *Old-Age Politics in California: From Richardson to Reagan* (Stanford, Calif.: Stanford University Press, 1970), chap. 8; Frank A. Pinner, Paul Jacobs, and Philip Selznick, *Old Age and Political Behavior: A Case Study* (Berkeley: University of California Press, 1959), chaps. 3–5; O. Otto Moore, *Mile High Harbor* (Denver, Colo.: Associated Publishers, 1947); Richard L. Neuberger, "Coast Has Revival of Townsend Plan," *New York Times*, September 15, 1946, p. 17; "George M'Lain, Pension Worker," *New York Times*, July 13, 1965, p. 33.

27. Pinner, Jacobs, and Selznick, *Old Age and Political Behavior*, chap. 6.

28. Arthur Altmeyer, "War and Post-war Problems," in *War and Post-war Social Security: The Outlines of an Expanded Program*, ed. Wilbur Cohen (Washington, D.C.: American Council on Public Affairs, 1942), pp. 20–30; Edward D. Berkowitz, "Social Security and the Financing of the American State," in *Funding the Modern American State, 1941–1995: The Rise and Fall of the Era of Easy Finance*, ed. W. Elliot Brownlee (New York: Cambridge University Press, 1995), chap. 4.

29. Wilbur Cohen, ed., *War and Post-war Social Security: The Outlines of an Expanded Program* (Washington, D.C.: American Council on Public Affairs, 1942); Edwin E. Witte, "American Post-war Social Security Proposals," *American Economic Review* 33 (1943): 825–38; Donald E. Spritzer, *Senator James E. Murray and the Limits of Post-war Liberalism* (New York: Garland, 1985), pp. 133–35; J. Joseph Huthmacher, *Senator Robert F. Wagner and the Rise of Urban Liberalism* (New York: Atheneum, 1968); Martha Derthick, *Policymaking for Social Security* (Washington, D.C.: Brookings Institution, 1979), pp. 111, 114.

30. Julian E. Zelizer, *Taxing America: Wilbur D. Mills, Congress, and the State, 1945–1975* (New York: Cambridge University Press, 1998), pp. 63–65; Mark H. Leff, "Speculating in Social Security Futures," in *Social Security: The First Half-Century*, ed. Gerald D. Nash, Joel H. Pugach, and Richard F. Tomasson (Albuquerque: University of New Mexico Press, 1987), pp. 243–78; Edward D. Berkowitz, *Mr. Social Security: The Life of Wilbur J. Cohen* (Lawrence: University Press of Kansas, 1995), pp. 49–55; Bartholomew H. Sparrow, *From the Outside In: World War II and the American State* (Princeton, N.J.: Princeton University Press, 1996), chap. 2; Coll, *Safety Net*, chaps. 6, 7.

31. "House Group Votes a 1% Security Tax, Dropping Rise Plan," *New York Times*, July 15, 1946, p. 1; Gordon W. Blackwell and Raymond F. Gould, *Future Citizens All* (Chicago: American Public Welfare Association, 1952); Ellen J. Perkins, "Old-Age Assistance and Aid to Dependent Children, 1940–50," *Social Security Bulletin* 14 (November 1951): 11–29.

32. The strongest stand about the power of the Social Security Administration is in Cates, *Insuring Inequality*, but many scholarly books portray the first fifteen years of U.S. social insurance as if it were a triumph waiting to happen. Altmeyer, however, labeled this period the "Crucial Years." *The Formative Years of Social Security*, chap. 7; Bureau of the Census, *Historical Statistics*, series H125, H127, H186, H193, H209, H210, pp. 197, 200, 201.

33. Steven Fraser, *Labor Will Rule: Sidney Hillman and the Rise of American Labor* (New York: Free Press, 1991), chaps. 16, 17; Bureau of the Census, *Historical Statistics*, series D 741, 745, p. 98; Derthick, *Policymaking for Social Security*, chap. 5; Sheryl R.

Tynes, *Turning Points in Social Security: From "Cruel Hoax to "Sacred Entitlement"* (Stanford, Calif.: Stanford University Press, 1996), pp. 111–14; David Plotke, *Building a Democratic Political Order: Reshaping American Liberalism in the 1930s and 1940s* (New York: Cambridge University Press, 1996), chaps. 7, 8.

34. A. H. Raskin, "Unions Will Press for Pension Gains," *New York Times*, December 27, 1949, p. 8; Beth Stevens, "Blurring the Boundaries: How the Federal Government Has Encouraged Welfare Benefits in the Private Sector," in *The Politics of Social Policy in the United States*, ed. Margaret Weir, Ann Shola Orloff, and Theda Skocpol (Princeton, N.J.: Princeton University Press, 1988), pp. 123–48; Frank R. Dobbin, "The Origins of Private Social Insurance: Public Policy and Fringe Benefits in America, 1920–1950," *American Journal of Sociology* 97 (1992): 1416–50; Tynes, *Turning Points in Social Security*, pp. 109–14; Steven A. Sass, *The Promise of Private Pensions: The First Hundred Years* (Cambridge, Mass.: Harvard University Press, 1997), pp. 113–42; Jacob S. Hacker, *The Divided Welfare State: The Battle over Public and Private Social Benefits in the United States* (New York: Cambridge University Press, 2002), pp. 126–34; Jennifer Klein, *For All These Rights: Business, Labor, and the Shaping of America's Public-Private Welfare State* (Princeton, N.J.: Princeton University Press, 2003), pp. 244–46.

35. Jill Quadagno, "From Old-Age Assistance to Supplemental Security Income: The Political Economy of Relief in the South, 1935–1972," in *The Politics of Social Policy in the United States*, ed. Margaret Weir, Ann Shola Orloff, and Theda Skocpol (Princeton, N.J.: Princeton University Press, 1988), chap. 6; Tynes, *Turning Points in Social Security*, pp. 106–7; Zelizer, *Taxing America*, pp. 70–74.

36. Bureau of the Census, *Historical Statistics*, series F87, H124, pp. 143, 197.

37. The four parts to the report were "Old-Age and Survivors Insurance," "Permanent and Total Disability Insurance," "Public Assistance," and "Unemployment Insurance." *Recommendations for Social Security Legislation: The Reports of the Advisory Council on Social Security to the Senate Finance Committee* (Washington, D.C.: U.S. Government Printing Office, 1949). For the best account of the advisory council, see Edward D. Berkowitz, *Robert Ball and the Politics of Social Security* (Madison: University of Wisconsin Press, 2003), pp. 58–72. See also Zelizer, *Taxing America*, pp. 64–65; Derthick, *Policymaking for Social Security*, chap. 4.

38. Congressional Quarterly, *Guide to U.S. Congress* (Washington, D.C.: Congressional Quarterly, 1985), p. 896; Porter and Johnson, *National Party Platforms*, pp. 430–47, 450–54. On the bid to provide veterans' pensions, see Richard L. Strout, "Veterans Pensions: Case History," *Christian Science Monitor*, March 26, 1949, p. 20. For Fair Deal legislation, see Richard L. Strout, "New U.S. Line-Ups Posted by Congress," *Christian Science Monitor*, October 20, 1949, p. 3; Richard L. Strout, "Truman Praises Congress—What of 'Fair Deal'?" *Christian Science Monitor*, September 25, 1950, p. 3. For a comparison with the previous Congress, see Susan M. Hartmann, *Truman and the 80th Congress* (Columbia: University of Missouri Press, 1971). On the national health initiative, see Paul Starr, *The Social Transformation of American Medicine: The Rise of a Sovereign Profession and the Making of a Vast Industry* (New York: Basic Books, 1982), pp. 280–89; Monte M. Poen, *Harry S. Truman versus the Medical Lobby: The Genesis of Medicare* (Columbia: University of Missouri Press, 1979), chap. 6.

39. Altmeyer, *The Formative Years of Social Security*, chaps. 6, 7; Wilbur J. Cohen and Robert J. Myers, "Social Security Act Amendments of 1950: A Summary and Leg-

islative History," *Social Security Bulletin* 13 (October 1950): 3–14; Leff, "Speculating in Social Security Futures"; Berkowitz, *Mr. Social Security*, pp. 56–70; Cates, *Insuring Inequality*, chap. 3; Coll, *Safety Net*, pp. 155–64; Hartmann, *Truman and the 80th Congress*, chap. 6; U.S. Social Security Administration, "History of Provisions," *Social Security Bulletin, Annual Statistical Supplement* (Washington, D.C.: Social Security Administration, 1991); Paul P. Kennedy, "Age Pension Bill Adding 10,000,000 Sent to President," *New York Times*, August 18, 1950, p. 1. Added to coverage were nonprofessional self-employed, farmworkers, nonprofit workers, and domestics. Another 1 percentage point increase in the tax was scheduled for 1953. The wage base on which taxes were to be paid was increased to $3,600 per year. The so-called increment, which increased the benefits of those who continuously paid payroll taxes, was eliminated, making it possible to increase "unearned" benefits. The number of OASI beneficiaries also receiving OAA actually increased in the 1950s, but most likely these were aged survivors of covered workers. Bureau of the Census, *Historical Statistics*, series H127, H129, H186, H210, pp. 197, 200, 201.

40. Angell and six other members of Congress testified in favor of Townsend legislation. Another seven were called but did not appear, and seventeen members submitted statements in favor of the Townsend Plan. John Doyle Elliot, the statistician for the Legislative Bureau of the Townsend Plan, Inc., provided most of the facts and figures regarding the legislation. *Hearings before the House Committee on Ways and Means, Social Security Act Amendments of 1949*, part I, pp. 601–81.

41. Ibid., pp. 691–791.

42. For Young's statement, see Hearings before the House Committee on Ways and Means, *Social Security Act Amendments of 1949*, H.R. 2892, part I, p. 615; E. J. Whitney, "Townsend Plan Stages Comeback," *New York Times*, January 22, 1950, p. 136; "Townsend Urges His Plan," *New York Times*, February 3, 1950, p. 13.

43. It is possible, too, that these Republicans may have been voting for a gag rule so as not to have to vote against a Townsend Plan amendment. See Edwin Amenta, Bruce G. Carruthers, and Yvonne Zylan, "A Hero for the Aged? The Townsend Movement, the Political Mediation Model, and U.S. Old-Age Policy, 1934–1950," *American Journal of Sociology* 98 (1992): 308–39.

44. Mills is quoted in Zelizer, *Taxing America*, p. 75.

45. A. H. Raskin, "Cost of Aid to Old Rises 250 Millions," *New York Times*, December 26, 1949, p. 31.

46. Raskin, "Unions Will Press for Pension Gains." An executive of Bethlehem Steel wrote to stockholders that it would not have to pay out much in pension benefits because most workers would either leave the firm or die before being able to cash in.

47. See the testimony of John B. St. John, U.S. Chamber of Commerce, Committee on Ways and Means, *Hearings on the Social Security Act Amendments of 1949*, pp. 581ff. A. D. Marshall of the Chamber of Commerce's Social Security Committee, argued along the same lines, as did Herschel C. Atkinson, the executive vice president of the Ohio Chamber of Commerce. U.S. Senate, Committee on Finance, *Hearings on H.R. 6000*, 81st Cong., 2nd sess., pt. 3 (Washington, D.C.: U.S. Government Printing Office, 1950), pp. 1465–1506. The quotation is from Marshall, p. 1483; Raskin, "Cost of Aid to Old Rises 250 Millions."

48. Aaron Paul, Director, Kentucky Department of Public Assistance, pp. 281–82; John H. Winters, Director, Texas Department of Public Welfare, pp. 288–89; Ellen

Winston, Commissioner, North Carolina State Board of Public Welfare, p. 297; Sanford Bates, Commissioner of Institutions and Agencies, New Jersey, pp. 304–5; W. B. Bond, Commissioner, Mississippi State Board of Public Welfare, p. 330; Arthur B. Rivers, Director, South Carolina State Department of Public Welfare, p. 331; Earl M. Kouns, Director, Colorado Department of Public Welfare, p. 354; Lawrence E. Higgins, Commissioner of Public Welfare, Louisiana, p. 364, all in *Hearings before the House Committee on Ways and Means, Social Security Act Amendments of 1949, H.R. 2892,* pt. 1.

49. Theda Skocpol, *Diminished Democracy* (Norman: University of Oklahoma Press, 2003). Townsend's son Robert, however, was unable to devote his full time to the organization. Cuneo, "The Townsend Plan in Retrospect"; "Dr. Townsend Dies; Led Old Age Pension Plan," *New York Times,* September 2, 1960, p. 1; "Townsend Plan, Once the Hope of Thousands, Is Near Death," *New York Times,* February 23, 1978, p. A16.

Conclusion: A Hero for the Aged?

1. See the introduction for the views of historians and contemporaries.

2. In 2004, Social Security accounted for $496 billion and Medicare $296 billion of a $2.3 trillion budget, with Medicaid costing another $176 billion, while national defense amounted to $456 billion. *Budget of the United States Government, Fiscal 2006* (Washington, D.C.: U.S. Government Printing Office, 2005), p. 56.

3. See chapter 1 for a more extensive discussion of these arguments.

4. I call them "prospective pro–social spenders" because of their greater willingness to back national and generous social spending. For evidence that members of Congress actually voted this way when push came to shove, see Edwin Amenta and Drew Halfmann, "Wage Wars: Institutional Politics, the WPA, and the Struggle for U.S. Social Policy," *American Sociological Review* 64 (2000): 506–28.

5. Moreover, the Townsend Plan did not have much influence when economic times were good, during the war and afterward, but its pattern of influence did not otherwise track economic activity.

6. *Townsend National Weekly,* February 6, 1943, p. 2; *Townsend National Weekly,* February 13, 1943, p. 1.

7. I refer specifically to assertiveness rather than the usual distinctions between "assimilative" and "disruptive" strategies. See chapter 1 for further discussion.

8. See chapter 3.

9. See chapter 4.

10. See chapter 5.

11. See chapter 6.

12. See chapter 6.

13. See also Edwin Amenta, Drew Halfmann, and Michael P. Young, "The Strategies and Contexts of Social Protest: Political Mediation and the Impact of the Townsend Movement in California," *Mobilization* 4 (1999): 1–24.

14. See chapter 7.

15. See chapter 8.

16. See chapter 9.

17. See chapter 9.

18. See chapter 9.

19. On the influence of the Social Security Board/Administration, see Martha Derthick, *Policymaking for Social Security* (Washington, D.C.: Brookings Institution, 1979), pp. 90–92; Jerry R. Cates, *Insuring Inequality: Administrative Leadership in Social Security, 1935–54* (Ann Arbor: University of Michigan Press, 1983); Sheryl N. Tynes, *Turning Points in Social Security: From "Cruel Hoax" to "Sacred Entitlement"* (Stanford, Calif.: University of Stanford Press, 1996). For an account of Aid to Dependent Children and its inferiority to social insurance, see Linda Gordon, *Pitied but Not Entitled: Single Mothers and the History of Welfare, 1890–1935* (New York: Free Press, 1994). For a discussion invoking the "big bang" imagery, see Theda Skocpol and G. John Ikenberry, "The Political Formation of the American Welfare State in Historical and Comparative Perspective," *Comparative Social Research* 6 (1983): 87–148. For the idea that "social security" was a response to short-term mobilizations, see J. Craig Jenkins and Barbara Brents, "Social Protest, Hegemonic Competition, and Social Reform: A Political Struggle Interpretation of the Origins of the American Welfare State," *American Sociological Review* 54 (1989): 891–909. See also Frances Fox Piven and Richard A. Cloward, *Regulating the Poor: The Functions of Public Welfare*, 2nd ed. (New York: Vintage Books, 1993).

20. Theda Skocpol, "How Americans Became Civic," in *Civic Engagement in American Democracy*, ed. Theda Skocpol and Morris P. Fiorina (Washington, D.C., and New York: Brookings Institution and Russell Sage Foundation, 1999).

INDEX

Italic page numbers refer to illustrations.

PRINCETON STUDIES IN AMERICAN POLITICS:
HISTORICAL, INTERNATIONAL, AND COMPARATIVE
PERSPECTIVES

IRA KATZNELSON, MARTIN SHEFTER, AND THEDA SKOCPOL, EDS.

*The Road to Nowhere: The Genesis of President Clinton's Plan for
Health Security* by Jacob Hacker

The Origins of the Urban Crisis: Race and Inequality in Postwar Detroit
by Thomas J. Sugrue

Party Decline in America: Policy, Politics, and the Fiscal State
by John J. Coleman

*The Power of Separation: American Constitutionalism and the Myth
of the Legislative Veto* by Jessica Korn

*Why Movements Succeed or Fail: Opportunity, Culture, and the Struggle
for Woman Suffrage* by Lee Ann Banaszak

*Kindred Strangers: The Uneasy Relationship between Politics and Business
in America* by David Vogel

From the Outside In: World War II and the American State
by Bartholomew H. Sparrow

Classifying by Race edited by Paul E. Peterson

Facing Up to the American Dream: Race, Class, and the Soul of the Nation
by Jennifer L. Hochschild

Political Organizations by James Q. Wilson

Social Policy in the United States: Future Possibilities in Historical Perspective
by Theda Skocpol

*Experts and Politicians: Reform Challenges to Machine Politics in New York,
Cleveland, and Chicago* by Kenneth Finegold

Bound by Our Constitution: Women, Workers, and the Minimum Wage
by Vivien Hart

Prisoners of Myth: The Leadership of the Tennessee Valley Authority, 1933–1990
by Erwin C. Hargrove

Political Parties and the State: The American Historical Experience
by Martin Shefter

Politics and Industrialization: Early Railroads in the United States and Prussia
by Colleen A. Dunlavy

The Lincoln Persuasion: Remaking American Liberalism
by J. David Greenstone

*Labor Visions and State Power: The Origins of Business Unionism in the
United States* by Victoria C. Hattam